RELIGION AND MORALITY

CLAREMONT STUDIES IN THE PHILOSOPHY OF RELIGION
General Editor: D. Z. Phillips

Published titles:

PHILOSOPHY AND THE GRAMMAR OF RELIGIOUS BELIEF
Edited by *Timothy Tessin and Mario von der Ruhr*

RELIGION AND MORALITY
Edited by *D. Z. Phillips*

CAN RELIGION BE EXPLAINED AWAY?
Edited by *D. Z. Phillips*

PHILOSOPHY AND THEOLOGICAL DISCOURSE
Edited by *Stephen T. Davis* (forthcoming)

Religion and Morality

Edited by

D. Z. Phillips

Danforth Professor of the Philosophy of Religion
Claremont Graduate School, and
Professor of Philosophy, University of Wales, Swansea

First published 1996 by
MACMILLAN PRESS LTD
Houndmills, Basingstoke, Hampshire RG21 6XS
and London
Companies and representatives
throughout the world

ISBN 0–333–62066–6

A catalogue record for this book is available
from the British Library.

10   9   8   7   6   5   4   3   2   1
05   04   03   02   01   00   99   98   97   96

Printed in Great Britain by
The Ipswich Book Co Ltd
Ipswich, Suffolk

 Published in the United States of America 1996 by
ST. MARTIN'S PRESS, INC.,
Scholarly and Reference Division
175 Fifth Avenue, New York, N.Y. 10010

ISBN 0–312–12868-1

Contents

Preface and Acknowledgements

This collection of essays is the second in the series *Claremont Studies in the Philosophy of Religion*, the first being *Philosophy and the Grammar of Religious Belief* edited by Timothy Tessin and Mario von der Ruhr. It is based on the proceedings of the fifteenth annual conference on the philosophy of religion at The Claremont Graduate School, California, in February 1994.

As in the first volume, I have included 'Voices in Discussion' as an afterword. Some readers may want to read this discussion first before turning to the papers as fuller elucidations of the philosophical perspectives expressed in it. Others may not want to do so, hence the general introduction.

I am grateful to the contributors to this collection, not only for participating in the conference, but for their generous support of the fund from which the annual conferences are funded. I also gratefully acknowledge contributions to the fund by The Claremont Graduate School, Pomona College, and Claremont McKenna College.

I am indebted to Stephen Davis, Jackie Huntzinger and Althea Spencer-Miller for administrative assistance with the conference and to all those graduate students who, in various ways, contributed to the success of the conference. I acknowledge the help provided in the preparation of typescripts by Lance Ashdown and Martha Bailey, my research assistants at Claremont, and Helen Baldwin, Secretary to the Department of Philosophy at Swansea. I am grateful to Timothy Tessin, my colleague at Swansea, for help with the proof-reading. The ready cooperation of people based at Claremont and Swansea is a happy by-product of my involvement in both institutions.

D. Z. PHILLIPS

Claremont and Swansea

Notes on the Contributors

Marilyn McCord Adams is Professor of Historical Theology at Yale University and an Episcopal priest. She is author of a two-volume study, *William Ockham*, and of numerous articles on medieval philosophy and theology, Anselm, Duns Scotus, and the problem of evil.

Robert Merrihew Adams is Professor of Philosophy and Religious Studies at Yale University. He is the author of *The Virtue of Faith* and *Leibniz: Determinist, Theist, Idealist*, and of articles on metaphysics, ethics, the philosophy of religion, and the history of philosophy.

R. W. Beardsmore is Senior Lecturer in Philosophy and Head of Department at the University of Wales, Swansea. He is the author of *Moral Reasoning* and *Art and Morality* and author of papers on ethics, aesthetics and Wittgenstein.

John V. Canfield teaches at Erindale College, University of Toronto. He is the author of *Wittgenstein: Language and the World* and *The Looking-Glass Self*.

James Conant is Assistant Professor of Philosophy at the University of Pittsburg. He is the author of articles on Kierkegaard, Nietzsche, Frege and Wittgenstein.

Raimond Gaita is Professor of Philosophy at the Institute of Advanced Research, Australia, and Lecturer in Philosophy at King's College, London. He is the author of *Good and Evil: An Absolute Conception* and editor of *Value and Understanding: Essays for Peter Winch*.

Frank J. Hoffman is Assistant Professor of Philosophy at West Chester University. He is the author of *Rationality and Mind in Early Buddhism* and co-editor of *Pali Buddhism*. He is Associate Editor of the *Journal of Comparative Literature and Aesthetics* (India).

John Hyman is Fellow and Praelector in Philosophy at The Queen's College, Oxford. He is the editor of *Investigating Psychology* and the author of *The Imitation of Nature*.

Clark A. Kucheman is Arthur V. Stoughton Professor of Christian Ethics at Claremont McKenna College. He is editor of *The Life of Choice: Some Liberal Religious Perspectives on Morality* and the author of numerous essays in journals and anthologies.

David McLellan is Professor of Political Theory at the University of Kent. His numerous books have been translated into many languages. His most recent publications are *Simone Weil: Utopian Pessimist* and *Unto Caesar: The Political Reference of Christianity*.

D. Z. Phillips is Professor of Philosophy at the University of Wales, Swansea and Danforth Professor of the Philosophy of Religion at The Claremont Graduate School. He is the author of *The Concept of Prayer; Moral Practices* (with H. O. Mounce); *Death and Immortality; Faith and Philosophical Enquiry; Sense and Delusion* (with Ilham Dilman); *Athronyddu Am Grefydd; Religion Without Explanation; Through a Darkening Glass; Dramâu Gwenlyn Parry; Belief, Change and Forms of Life; R. S. Thomas: Poet of the Hidden God; Faith After Foundationalism; From Fantasy to Faith; Interventions in Ethics; Wittgenstein and Religion; Writers of Wales: J. R. Jones*. He has edited many books including *Wittgenstein: Attention to Particulars. Essays in Honour of Rush Rhees* (with Peter Winch). He is editor of the journal *Philosophical Investigations* and of the Macmillan series, *Swansea Studies in Philosophy* and *Claremont Studies in the Philosophy of Religion*.

Philip L. Quinn is John O'Brien Professor of Philosophy at the University of Notre Dame and was formerly William Herbert Perry Faunce Professor of Philosophy at Brown University. He is the author of *Divine Commands and Moral Requirements* and numerous articles on philosophy of religion, philosophy of science, ethics and metaphysics. He has served as editor of *Faith and Philosophy* and president of the American Philosophical Association, Central Division (1994-5).

Joseph Runzo is Professor of Philosophy and Griset Professor of Religion at Chapman University. He is the author of *World Views* *and Perceiving God; Relativism and God*; editor of *Is God Real?* and *Ethics, Religion and the Good Society, New Directions in a Pluralistic World*, and co-editor of *Religious Experience and Religious Belief: Essays in the Epistemology of Religion*. He is founder and president of the Philosophy of Religion Society.

Richard Schacht is Professor of Philosophy and Jubilee Professor of Liberal Arts and Sciences at the University of Illinois at Urbana-Champaign. He is Executive Director of the North American Nietzsche Society and editor of the University of Illinois Press series *International Nietzsche Studies*. His books include *Alienation; Classical Modern Philosophers; Hegel and After; Nietzsche*; and, more recently, *The Future of Alienation; Making Sense of Nietzsche*.

Rowan Williams is the Anglican Bishop of Monmouth, Wales, Honorary Professor of Theology at the University of Bristol and Fellow of the British Academy. He was formerly Lady Margaret Professor of Divinity, University of Oxford. He is the author of *The Wound of Knowledge; Resurrection; The Truth of God; Beginning Now: Peacemaking Theology* (with Mark Collier); *Arius: Heresy and Tradition; Theresa of Avila* and editor of *The Making of Orthodoxy*.

Introduction

D. Z. PHILLIPS

For some contemporary philosophers, an emphasis on guilt in morality is infantile, the sign of a narrowly conceived ethics. Raimond Gaita argues that this is not so. Guilt is the essential means by which we recognise the harm we do to others. In such a revelation, guilt is related to that first-person affective response we call remorse. Remorse is not the psychological consequence of recognising the harm, but is constitutive of what such recognition amounts to. It is the recognition of a violation of human beings which Gaita thinks can be described best as the violation of the sacred. Once again, however, Gaita wants to emphasise that the affective response does not occur *because* the other is seen to be sacred. Rather, the sense of the sacred is given in the possibility of such a response; a response which reveals the absolute worth of human beings.

Gaita recognises that the notion of the sacred has its roots in certain religious responses, but he hopes to show that it has a meaning independent of these origins. The possibility of showing this raises an issue which runs through all the papers: the interrelations between moral and religious concepts. Richard Schacht is suspicious of the transposition of concepts Gaita seems to contemplate, and Gaita himself comes to have misgivings concerning it. Both symposiasts agree on the confusion involved in looking for metaphysical underpinnings for our affective responses. Schacht argues, however, that talk of absolute values and absolute worth, which Gaita wants to maintain, itself depends on such metaphysical support and cannot be sustained without it. We must realise, Schacht argues, that we are interpreters of our own conditions. The vital issue for him concerns what there is to guide us in these interpretations. In them, we are always creating more than we know, but without such efforts we are condemned to prosaic speech. Schacht believes that after the demise of transcendental metaphysics and the transcendental religion which depends on it, we have the resources to explore the possibility of other forms of discourse which constitute a celebration of life.

In the second symposium, we meet a very different perspective. It should not be confused, however, with the view that the good is good because God commands it. That is not what Robert Adams means by a Divine Command Theory. On the contrary, the theory, on his view, presupposes our conceptions of human good and harm. We can appreciate that torture is wrong independently of the theory, and the harm involved is not elucidated in terms of it. What the theory explains is the notion of obligation. We must obey because it has been commanded, but the command is not the reason for the goodness involved. Yet, the theory does involve belief in a revelation in which what is communicated to us is not a mere wish, but the direct command of God who is the source of highest value. It follows, therefore, that our moral responses are grounded in an objective state of affairs. God's commands may not be accessible to all people at all times, in which case they are under no obligation to obey them. Yet, people still retain a sense of good and evil. Adams argues that in such contexts we have a relativity of obligation, but no relativity of value. Here, the emphasis is clearly different from that found in the first symposium where moral responses are said to occur, not *because* human beings have absolute worth. Rather, the notion of absolute worth is found in the possibility of such responses.

Clark Kucheman, like Adams, seeks an objective grounding for our moral responses, something which no person would be justified in not accepting. He finds this in a version of Kant's categorical imperative; a grounding which we must not surrender to an alien will. The grounds of our moral responses can be found in the respect due to others. Unlike the first two symposiasts, Kucheman does not want to say that this respect has its sense in our affective responses, since if those responses are wanting, he wants to argue, the respect is due, nevertheless.

How does any reference to God inform our lives in face of the actual evils, some of them horrendous, which human beings have to face? In the third symposium, Marilyn Adams thinks that some kind of theodicy is needed if this question is to be answered satisfactorily. Yet, a great deal depends on the kind of theodicy which is advanced. How is sense to be made of one's life in such a way that its fragmented parts can be seen in the context of a meaningful whole? Marilyn Adams has little time for attempts made by analytic philosophers of religion to justify and explain evil by appeals to possible worlds or the free-will defence. Such theories simply do not work. Things are too bad for them, and we are right to reject them. For Marilyn Adams, the only hope of making sense of things, including the horrendous evils people suffer, is to be found in post-mortem experiences in which encounters with God will transform our understanding of our present condition. It is not that the evils suffered cease to be horrendous, but that their meaning changes. This change of meaning is a form of redemption received by all in the end, even the most evil person imaginable, since God would not create a creature beyond his own powers of redemption. In a post-mortem context, those powers may include forms of coercion to change people's views.

Rowan Williams is unhappy with the language he takes Marilyn Adams to be offering us to cope with the fact of horrendous evils. He does not want even to begin talking of what solutions would be proportionate or disproportionate in relation, say, to years of sexual child abuse. He thinks such language destroys both our sense of such evils and the religious notion of beatitude. The task of correlation he thinks such talk involves invites us to entertain misleading pictures of our experiences as atomic units. These pictures cannot do justice to the diverse ways in which people have come to terms with horrendous evils in their lives, ways which are by no means always religious. When the reactions are religious, Rowan Williams argues, the account Marilyn Adams gives of them is too reactive, as something introduced post-mortem when all else has failed. This raises the whole issue of the grammar of divine action. Robert Adams and Marilyn Adams acknowledge that their views involve a degree of anthropomorphism, whereas, for Rowan Williams, divine action is incommensurable with finite agency. To see what it involves we must pay attention to the form concept-formation takes where the notion of grace is concerned. Talk of grace must remain faithful to the facts of human suffering, a faithfulness which, for Rowan Williams, involves giving up talk of balancing horrendous evils against something else. He is suspicious of all theoretical attempts at resolving the problem of evil since, in the end, he believes they involve not only evasions of humanity, but of divinity as well.

Undoubtedly, among horrendous evils we find torture. Yet, can we say it is always wrong, everywhere and for everyone? This is the issue Philip Quinn addresses in the context of religion and moral relativism in the fourth symposium. He argues that, if we are religious, we can say that we should not torture others because they are sacred, a fact derived from their being created by God. For Quinn, this is a metaphysical sacredness, although he admits that it can sometimes stand alone apart from its metaphysical grounding. This recalls issues in the first symposium. The problem, Quinn argues, is that the metaphysical religious grounding does not work for everyone and there is little reason to suppose that it ever will. The only hope in such a situation is to seek to influence the moral teaching of children, or to work towards such moral consensus as can be attained. But Quinn is suspicious of those who argue that there is such a thing as the moral point of view which, if recognised, will show us why we should not torture others. This moral view, it is said, involves respecting others as persons, taking into account the good of others, abiding by the principle of universalisability, and commitment to certain moral principles as normative. But these characteristics belong, Quinn argues, not to *the* moral point of view, but to *a* moral point of view, that of Western Enlightenment Liberalism. Quinn is, in fact, an adherent of such liberalism, but he is under no illusion that he and his fellow liberals alone occupy the moral point of view. Worse, even within such a point of view, agreement relating to torture in a particular case is by no means guaranteed. He concludes, with some regret, that moral pluralism is here to stay.

Clearly, Quinn's difficulties contrast with the Kantianism advanced by Kucheman in the second symposium. One aspect of this Kantianism is taken up by Joseph Runzo in his reply to Quinn. He agrees that there are no overreaching religious or secular arguments which can command a universal audience where the prohibition of torture is concerned. Yet, he still wants to maintain that it is a universal prohibition. How can this be said? According to Runzo, it is rooted in a respect for persons, which overlaps many different perspectives. All human beings have the duty to show this respect, whether they recognise it or not. For believers, this respect is grounded in seeing others in the image of God, but this conception is not shared widely enough to work as a final appeal. Runzo wants to argue that no circumstances should constitute exceptions to the rule prohibiting torture, since it violates the respect for others most people acknowledge. Those who do not recognise it are beyond the moral pale. To admit exceptions to the rule would be to embark on a slippery slope which ends in the direst atrocities.

In the subsequent discussion, difficult situations and moral di-

lemmas loomed large; situations which Quinn readily acknowledged. Apart from cases where the moral descriptions of the situations would be disputed, some admitted that even when it is
appropriate to speak of torture they would, in certain circumstances, commit it. For some, this meant regarding such situations
as exceptions to the moral rule, while others would not speak of
'exceptions' but of involvement in tragic, moral dilemmas where
we discover what we have to do without necessarily talking of
the right thing to do. In some cases, it was argued, torturing a
terrorist would not constitute a violation of respect for persons
even in relation to the terrorist.

The connection with issues in the first three symposia arises
from the attempt to give a central role to the notion of respect
for persons. For some participants, the notion is a highly theoretical one of a Kantian or Hegelian kind. For others, talk of rules
and principles in this connection is of limited value. They argued
that when we say that torture is wrong because we have failed
to respect others, this creates the illusion that we have been told
why torture is wrong. The 'respect' itself can only be cashed out
in moral terms which limit what we should be prepared to do to
others. So talk of principles does not underwrite our moral practices, since it is in terms of these practices that the principles have
their life. This reminds us of the issues concerning whether our
affective responses, in respecting others, are grounded in something independent, whether it be post-mortem experiences, a
metaphysical system or a set of principles, or whether the respect gets its sense from our affective responses.

Once we ask for a further elucidation of what respect for others involves further issues return which are present in the preceding symposia. If we say that the respect expresses a sense of
the sacred in others, this leads to the question of the extent to
which a sense of the sacred can have sense independently of its
religious roots. This question leads us to the concerns of the fifth
symposium, concerns which are intimately connected with the
discussions which preceded it.

John Canfield is concerned to bring out the practical import of
the notion of 'no-self' in the practice he calls post-Zen. He shows
that this has to do with the possibility of a certain kind of enlightenment which shows itself in what is called 'fine behaviour',
free of our normal egocentric preoccupations. This is not the notion of the self which philosophers usually worry about, or the

kind of self-consciousness they normally discuss. The reason for mentioning the philosophical preoccupations is that they can easily obscure the whole point of the striving for no-self. The metaphysical preoccupations obscure the practical context in which the notion has its life. That is why John Canfield speaks of post-Zen. He is referring to a practice which has deliberately divorced itself from the metaphysical doctrines of Buddhism, such as the doctrine of rebirth, but which, at the same time, has kept those practices which constitute the path to enlightenment. Some may see this as an attenuated form of Buddhism, but Canfield sees it as the separation of the essential from the inessential, the separation of the spiritual from the metaphysical.

It is the character of this separation which concerns Frank Hoffman. Why cut post-Zen off from the main tenets of Buddhism? Although Canfield does not say a great deal about why he cannot swallow the metaphysical aspects of Buddhism, it is clear to Hoffman that it is because Canfield thinks they obscure what really matters in Buddhism. But, then, there are philosophers who think that metaphysical theories have done Christianity an equal disservice. They do not, for that reason, speak of the need for a different practice called post-Christianity. The intriguing question is this: has the notion of rebirth a spiritual significance which is itself obscured by metaphysical accounts of it? If this question is answered in the affirmative, giving up the notion of rebirth would be to lose a form of practice in which the enlightenment made possible by the use of the notion would show itself. Of course, none of this has any implication for the nature of the enlightenment Canfield discusses in his elucidation of the practice of post-Zen.

These issues lead us to the concerns of the final symposium, concerns which are connected with the earliest discussions of the interrelations between moral and religious conceptions. It is no part of R. W. Beardsmore's intention to deny that there are religious conceptions which have no counterparts in morality. But he also wants to reject the claim that moral concepts are necessarily parasitic on religion. He is well-aware of the condescending misunderstanding to which religion is often subjected and wants no part of it. On the other hand, he thinks that it is equally necessary to recognise that atheism can be subjected to a condescending misunderstanding too. He illustrates what he means by considering what is involved in gratitude for life. Even if it could be shown that gratitude for life originated in religion, why should it follow that it must have those associations for us now? It is tempting to say that the atheist feeds on some vestiges of religious faith, so that they cannot really say what they want to say in expressing gratitude for life. Their speech is an implicit recognition of God. Beardsmore wants to resist the temptation to think in this way. We have to look to the role gratitude for life plays in a person's life to see what it amounts to. Beardsmore provides examples of such gratitude which do not take a religious form. They need not have a religious origin. If we think of certain general facts of nature, laughing, crying, reacting to miraculous escapes with gratitude, why shouldn't we say that religious and atheistic conceptions of gratitude are derived from the last of these?

Beardsmore argues that such considerations count against the tendency in some philosophers to advance general claims about the relation of morality to religion. In particular, some philosophers have argued that we are in a state of moral unintelligibility. This comes about by our attempt to use concepts disconnected from the religious context in which they have their intelligibility. Beardsmore finds such a thesis in the work of Elizabeth Anscombe. He believes that she conflates two theses: that certain words may survive the demise of a divine law conception of ethics, and that certain concepts can do so. If Anscombe is saying that we cannot have a divine law conception of ethics without a conception of divine law her thesis is a tautology. It is manifestly false to say that words can't survive the demise of the context in which they had their original sense. Beardsmore's thesis is quite different, namely, that there are moral notions of obligation, moral necessity and gratitude for existence which are distinctive concepts, not dependent on religion for the sense they have in people's lives.

In his reply, much expanded from his original paper, James Conant concentrates on what is involved in the claim that people can be in the grip of a certain kind of moral unintelligibility. He explores, in illuminating detail, what this claim amounts to in the work of three very different thinkers: Nietzsche, Kierkegaard and Elizabeth Anscombe. He thinks that this claim needs to be clearly distinguished from any general philosophical thesis. To the extent that Beardsmore attributes such a general thesis to Anscombe, Conant argues, this is to miss the main thrust of her far more specific observations; observations which have to do with the way many philosophers and others attribute sense to notions of moral necessity and obligation which depended for their sense on a divine law conception of ethics no longer in evidence.

Conant admits that Anscombe is not as careful as she might be about the distinction between the survival of concepts and the survival of words. She speaks, sometimes, of the survival of concepts outside the framework which once made them possible. But that supposition is meaningless since, in that event, we do not have the concept. Only nominal words survive. It may seem that this thesis is obvious, but uninteresting. It gets its interest from the fact that people may not realise what situation they are in. They employ the words in contexts which seem to resemble those which gave them their sense, but they do not recognise this; thus people are in a state of moral unintelligibility without realising it. This is a common theme in Nietzsche, Kierkegaard and Anscombe, although their diagnoses of the reasons for and the consequences of such situations differ in important respects. Unlike MacIntyre, however, their concerns are quite specific. MacIntyre propounds a thesis about the state of *all* our moral concepts, which is why Conant parts company with him.

Anscombe, Conant argues, is quite specific. She claims that the sense we try to give to a moral use of 'must' is confused in the absence of a divine law conception of ethics. Once that conception is lost, her claim is that we have nothing similar at that level of generality. Our sense of an absolute prohibition is lost. As a result, we are tempted to indulge in the corruption of contemplating evil so that good may come. Other concepts of obligation, independent of this absolute conception are, of course, unaffected by this specific claim.

Even in this specific context, Beardsmore and Gaita recognise that Anscombe is looking for a moral 'stopper'. But they insist that 'It is commanded by God' is only one stopper among many. Wittgenstein, for example, reminds us of another use. If we told someone he ought to act decently and he said that he was not interested in doing so, we'd say, 'But you ought to.' That use is perfectly intelligible without reference to religion. The necessity expressed is not a psychological consequence of recognising the harm, but is constitutive of what the moral response to it amounts to. Conant agrees that a successful elucidation of the concept of moral necessity involved in such contexts would constitute a refutation of Anscombe's claim regarding its dependence on a divine law conception of ethics.

The issues in the final symposium have brought us full circle to the central concerns which we met in the first symposium, concerns which are seldom far away at any point in the collection. They may be summed up in the following fundamental question: are our affective responses, moral or religious, grounded in the recognition of what is decent or sacred, or is the sense of decency or the sacred shown in these responses? However readers answer this question in the end, their reflections on it will, hopefully, be furthered by the discussions in and after the symposia in this collection.

Part I
Religion as Infantile

1

Is Religion an Infantile Morality?

RAIMOND GAITA

I

In his 'Lecture on Ethics', Wittgenstein spoke of experiences which he hoped would convey to his audience a particular sense of absolute value. One of them was the experience of remorse. Two things in particular about what Wittgenstein said would seem odd to many moral philosophers: first, that he should distinguish between absolute and relative value, yet not speak of what John Finnis calls 'exceptionless moral norms'; and, second, that he should place such weight on what he called 'experiences'. Later I shall argue that Wittgenstein was right and try to show why and what interest there is in it. I will now merely remark that what he said draws attention to an important divide in moral philosophy. Some moral philosophies express a preoccupation with rules, principles, prescriptions, virtues and vices, and so on, usually in order to see how these stand in relation to reason. Others – far fewer – are inspired by an experience of morality as something extraordinary – often as something mysterious. Or, to put the point in a way whose significance will emerge later, they are haunted by a certain sense of good and evil.

There are many ways of conceiving of morality which are inspired and bear witness to no such wonder. The reason is not because they are reductive, as are, for example, utilitarianism or certain functional accounts of the virtues. Morality may be acknowledged to be *sui generis* – as when for example we acknowledge that the nobility we prize in courage is not reducible to the functional value of courage – without occasioning wonder, or not at any rate a wonder that there should be in the world such a quality as nobility. That kind of wonder comes with experiences of good and evil. Of course, when courage or some other virtue exemplifies goodness rather than nobility then it will also evoke that wonder. R. F. Holland said:

> A stance has to be taken unless it goes by default, towards the difference between judgments that are of the highest significance for ethics and judgments that are not. In the former case I would say that it is more a matter of registering an experience or marking an encounter, than passing a judgment. I am thinking now of what can be seen in the unprofitable fineness of certain deeds or characters – and is pointed to by the unprofitable vileness of others; the difference between the unqualified goodness attested or offended against there and the ordinary run of merits and demerits among people and their works.[1]

I will say something similar about evil as it is experienced in remorse. I will argue that we could not speak of goodness as Holland does were it not for our experience, in remorse, of evil; and also that remorse would not be what it is for us, distinguished so sharply from shame, were it not for our experience of goodness of the kind Holland speaks of.

It is often said that the belief in absolute value, conceived as exceptionless moral norms, is the expression of an infantile longing for certainty which seeks its justification in a religious underwriting of those norms. That invokes a colloquial sense of 'infantile' and the thought is not very interesting. It is often itself the expression of an infantile (again, in the colloquial sense) fantasy of those who flatter themselves that they have seen through things and that they live courageously in the light of their disillusionment. However, the thought that it is an infantile morality which secures its authority and seriousness from the preeminence it accords to guilt and remorse is more interesting and has been developed more profoundly. Freud thought that psychoanalysis would reveal the deep psychological structure of our illusions about the nature of morality's authority. His account of guilt-feeling deploys a detailed psychological theory to support the more general (sceptical) claim that something can be so deeply inner that it can appear to represent an outer authority of a kind quite unlike familial, social or political authority.

This sceptical theme has been taken up in recent philosophy

by Bernard Williams and developed more specifically by Richard Wollheim.[2] Their target is a guilt-centred morality with a Kantian emphasis on obligations which fall upon a thin, characterless moral agent. They hope to persuade us from allegiance to a sense of morality as being ubiquitous and overriding; which allows for no other values seriously to compete with moral value; and which is marked by a psychologically destructive preoccupation with a sense of guilt that is radically distinguished from shame. They believe that a critical philosophy which is historically informed and supported by a sophisticated moral psychology will locate the nature of the value that we call moral – or, as much as they believe can be retrieved from the distortions of religion and religiously influenced philosophy – firmly in the natural conditions of human life. Wollheim argues that morality, or as he sometimes puts it, 'morality narrowly conceived', is structured by the largely alien and persecutory voice of the superego, and is thus 'oriented towards guilt and preoccupied with what to do rather than with what one should be'. He argues that morality 'inherits from the superego certain baneful features' which are internal to it, and that to move beyond them we should 'think of shame as the prime moral sentiment of evolved morality, of morality beyond the superego'. It is the task of a 'genetic moral psychology' to free us of the illusion that we can have 'an idealised version of morality free of [morality's characteristic] failings'. He says that 'Morality broadly conceived is an amalgam of morality narrowly conceived and the sense of value: it is morality constructed at once upon obligation and upon goodness.'[3]

Such is the background and context of my discussion. Nietzsche and Freud haunt it at various points. I will discuss remorse (which I take to be the pained recognition of one's guilt) in a way that I hope will relieve one of the feeling that something like what Freud says *must* be right, by relieving one of the idea that the alternatives to believing something of that kind are either to be naive about the appearances or to have false metaphysical or religious beliefs that one hopes will save the appearances. I will discuss goodness in an example which would provoke Nietzsche's contempt and hope to show up that contempt. I also hope to show that certain experiences of good and evil reveal a substantial sense of absolute value that does not require, and could not have, metaphysical or religious underpinning.

II

'What have I done!' 'How could I have done it!' These are characteristic expressions of remorse. They express a realisation of the
significance of what one has done, a shocked remembrance of
the fact that something *could* have that kind of significance. They
are not really questions. To the extent that they may be taken as
such, their answers at any level of description that would interest
a court are obvious. In so far as they carry an implication that
one did not fully know what one was doing, then such ignorance
is not of the kind suffered by, for example, Oedipus; nor is it of
the kind that leads us to say that the criminally insane do not
know what they do or that they do not 'know right from wrong'.
Just as the contact with the goodness that Holland describes in-
spires the wonder that there could be such a thing in the world,
so in the case of remorse we are painfully struck by the reality of
evil, and by the way remorse differs from natural suffering, from
the afflictions of Job, and from shame and dishonour.

Some people look upon the suffering I have described as a
morally suspect addendum to the properly moral dimensions of
remorse, these being the repudiation of one's wrong-doing and
the requirement to make reparation when it is possible. On this
view the suffering associated with remorse is not one of its morally essential constituents. A contrary position for which I will
argue can be put by paraphrasing the later Wittgenstein: the suffering of remorse is not an emotional effect of the recognition
that one has wronged someone, but is the primary form of that
recognition. Remorse is not recognition plus suffering: it is the
indivisible suffering–recognition of the *meaning* of what one did.
It is, however, suffering unlike any other. We cannot legitimately
seek consolation in the knowledge that others are as guilty as we
are, or even more so.[4] The lucid, remorseful recognition of one's
guilt leaves one, as I have put it elsewhere,[5] radically singular
because we cannot seek uncorrupted consolation in fellowship
with others who suffer as we do. This makes remorse unique
amongst forms of suffering and gives to us that distinctive concept of evil that Hannah Arendt tried to convey when she said
that the men of the eighteenth century had no understanding of
goodness beyond virtue or of evil beyond vice. If that is so, then
the lucid refusal of consolation in a fellowship of the guilty is
not a form of pride and is not morally or psychologically un-

realistic. It is not a consequence of setting standards that are too
high, nor is it the expression of a severe and persecutory conscience. It is merely the acknowledgement that such is the nature
of guilt. Why is remorse as it is? How could there be such a
phenomenon? These questions are no more an invitation to psychological inquiry than is the cry, 'How could I have done it?'

The pained realisation of what one has become is internal to
the remorseful realisation of what one did. But, in this connection, the concept of 'what one has become' is complex for at least
two reasons. First, there may be nothing more substantial to be
said about one's character or personality than that one has become the doer of a deed of such and such a kind, that one is a
traitor, for example. To be sure, that invites elaborations which
reveal more fully the significance of what one did, but these too
need say nothing more substantial about our personality or about
our character. Often deeds of which we are guilty are also deeds
which reveal our vices, and elaborations of what we have done
will include both what is properly the object of remorse and what
is the object of those responses which focus on what our deeds
have revealed about us. But it *need* not be so.

Second, the concern with what one has become may appear to
be of an unsavoury kind which distracts attention from one's victim
who should be the proper focus of our concern. Of course that
may happen, but when it does it is a failing whose character is
revealed in the light of a lucid remorse. Remorse is the perspective in which a deepened appreciation of the meaning of what
one has done, of what one has become through doing it, and of
what one's victim has suffered, are inseparable. If that still raises
the suspicion that a remorseful concern with what one has become competes with a proper concern for one's victim, then it
might help to think of other examples. Grief, when it is not self-
indulgent, is a heightened form of the awareness of another, but
hardly anyone would say that the pain of grief must distract our
attention from the person over whom we are grieving. Or, consider the example with which Williams introduces what he calls
'agent-regret', when it matters to the lorry driver who (blame-
lessly) runs over a child that *he* did it.[6] The fact that we experience such regret is no reason for wishing that we would experience
only the regret of an ideally compassionate spectator, under pain
of self-centredness. Indeed, there is reason to believe that the fact
of agent-regret plays an important role in the formation of those

very concepts which make such responses appropriate.

The reason for that conclusion can be sketched as follows. The *generality* of agent-regret partly conditions the sense of the concepts with which we make sense of it in the individual case. In Williams's example they are the concepts which express, and which enable us to explore in ever deepening ways, our understanding of what it means to kill a child. If that is so, then someone who insists that what really matters (morally) is the child's death and the parents' suffering, rather than by whom these were caused, would fail to see what conditions the concepts to which they appeal. They are the ones that reveal to us the significance of, and which thereby properly place, the insistence that the agent should attend to the 'independent reality' of the child. These concepts also determine the nature of the spectator's reactions. Spectators of agent-regret respond to something whose meaning has been partly constituted by such agent-reactions. They cannot, therefore, idealise their own position as the one which secures an objective perception of how things are without actually losing sight of what is there to be seen. Whatever conception we have here of what it is to see things rightly, it must be informed by the recognition that the grammar of the epistemic and critical concepts under which the phenomena present to us is conditioned by the encounter of agent and victim.[7]

Much the same can be said about remorse. It need not diminish one's sense of the independent reality of one's victim, and if it is lucid it will not. On the contrary, it is both constitutive and revelatory of our sense of other human beings as a unique limit to our will of the kind we express when we say that they are ends in themselves, or of absolute value, or the bearers of inalienable natural rights, or that they are infinitely precious, or, more simply, that they are sacred. The unique character of guilty suffering has its counterpart in a particular sense of the preciousness of other human beings. The sense that it is extraordinary that there could be such a state as guilt and such suffering as remorse has its counterpart in the wonder that other human beings whom we might otherwise not care for, and whom we might otherwise despise, could matter so to us.[8] But the sense of incomprehension that is often expressed in remorse is not about how one could have failed to realise that other human beings are in that way precious, or how, given that one realised it, one failed adequately to respect it. It is the bewildered realisation that there could be something which is in this way precious. I say *in this way precious* because, of course, things are precious in different ways. And 'precious' is, anyhow, an inadequate word here. The mainstream philosophical tradition has given us only Kant's 'ends in themselves', but it has more problems than are tolerable. The religious tradition has given us the word 'sacred'. Let me for the moment use it and say that remorse is a bewildered contact, through its violation, with what is sacred.

We may, for philosophical purposes, try to express that sense of violation by noting that someone who is wronged suffers not only whatever natural form of harm is consequent upon it, and horror or disgust at the vice which may be expressed in it, but also and in a way not reducible to these, the harm of being wronged. However, that (formal) point – that the victim of evil suffers a harm *sui generis* as does the agent – will not, of itself, take us to the idea that a person should be that kind of limit to one's will which we express when we say that he or she is sacred, when we express our sense of the evil of murder by saying that it violates something sacred. On some readings, Aristotle held a form of the first view, but on no plausible reading did he hold the second. What the formal point comes to depends upon other features of the conception of value to which it gives formal and general expression. I am suggesting that a sense of an individual as sacred is partly expressed in the realisation of what they suffer when they are wronged, and that remorse is the primary form of that realisation. The recognition in remorse of what one has done is the recognition of the preciousness of one's victims as that is revealed in the character of what they suffer because, and only because, they have been wronged. Or, to put the point backwards in a way that stresses the interdependence of the concepts involved: that they are precious is revealed in the fact that the murdered dead suffer not only the natural evil of death, but also the evil of having been murdered; but what *that* amounts to – the sense in which they are precious and the way it is internal to the wrong they suffer – is revealed to us in remorse and is partly constituted by it. The harm, *sui generis*, which is suffered both by the victim and the agent, the sacredness of the victim (and, indeed, of the agent) and the unique kind of suffering which is remorse – these are interdependent. The form of their interdependence gives to us a distinctive concept of evil. This shows, I think, that it would be misleading to think, as Williams seems to, that one could best understand the relations and differences between remorse (guilt-feeling) and shame by seeing them as focusing on the two faces of action; with shame turning inwards towards what has been revealed about the agent and guilt turning outwards to the effect of his or her actions. Remorse does not merely turn us towards our victims: it is revelatory and partly constitutive of our sense of what it is for them *to be our victims.*[9]

III

Freud argued that the authority that a sense of guilt seems to confer on moral imperatives derives from the nature and intensity of the guilty person's response to an internalised human presence that keeps him or her answerable to something more than an abstraction, such as the moral law or the embodiment of rationality in another. The point is important but is, I think, a distortion of the one I made in Section II. When seen from the standpoint of one who, in remorse, confronts the realisation of what it means to be guilty, many of the traditional accounts of the seriousness of the ethical appear as parodies. 'My God, what have I done! I have violated the moral law; I have violated the rationality in another.' Their preoccupation with reasons that would give all rational agents to be moral distracted philosophers from the realisation that the reasons to which they implicitly or explicitly appeal provide no account of the gravity of the experiences – our encounters with good and evil – that underlie the authority of the rules and prescriptions that they tried to rationalise. The reason – that the victim is insufficiently present in the implicit account of what it means to have wronged him – was misunderstood by Freud, but he was alive to it.

Freud's misunderstanding of this led him to mistake remorseful suffering for the persecutory voice of the superego and to connect it with a substantive sense of self-hatred and worthlessness. He failed adequately to distinguish between remorse and those forms of moral response which focus on character and personality. To oversimplify, but in a way which takes us back to the contrast invoked by Wollheim, Freud failed adequately to distinguish guilt from shame, and thereby, evil from vice. The moral focus of shame is on what one has been revealed to be. Often it is on character because one's virtues and vices reveal what kind of person one is. But, as Aristotle pointed out, that is relative. He rightly observed that there are fears which are beyond human endurance. Acknowledgment of that fact places limits on accusations of cowardice and enables us to find legitimate consolation in our shame over our cowardice when we discover, for example, that others, braver even than we, fled in circumstances similar to ours. Our shame, like other forms of human suffering, may be consoled when we see it in the light of the shame suffered by others. Similar things can be said about some forms of agent-regret. This is the source of the consoling power of much psychotherapy. We often regard excesses of shame as a kind of hubris, as a failure to acknowledge that one is 'only human'. That is why reflection on shame can inspire the thought that moral philosophy is in need of a realistic moral psychology.

We would not, I think, feel guilty if we did not feel ashamed. We would not have the concept of evil if we did not have that of vice. I have not argued for these claims but my opponents would, I believe, readily grant them.[10] Guilt does not focus on character but it stands in complex relations to it. It is dependent on it, but it also transforms our sense of its virtues and vices. Its dependence on character will be obvious to anyone who sees the need for a serious account of the virtues. Nothing I have said lessens the need for such an account, and I would emphasise the ineliminable role of the virtues of character in the constitution of the epistemic virtues that are needed by anyone who wishes to be lucid about the nature of their guilt, and who wishes to avoid the many corruptions of remorse that were brilliantly, if venomously, diagnosed by Nietzsche. But a sense of remorse as I have characterised it will alter our sense of the virtues and vices by connecting them with a sense of good and evil. That sense of good and evil is inseparable from the radical change in our sense of what it is to be a human being, which comes through a transformed sense of self and others, as these are experienced in remorse.

My characterisation of remorse is logically independent of pessimistic or optimistic views of human nature. It is logically independent of any claim that we are by nature sinners. The horror which I spoke of is not an expression of self-hatred, nor of a sense of worthlessness, in so far as these focus on character, desires, dispositions and so on. It need, therefore, have nothing directly to do with self-esteem. Much of the talk of the poisonous nature of remorse expresses confusion about this and confuses remorse with its corruptions. The deep woe which is sometimes expressed in remorse may be the natural expression of the despair of those who realise that the evil they have done has spread through their lives, depriving the things which gave sense to their lives of the power any longer to do so. Often, when things which give sense to people's lives are redescribed in the light of their guilt, they can no longer be a source of energy for them. The evil we do can spread through our lives destroying the meaning of the very things for whose sake we did it, compounding the horror of remorse with the sense that we were, necessarily, involved in a self-defeating project.[11] The horror of that is consistent with there being nothing within the person to whom it applies – no desires or dispositions – which would appropriately be an object of his or her loathing.

My emphasis on the radical singularity of the guilty, and the way it distinguishes remorse from shame, is not the unrelievedly bleak one which would deny an end to guilty suffering. But it reveals, I believe, that the consoling power of forgiveness, expiation, atonement and punishment differs in kind from the consolation to be found in psychotherapy and *from whatever other forms of consolation come from a sense of fellowship with others who suffer as we do*. When it comes from the acknowledgment of one's guilt, the need to make reparation is different from when it comes from the kind of regret suffered by Williams's lorry driver. The lorry driver does not suffer remorse, but the fact that his suffering has much in common with remorse encouraged Williams to believe that he had found, in the concept of agent-regret, the key to what is retrievable in the concept of remorse as it had been distorted by the 'morality system'. I hope to have shown that he was mistaken.

If what I have said is true, then Wollheim was also mistaken to contrast morality and value as he did, placing guilt and remorse on the side of morality. For if, as I have argued, these are not merely expressive of the austere morality of obligation, but are constitutive of our sense of the infinitely precious character of each individual human being, then *they are amongst the most important determinants of any sense of value which might profitably be contrasted with a morality centred on obligation or which might be offered to deepen it*. It is, therefore, also wrong to contrast a sense of value that centres on guilt and remorse with one that centres (more *positively*, some would say) on compassion, and which emphasises the virtues of charity and friendship. As I have already suggested, the ethically conditioned individuality, manifest in remorse and (partly) constituted by it, radically effects any account of what these (and other) virtues may be. What it is to be a friend, a comrade, a wife or husband, a fellow citizen or a foreigner – our understanding of these and of the requirements and the qualities of character which are internal to them, and of what pride and shame may be in relation to them, is transformed under the shock of what a lucid remorse reveals human beings to be.

IV

The nature of the interdependence between remorse and our understanding of evil might become clearer if we consider an example provided by Peter Singer. He has wondered whether there is a moral difference between 'going over to India and shooting a few peasants' and failing to give money to Oxfam when the latter results in the death of people in, say, India.[12] Philosophers will be familiar with his reason for wondering this: it is because he is interested in what we make (morally) of the difference between acting and failing to act. He concludes that there is a moral difference although it is by no means as great as we think it to be, and he seems to suggest that a saint would probably make little of it.

Suppose that we go to Singer's room and find him trying to hang himself from the rafters. We ask what he is up to and he replies that he intends to kill himself because he can no longer live with the (multiple) murderer he became when he failed to renew his monthly bank order to Oxfam. Would even those of us who read his book and were unable to fault the argument conclude that Singer was a man of impressively severe principles and saintly character, whereas poor Fred who shot himself last week after 'going off to India and shooting a few peasants' was a man of no more than common conscience?

I will not try to convince those who do not feel the rhetorical pressure of that question. My concern is to understand why many people do. The general answer seems to be that the professed belief that failing to send money to Oxfam could be much the same morally as murder cannot find expression in someone's life sufficient to convince us that they could seriously hold it. The difficulties in that general answer – the interesting and revealing difficulties in it – may be appreciated by considering a natural response to it. It is this. I am able to count on cheap laughs from this example because I trade on the (by no means uncommon) fact that emotions which characteristically accompany certain beliefs may not accompany radically new forms of them. Our psychological life might not keep pace with the radical discoveries of our reason. In the case of the example we are discussing (the thought continues), the emotional part of remorse – the part of remorse which is not logically connected with moral judgement as are repudiation and (perhaps) the requirement to make reparation – has not kept pace with our judgement that this kind of omission is akin to murder. Similarly, Singer would argue, our emotional life may not keep up with the rational acknowledgement that blacks and women are in every moral respect our equals, or that the killing of chimpanzees is morally little different from the killing of human infants whose morally relevant capacities are not as developed as are those of the chimps. Our emotional responses may change in time or they may not, but unless emotivism is true (and possibly even then), whether or not they do is irrelevant to the cogency of the argument. Thus goes the deflationary diagnosis of the force of my rhetorical question.

I think that the diagnosis is mistaken for two reasons. I have already discussed the first. While the diagnosis acknowledges that remorse may have causal influence on our epistemic capacities, it denies it any intrinsic epistemic potential.[13] It therefore has no serious room for the thought that remorse may reveal to us the meaning of what we have done. Or, and this is just another aspect of the same incapacity, to the extent that it will acknowledge a connection between remorse and our sense of the meaning of what we have done, it will not acknowledge that the realisation or understanding of meaning is a cognitive achievement. The second reason is even more fundamental and is expressive of something deep and pervasive in philosophy. Its nature and (in my judgement) its error was exposed by Wittgenstein. The deflationary diagnosis treats certain facts of our human life – certain psychological states and practices – which condition the grammar of the *concepts* that we express in our beliefs as standing in only causal relations to those *beliefs*. Certain psychological responses are invoked to explain why we sometimes find it hard to believe what our reason requires us to believe. G. E. Moore spoke for a long and powerful tradition when he said that some things are doubtful (that is to say, our reason tells us they are dubious), but it is (psychologically and practically) impossible for us to doubt them. It is easy to see that the reply I sketched on Singer's behalf belongs to that tradition. Wittgenstein's dissenting claim was that some aspects of human life which philosophers denigrate as thwarting the radically critical ambitions and achievements of Reason sometimes determine the grammar of what the philosophers are investigating – the concept of pain, for example – and, more significantly, of the critical concepts that mark what it is to think well or badly about what they are investigating.

We may now see why the *reductio* works. It is not because there are insuperable psychological obstacles to our believing what Singer invites us to believe. Nor is it because we should give more weight than he does to the beliefs of common sense or what we ordinarily believe. Nor is it because Singer's conclusion is so radically discrepant with our pre-theoretical intuitions that theory and pre-theory cannot meet in reflective equilibrium. That Rawlsian thought is of a piece, albeit in a dissenting form, with what Singer says. They share the same assumptions. The *reductio* works because the responses which Singer dismisses as of merely psychological interest condition (determine the grammar of) the concepts under investigation. If we attempt to prescind radically from them in the name of reason, then we will succeed only in sawing away the conceptual branch on which we are sitting. We will then be in the comical position of losing our subject-matter at the very time when we believe that we have made radical discoveries about it.

I think that account of why the *reductio* works is truer to most people's responses to the rhetorical question which followed my thought experiment. When we cannot take seriously the idea that people might kill themselves because they failed to renew their bank order to Oxfam, it is because we do not know *what it would be for them seriously to believe they are murderers.* Singer invites us to judge whether something is morally much the same as murder while inviting us radically to prescind from those responses that determine a significant part of our sense of the relevant kind of seriousness. He invites us to measure one thing against another while inviting us to undermine exactly those things which are constitutive of our measure.

If we cannot find it intelligible that someone should feel such remorse as they might about murder because they failed to renew their contributions to Oxfam, then we will not know what to make of the idea that these omissions could be morally much the same as murder. This is because we will have lost our grip on the concepts which determine the relevant 'sameness'. The concept of moral seriousness, the kind of seriousness which morality has for us and which informs our sense of the seriousness of murder, has been deprived of one of the main determinants of its sense. This does not, of course, mean that the readiness to kill oneself is a criterion for understanding what one has done if one has committed a murder. But it does mean that we must find it intelligible that murderers might, in their despair, be driven to commit suicide. Remorse is partly constitutive for us of what it is for something to be a moral matter because it is constitutive for us of the kind of seriousness which we think to be internal to such matters. Singer trades on that sense of seriousness in order to convince us, but he falls into absurdity because he does not understand what underlies it.

It is important, therefore, to see that my point is not that someone could make the judgement that Singer invites us to make only if they were unhinged, and that therefore, it cannot be recommended to us as a requirement of reason. If we imagine a person who kills himself or herself after telling some such story as Singer invites us to accept, then we are not imagining someone who makes outlandish moral judgements, but who retains intact those concepts which inform our sense of seriousness of moral matters. We are imagining someone who has lost their grip on what it means be a murderer to an extent that is so radical that we must doubt whether they have any serious understanding of morality. The psychological state which is both cause and effect of this conceptual impairment, and which might drive such a person to commit suicide, would be an emotional shadow of remorse.

Suppose now someone who grants that what Singer says is unintelligible (where that is not just a hyperbolical way of saying that it is outrageously false), but who also points out that people had found it unintelligible that one should feel serious remorse if one murdered a negro. That reminder will not work in Singer's favour unless it is (wrongly) assumed that I have claimed remorse to be an epistemic guide to when something is morally wrong to do, as something whose presence we might (even if cautiously) take as a guide to true moral beliefs. People sometimes speak of conscience in this way. Nonetheless, the point gets at something important. But, properly developed, it undermines even more radically the perspective from which Singer mounted his argument and from which it could be defended. That development centres on what is involved in coming to find something morally intelligible when one had not found it so before.

V

It is, I think, a mistake to believe that we can, altogether independently of the way remorse shows itself in people's lives, determine what are its rationally appropriate objects. The point, of course, extends beyond remorse. Often we may not know what is an appropriate or even an intelligible object of love until it is revealed to us by the quality of someone's love. I will elaborate this in some detail in the next section. But the idea of something as revealed to us through the way in which it shows in a person's life is a complex idea. There is a thin, but philosophically pervasive, idealisation of the subject to whom it is revealed, which is that of a *res cogitans* whose properly cognitive achievements and the capacities which make it possible are essentially unconditioned by the particular conditions of human life. And there is a conception of what there is for such a subject to understand (of the objects of its cognitive achievements) which centres on a correlatively thin conception of expressive behaviour in certain circumstances. I want to show how and why these are inadequate. In the discussion of the example which follows, I shall characterise the background of common understanding within which it becomes intelligible that we should be moved, and through being moved find depth, or even sense, where we had not found it before. That background is often called a 'conceptual framework', but I hope to reveal why that phrase invites readings which are too intellectualist.

Consider this passage from the *Iliad*:

Meges in turn killed Pedaios, the son of Antenor,
who, bastard though he was, was nursed by lovely Theano
with close care, as for her own children, to pleasure her
    husband.
Now the son of Phyleus, the spear-famed, closing upon him
struck him with a sharp spear behind the head at the tendon,
and straight on through the teeth and under the tongue cut
    the bronze blade,

and he dropped in the dust gripping in his teeth the cold
  bronze.

Homer reveals the brutality of war and, at the same time, the
humanity of a soldier who is its victim. Simone Weil has written
powerfully, in her essay on the *Iliad*, of the way that war may
turn human beings into things.[14] Such ways of speaking of human beings, of how they may recover, lose or never fully attain
their humanity, come naturally to us. It is natural to think that
there are conditions which make it impossible to recognise the
humanity in someone. To dehumanise people, in prisons or in
concentration camps for example, is to create such conditions with
varying degrees of awareness and intent.

Two things may strike one when one reflects on this example.
First, it is natural to invoke here the concept of a human being in
a way that is resistant to the philosophical insistence that it is
really the concept of a person that carries its frequent ethical connotations. The concept of a person, when it is not used inter-
changeably with that of a human being, but offered as a corrective
to its use, invites us to prescind from exactly those aspects of
human life which seem to be important in the passage I quoted.
The passage reminds us of the importance to our moral identity
– indeed to our identity *simpliciter* – of our place in the network
of personal relations whose character and content seem not easily separable from the forms they take in human life.

Second, when we speak of seeing the humanity in someone, or
of acknowledging someone as fully human, or conversely of de-
humanisation, we imply the acknowledgement or the denial of a
certain kind of individuality. This might appear to be a pecu-
liarly modern way of thinking which it would be far-fetched to
attribute to Homer. Indeed, one might note that Homer does not
draw our attention to anything that strongly individuates his
character; that, on the contrary, our attention is drawn to the
soldier's place in personal and institutional relations whose significance to our sense of his humanity derives from the fact that
they are common to human kind. We should, however, not be
misled by this, for the kind of individuality we are here concerned with has little to do with the celebration of what in modern times we call individualism. Parents who mourn a dead child,
or the wife or husband who mourns a dead spouse, grieve because the one they have lost is irreplaceable, but not in the sense

in which something is irreplaceable because it has characteristics which we will not find elsewhere. That (latter) kind of individuality, marked by individuating characteristics or achievements, is also prominent in the *Iliad*, in the celebration of the feats of the great heroes, Achilles, Hector and others. But the individuality whose nature marks our mourning is what is prominent in the passage that I quoted. It is fundamental to our sense of the 'intrinsic dignity' of each human being irrespective of anything which might make him or her stand out from a crowd.

We sometimes express that kind of individuality by saying that each of us necessarily experiences the world differently or that each is a unique perspective on the world. That is right, I think, but the emphasis should not be on the idea that our subjectivity is at important levels inaccessible to others. The recognition that the kind of individuality which I am emphasising is connected with the idea that each person is a unique perspective on the world may be developed differently. The difference turns on a sense of inner life as we mean it when we say that some people have rich and others have impoverished inner lives. We mean something different when we speak this way of the inner life than when we say that sensations, for example, are inner and subjective whereas behaviour is outer and objective.

In the first way of speaking of the inner life, the reference to depth and shallowness is essential because the inner life, thus conceived, consists of states – love, grief, joy and so on – which present themselves under concepts that require us to distinguish between the real and counterfeit forms of what falls under them. We call something love only because we can distinguish it from its false semblances; because, for example, we can distinguish love from infatuation. And we call something grief only because it is answerable to the standards which distinguish genuine forms of it from, for example, sentimental and self-absorbed indulgence – a distinction which requires a conception of the independent reality of others. The individuality I have been describing is essential to the epistemic and critical grammar of those standards that inform our sense of what we mean when we speak of appearance and reality as it concerns the inner life; standards that determine what it is critically to probe the appearances and whose authority imposes on us a requirement to do so under pain of superficiality.

The inner life, as I am suggesting we think of it, is partly constituted by the attitudes we take to certain defining facts of human life – facts such as that we are mortal, that we are vulnerable to suffering, that we may be destroyed by our passions and so on. I say *partly* because, of course, there are other things – a commitment to justice, to duty, to an impersonal concern with the interests of people who are distant from us literally and emotionally, to take salient examples. However, our sense that there may be something profound in these other things depends on our seeing, or assuming, their connection with our responses to those facts which I suggested are primary. Failing that connection we could have no serious sense of their claim on us.

The attitudes I mentioned earlier determine our sense that we belong with others to a common kind whose character is marked by the fellowship we register when we speak of the human condition as a common fate. Much reflection that is, in a broad sense, ethical or spiritual, and much of our art and literature is in response to such facts and to the ways our reflective attitudes to them enter our sense of common humanity. I call them defining facts of human life, because our responses to them define our sense of belonging to a common kind in ways that condition what we mean when we speak of human beings when we mean more than that they belong to the species *Homo sapiens*, and of what we mean when we speak of a shared humanity against whose background we understand one another. Much of this is marked by two ways in which we use the first person plural. I shall call one a 'we' of fellowship and contrast it with a use of 'we' that is merely classificatory. This distinction is important to the idea of a common understanding in so far as that implies a conceptual space which enables those within it to converse about what it means to live a human life. That space is defined by the 'we' of fellowship: it marks the kind of commonness we are here concerned with and the kind of publicness necessary for the (broadly) ethical concepts to have the grammar which they do.

Philosophers often say that utterances or statements or propositions or thoughts are the subject-matter for (philosophical) ethical reflection. We may be alerted to a different possibility if we reflect on the significance of Socrates' persistent demand that his interlocutors speak for themselves. He did not do this because he was primarily concerned with the consistency of his interlocutors' sincerely held beliefs. He did it to awaken in them an obligation to a discipline of thought, to a mode of seriousness and sobriety, whose constitutive categories cannot be specified independently of the moral disciplines of the Socratic form of dialogical engagement. Socrates' insistence on the individual voice does not attenuate the rigours of reason: it is a reminder to his interlocutors of the connection between the forms of sober judgement that are fundamental to ethical thinking and the need to find one's own voice; and of the connection between these and what is thought about ethical and spiritual matters to be true and truthful and 'in tune with reality'. The subject-matter for Socratic reflection is not utterances whose cognitive contents are typically independent of who made them. It is action and speech which have a certain authority, and when it is speech, it is what has been said in the sense we mean when we say that some people have 'something to say'. That sense connects with an authority which derives from the way they have lived and with the integrity with which they answer to the obligation to self-knowledge.

The contrast between appearance and reality is, of course, central to the Socratic and Platonic dialogues. The subject-matter was often the virtues, or to the extent that they are different, psychological or spiritual states, dispositions or responses, such as love, the true object of desire, the proper response to mortality and so on. It is well-known that Socrates was concerned to test the appearances by argument. He insisted that he and his interlocutors follow the argument wherever it led them. Peter Singer insists on that too. What I have said should at least raise the suspicion that he and Socrates do not have the same thing in mind. It was Wittgenstein who raised the possibility that if we were to try to purify our critical concepts from their embeddedness in human life and of their expression in natural languages – rich in resonance and local association – then we would leave ourselves with only a shadow play of the grammar of serious judgement. It would be absurd to attribute a theory of the matter to Socrates. However, something like Wittgenstein's thought was, I think, presupposed in the importance that Socrates attached to the need for participants in argument to answer for themselves – to find their own voice – and in the connection he saw between this and the concepts that mark sober judgements about the appearances. It was, therefore, presupposed in his conception of what it is soberly to follow an argument wherever it goes.

The sobriety he demanded of his interlocutors and himself presupposed a self whose authenticity partly constituted, and was partly constituted by, forms of truthfulness, sobriety and responsibility. Their interdependence gave Socratic inquiry its distinctive intellectual discipline. That is why the dialogical form of Socratic inquiry was essential to the logical character of the critical concepts which marked its successes and failures. That is also why standards of intellectual rigour and standards of responsibility are interdefining in the dialogues. Socratic argument demanded a kind of seriousness, which could only be answered by a self considerably more substantial, more personal, less punctual (as Charles Taylor puts it) and more essentially and fully human than the one Singer implicitly hypostatises as the respondent to the demands of Reason.

When I asked why my *reductio* against Singer worked, I said that when we looked to how it might show itself in a life, we could not take seriously the claim that people could kill themselves because they seriously believed they became murderers when they failed to send money to Oxfam. Then I spoke of the interdependence between remorse and our sense of good and evil, between remorse and our sense of the seriousness of murder. The argument there was more specific to particular moral concepts. The argument in this section has tried to focus more generally on what is involved in the concept of taking something seriously in this kind of area, and in the concept of something being revealed to us in a person's life. These, too, are interdependent in various ways.

Singer says that a belief may be taken seriously – may be taken seriously as a motive for a serious person – if we can see how an argument for it could reasonably convince that person. In a way I agree. But my question is how we should understand the idea of an argument compelling someone to a conclusion. Singer would reply that the answer is relatively simple and is provided in the logic textbooks. My argument has been that what we find in the logic textbooks presupposes a certain background in whose absence nothing we find in the textbooks could compel us seriously to believe anything. Sometimes the discrepancy between what an argument appears to compel us to conclude and what we can seriously conclude (seriously profess as our belief) is dramatic. Scepticism of the external world or of other minds provides examples to those who do not believe that such doubts can seriously be entertained. *Reductios* of the kind I presented against Singer are less dramatic but essentially similar examples. Both provoke the question why someone cannot seriously believe a conclusion even though they may not be able to fault the argument which led to it.[15]

The answer in very general terms is that if we try to form a conception of the rigours of argument that disengages radically from the characteristic forms of human life – as do conceptions of argument that inform the contrast between the rational and the psychological as we have it in the defence I sketched of Singer – then we are liable to a light-headedness that will make our arguments vulnerable to the kind of *reductio* I directed against Singer. Socrates noticed in the orators their tendency to flights of fancy, their tendency to proliferate the appearances while making a great display of penetrating them. He said that they were good at oratory but unable to submit to the disciplines of conversation which alone could yield sobriety. Ironically, Singer – and in this he is quite representative – sees himself as an heir to Socrates, whereas in his vulnerability to the heady excesses of a particular rhetoric about reason and its demands, he is closer to Polus.[16]

There have been two strands to my argument in this section. First, a general argument, heavily dependent on the work of the later Wittgenstein, against an ideal of reason which is best represented in the persona of Descartes's *Meditations* – the *res cogitans* who represents thinking as such, thinking as it would be in its essence for any thinking thing. Second, a more particular argument about how to conceive the subject who wishes seriously to see things as they are, to penetrate the appearances about matters which come broadly under the head of the ethical. My argument has been that any account of what it is to rise to the requirement of rigorous argument in order seriously to understand these matters must include an account of what it is to find one's own voice – of the kind of individuality expressed in it. That will entail an elaboration of the interdependencies between finding one's voice and the concept of life as we use it when we speak of what life may teach us, of what may be revealed in a life, of the way grief, remorse, and so on, can show in a life in ways that have the power of revelation.

All this is necessary (but I do not say sufficient) to understand what Wittgenstein meant when he said that he had to speak personally of his experiences of absolute value – necessary to understand what he meant by 'personally' and what he meant by 'experience'. On the account that I am criticising – the account implicit in Singer's defence against my *reductio* – when we announce that

we speak personally, then we disclaim responsibility to the rigours
of reason, which are thought to be essentially impersonal. There
was indeed a disclaimer concerning the limits of a certain kind
of discursive reasoning in what Wittgenstein said, but there was
nothing which suggested a failure of the disciplines which must
inform understanding. If there were, then he would have said
nothing to deserve our attention and nothing to claim our trust.

When Wittgenstein said that he spoke personally, he expressed
the hope that he shared a common understanding with at least
some of his audience. The understanding he sought was not the
common understanding I characterised earlier when I spoke of a
sense of fellowship that was conditioned by our responses to the
defining facts of the human condition. However what he sought
presupposed that form of common understanding and had fundamental features in common with it. I can perhaps explain why
by appealing to a distinction made famous by Martin Buber.[17]
The 'we' of fellowship that marks the kind of commonness we
mean when we speak of a common human understanding is conditioned by the primacy of the encounter between I and Thou –
by its primacy to our sense of the kind of commonness it is. Or,
to put the same point with the help of Socrates: the character of
that commonness is determined by the primacy of Socratic inter-
locution; by the way we are each potentially a respondent to another's call to seriousness. Or, to put the point differently again
and in a more linguistic/grammatical idiom: the common understanding whose existence gives the grammatical shape to our ethical
concepts has a character determined by the encounter between
first and second person rather than between first and third. That
is the kind of publicness revealed in the grammar of our ethical
concepts. That is the logical space in which ethical examples may
'speak' to us, the logical space which determines the epistemic
and critical grammar of the authority that we attribute to words
and deeds which have the power to move us and which may
reveal something to be intelligible whereas we had previously
not found it so.

Buber noted the interdependence between I and Thou and, also,
the fact that what they have in common to reflect upon and respond to is conditioned by that interdependence. Iris Murdoch
complained that the impersonal public character of ethical concepts was inadequate for ethical understanding. She sketched a
form of understanding whose personal character she believed to

be opposed to the spirit of Wittgenstein's argument against private languages. She thought that the privacy she appealed to had been denied by moral philosophies influenced by behaviourist conceptions of the mind.[18] She was, I think, instructively mistaken. I believe that we get a better sense of the relation between inner and outer, between personal and public, by conceiving of the public space as constituted by the dialogical encounter between individuals, each a unique perspective on a common world, whose existence as a domain of meanings depends on a common understanding that is both presupposed and constituted in those dialogical encounters. To put the point more simply and in summary form: what is at issue in the discussions of privacy and publicness, individuality and commonness, as these bear on concept formation, will seem radically different according to whether one conceives of the public realm as essentially constituted by the encounter of I and Thou or by the encounter of I and Them.

If what I have said is right, then we may understand more deeply why it is virtually a tautology – why, at least, it is a conceptual point – to say, first, that moral or ethical concepts must deepen rather than cheapen what they speak to; and, second, why they must speak to those common responses to certain big facts of life that condition our sense of a common humanity. What is true of the ethical is also, I think, true of the religious and the spiritual. In whatever sense they disengage from the world, they must deepen rather than cheapen our sense of the world as constituted by our common human concerns. The experiences reported by Wittgenstein were of a kind we would call spiritual, and some would call them religious. We may now see why I said earlier that the more restricted common understanding he hoped for when he gave his lecture depended on that more general understanding whose nature I have been trying to elucidate.

Finally, if standards of intellectual rigour and standards of responsibility are interdefining, as I claimed they were for Socrates, then we may see more clearly the relation in ethics between truthfulness and truth, and the relation between these and our sense of the requirement to follow the argument wherever it takes us.

I suggested earlier that the kind of argument defenders of Singer would mount against my *reductio* depended upon an edifying, but un-Socratic, fantasy about what it is seriously to care for the truth and to seek it courageously. It is natural and common to believe that in a discussion like this we should distinguish at least two kinds of necessity: first, the necessity, explained in logic books, that requires one to assert q if one has asserted p; second, the necessity that marks the compulsion to follow the inquiry wherever it leads. My argument has been that they are not so easily separable. The concept that mediates their connection is that of seriously professing a conclusion. I argued earlier that the idea of following an argument wherever it went could not be separated from the interdefining disciplines of character and intellect as these were revealed in Socratic conversation. These disciplines are marked by the critical concepts that record our sense of sober judgement. Any conception of argument presupposes them if it has the resources adequately to distinguish between sincerely assenting to whatever sentence follows the 'therefore' sign in an argument and seriously professing the conclusion of that argument. But, of course, it is important that I appealed here to the character in the Platonic dialogues – a character given to us by an artist of genius. It is important because what the Socratic call to seriousness amounts to can only be revealed in a life. It is profoundly ironic that the edifying conception of truth that underlies our fascination with the *res cogitans* depends, both for its content and for its rhetorical power, on exactly those forms of life from which it would disengage. To rely on that conception of truth and of its value to us to support a radical contrast between the rational and psychological is just another way that someone like Singer saws away the branch on which he or she is sitting. That is the deepest reason why that false paradigm of reason cannot run faster than what we find an intelligible object of remorse as that may be revealed authoritatively in a person's example.

VI

Earlier I said that I would speak of goodness – the goodness in whose light those who are lucidly remorseful understand the meaning of what they have done – by way of an example which would earn Nietzsche's contempt. I want now to do so also to illustrate again the interdependence between good and evil and the idea that human beings are precious in the sense we mark when we speak of the sanctity of human life. I want also to develop the Wittgensteinian thought that the concepts which most seriously mark our sense of mystery and of transcendence are rooted in particular practices, in particular conditions of human life.

In the early 1960s I worked as a ward-assistant in a psychiatric hospital. Some of the patients had been there for over thirty years. They were judged to be incurable and they appeared to have irretrievably lost everything which gives meaning to our lives. They had no grounds for self-respect in so far as we connect that with self-esteem; or none which could be based on qualities or achievements for which we could admire or congratulate them without condescension. Friends, wives, children and parents if they were alive had long ceased to visit them. More often than not they were treated brutishly by the psychiatrists and nurses. There was a small number of psychiatrists who worked devotedly to improve their conditions. They spoke, against all appearances, of the inalienable dignity of even those patients. Most of their colleagues believed them to be naive, even fools, and some of the nurses despised them with a vehemence that was astonishing. One day a nun came to the ward. Everything in her demeanour towards these patients – the way she spoke to them, her facial expressions, the inflexions of her body – contrasted with and showed up the behaviour of these fine psychiatrists as being, despite their best efforts, condescending. She revealed that even such patients were, as the psychiatrists had sincerely and nobly professed, their equals; but she also revealed that the psychiatrists did not, in their hearts, believe it.

I do not know how important it was that she was a nun. One is, of course, inclined to say that her behaviour was a probably a function of her religious beliefs. Perhaps, but typically, beliefs explain behaviour independently of their truth or falsity. However, seeing her one felt irresistibly that her behaviour was directly shaped by the reality which it revealed. One wondered at her, but not at anything about her except that her behaviour should have, so wondrously, this power of revelation, and therefore, of course, at what it revealed. She showed up the psychiatrists, but if one asked how exactly, then there would be no substantial elaboration on defects in their character, or their imagination, or in what ordinarily would be called their moral sensibility. Of course her behaviour did not come from nowhere, and virtues of character, imagination and sensibility, given content and form by the disciplines of her vocation, were essential to her becoming the kind of person she was. But in another person such virtues and the behaviour which expressed them would have been the focus of one's attention, as it was in the case of the psychiatrists. In the nun's case they issued in forms of behaviour which were striking not for the virtues they expressed, nor for the good they achieved, but for their power to reveal the full humanity of those whose radical affliction had made their humanity invisible. We rightly call such behaviour the expression of love, but in this case love does not work in conjunction with the recognition of some independently specifiable aspect of the person who is loved, such that together they – the love and the recognition – produce such behaviour. Behaviour of this kind *is* the form of her recognition of the reality of another; and love is the name we give to it. If she were questioned she may have told a metaphysical story about the people to whom she responded with a love of such purity. But one need not believe it or substitute any other metaphysical story in its place to be certain about the revelatory quality of her behaviour. That certainty is not a blind refusal to acknowledge the possibility of a mistake. It rests on the fact that here there is no clear application for the concept of a mistake as it would normally be understood in connection with claims about the metaphysical or empirical properties of the people in question.

Hers was a form of unconditional love. So too is parental love. They are unconditional but they are not unconditioned. Their existence depends on certain practices and customs as much as it informs them, and also upon certain facts of the human condition. Neither is universally an ideal amongst the peoples of the earth, and even in cultures such as ours where they are (or have been) celebrated, people's hold on them is often fragile. They are, I believe, dependent upon one another. I doubt that such love as was expressed in the nun's demeanour would have been possible for her, were it not for the place which the language of parental love had in her prayers. Theology and philosophy, both being discursive disciplines, seek ways of formulating this which are more abstract and more tractable to that conception of reason which I criticised in the previous section. Generally, such formulation could not find their way into her prayers. Philosophers and theologians are (for deep reasons) inclined to say that the language of prayer and worship, anthropocentric and often poetic, may make psychologically accessible and moving things whose intellectual content is more clearly revealed in the abstract deliverances of theological and philosophical theories. I suspect that the contrary is closer to the truth – that the unashamedly anthropocentric language of worship has greater power to reveal the structure of the concepts under which the nun's behaviour and what it revealed are intelligible to us.

It is an important aspect of parental love as we know it that a child appears as precious to its parents in ways that transcend its relations to and with them. Parental love, like other forms of love, must rise to the requirement to respect the independent reality of the child. We have, of course, a range of moral concepts with which we express that requirement and the various ways we fail to rise to it, but our clearest vision of it is attained when it is illuminated by the compassionate love of saints. The parent who is able to love a child who has become a vicious and vile adult reminds us, when that love is pure, that not only is this a requirement rather than a supererogatory ideal of parental love, but also and inseparably from that, that this person, however vile, is fully our fellow human being. The requirement is not external to parental love, a standard imposed from elsewhere; it is fundamental to the standards which determine real from counterfeit forms of it. It is fundamental to an account of the way in which the child appears as precious to its parents if their love is pure. But the power of parental love to reveal that – its having that to reveal – depends, I think, on the impersonal love of saints. For it is because of the place of such impersonal love in our culture that there has developed a language of love whose grammar has transformed our sense of what it is for a human being to be a unique kind of limit to our will. We express our sense of that limit when we say that human beings are owed unconditional respect, or that they have inalienable rights, and similar things. These ways of speaking express a disposition to find a basis for what love revealed which is more secure than is love itself, and to find a way of characterising it which makes it more secure to reason.

Kant is virtually alone amongst the great philosophers in emphasising the importance of our sense of the individual to the authority which morality claims over us. It is captured in his famous injunction that one act so that one always treats a person as an end and never merely as a means, and in his ideal of rational beings fully and unconditionally respectful of each other in the Kingdom of Ends. He also said that the biblical command to love one's neighbour could not be taken literally because love cannot be commanded. He took it to be a rhetorical way of expressing the duties whose nature he believed was more perspicuously revealed in his philosophy.

It is not straightforwardly true that love cannot be commanded, if that means that we cannot be required to love better. But most human beings are not saints and we come closest to loving our neighbour when we love our children as we ought and when we acknowledge our duties to others. Kierkegaard remarked that the commandment to love one's neighbour does not mean that one should love one's neighbour in one way and one's wife, children and friends in another. Rather, the partial love of one's wife, children and friends should also be the love of one's neighbour in them. This is the point I made earlier when I said that parental love aspires to be responsive to a sense of the preciousness of the child which is partly determined by the language of love as that has been informed by the compassionate love of saints. Of course morality is not merely an imperfect substitute for love. But the question is whether that aspect of our morality which is responsive to a sense of the preciousness of each individual can adequately be expressed without acknowledging the fundamental place which love plays in the formation of the concepts through which we understand that preciousness – the kind of preciousness which it is.

I think that it cannot. But when I speak of love I do not mean only the more edifying forms of it. I mean Othello's egocentric love of Desdemona as much as the love of Mother Teresa: to deny the former in the name of the latter would be as mistaken as denying the latter in the name of obligation. Here I disagree with Kierkegaard. We may be tempted to say that Othello did not really love Desdemona, but such moralisation of the standards by which we distinguish real love from its semblances is likely to undermine the very thing on which such judgements depend, namely, our sense of other human beings as irreplaceable. This would be yet another case of sawing away the branch on which one is sitting. Love takes many forms, some of which are in tension with one another and some of which are in tension with morality. I suspect that those forms of love which are in tension with morality are also essential to our sense of the preciousness of individuals. If that is so, then morality is in tension with what (partly) conditions its most fundamental concept.

It is important to our understanding of racism – at least the kind that prompts us to say that racists do not see the victims of their denigration as human beings – that someone who saw blacks as they were caricatured in the faces of the *Black and White Minstrel Show* could not believe them to be capable of the kind of suffering portrayed in *Othello*. We could not cast as Othello someone who looked to us like that. That fact is fundamental to understanding why racists are often able so utterly to disregard the sufferings of their victims. It is because they do not find it intelligible that their victims have inner lives of the kind which enable the wrongs they suffer to go deep.

Something similar is true of those who suffer severe and ineradicable affliction. When the nun revealed the compassion of the psychiatrists to be condescending she revealed that they did not perceive their patient's affliction and the wrongs done to them as being of a kind suffered by those to whom they unhesitatingly respond as to an equal. That is why I said earlier that the nun's love was the recognition of the humanity of those patients rather than being an affective state which, together with beliefs about their status, caused her to behave as she did. And that is why it is both true that the psychiatrists were shown up and that they were not morally to be faulted. The inadequacy of the concept of morality obscures what is here most deeply at issue, as was revealed when the psychiatrists spoke of the inalienable dignity of the patients. To talk of inalienable dignity is rather like talking of the inalienable right to esteem. Both are alienable; esteem for obvious reasons and dignity because it is essentially tied to appearance, and like the protestation of rights to which it is allied, will survive only if one is spared the worst. Those who are not spared, those whom Simone Weil described as having been 'struck one of those blows which leave a being struggling on the ground like a half crushed worm' depend on the love of saints to make their humanity visible. That is why Weil also said that 'when [compassion for the afflicted] is really found we have a more astounding miracle than walking on water, healing the sick, or even raising the dead'.

VI

I argued that Freud was right to believe that our sense of the authority of morality was connected with remorse (guilt-feeling) and that an account of the victim as he or she haunts those in remorse is fundamental to it. He was, as I have already indicated, inclined to a reductive view, partly because he believed that what I have described was merely the appearances and that our understanding of them would be deepened either by religion and metaphysics which lay in one direction or by psychology which lay in the other. He was hostile to metaphysics and therefore turned to psychology. It is not difficult to see why Freud would see in the account that I have sketched of remorse a mere phenomenology of the appearances as they have been structured by bad philosophy and bad religion, each serving the other. He would argue that the sense of the radical singularity of the guilty is a psychological echo of the religious claim that sinners will inescapably find themselves alone under judgement, which is itself an illusion whose nature psychoanalysis will make plain. Others who thought that this amounted to the reduction of morality to psychology, but who shared Freud's assumptions about what constituted the surface phenomena and his beliefs about where we could (in principle) look for a deeper understanding, turned to metaphysics. The latter impulse is well-expressed by Martin Buber in the following:

> Freud, a great late-born apostle of the enlightenment presented the naturalism of the enlightenment with a scientific system and thereby a second flowering. As Freud recognised with complete clarity, the struggle against all metaphysical and religious teachings of the existence of an absolute and the possibility of the relation of the human person to it had a great share in the development of psychoanalytical theory . . . There is in Freud's materialism, no place for guilt in the ontological sense . . . The psychologist who sees what is here to be seen must be struck by the idea that guilt does not exist because taboos exist to which one fails to give obedience, but rather that taboos and the placing of taboo have been made possible only through the fact that the leaders of early communities knew and made use of the primal fact of man as man – the fact that man can become guilty and know it.[19]

For Freud, as Buber seems to understand him (and I suspect rightly), a taboo was constructed out of two independently characterisable elements – a prohibition and independently characterisable psychological reactions to it which, when mediated by complex psychic mechanisms governing the relations of parents and children, create the sense of gravity – even of awe – which surrounds the prohibition and which give the word 'taboo' its particular connotations. According to Freud, the reasons for not committing incest are the prudential, functional reasons upon which the psyche projects an apparently reason-giving authority of a quite different kind. For Buber, the realisation of guilt is a response to a reality, a condition *sui generis*, whose significance informs our understanding of the kind of wrong-doing implied by the word 'taboo'.

Guilt as a condition *sui generis* and mysterious, irreducible to psychological explanation, is partly what Buber means by 'guilt in the ontological sense'. I think that is about all that he can mean by it, for we have no way of characterising that terribleness which is realised in remorse, the terribleness which Buber calls the 'ontological fact of guilt', apart from how it shows itself to remorse and in the life of the person who is remorseful. The point is not that remorse is a peculiar and privileged epistemic route to a condition which exists independently of our disposition to it. The point is that there is nothing else which that terribleness could *be*, nothing else which *is* the evil-doer's condition. It has been my argument that we cannot look upon the way remorse shows itself in a life as a response to an independently intelligible conception of the reality of evil.

The metaphysical point then is confusion and rhetoric: a way of defending what is *sui generis* and mysterious from reduction. But the psychologically reductive claim is driven by the same mistake about what the options are if one is not to rest uncritically with the appearances. The desire for the metaphysical account and for the psychological reduction are expressions of the same mistake about what counts here as merely appearances and, therefore, of what might intelligibly be canvassed as a means to a deepened understanding of them. My point is not that we should uncritically accept the appearances, but that we should not think of the features of remorse which I described as being mere appearances. They look that way only to someone who assumes the metaphysical account – the kind of account that Buber offers of the 'ontological' nature of guilt – to be intelligible. I have suggested that it is not and that the moral psychologist who realises it will be freed from some of the strongest pressures to reductionism.

If I am right, we may have the material for a deeper acknowl-edgment of the fact that so much of what I have been saying resonates against a religious language. The conceptions of good and evil, guilt and remorse, love and sacredness are, in my judge-ment, as we have made them, partly within a religious life and language and partly independently of them. I have tried to show how they may now stand independently of religion and of meta-physics, however it may have been with their origins. I have tried to display how things which grow in one place may take root elsewhere.

POSTSCRIPT

In discussion, Dick Schacht and I found that we agreed much more over matters to do with realism, ontology and interpreta-tion that would appear to be the case from his reply in this vol-ume. However, I suspect that there remains some substantial disagreement. It might clarify what I have said in my paper if I try to locate some of it.

At one point Schacht asks:

> But how are we to take [Gaita] here? Is he saying that *what these concepts really come to* is to be understood in terms of their genealogies, and thus in terms of the practices and conditions of life in which they are noted *together with the emotional invest-ment we make in them*? [my italics] or is he suggesting that this is *how such notions get going* and establish a foothold in our lives – how they are constituted genetically, as it were – but that, once they are available to us, they then may outstrip their origins and vault us towards the truly transcendent? That would ally him not with Nietzsche but with C. S. Lewis (p. 48).

I do not quite want to accept either of the possibilities Schacht offers me here, but I find his Nietzsche more congenial than C. S. Lewis. I have in mind these kind of remarks:

> it may be that [Gaita's] realism and cognitivism are actually not very different from the Nietzschean brands I favour. To some, the very mention of 'Nietzschean realism and cognitivism' may seem oxymoronic, like 'Schopenhauerian optimism'; but

that is because they have misunderstood the moral of Nietzsche's story (in *Twilight of the Idols*) about 'How the "True World" Became a Fable' and other such reflections. Once we drop the idea of a 'true world' in relation to which this life and world are merely apparent, the stock of what goes on in this life rises markedly. Human life is as real as anything can be – warts and genealogies and all (pp. 46–7).

R. F. Holland, criticising certain forms of moral realism, said that the reality of value was not that of fact but that of meaning. A considerable amount of what I said in Section V could be taken as elaboration on that, and as a defence of the claim that this way of bringing together reality and meaning invokes a substantial conception of reality; one that brings with it correlatively substantial conceptions of understanding and of what it would be for ethical thought to be in tune with reality. A considerable amount of my argument is meant to reveal why, when we speak this way of reality and meaning, we are speaking about reality, not 'reality', about understanding, not 'understanding', about seeing things as they are, and not about 'seeing things as they are', and so on. The pressure to insert the inverted commas depends upon a conception of when these words and phrases deserve to be free of them, that is not false but incoherent. Often Dick Schacht seems to agree about this. Much of what he says about interpretation is what I intended to convey when I spoke of, for example, the meaning of what an evil-doer had done.

Sometimes, however, his debunking tone suggests otherwise. It seems to require that the conception is seductive *in such a way* that resistance to its power calls upon qualities of mind and character whose nature presupposes that the conception is coherent. Thus, for example:

No eternal verities are involved, no necessary and universal truths or structures of reason – and no absolute value either, of a kind that might be conceived apart from the contingently developing configurations of human life. There are, moreover, actually a multiplicity of such tapestries. As best I can see, all this is neither more nor less than an unfinished collection of episodes in the multiplicity of careers of our no-longer-merely-animal, unevenly lovable, frequently all-too-human, occasionally appalling but sometimes admirable human family. Is it just

sound and fury signifying nothing. Well there is plenty of sound
and fury, and I see no reason to suppose that it signifies anything
beyond itself; *but it is rather remarkable as an accomplishment in a
world that couldn't care less* [my italics] (p. 46).

The phrases I have italicised in this quotation and in the first in
this postscript raise a suspicion that their rhetorical effect presupposes a separation of fact and value of a kind that Schacht
agrees should be rejected as unintelligible. Here is another one:
'Both Hegel and Nietzsche were convinced that something like
this interpretation is better than any other they could think of in
terms of soundness and justice, *and moreover offers us the best deal
we can get* after the demise of its religious and metaphysical rivals
(which advertised more and went bankrupt)'.

I said in our discussion that one couldn't hanker for something
that is unintelligible. James Conant convinced me that is not quite
right. If it were then we could give no account of how philosophy has been haunted by what is unintelligible. Nonetheless,
finding *p* incoherent rather than merely false must effect what it
can be to wish that *p*, long for *p*, be seduced by *p*, renounce *p*,
and so on. Schacht's debunking depends upon a more robust sense
of what we should courageously renounce than he is permitted
once he has admitted that it yields no coherent specification. When
we realise that talk of an Archimedean point, or of seeing the
world as from no place within it, is unintelligible, then we cannot be tempted by it in the way that we could were it intelligible
but false. Our vulnerability to it cannot, therefore, attract the dis-
dain whose rhetorical force depends upon the many kinds of occasions when we seek consolation in believing something that is
false. If I am right, then the implications for what interpretation
amounts to are likely to be quite different from those Schacht
develops in his paper.

The same is true for one's understanding of what talk of mystery might amount to. Schacht suspects it to be a sign of the same
refusal squarely to face the facts of our human condition – a ref-
uge in obscurantism when all argument has failed to reveal the
existence of 'the truly transcendent'. But that takes talk of mystery to be a polemical move – an appeal – in a metaphysical argument that I have renounced. When I said that our sense of
good and evil introduces us to something mysterious, I did not
mean that it introduces us to something which is mysterious to

us only because of our limited epistemic capacities, that it is something which could be penetrated without residual obscurity by a vastly superior intelligence – by the omniscient God of the philosophers, for example. I wanted to create space for a way of speaking about mystery – a space whose existence does not depend upon the outcome of the traditional metaphysical/ontological battles. That does not mean that it cannot be rejected as obscurantist or high-minded nonsense. It means only that it cannot rightly be rejected on the assumption that it presupposes a metaphysical doctrine.

Finally, I must admit that Dick Schacht was right to suspect that when I spoke of the sanctity of life, I wanted to have my cake and eat it too. I now regret speaking that way. The proper use of words like 'sacred' and 'sanctity' are, I think, tied to the religious background which I claimed is not necessary to the sense of absolute value that I want to articulate.

Notes

1. R. F. Holland, 'Is Goodness a Mystery?', in his *Against Empiricism* (Oxford: Blackwell, 1989), p. 186.
2. Bernard Williams, *Shame and Necessity* (Berkeley: University of California Press, 1993) and Richard Wollheim, *The Thread of Life* (Cambridge: Cambridge University Press, 1984).
3. Wollheim, *The Thread of Life*.
4. When I say they cannot, this 'cannot' is both conceptual and moral. It is a point about the concept of remorse as that appears within a moral tradition, that is, inexpungeably from a moral conception which no mastery of logic and language together with a knowledge of the facts of human nature can compel one to occupy.
5. Raimond Gaita, *Good and Evil: An Absolute Conception* (London: Macmillan; New York: St Martin's Press, 1991), ch. 4.
6. Bernard Williams, 'Moral Luck', in his *Moral Luck* (Cambridge: Cambridge University Press, 1981).
7. I think, however, that Williams is mistaken in believing that this is a basic fact about the nature of agency.
8. Dostoevsky portrays this brilliantly in *Crime and Punishment*.
9. Williams, *Shame and Necessity*, p. 92.
10. Williams says: 'The structures of shame contain the possibility of controlling and learning from guilt, because they give a conception of one's ethical identity, in relation to which guilt can make sense. Shame can understand guilt, but guilt cannot understand itself' (*Shame and Necessity*, p. 93). My argument has been that while that is partly

true, there is just as much reason for saying more or less the opposite. My argument in the main body of the text shows why.

11. See Gaita, *Good and Evil*, pp. 231–7.

12. Peter Singer, *Practical Ethics* (Cambridge: Cambridge University Press, 1979), p. 162.

13. I do not know whether this is a reason for saying that remorse is not a psychological phenomenon, or for saying that it shows how inadequate is our concept of the psychological. There are reasons which speak for both. If one decides for the second, then, clearly, one will wish to save the psychological from reduction to the 'merely psychological', to be contrasted with the rational and the moral.

14. Simone Weil, 'The *Iliad*, Poem of Might', in her *Intimations of Christianity among the Ancient Greeks* (London: Routledge & Kegan Paul, 1976).

15. For development of this argument as it applies to Cartesian types of scepticism, see Raimond Gaita, 'Radical Critique: Scepticism and Commonsense', in D. Cockburn (ed.), *Human Beings* (Cambridge: Cambridge University Press, 1992).

16. For further development of this line of argument see Gaita, *Good and Evil*, ch. 15 and 16.

17. Martin Buber, *I and Thou*, trans. R. Gregor Smith (Edinburgh: T. & T. Clark 1953). For discussion relevant to the point about the public nature of language, see Buber, 'The Word that is Spoken', in M. Friedman (ed.), *The Knowledge of Man* (London: George Allen & Unwin, 1965).

18. Iris Murdoch, *The Sovereignty of Good* (London: Routledge & Kegan Paul, 1970), ch. 1.

19. Martin Buber, 'Guilt and Guilt Feeling', in his *The Knowledge of Man*, pp. 123–4; 125; 126 (excerpts).

2

Reply: Morality, Humanity and Historicality: Remorse and Religion Revisited

RICHARD SCHACHT

I am grateful to Rai Gaita and to the organisers of this conference for the opportunity to return to the very topic that was the focus of my attention in my very first substantial piece of work in philosophy: my undergraduate honours thesis at Harvard, written more than thirty years ago, under the supervision of David Sachs, with John Rawls as second reader. Entitled 'The Feeling of Guilt', it dealt with precisely what Gaita in his paper calls 'remorse' – which he without further ado simply defines as 'the pained recognition of one's guilt'. In it I too explored some of the relevant language, did some moral phenomenology, dismissed Freud's account as failing to do justice to the guilt-feeling, and took a look at various thinkers in the Continental tradition who offered other, more 'ontological' rather than naturalistically psychological accounts; but like Gaita, I devoted most of my essay to reflection on what I took to be the larger and profoundly important human reality reflected in the experience of genuine guilt.

So while I may have been paired with Gaita for ticket-balancing reasons – perhaps to play naturalistic *advocatus diaboli* to his advocacy on the side of the angels – it turns out that guilt and I go way back. And the account I offered back then resonates strongly to what I take Gaita to be saying. It seems to me that both of us were and are on to something important, which I analysed in terms of the deep connection between the feeling of guilt and the call of care, and which Gaita expresses in somewhat similar language and imagery. But I also have come to think that some recasting is necessary.

Gaita puts before us a rich array of profoundly important issues. They would seem to have very little relation to his title; but to my mind that is all to the good, for the things he does discuss are much more interesting than the question his title poses – to which, as far as I can see, he does not even hint at an answer. He evinces considerable friendliness to religious figures and language; but he also suggests in several places that he takes his main points to be independent of and even at variance with religious thought. I must confess that his ready appropriation of terms like 'sacred' and 'sanctity' makes me wonder about his tactics if not his intentions in this respect; and I am not at all sure wherein the variance consists. Still I am quite happy to take him at his word on this point.

The more pressing questions looming behind this issue are how to construe the points Gaita wants to make about value, morality and our humanity, and what to make of them. What is at stake here is the status of the phenomena to which he draws our attention. The language he employs in talking about them has a strongly realist flavour. 'Absolute value', 'inalienable rights', 'ends in themselves', 'infinite preciousness', 'defining facts of human life' – the list of such things to which he is not only willing but eager to commit himself is quite impressive. As we all are well aware, one must in some way or another establish one's right to retain and employ notions like these. They are the heavy artillery of philosophical reflection on matters human and normative, and are to be neither used nor taken lightly.

Gaita strides boldly in where the existential eager beavers of my generation were made to fear to tread by the paragons and guardians of the erstwhile analytical establishment. He sallies forth with Wittgenstein as well as Buber by his side; and at different points in his paper I found myself hearing amplified echoes not only of Kant and Kierkegaard but also of Husserl, Scheler, and (even more loudly and clearly) Karl Jaspers, my personal favourite among the existential contingent. Gaita takes us back to those thrilling days of yesteryear, when we of the Continental counterculture would endeavour phenomenologically (in Gaita's words) 'to see things as they are' in the morning ('*An den Sachen selbst*'), reflect existentially on 'what it means to exist as a human being' in the afternoon, and agonise axiologically about what values (if any) are absolute far into the evening. One would almost think we are witnessing the rebirth of existentialism here and now, under the aegis of the later Wittgenstein!

Actually, this is no mere jest; and in drawing attention to these parallels my intent is far from pejorative. I do so in part because when I read Gaita's paper, I was powerfully struck by a kind of shock of recognition. For these are the very kinds of matters, gone at in a different surface style but in much the same basic sort of way, that made existential phenomenology so greatly appealing to many of my generation when it first hit these shores. It may not have much in common with French existentialism; but Gaita very commendably and courageously is linking up with and resuming a current of philosophical thought that ran strong on the other side of the Rhine, from Kierkegaard to Jaspers and beyond. Jaspers is a particular favourite of mine precisely because he is attentive to many of the same matters that interest Gaita. Gaita's 'facts of life', for example, recapitulate Jaspers' *Grenzsituationen*; and Gaita's 'fellowship' recalls Jaspers' 'communication'. But because Gaita enters the lists with a different lineage and philosophical sensibility, he is by no means simply reinventing the wheel. Rather, he is giving it a welcome new twist and spin.

Despite the fact that I was subsequently drawn towards Hegel and Nietzsche, therefore, I am highly sympathetic to much of what Gaita is saying and trying to do. And I also want to suggest that he and Nietzsche actually may not be as far apart as he seems to think. He remarks that Nietzsche and Freud haunt his discussion at various points. I get the impression that he thinks they haunt it rather in the manner of sinister spectres that require to be exorcised if possible. But the Nietzsche with whom I am acquainted would neither be contemptuous of Gaita's nun in his example, nor hostile to the spirit of his concluding remarks. Indeed, it seems to me that, in the kind of undertaking Gaita is pursuing, one needs philosophical companions like Nietzsche and Hegel no less than one needs others like Buber and Jaspers – and the later Wittgenstein too, of course – on one's team.

What I find most disconcerting in Gaita's discussion, owing perhaps to my modified post-phenomenological sensibility, is his confidence that there are not only 'absolute values' but also something like absolute *facts*, and his seeming obliviousness to what I would take to be the highly and problematically interpretive character of many of the accounts he provides as though he were simply giving us the news. And where I think I more specifically part company with him – although some of his disclaimers leave me less than sure – is over the status of those things about ourselves and value that he takes to be reflected and revealed in the experience or phenomenon of remorse.

It has been some time since I have encountered a philosopher who comes as close as Gaita does to sharing Husserl's conviction that if we will just do it right we should be able to lay hold of *den Sachen selbst*. But here he is, setting about to 'penetrate the appearances about matters which come broadly under the head of the ethical' and 'see things as they are' (p. 23). Moreover, he simply *tells* us that 'Whatever conception we have here of what it means to see things rightly, it must be informed by the recognition that the grammar of the epistemic and critical concepts under which the phenomena present to us is conditioned by the encounter of agent and victim' (p. 8). I see nothing obvious about this, and am rather inclined to think that the conditioning here may well go the other way.

Gaita further refers repeatedly to the revelatory character of remorse with respect to nothing less than what it is to be a human being – as, for example, in speaking of 'what a lucid remorse reveals human beings to be' (p. 13). Towards the end he does issue the disclaimer that 'The point is not that remorse is a peculiar and privileged epistemic route to a condition which exists independently of our disposition to it' (p. 33). Yet he pretty clearly does take it to have what he calls 'intrinsic epistemic potential', chiding those who fail 'to see the revelatory dimension of remorse'. And remorse is held to be revelatory of a great deal – 'full humanity', human 'individuality' and 'inner life', the 'preciousness' of each and every one of us, 'absolute value' and much more, all of which he takes to be 'partly constituted' as well as distinctively revealed by or through remorse.

The experience of remorse is not, however, taken to be our only mode of access to this complex of states of affairs; for the same realities are also said to be 'revealed' with particular clarity by the loving 'demeanour' of the nun in Gaita's example. He does not say whether he thinks her kind of 'unconditional love' likewise 'partially constitutes' the 'full humanity' of the patients she visited that day; but I do not see how he coherently could. After all, the whole point of the story was that, prior to her visit, their 'radical affliction had made their humanity invisible' – to the obtuse psychiatrists in particular, and perhaps even to Gaita himself. Invisibility entails reality.

Another kind of reality that Gaita takes to be revealed in the remorse experience is that of *moral meaning*, which he thus likewise appears to suppose to be a kind of true fact that one may or may not rightly comprehend. Thus he lays it down that 'Remorse is not recognition plus suffering; it is the indivisible suffering–recognition of the meaning of what one did' (p. 6). He also asserts that 'remorse is a bewildered contact, through its violation, with what is sacred' (p. 9). And the list of things to which we are granted epistemic access by moral experience extends to Gaita's counterpart to Jaspers' *Grenzsituationen*, 'certain defining facts of human life – facts such as that we are mortal, that we are vulnerable to suffering, that we may be destroyed by our passions and so on' (pp. 19–20).

All of this and more is pretty much simply stated, with little argument or case-making apart from the examples Gaita provides in an attempt to engage and enlist our intuitions. He in effect announces that he will be proceeding in this way at the outset, by quoting Holland's remark that 'judgments that are of the highest significance for ethics' are 'more a matter of registering an experience or marking an encounter than passing a judgment' (p. 4). His examples are made to bear much of the burden – and if one happens not to 'feel [their] rhetorical pressure', so be it; for Gaita modestly claims to be concerned only 'to understand why many people do' (p. 13).

But how concerned really is he to do so? Is he concerned to sort out and explore and weigh different interpretations of 'why many people do', and to try to ascertain which of them is most deserving of our acceptance? Or is he wedded to one such understanding that he is seeking to preserve in the face of the onslaught of the likes of Freud and Nietzsche, by showing that enough nonnaive and non-fictitious sense can be made of it to deflect the worry that they '*must* be right'? That is what he seems to admit early on, and what his general procedure seems to suggest – reminding me of Kierkegaard even more than Wittgenstein. If his objective truly is only to deflect that worry, I am quite willing to grant him success. But if he further aspires to convince those who are not already converted to side with him, he has more work to do.

Perhaps I have been hanging around with Nietzsche too long;

but where Gaita sees facts, realities, true meanings and absolutes being revealed, I see a lot of interpretations; and when he states what 'individuality' and 'inner life' and 'full humanity' are, and employs notions like 'sacred' and 'preciousness' in doing so, I see more of them. I have seldom seen a paper as rich in interpretations of so many important matters as Gaita's. This itself is no problem for me; for with Nietzsche I believe that we philosophers are in the interpretation business, along with the evaluation enterprise, and that philosophy has to do above all with the examination, development and assessment of interpretations and evaluations. What I take to be missing in Gaita's paper is due acknowledgement that this is what he is doing, sensitivity to just how interpretation-laden so much of what he says is, and awareness of the implications of this circumstance for his undertaking.

I have in mind at least two different ways in which interpretations figure in Gaita's discussion, wittingly or no. There are, of course, his own interpretations, which are reflected in some of the more notable things he has to say about remorse, value, inner life, the nun, the revealing–constituting matter, and the like. And then there are interpretations that have come in the course of cultural–historical–human events to be woven into our languages, ways of acting and interacting, emotional responses, and other facets of our lives and forms of life.

Gaita's interpretations are to some extent reflections of such entrenched interpretations, and are to some extent his own attempts to make sense of them. It is a nice question which are which. It is an important question too. But it is a question with which he does not give us much help, because his philosophical sensibility seems not to be very much attuned to what our German colleagues call the 'problematic' of interpretation. His mode is analytical rather than hermeneutical, and phenomenological rather than genealogical. But interpreting is what he is doing, and interpretation is also at the heart of the phenomena with which he is dealing; and it seems to me that he would be well-advised to be more mindful of and explicit about this, and to see what he can do by way of case-making pro and con (as the interpretation game requires).

So, for example, the experience of remorse *involves* interpretation, since it relates to the way in which one understands 'the meaning of what one did', as Gaita observes. Such meanings are not simply worn on the sleeves of our actions in such a way that no one whose eyes are open can miss them or understand them any differently. And Gaita is himself then interpreting what is going on in this interpretive experience (and rejecting another interpretation of it that is not patently absurd) when he asserts that 'the suffering of remorse is not an emotional effect of the recognition that one has wronged someone, but is the primary form of that recognition' (p. 6).

Gaita not only offers us a good many other such interpretive remarks with respect to remorse (which are in competition with other interpretations of this kind of experience, and may or may not do greater justice to it than any other), but also advances contestable interpretations of a good many other interpretive phenomena. For example: 'I am suggesting that a sense of an individual as sacred is partly expressed in the realisation of what they suffer when they are wronged, and that remorse is the primary form of that realisation.' When notions like 'being wronged', 'suffering' in consequence of it and 'sacredness' are in experiential play, a lot of interpreting is going on; and when suggestions of this sort with respect to their relation are advanced, a significant interpretive move is being made.

Another very important case in point has to do with the idea of humanity with which Gaita operates, and which he is at pains to distinguish from mere instantiation of our biological species. It is related to what he calls 'our sense of the "intrinsic dignity" of each human being'. He glosses it in part in terms of a 'kind of individuality', which in turn is glossed (among other things) in terms of 'a sense of inner life' (p. 19). And there is more: 'The inner life', he tells us, 'is partly constituted by the attitudes we take to certain defining facts of human life' (pp. 19–20). Interpretations upon interpretations! And we have not reached bedrock even yet; for these 'facts of human life' – those Jaspersian boundary situations – are themselves interpretation-laden rather than brutally factual. Our 'mortality' and 'vulnerability to suffering', for example, are not simply matters of biological fact. These notions are much richer than that – because they bear the traces of a great deal of interpretive activity with respect to what happens to us.

Mortality, suffering, being wronged, guilt, remorse, love, respect, grief, joy, and a host of other phenomena Gaita mentions are indeed of great significance both for morality and our humanity and for their understanding. They also are deeply and intimately related. Or so Gaita contends – and on these points I am in complete agreement with him. I am further in agreement with him that their relations in many instances are not of a one-way deriva-tional or causal nature, but rather would appear to have a mutu-ally constitutive and revelatory character.

All of these human phenomena, I would submit, and our very version of humanity itself that is woven of them and others like them, have *become* what they are, in the manner of a tapestry. Its warp may be the elements of our fundamentally similar biologi-cal constitution, but its woof is the yarn of our diversely devel-oping cultural life, creatively elaborated as the shuttles of interpretation and praxis-formation cross the warp again and again, in ways related to but not determined by prior passes.

To my way of thinking (closer to Nietzsche's than to Hegel's here), this is not only a historical but also a fundamentally *artis-tic* affair, according with no Platonic *eidos* and realising no Hegelian *Begriff*. No eternal verities are involved, no necessary and univer-sal truths or structures of reason – and no absolute values either, of a kind that might be conceived apart from the contingently developing configurations of human life. There are, moreover, actually a multiplicity of such tapestries. As best I can see, all of this is neither more nor less than an unfinished collection of epi-sodes in the multiplicity of careers of our no-longer-merely-animal, unevenly lovable, frequently all-too-human, occasionally appalling but sometimes admirable human family. Is it just sound and fury signifying nothing? Well, there is plenty of sound and fury, and I see no reason to suppose that it signifies anything *beyond itself*; but it is rather remarkable as an accomplishment in a world that couldn't care less. Anyhow, it's our thing, and it's all we've got – and so it certainly would seem to behoove us to make the most of it.

There are times in Gaita's paper when he says things that seem pretty close to this way of thinking; and it may be that his real-ism and cognitivism are actually not so very different from the Nietzschean brands I favour. To some, the very mention of 'Nietzschean realism and cognitivism' may seem oxymoronic, like 'Schopenhauerian optimism'; but that is because they have mis-understood the moral of Nietzsche's story (in *Twilight of the Idols*) about 'How the "True World" Became a Fable' and other such reflections. Once we drop the idea of a 'true world' in relation to which this life and world are merely apparent, the stock of what goes on in this life and this world rises markedly. Human life is as real as anything can be – warts and genealogies and all; and the possibility of comprehending a good deal about it, far from being precluded or incoherent, turns out to make good sense, once we catch on to the need to align our interpretive practices with the human phenomena we investigate. That is what Nietzsche is up to in his *Genealogy of Morals*; and it may be what Gaita is at least moving towards in his paper.

This depends on how we are to take Gaita's talk about the relations between what he calls the 'grammar' of remorse (and other such notions) and the states of affairs (both experiential and referential) with which they are associated – and about the relations between experiences such as remorse and the matters of which they are said to be 'both constitutive and revelatory': for example, 'our sense of other human beings as a unique limit to our will' (p. 8), 'our sense of the infinitely precious character of each individual human being' (p. 12), 'our understanding of evil' (p. 13), and our idea of 'what it is for something to be a moral matter because it is constitutive for us of the kind of seriousness which we think to be internal to such matters' (p. 29). If the 'constitutive' theme wears the trousers, Nietzsche and I can embrace Gaita with open arms; while if the 'revelatory' theme is cut loose from it and predominates, that would seem to place him among those for whom (as Nietzsche might put it) God's requiem remains to be said.

I have already observed that Gaita's way of telling the nun's story weighs in favour of the latter construal, since it would seem highly implausible to suppose that the nun's demeanour and love *constituted* as well as revealed the 'full humanity' of the patients. On the other hand, Gaita goes on to say something in elaboration of one of the most astonishing claims he makes that may tip the scales in the other direction. The astonishing claim is about 'the way in which the child appears as precious to its parents if their love is pure'; and the claim itself is that 'the power of parental love to reveal that [preciousness] – its having that to reveal – depends, I think, on the impersonal love of saints'. I will let that pass, however, because it is what Gaita goes on to say that is of particular significance for present purposes:

> For it is because of the place of such impersonal love in our culture that there has developed a language of love whose grammar has transformed our sense of what it is for a human being to be a unique kind of limit to our will (p. 29).

This purported state of affairs presumably is meant to be an instance and illustration of what Gaita has in mind when he says that he is attempting 'to develop the Wittgensteinian thought that the concepts which most seriously mark our sense of mystery and of transcendence are rooted in particular practices, in particular conditions of human life' (pp. 26–7). But how are we to take him here? Is he saying that *what these concepts really come to* is to be understood in terms of their genealogies, and thus in terms of the practices and conditions of life in which they are noted together with the emotional investment we make in them? Or is he suggesting that this is *how such notions get going* and establish a foothold in our lives – how they are constituted genetically, as it were – but that, once they are available to us, they then may outstrip their origins and vault us towards the truly transcendent? That would ally him not with Nietzsche but with C. S. Lewis.

Much of Gaita's rhetoric seems to reinforce that interpretation. Yet at the end of his paper he would appear to swing back the other way. Rather surprisingly to me, he remarks that 'so much' of what he has been saying 'resonates *against* a religious language'; but be that as it may, what he goes on to say in conclusion is of great importance:

> The conceptions of good and evil, guilt and remorse, love and sacredness are . . . as we have made them [!] partly within a religious life and language and partly independently of them . . . I have tried to display how things which grow in one place may take root elsewhere (p. 34).

Gaita's observation about the origin of these conceptions is surely true; and I likewise am in complete accord with the thought he expresses in his final sentence. So, for that matter, is Nietzsche. Such transplants and graftings may not always be successful, and some that have been or might be made may be highly unfortunate; but experiments of this sort are among the most pressing orders of business of philosophy today, as it attends to the disposition of its religious and metaphysical inheritance and looks to what Nietzsche called a 'philosophy of the future' beyond 'the death of God'. It would be the height of folly to toss out everything acquired in the course of the development of the old estate, or to let it go at garage-sale prices to anyone who might be interested.

A variety of forms of love will be well worth hanging on to;

and the same may well be true of guilt and remorse. Gaita seems to me to be quite right to stress, for example, 'the fundamental place which love plays in the formation of the concepts through which we understand [the] preciousness [of each individual human being] – the kind of preciousness which it is' (p. 30). But it further seems to me that he has no good reason to hedge his bets in this way. Why assign love a fundamental role only in *the formation of the concepts through which we understand* this preciousness? Why not bite the bullet and accord love a crucial role in the emergence of *this preciousness itself* – of the very idea, sense, phenomenon and reality of such preciousness – which thus would be inextricably bound up with learning to love in that manner (as matters arguably stand in the case of beauty)?

The only good reason I can see not to do so is the reason Gaita hints at with his 'constituting/revealing' and 'interdependence' talk, as when he refers to what he takes to be the 'interdependence between remorse and our understanding of evil' – and this, I believe, is a very good reason indeed. For it seems to me quite right of him to make so much of the interrelations among the various notions and forms of experience that are in play in his discussion, and in the lives of people for whom they are realities. I think he is on to something important, for example, when he remarks that 'we cannot look upon the way remorse shows itself in a life as a response to an independently intelligible conception of evil' (p. 33). Our capacity for anything like remorse and our notion of something like evil go hand in hand, developing together or diminishing together; and if the one is absent in a person, the other almost certainly will be absent as well, in any real sense. They may be conceptually distinguishable, but they would seem to be existentially inseparable. Neither is truly primary to the other; rather, they would seem to be coeval, each *funding into* the other (to borrow an apt phrase from Dewey) phenomenologically, psychologically and culturally.

I would further agree that the same sort of thing applies with respect to love and preciousness, when one adds them to the picture. And much of morality as Gaita understands it has to do with this very tapestry of phenomena. They constitute the greater part of its substance, fleshing out the skeleton of abstract principles and rules that are sometimes mistaken for its essence and supposed to be capable of some sort of independent derivation.

Does this put me in Gaita's corner? I am far from certain. Because

I am not at all sure how seriously he is prepared to take a point
that he himself touches upon in connection with our debt to 'the
impersonal love of saints'. As noted above, he suggests that 'it is
because of the place of such impersonal love *in our culture* that
there has developed a language of love' that has transformed our
sense of human being and worth (p. 29). Yet I suspect he is not
prepared to embrace the view that the whole configuration of
phenomena to which he here refers is fundamentally *a cultural
affair through and through*, answering to and reflecting nothing whatsoever beyond the horizon of human life and history – and an
entirely contingent affair at that, with nothing either necessary or
universal about it. Gaita does make a point of emphasising the
'rootedness' of even our 'most serious' conceptual markers of 'our
sense of mystery and transcendence' in 'particular' and therefore
contingent 'practices' and 'conditions' (pp. 26–7). He does not seem
to want to go all the way, however, restricting his claim of contingent rootedness to 'the concepts which mark' this sense rather
than this sense itself, and the whole business of 'mystery and
transcendence' along with it.

The fact that Gaita sees himself as fighting to preserve the plausibility of an alternative to the naturalism of Freud, Nietzsche,
Wollheim and Williams pretty much clinches the case. He concedes the conceptual markers to naturalism, but wants to hang
on to the mystery and transcendence; and he appears to want to
do something akin to sanctifying the morality of good and evil
and the humanity of equally and intrinsically precious individuality by means of them. That may not be religion, and it certainly
is not an infantile morality; but it sounds to me like the sort of
Jaspersian substitute for religion and religiously-based morality
that Nietzsche would have placed among what he called the
'shadows of God' lingering on after the demise of the source. I
quite agree with Gaita's observation that 'the unabashedly anthropocentric language of worship has greater power to reveal the
structure of the concepts under which the nun's behaviour and
what it revealed are intelligible to us' (pp. 28–9). yet he would be
doing all of us a favour if he would get clearer and be clearer
about the upshot of demythologising this language and our thinking
about these matters.

Gaita and we need to take seriously the idea that not only the
concepts expressing the things he takes to be fundamental to our
sense of morality and humanity but also *the very fabrics of our*

morality and humanity themselves are historically constituted cultural phenomena inside and out, and that everything about them
and about human life more generally beyond the biological level
has a thoroughly mundane genealogy. It may be that forms of
life have emerged in which the concepts with which he is concerned have genuine purchase, 'coming true' (as it were) as his
'constituting revealing' relations serve to transform the very character of human reality among those whose lives they inform. This
would amply deserve to be regarded as a wondrous alchemy, in
connection with which it would be at least as understandable to
feel a sense of mystery – and to discern a kind of transcendence
of the merely natural – as in the case of artistic creation, to which
it is akin. But on this interpretation the only higher reality involved in either case is that which is engendered in the course of
human events, as human beings creatively transfigure elements
of their world and themselves. As in the case of procreation, in
which we likewise create better than we know, awe and mystery
have place – but no extranaturalistic upshot.

This interpretation, which I associate with Hegel and Marx as
well as Nietzsche, has some fairly radical implications, which I
am prepared to embrace. On this view the configuration of concepts, experiences and elements of humanity with which Gaita is
concerned is reality-licensed, but is not granted exclusivity rights.
It is accorded (and thus, in the eyes of its champions, is relegated
to) the status of one contingent set of human possibilities among
others, with no teleological guarantees or certificates of metaphysical
merit. There is nothing whatsoever inherent in our human nature,
amorphously plastic as it is (except perhaps for a few dispositions from our evolutionary–biological inheritance), that predis-
poses all human beings as such to it. We all may come into this
world with the capacity to realise it, under the right conditions;
but we all likewise come into the world capable of turning out
very differently under other circumstances – and there is no more
basis for taking this sort of humanity to be *the right one* than there
is for taking English to be the right language for human beings
to speak.

This is not to say that its realisation thereby becomes a matter
of mere indifference. We may be attached enough to it to be willing to fight and die for it; and we may be prepared to give up
our lives rather than betray it or allow ourselves to be turned
into something else – as Socrates might be considered to have

done, albeit for immortality-related reasons as well. Such a stand might be well-warranted, not merely on psychological grounds, but (for example) as an expression of commitment to the sort of life-enhancement that endows human existence with worth. There may be no absolutes or clear criteria to which appeal can be made in this context, any more than there are in art; but it does not follow in either case that the situation is the nihilistic counterpart to Hegel's 'night in which all cows are black'.

Both Hegel and Nietzsche were convinced that something like this interpretation is better than any other they could think of in terms of soundness and justice, and moreover offers us the best deal we can get after the demise of its religious and metaphysical rivals (which advertised more but went bankrupt). Hegel is often derided for his talk about different periods in which one or some or all are free, about different forms of life among different peoples, and about the indispensability of social institutions to everything that matters in human life. Nietzsche likewise is often taken to task for his talk of masters and slaves and other exhibits in his human menagerie, for his emphasis upon human differences, and for his genealogical treatment of even our loftiest attainments. But it seems to me that they were both on to something important. Both would have a real problem with Gaita's contention that, except in a trivial biological sense, each and every member of our species, 'however vile, is fully our fellow human being' (p. 29). And I would too.

With them, I am inclined to think that the contours of whatever sort of humanity we attain are both revealed and constituted by the interpretive, evaluative and normative concepts that come to inform our experience and conduct – and that these conceptual configurations have differed markedly in the course of human events. The humanity revealed and constituted by Gaita's configuration may be a reality; but is it the sort of reality he suggests it to be when he universalises his notion of being 'fully our fellow human being' in this manner, with every *Homo sapiens* mother's child there is and ever has been deserving to be reckoned the same sort of (precious) individual? I am doubtful, to say the least. Human beings have not always shared our modern Western *sensibility with respect to* human individuality, dignity and preciousness, equality of worth, morality, doing and suffering wrong, guilt and remorse (to mention just a few of the matters at hand). One might well wonder whether there is any good reason to suppose that matters stand otherwise with respect to their reality.

Thus I would venture to suggest (with Hegel and Nietzsche) that there have been cultures and societies in which the kind of individuality, inner life, responsibility and worth to which Gaita directs our attention simply did not exist; in which humanity amounted to a variety of things quite different from what it is in his account; and in which his notions of good and evil, wrong done and suffered, guilt incurred and remorse warranted would be as alien as we might find the ways of thinking informing the lives and judgements of their populations. Just within the past few thousand years, for example, there really have been rulers and subjects, royalty and commoners, masters and slaves, nobles and peasants, lords and serfs, brahmins and untouchables, knights and knaves, saints and sinners, monks and reprobates, nuns and maenads, brigands and bourgeoisie. There have been and are human identities engraved and sculpted in accordance with a hodgepodge of different religions, races, ethnicities, classes, ideologies, sexual orientations, and a host of other ways of being human beings. There are even men and women.

The meanings of all of these and other such distinctions are constructs, as are the human realities they designate, at once revealed and constituted – and elaborated, sustained and perpetuated – in the same sorts of ways Gaita indicates. Indeed, the 'revealing and constituting' go on even as we speak – as, for example, where Gaita writes: 'Similarly, Singer would argue, our emotional life may not keep up with the rational acknowledgement that blacks and women are in every moral respect our [!] equals'. And we do it all the time, one way or another, politically corrected or not; for we can only exchange one interpretive construct for another.

It seems to me that the phenomena Gaita discusses, for better or for worse, are of a piece with all other such phenomena involving the interpretively creative characterisation and evaluative rendering of human beings, their traits and their doings and undergoings. We may decide to accord special importance to Gaita's phenomena, and so to promote what might be called his script of humanity and morality over any others that have been or might be prepared and proposed. We may also choose to modify it in certain respects – as I (in company with Hegel and Nietzsche) would favour doing. In either event, we had best do so with our eyes open and unclouded by the mists of mystery.

But what is to guide any such choices? How are we to chart our course as we sift through our human possibilities and contemplate which of them might be worth aspiring to, in the aftermath of the demise of all gods? That was Nietzsche's question too, with nothing like Hegel's answer – not to mention those of Kant and Kierkegaard – available to him. The reinterpretation of our humanity and the revaluation of values he felt obliged to undertake distances him from much of what I take Gaita to be trying to hold on to as well; but they certainly did not detract from the intensity of Nietzsche's affirmation of life and his concern with its enhancement. In the end, as at the beginning, he thought that we will have to make do with something like aesthetic considerations, informed by an understanding of what we're up against in this world and what we've got to work with in terms of our own resources. I suspect he was right.

But should friends and philosophers of religion think of Nietzsche as anything other than either a threat or a menace? After all, he not only proclaimed the death of God but styled himself anti-Christ(ian), and is often regarded as a quintessentially anti-religious thinker. Yet that may be to do both him and religion a serious injustice, or at any rate to sell both short. Paul Tillich used to delight in causing a stir by proclaiming Nietzsche to have been a deeply *religious* thinker, his anti-Judeo-Christian polemics notwithstanding, and to have had an intense and profound sense of the divine second to none. Tillich likened Nietzsche to Spinoza in this respect – and likened his own religiousness to theirs. 'Ecstatic naturalism', he called it, featuring a 'God beyond God' that is more properly to be conceived as a divine immanence rather than a hypostatised transcendence. I see plenty of evidence in Nietzsche that he would not at all have minded being thought of as religious in this sense. Religion as the recognition and celebration of the de-deified divinity of life and the world, as he sketched it in such passages as the wonderful notebook entry of 1885 that has come to be known as Section 1067 of *The Will to Power*, was at the very heart of his thought, without which his fervent affirmation of life in the face of Schopenhauer's indictment of it is inconceivable.

To be sure, religion without God may seem strange if not downright perverse to many; but I can well imagine Nietzsche responding that this is their problem, not his. And in view of his professed immoralism and call to advance to a kind of thinking that would be 'beyond good and evil', one can easily imagine what little patience he would have with any attempt to hang on to a vision of morality conceived in God's image. But the demise of such a conception of morality is no more tantamount to the end of all normativity than the death of God spells the end of all religion; for the former is as inseparable from all enhancement of life as the latter is wedded to its affirmation, when reconceived as its celebration.

Gaita was quite right – perhaps even more so than he realised – to remark that his paper is haunted by Nietzsche. Indeed, it occurs to me to suggest, in an ecstatically naturalistic sort of way, that a more interesting version of his title question might be its inversion. After all, Nietzsche's idea of going beyond good and evil, like his idea of the death of God, makes good and constructive sense if absolutising good-and-evil moralities, along with deistic mythologies, are deemed something like varieties of infantile religion, to be dispensed with when we outgrow them and are capable of improving upon them. And perhaps that's just what they are. If so, their passing will not mean the nihilistic end of morality and religion, but rather their – and our – coming of age.

Part II
Morality and Divine Commands

3

The Concept of a Divine Command

ROBERT MERRIHEW ADAMS*

I   DIVINE COMMANDS AND THEISTIC ETHICAL THEORY

The concept of a divine command may be approached from more
than one angle. It plays a major role in the scriptures, and the
ethical thinking, of several religious traditions. I am particularly
interested in questions about the viability of a theistic ethical theory which would explain the nature of ethical obligation in terms
of commands of God. There is much in the phenomenology of
obligation, and the related phenomena of wrong-doing and guilt,
that supports an understanding of obligation in terms of social
requirements. The great difficulty with such a view, to sum it up
bluntly, is that human social requirements are not good enough.
If we seek a better sort of social or quasi-social requirement, something transcendent, that might ground a more perfect system of
ethical obligations, the most obvious candidate is divine commands.

A number of issues arise about this idea. I have treated some
of them elsewhere.[1] One that I have not dealt with, however, and
that has not been much discussed in the philosophical literature
on divine command theories, is particularly basic. This is the
question, what it is for something (and indeed for one thing rather
than another) to be commanded by God. A divine command theory of the nature of obligation requires a rather strong answer to
this question. According to such a theory, God's commands are
the standard, conformity to which constitutes the ethical validity

---

*I am indebted to the members of my Spring, 1988, seminar at Yale Divinity
School for pressing on me the problem addressed in this paper, and to them
and the members of my Spring, 1990, seminar at UCLA for helpful discussion
of my earlier attempts to deal with it.

of human social requirements, and the correctness of one against another when they disagree. And God's commands may go beyond human standards, revealing new ethical obligations not previously known. If divine commands are to fill these roles, there must be a fact of the matter about what God commands. It must be an objective fact, independent in some ways of human social requirements; and it must be richly determinate, containing answers (whether we can prove them or not) to ethical issues on which humans disagree. A divine command theorist is confronted, therefore, with the question, what would constitute such a fact.

This is a difficult question, as we shall see. Its difficulties are connected with the fact that commands are a form of communication, a type of speech-act. The concept of a command of God falls under the wider concept of God's speaking, or the word of God. It may be suspected that all these concepts are metaphorical, since God is not a literal, or at any rate not an ordinary, participant in any linguistic community.

One might be tempted to escape these difficulties right at the outset by replacing the concept of God's commands with that of God's will. The two concepts often seem interchangeable in theistic ethics, and believers may think of their ethical reflection as an attempt to 'discern the will of God'. And God's will, unlike God's commands, seems to exist and have its content independently of what God does to communicate it. There are several weighty objections to the proposed replacement, however. The most obvious is that a shift of attention to the concept of divine will can hardly dispense the student of religious ethics from the task of trying to understand a concept that plays such an important role as that of divine commands does in the ethics of most theistic traditions. Two other objections are more complex and require more explanation.

1. One problem is that, according to most theologies, not everything wrong or forbidden by God is in every way contrary to God's will. It has commonly been taken as following from God's omnipotence and providence that nothing happens that is totally contrary to God's will, though deeds are in fact done that are wrong and contrary to God's commands.[2] Christian theologians have distinguished between God's *antecedent will* and God's *consequent will*. God's antecedent will is God's preference regarding a particular issue considered rather narrowly in itself, other things being equal. God's consequent will is God's preference regarding

the matter, all things considered. It has commonly been held that nothing happens contrary to God's consequent will, though many things happen contrary to God's antecedent will. On the typical view, to be sure, God's consequent will is partly permissive; some things are permitted by God that are not fully caused, or even intended, by God. Clearly, the ground of our obligations is not to be found in God's merely *permissive will*, or more broadly in God's consequent will, inasmuch as all the wrong-doing that actually occurs is not contrary to them. Neither can the ground of obligation be identified with God's antecedent will as such; for it seems that we are sometimes morally obliged to make the best of a bad situation by doing something that a good God would not have preferred antecedently, other things being equal. With what divine will, then, can we identify the ground of ethical obligation? The usual response has been to say that the divine will by which we are ethically bound is God's *revealed will*. And what is God's revealed will? Either it is the same as God's commands; or, if it includes something else, perhaps advice or 'counsels', the commands will be the most stringently binding part of it. Either way it will be God's commands that will ground obligation as such.

2. This point about the *revealed* will of God is a key to another objection to replacing divine commands with divine will as the ground of ethical obligation. Commands must be communicated in order to exist as commands, and revelation is God's communication addressed to humans. So it is by revelation that God's will gives rise to divine commands. Divine will is not really different from divine commands as a ground of ethical obligation if revelation is essential to the grounding of obligation in the divine will. And the problems attending the concept of divine commands, as we shall see, are largely problems about revelation. So the point of replacing divine commands with divine will in a theory of obligation would depend on the assumption that God's will can be what it is without being revealed. But this yields an unattractive picture of divine–human relations, one in which the wish of God's heart imposes binding obligations without even being communicated, much less issuing in a command. Games in which one party incurs guilt for failing to guess the unexpressed wishes of the other party are not nice games. They are no nicer if God is thought of as a party to them. Also, basing obligation on unrevealed as distinct from revealed divine will deprives God of the freedom to choose whether or not to impose an obligation. It closes

off the possibility of supererogation, important in some theistic
ethical theories, the possibility of an action that is preferable from
God's point of view but not ethically required.

II   A PROBLEM ABOUT INTERPRETATION

An example may help us to grasp the problem that most concerns me here. Let us focus on a command widely believed divine, a short one, though by no means a simple one, the Sixth of
the Ten Commandments in the usual Jewish and Protestant num-
bering, *lo' tirzakh* (Exodus 20: 13), variously translated into English as 'Thou shalt not kill' and 'Thou shalt not commit murder'.
Both translations have been criticised; so right away we have an
issue for interpretation. Certainly the verb *rarzakh* does not sig-
nify any and every sort of killing, but there is room for argument
about what sort it signifies here. Philologically and historically,
we might also entertain the hypothesis that it signified one sort
of killing at the time of the exodus, and a somewhat different
sort centuries later when the Hebrew text of Exodus received its
canonical form.[3]

But if we are thinking of *lo' tirtzakh* as a divine command, our
interest in it is not purely philological and historical. In asking
what it means we want principally to know what *God* meant and/
or means by it. And this opens an even wider range of interpretive issues. Is God's meaning determined by the words' linguistic
meaning at the time of the exodus, or at the formation of the
canon, or both, or neither? And to whom is God's command addressed? Is it addressed only to Israel, or also to some or all non-
Israelites? Is it addressed to anyone now living, or only to members
of some past generation or generations? And if it is binding on
people today, how are we to apply it in modern circumstances?
Does this command of God tell us whether or not we may turn
off the respirator of an irreversibly comatose patient?

How are we to answer such questions of theological interpretation? Can we and should we rely solely on philological and historical investigation? Is there some other authoritative source for
the religious interpretation of the text – perhaps rabbinic tradition, or the words of Jesus? It is well-known that the commandment is interpreted rather broadly in the reported sayings of Jesus,
as forbidding hatred as well as murder. Broad interpretations have

flourished in Christian tradition. According to the Westminster Larger Catechism (qu. 135), for example, 'The duties required in the Sixth Commandment are: all careful studies, and lawful endeavours, to preserve the life of ourselves and others'; and these are itemised at length, including 'a sober use of meat, drink, physic, sleep, labour, and recreation' and 'comforting and succouring the distressed, and protecting and defending the innocent'. Christians debate with each other whether the commandment should be interpreted today as supporting pacifism or opposing capital punishment.

Some of us may think we know the answer to some of these questions. And some of us will disagree about some of them. But I am not asking here which interpretation is correct on any of these points. My question is rather *what it means* to identify something as the correct interpretation of 'what God commands'. I am not asking this against the background of a general scepticism about meaning or interpretation. I assume that there are many human interactions in which a command is correctly interpreted, cases in which the person who issues the command and those who receive it *know*, precisely enough for all practical purposes, what was commanded; and also cases, less numerous but common enough, in which commands are clearly *mis*interpreted. But there are particular problems about what constitutes correct interpretation of a command of *God*, or what it is for *God* to have commanded this rather than that; and those problems are my topic.

III LINGUISTIC MEANING

Most people, on hearing a discussion of divine commands, think first of something like the Ten Commandments – that is, of actual texts in a human language, sacred texts in more or less imperative form, claiming God's authority more or less explicitly. It is not only such texts that have been thought of as divine commands. Natural laws 'written on our hearts', and an individual's sense of vocation, have often been thought of as divine commands; and while such commands can be expressed in language, the linguistic expression, in these cases, is not usually identified with God's command itself, but is seen as an interpretation of something else in the person's heart or soul that is pre-linguistic or at least variable in its linguistic expression. But it may still be thought that the simplest theory of the nature of divine commands is one that identifies them as sacred texts. On this theory, God commands by causing words to be spoken or written in some human language, and what God commands is what those words mean in that language at the time of utterance.

We can see right away that theories of the nature of divine commands are not always theologically or hermeneutically neutral; for this theory yields a rather fundamentalist hermeneutics. Some will like it and others will dislike it on that account. I am among those who dislike it; but I will try to confine my objections to it here to those that do not depend on what might be regarded, in relation to the present inquiry, as a theological prejudice. Several such objections claim our attention.

1. This straightforwardly linguistic and textual understanding of the nature of divine commands is much less flexible than one that allows, for example, for laws of nature 'written on the heart'. And this may be important for a comprehensive divine command theory of the nature of ethical obligation. May there not be people who have never been exposed to the relevant sort of sacred texts? Are they under no ethical obligations? Or how are any obligations they may have related to God's commands? And is our belief that slavery is wrong, for example, to depend on finding a prohibition of slavery in a strict construction of the original meaning of a text we accept as sacred? But these questions reflect my meta-ethical concerns. We ought perhaps to seek objections more internal to the linguistic meaning theory.

2. The theory does not really tell us how to understand the difference, among texts purporting to convey divine commands, between those that do and those that do not in truth convey them. What is it for a text to have been *authorised*, as we might say, by God? The theory implies that those that have been have been *caused* by God. But on most theistic views, the divine causality is so comprehensive that God is among the causes of everything. If the difference between texts that are backed by divine authority and those that are not is to be understood in terms of causality, there must be some special way in which God causes those texts, and only those, that are divinely authorised. Advocates of the linguistic meaning theory might propose *inspiration* as the relevant form of divine causality; the texts authorised by God, on this view, would be those that are divinely inspired. On this construal, the linguistic meaning theory requires for its comple-

tion a theory of inspiration; and its fundamentalist hermeneutics would not be supported by just any theory or theology of inspiration. Maybe the theory it needs can be supplied, but I won't pursue issues about inspiration here. The linguistic meaning theory, as thus far presented, is designed not so much to answer questions about what commands are and are not divine, as to answer or avoid questions about the interpretation of commands taken to be divine. The most obviously pertinent objections to the theory, therefore, will be those that address its capacity to deal with issues of interpretation.

3. Reflection on problems of interpretation in the law makes it clear that in many cases linguistic considerations do not suffice to determine how a rule or command, formulated in words, should be interpreted. So if what God commands is simply a function of linguistic meaning, God's meaning in many cases will be (and not merely appear) quite indeterminate. This is a serious difficulty for an ethics of divine commands.

4. This problem is aggravated by temporal and cultural distance. The simplicity attained by the theory under consideration depends on its strict constructionism. It maintains that what God means by a divine command is just what is meant, no more and no less, by the words of the sacred text, in their original language, at the time of the original composition of the text. If the texts are relatively ancient, this will limit the applicability of God's commands in the present day. God's meaning will depend on the original cultural meaning of terms like 'murder' or 'ratzakh', and a considerable part of the ethically relevant nuances of those cultural meanings has long been permanently inaccessible. Even if we had perfect knowledge of those nuances, moreover, they would yield no answer to many questions about the application of the concept of murder to present circumstances unforeseen in ancient times. Thus there would be no fact of the matter as to whether turning off the permanently comatose patient's respirator is forbidden by God's commands or not.

5. Even within the original cultural context of the sacred text, if the linguistic meaning theory is right, what God means by the command *lo' tirtzakh*, 'Thou shalt not commit murder', depends on the cultural meaning of the term 'ratzakh' or 'murder'. This is a normative term. Its cultural meaning depends on what the culture accepts as right and wrong in killing. The command of God cannot, on this view, be a standard that determines what really

is wrongful murder where there is disagreement about that in the culture. The possibility of a prophetic interpretation amending the cultural understanding of murder to bring it more nearly in correspondence with God's intention would also be excluded. These consequences would severely limit the ethical role of the concept of divine commands.

IV   SPEAKER'S MEANING AND INTENTIONS

For reasons such as these we may abandon the attempt to explain the meaning of divine commands simply in terms of linguistic meaning – that is, in terms of the meaning that the words of a sacred text have in a language. An obvious alternative to consider at this point is a theory in terms of *speaker's meaning* – that is, in terms of what the speaker (or writer) of a particular utterance means by it on a particular occasion. This is certainly not totally independent of linguistic meaning, if the utterance is linguistic; but it has other determinants besides linguistic meaning, and may therefore provide more adequate resources for a conception of the meaning of divine commands.

Much of the discussion of this topic in analytic philosophy has been focused on the late Paul Grice's proposal to analyse speaker's meaning in terms of the speaker's intention 'to produce some effect in an audience by means of the recognition of this intention', so that 'to ask what [the speaker] meant is to ask for a specification of the intended effect'. In commanding, Grice suggests, one utters something with the intention of impelling an audience to do something, and to have as a reason for doing it their recognition of this intention in one's utterance.[4] Various objections and counter-examples to Grice's analysis have been proposed, and Grice has offered amendments of it to deal with some of them. A fairly obvious question with regard to commands is whether one could not command something without the intention of actually impelling anyone to do what was commanded, rather hoping, for one reason or another, to be disobeyed (though I suppose the *communication* of that hope to one's audience might invalidate the command). This question, and most others like it, need not detain us here, however. My project is quite different from Grice's. I am not seeking a reductive analysis of the notion of meaning,[5] but only asking whether there are general truths about meaning that might determine what *God* means by a command. It is therefore not necessary for us to debate every feature of Grice's analysis. But the general point that speaker's meaning is a matter of intentions seems correct; and one thesis suggested by Grice's view about commands has much plausibility: that in commanding anything one must intend one's audience to recognise and understand that one is commanding that.

Applying this point to our problem, we get the hypothesis that what God commands, or what God means by a command, is what God intends to be understood as commanding. This view seems to avoid some of the disadvantages that I noted above for the simple linguistic meaning theory. (1) It is more flexible inasmuch as it is not limited in its application to linguistic texts. We can issue commands by gestures or any other sort of sign that can be recognised as intended to communicate the command. God's commands can presumably be 'written on our hearts' in the form of inclinations to moral attitudes, provided God intends us to recognise these as signs intended to communicate a divine command. (2) To the question, which purported divine commands are truly authorised by God, we can answer, on this view, that it is those that are intended by God to be received as divine commands. (3) Similarly, questions about what God's commands mean will be answered in terms of God's intentions; and that seems to be as it ought to be, at least in a general way.

However, serious difficulties attend this view too. They arise from the claim that in commanding people to do anything, God must intend to be understood by those people as commanding them to do that. To this we may add the widely accepted thesis that, as Grice puts it, 'one cannot have intentions to achieve results which one sees no chance of achieving'.[6] The latter thesis will limit God's intentions more narrowly than ours, because God knows more. Suppose in particular that God has perfect and certain knowledge of the future, as has commonly been believed. Then if any people do not in fact recognise a given text or sign s as conveying a command from God to perform action a, God must always have known with certainty that they would not so recognise it. It follows that God cannot have intended to obtain that recognition from them, and hence, on the view now before us, that God cannot have used s to command those people to do a. In short, the view seems to have the consequence that divine commands cannot be unrecognised or misunderstood by those to whom they are addressed. This is a serious disadvantage of the view, for several reasons.

1. If we are interested, as I am, in the possibility of understanding the nature of ethical obligation quite generally in terms of divine commands, we will hope to understand the concept of a divine command in such a way that ethical imperatives to which non-theists see themselves as subject might be understood, at least in some cases, as commands of God addressed to them. But if God's commands must be intended by God to be recognised by their addressees as commands of God, and if God knows with certainty that the non-theist will not recognise anything as coming from God, it follows that God does not address any command to the non-theist. This is perhaps the least of our problems. For we can relax the requirement of intended recognition of the speaker without drawing all the teeth of the theory. We can suppose it is enough for God's commanding if God intends the addressee to recognise the command as extremely authoritative and as having imperative force. And that recognition will be present in virtually all of the cases in which one would be most tempted to speak of non-theists as receiving divine commands.

2. Problems about the possibility of conflicting interpretations of divine commands cannot be dismissed so easily. Such conflicts are a central part of the history of theistic religions. One of my objections to the simple linguistic meaning theory was that it seems not to provide for the possibility of one interpretation of a divine command being correct against another in many cases where both interpretations have some basis in the linguistic meaning of the relevant text. Now it seems that a theory in terms of speaker's meaning may have a similar or perhaps even more radical difficulty at the same point. For if there is actually disagreement about the meaning of a supposed divine command, and if God (being omniscient) knew there would be, then there is no meaning that God can have intended the supposed command to be recognised by all the parties to the dispute as having, on the disputed point. And hence, on the speaker's meaning theory we are considering, God cannot have addressed the same command on that point to all the parties. A theory of divine commands that so radically undercuts the possibility of correctness in a disputed interpretation is very unsatisfying.

3. Even apart from disagreements, the possibility of imperfect understanding is very important to the role of the idea of divine

commands in theistic religious traditions. A great deal of study, discussion, and reflection makes sense only in relation to the belief that it is possible to come to a fuller understanding of God's commands than one now has. This belief is threatened if God's commands cannot mean anything that God did not know would be recognised by all their addressees.

I think there is a serious problem here about divine foreknowledge, and one that has not received much attention in the voluminous literature on that subject. The idea of God's meaning something that may be misunderstood, and that religious interpretation strives to discern, is of fundamental importance to the treatment of revelation in theistic religious traditions. But our ordinary concepts of meaning-misunderstood-and-discerned-with-effort certainly originate in contexts where a communicator is seen as *trying* to be understood without knowing for sure whether, or how far, the effort will be successful. It is not obvious how much of this conceptual framework can be applied to a communicator who is omniscient about the future. There may be a motive of some weight here, to be added to others which have been alleged, for abandoning the dogma of divine omniscience about the future. I do not mean to disparage that possibility, but in the remainder of this paper I will explore possibilities of solving the problem on the assumption that God does foreknow everything with certainty. These possibilities should be of interest even to those who would abandon the foreknowledge doctrine; for they, in general, will still ascribe to God enough knowledge for God to be certain in advance that there would be much of the misunderstanding implied by religious accounts of the vicissitudes of revelation and interpretation.

V   SPEECH-ACT INTENTIONS AND ESCHATOLOGICAL INTENTIONS

This problem in applying to divine commands a Gricean account of speaker's meaning stems from the fact that the intentions central to the account are concerned with the effects of an utterance on an audience. We might therefore avoid the problems, while retaining the more fundamental insight that a speaker's meaning depends on the speaker's intentions, if we could account for the meaning of commands in terms of a different sort of intention.

The obvious hypothesis to explore along these lines is that the intention that is crucial to one's commanding a person p to do an action a is simply one's intention to command p to do a.

In adopting this hypothesis we would be renouncing, in a more extreme way than we have thus far, Grice's project of reducing such linguistic or communicative notions as meaning and commanding to prior psychological notions. But I am sceptical about that project anyway. I am sympathetic to the idea that linguistic facts are grounded ultimately in psychology, but that does not mean that a reductive definition of the former can be given in terms of the latter. Linguistic and other social practices can create types of action of which no precise definition can be given independent of the practice. And it is typical of such actions that they cannot exist in the absence of a concept of them. You cannot hit a home run, for example, unless you are playing a game where people have the concept of a home run. Because Grice wants commanding to be reducible to psychology, he wants commanding to be just doing something that is naturally possible even prior to any *practice* of commanding; but that seems to me wrong. Merely attempting to impel someone to do something by expressively revealing one's intention to do that is not yet commanding; and what it lacks is precisely a relation to a practice of commanding. So I think it is plausible to say that the intention crucial to one's commanding p to do a is one's intention to command p to do a.

This is not to say that such a *speech-act intention*, as we may call it, could plausibly be regarded as implying nothing about one's intentions regarding audience understanding. Under normal circumstances one could neither command nor intend to command a subordinate to load a truck by saying, in English, 'Bring me a cup of coffee'. For one could not intend to issue such a command in English without knowing enough about commanding and about English to know that no one (in normal circumstances) could understand 'Bring me a cup of coffee' as a command to load a truck. It follows, I think, from the concept of commanding that one does not intend to issue a command to do a unless one believes that the signs one employs could be understood by one's intended audience (or at least by part of it) as a command to do a.

But this may still be thought to impose a looser restriction on a commander's beliefs about the audience than a requirement that the commander intend to be understood by the audience precisely as commanding a. This thought may be supported by an experience that I imagine is familiar to all of us. One sometimes says something, meaning one thing by it, although one knows that there is another interpretation that one's words will bear. There is, after all, a limit to how far it is practical to go in eliminating possibilities of ambiguity. In such cases, nevertheless, we commonly think we know what we *meant*, and what we meant was certainly what we intended to say. And we think it was what we actually *asserted*. It may not be quite right, however, to say that what we meant was what we intended to be understood as saying. For we may believe it virtually certain that we will be misunderstood by part of our audience; and believing that, we cannot exactly *intend* to be understood by our whole audience as saying what we in fact mean.

Perhaps my meaning one thing rather than another in such a context must be understood against the background of my *reasons* for what I am saying. One reason that will often be important is that the meaning that I do intend fits into a larger pattern of thought that I am presenting or at least developing. My awareness that the larger pattern is better-known to me than to my audience may help to explain how I can intend to say something that I know they may find it difficult to understand.

A similar problem can arise even where we are aware of no particular ambiguity. I would not want to be deemed to have meant, and said, in my undergraduate lectures on Kant's *Critique of Pure Reason*, only what I thought it epistemically possible that virtually everyone in the class would understand. On some topics, with most audiences, a lower standard of communicative success than that is reasonable. I may *want* everyone to understand exactly what I mean; but I can hardly *intend* it, because I know it is virtually certain that some will not understand. Conversely, I may think that I now understand better than I ever did before, and better than most other readers have, what Kant meant by a certain passage of the *Critique*. I believe, controversially no doubt, that such interpretive beliefs can in principle be objectively correct. And I think their correctness is to be understood in terms of what Kant intended to *say*, not in terms of any hopelessly unrealistic intentions he may have had about being *understood*.

These views can be used to give an account of the notion of *God's* meaning something by a sign or revelation or 'word of God', an account in terms of speech-act intentions. Like the simple linguistic meaning theory discussed in Section III above, it will present

God's 'saying' something and meaning it as dependent on the existence of linguistic practices, and hence of creatures that have such practices. But that seems right in any case; there would be no such thing as commanding or promising for God to do if there were no practices of commanding and promising.

On a speech-act intentions account, then, we can say that if God produces or in some way brings about a relevant sign, God thereby 'says', and means, exactly what God intends *to say*, or more precisely to command or promise or declare, as the case may be. No doubt God must also intend that at least some of the intended audience be able to understand, or come to understand, what God meant and 'said'. But God may know that some will not understand, and that none will understand very well at first; and knowing that, God cannot *intend* otherwise. The relation of a speaker's meaning to a larger pattern of thought may be important here. Theists commonly believe that any divine revelation has a place in a very large pattern that God has in mind; and theologians sometimes argue that particular passages of scripture should be interpreted in the light of their place in a whole body of scriptures.

The larger pattern may be a pattern not merely of thought but also of historic purpose, and specifically of communicative or revelatory purpose. According to some theistic traditions, God intends to bring all of us in the end to a correct understanding of the divine meaning in revelation, and will in fact do so. This involves belief in life after death, and is part of some ideas about 'the last judgement'; so we may speak here of ascribing *eschatological intentions* to God. In terms of them we may frame a hypothesis that retains an intention to be understood as a standard of the correct interpretation of God's meaning. What God means, and 'says', by a sign or revelation is what God intends to bring all of us, in the end, to understand as its divine meaning.

Unfortunately, this account in terms of eschatological intentions and the account I have given in terms of speech-act intentions may both be less satisfactory in dealing with commands than with other types of communicative act that God may perform. The relation of commands to responsibility and the possibility of disobedience makes it difficult to prise the intention to command something apart from the intention to be understood or recognised as commanding it. For if you intend to command p to do a, you intend to bring it about that p will have disobeyed if p does not do a. But p's not doing a will not constitute disobedience if p

does not recognise you as commanding *p* to do *a*. So it seems to follow that if you intend to command *p* to do *a*, you do intend *p* to recognise you as commanding *p* to do *a*. And this problem cannot be solved by an appeal to eschatological intentions. For if the command is a command to do *a* now, or at any rate before the end, *p*'s not doing *a* before the end will not constitute disobedience if it is only in the end that *p* recognises you as having commanded *a*. So it seems that you must intend your command to be understood by your intended audience – that is, by anyone who is subject to it – and to be understood by them not later than the time by which they are to have complied with the command. This reasoning seems to apply to God as well as to any other commander. And its conclusion agrees with our sense of fairness; it is not in general fair, we think, to regard people as subject to a command that they have not understood.

VI SUBJECTIVE AND OBJECTIVE OBLIGATION

The problem that stubbornly recurs at this point is reminiscent of an old discussion in ethical theory about objective and subjective obligation. Does an agent have an obligation, and responsibility, to do just what the agent thinks she ought to do, which we may call her *subjective obligation*? Or if an agent's ethical views are erroneous or incomplete, can she have *objective obligations* that are different from what she thinks she ought to do? Once we admit the possibility and gravity of error in moral beliefs, we might expect to draw the conclusion that our true obligations are the objective ones. But some moralists have argued that subjective obligations, and they alone, are really binding.[7] It will be convenient to divide the issue in two. We can ask whether subjective obligation is *always* binding, and whether *only* subjective obligation is binding.

The principal reason for thinking that an agent is truly obliged, morally, to do *whatever* she thinks she is obliged to do, even if her ethical beliefs are erroneous, is related to the value of *conscientiousness*. Suppose (1) you believe you are obliged to action *a*, but (2) if all your ethical beliefs were correct you would think it better to do something else instead. Given your actual belief, you would be unconscientious in failing to do *a*. And unconscientiousness is a moral fault. Hence it seems you would be blameworthy in failing to do *a*, and that is taken as implying that your subjective obligation to do *a* is morally binding.[8]

This conclusion can be scandalous in some cases, however. Consider that stock example, the conscientious Nazi, who believes he has a morally binding duty to do what most of us regard as crimes against humanity. It is highly counter-intuitive to say that therefore this Nazi has a subjective obligation that is morally binding to do what, objectively regarded, is a crime. And if, at the moment to act, he is overcome by compassion for the designated victim and pulls back, it will be hard to say that he has violated a moral obligation. In this case the value of conscientiousness seems to be not merely outweighed but overwhelmed or obliterated by the heinousness of the deed to which it prompts.

I believe that in any case there is a confusion involved in the argument from conscientiousness for the validity of subjective obligation. Violations of obligations are not the only type of moral fault. One may be subject to warranted moral criticism for actions manifesting a vice, such as intemperance or cowardice or stinginess, even if the action itself wrongs no one and violates no obligation. This possibility might be thought not to arise for actions manifesting unconscientiousness, since the standard way of being unconscientious is by doing something that really does violate an obligation. But where it is only by moral error that you think you have an obligation to do what you are refusing to do, I think it is implausible to say that you are violating an obligation, or wronging anyone, by not doing it, though you may be criticised for a lapse from conscientiousness.

Something similar can be said about commands and disobedience. Suppose you command *p* to do *a*, and *p* does *a* but, misunderstanding your command as a command to do both *a* and *b*, nonetheless fails to do *b*. *p* may thereby have manifested a disobedient frame of mind, but has not disobeyed the command you actually gave. The ascription of disobedience implies that the subject acted contrary to the commander's intentions as well as the subject's beliefs. Therefore you can have intended to issue, and thus have issued, a command that was only a command to do *a*, even if you knew it would very likely be misunderstood as a command to do *b* as well. To be sure, this is possible only if your command is given in such a form that it is not absurd to say it is a misinterpretation to regard the command as requiring *b*. If you knowingly give it in the form 'Do *a* and *b*', you have commanded *b*, whether you are willing to admit it or not.

This applies to divine commands too. We have not disobeyed a divine command (though we may have shown a disobedient spirit) if we have acted contrary to what we thought God commanded but not contrary to what God really meant to command. Such a case will be impossible if we have received such signs that it would be absurd not to interpret them as revealing the divine command we took them to reveal. But little if anything in this world is as religiously unambiguous as that. Even if we assume as given the divine authorisation of a particular text in imperative form, such as 'Thou shalt not commit murder', we cannot exclude in principle the possibility of misinterpreting the text as requiring more than God means to require. There are doubtless some crimes so unambiguously instances of murder that the only way in which God could not have forbidden them is by not commanding 'Thou shalt not commit murder'. But what about turning off the respirator of an irreversibly comatose patient? The possibility that that does not fall under the prohibition that God intended in commanding 'Thou shalt not commit murder', but that some people mistakenly think that it does, seems perfectly intelligible. I think it is no less intelligible if we add that God foreknew the misunderstanding – particularly if we also add that God intends to bring everyone to a correct understanding in the end. Thus I am inclined to dismiss the thesis that subjective obligation always binds morally, and to accept as relatively unproblematic the possibility of misinterpreting divine commands as requiring more than God meant them to. In this I see no need to depart from the speech-act intentions and eschatological intentions theories of divine commands.

The thesis that only subjective obligation binds is harder to dismiss and more troublesome, however. This is the thesis that engages our sense of fairness. Is it fair to hold me responsible for obeying a command to do *a* if I did not understand that I was commanded to do *a*? This is also the basis of the objection from the possibility of disobedience that I posed for the speech-act intentions and eschatological intentions theories at the end of Section V above. The crux of that objection is that I cannot in general be held to have disobeyed a command if I have not acted contrary to my understanding of it. The ascription of disobedience implies that the subject acted contrary to the subject's beliefs as well as the commander's intentions. So it seems that I cannot be subject to a divine command to do *a* if I do not recognise it as such, and indeed that such a command cannot be addressed to me by a God who knows that I will not recognise it as such, because in that case God could not intend by commanding to bring it about that my not doing *a* constitutes disobedience. I think a measure of truth must be granted to this conclusion. I believe that the speech-act intentions theory is sound as a general framework for thinking about divine commands and their meaning, but must be qualified to allow that people may be counted as not subject to a divine command, and even as not addressed by it, not part of its intended audience, if God foreknew that they would not understand it.

We must not make too sweeping a concession at this point, however. The thesis that only subjective obligation binds is plausible only up to a point. If I do something I think is right, but you think I *should* have known it was wrong, you may well think that I have violated a morally binding obligation thereby. This point may be put by saying that *culpable ignorance* does not release from obligation. There are issues about culpable ignorance that need not detain us here.[9] For present purposes we can confine our attention to questions directly related to commands, particularly divine commands, and disobedience.

VII SINFUL MISUNDERSTANDINGS

The idea that one can be addressed by a word from God, and be subject to it, and can indeed be disobedient to it, without having recognised and understood it is certainly present in the Bible. It is particularly prominent in the oracles of Isaiah. The record of his inaugural vision contains an oracle that explicitly says it is addressed to people that God does not intend it to be understood by. God says to Isaiah,

> Go and say to this people:
>   'Hear and hear, but do not understand;
>   see and see, but do not perceive.'
> Make the heart of this people fat,
>   and their ears heavy,
>   and shut their eyes;
> lest they see with their eyes,
>   and hear with their ears,
> and understand with their hearts,
>   and turn and be healed.[10]

Here it is clear that the people to be addressed will be held responsible for responding or not responding appropriately, and clear enough (though not fully explicit) that it is because of their sinfulness that they are expected not to understand. These themes recur in other oracles. The declaration that 'the vision of all this has become to [people] like the words of a book that is sealed'[11] is surely connected with the charge that 'they are a rebellious [or disobedient] people ['*am meri*]' who do not want to hear what God will say to them.[12] Similarly God tells Ezekiel that the people to whom he is sent 'will not listen to you; for they are not willing to listen to me; because [they] are of a hard forehead and of a stubborn heart'. Nonetheless, 'you shall speak my words to them, whether they hear or refuse to hear; for they are a rebellious house'.[13]

The presupposition of these texts, that one can be counted as disobedient to a command that one does not understand, if it is only because of one's sinfulness that one does not understand it, is plausible enough. This suggests another way of trying to understand the meaning of a divine command in terms of God's intentions about audience understanding. We might suppose that for God to command p to do a is for God to present p with signs that God intends to be such that if p had no sinful attitude, p would recognise by these signs a divine command to do a.[14]

How does this fare as a theory of the meaning of divine commands? It nicely complements a religious sense of ethical reflection as a spiritual exercise. For it suggests that the attempt to achieve a fuller understanding of God's commands can be understood, at least in part, as an effort to attain a better frame of mind, a fuller harmony with God, for understanding them. And there are some possibly undesirable implications with which the theory need not be burdened. (1) It need not be taken as implying that whoever receives a divine command would be a theist if sinless. Recognising a divine command in the signs might amount to no more than finding in them something extremely authoritative and having imperative force, as suggested in Section IV above. (2) It also need not imply that those who are wrong in a dispute about the interpretation of a divine command are more sinful than those (if any) who are right. Both may be equally sinful (which does not mean monsters of sin); for even without being totally pure one may arrive at the conclusion one would reach if one were totally pure. The theory does imply, however, that in any such dispute about a command that really has been issued to them by God, at least one party's views are influenced by sin. I am Calvinist enough to find that plausible; but some may find it objectionable.

I am less reconciled to another implication the theory does have, that the meaning of a divine command is determined by what a sinless recipient would take it to mean. This makes the ethical status of certain attitudes as sinful, or as good and bad, prior in the order of explanation to the meaning of divine commands; but that is not what troubles me here. It would trouble me if I thought that *all* ethical facts should be explained in terms of divine commands; but it seems quite implausible to me for more than one reason to suppose that facts of good and bad, as distinct from facts of right and wrong, should be so explained. It is only the obligation family of ethical facts that can plausibly be explained in terms of commands of any sort. We are seeing here one of the reasons why divine commands, and indeed any decent practice of commanding, are likely to have to presuppose judgements of good and bad.[15]

What disturbs me more is the dependence of this theory on counterfactual conditionals about human responses. I am sceptical about such conditionals.[16] I suspect that in many cases there is no single interpretation that a person definitely would give if sinless. If we want a theory that assures a single determinate meaning to divine commands, we are probably better off with a theory in terms of speech-act intentions, according to which the meaning of a divine command is determined by what God intended to command. We must still take into account the fact that the ethical goodness or badness of a person's attitudes affects whether she can fairly be deemed to have disobeyed, or to be responsible for obeying, a divine command she has not understood. But instead of making this fact the basis of our theory of the *meaning* of divine commands, we can simply take it as imposing a condition on a person's being subject to, or even addressed by, a divine command.

We can say that if God's command to do a is addressed to p, then God must intend (and if omniscient must know) the signs presented to p to be such that p either will recognise, or would in all probability recognise thereby a divine command to do a, if p had no sinful attitude. This is a necessary, not a sufficient, condition of p's being addressed by a divine command. What it requires is that *p*, if sinless, would recognise as commanded everything that is commanded. For reasons indicated above in rejecting the claim that subjective obligation always binds, the condition now laid down does not require that *p*, if sinless, would recognise as commanded no more than what is commanded. That is unnecessary, since this is not a complete theory of the meaning of divine commands. We are still relying in this condition on counterfactual conditionals about which I am somewhat sceptical, about how people would respond if sinless; but we should be able to tolerate an area of indeterminacy here, since responsibility and culpability are commonly matters of degree in any event.

VIII CONCLUSION

In the end the view that what God commands is simply what God intends to command by signs that are in fact given seems to me to provide the most plausible framework for an account of the meaning of divine commands. I have not considered in detail what signs are or could be used by God in this way, though scriptures and natural ethical inclinations are obvious candidates. The theory in terms of speech-act intentions must be supplemented with provisos in terms of intended audience-understanding. One is not addressed by a divine command that one does not recognise unless the relevant signs were intended by God to be such that if one were sinless, one would in all probability recognise in them a divine command requiring at least what God meant to require. And no doubt the nature of communication requires further that any command actually given by God be intended by God to meet with at least a measure of recognition and understanding in some recipient.

Notes

1. Robert Merrihew Adams, *The Virtue of Faith and Other Essays in Philosophical Theology* (New York: Oxford University Press, 1987), chs 7–9; and 'Divine Commands and the Social Nature of Obligation', *Faith and Philosophy*, 1987, vol. 4, pp. 262–75.
2. This problem for divine will theories of the nature of obligation might of course be avoided if God's power were sufficiently limited; but, as we shall see, our difficulties in understanding the concept

of a divine command might also be eased by limiting one of the traditional attributes of God – specifically, by limiting God's knowledge.

3. As argued by Brevard Childs, *The Book of Exodus* (Philadelphia: Westminster Press, 1974), pp. 420f. I am relying on Childs in my delineation of philological options in this paragraph.

4. Paul Grice, 'Meaning', first published 1957, reprinted in Paul Grice, *Studies in the Way of Words* (Cambridge, Mass.: Harvard University Press, 1989), pp. 219–21.

5. As he explicitly was: see Grice, *Studies in the Way of Words*, pp. 351–9.

6. Grice, *Studies in the Way of Words*, p. 98.

7. For a careful presentation and defence of a position of this sort, see Sir W. David Ross, *Foundations of Ethics* (Oxford: Clarendon Press, 1939), pp. 159–67.

8. Ross seems to be relying on an argument of this sort in *Foundations of Ethics*, p. 163f.

9. I have discussed some of them in 'Involuntary Sins', *Philosophical Review*, 1985, vol. 94, pp. 3–31.

10. Isaiah 6: 9–10. I quote in this section from the Revised Standard Version, except as otherwise indicated.

11. Isaiah 29: 11; cf. 28: 9–13.

12. Isaiah 30: 9–11.

13. Ezekiel 3: 7, 2:7.

14. This formulation is inspired by one of Grice's modifications of his theory; see Grice, *Studies in the Way of Words*, pp. 114f. I leave open here the question whether one who held this theory would want to extend it to a general theory of the meaning of a communication or revelation from God, based on the assumption that any misunderstanding of a divine revelation must be due to sin.

15. I have suggested other reasons in Adams, 'Divine Commands and the Social Nature of Obligation'.

16. One aspect of this scepticism is developed in my paper, 'Middle Knowledge and the Problem of Evil', reprinted in Adams, *The Virtue of Faith*, pp. 77–93; but the present case is significantly different from the cases discussed there.

4

Reply: Moral Duty and God: A View from the Left

CLARK A. KUCHEMAN

I

After revealing by writing on the board that I am left-handed I often let it be known to the students in my classes that, having been made to suffer in many ways by right-handers over the years, I intend to 'get even', at least in a small way, by grading right-handed students by exceptionally rigorous standards. Almost invariably, though (with the exception, perhaps, of a few similarly resentful left-handers), the students object. 'No matter how badly you may want to get even with right-handers,' they say, 'you ought not to do that. You ought to grade right-handers and left-handers alike by the appropriate agreed-upon academic standards.' 'But why?' 'Because we'll complain to Dean Fucaloro if you don't grade everyone by the agreed-upon criteria, and he'll punish you for it.' 'No he won't,' I respond. 'Not only will I be very subtle about it, but, I assure you, I'll be able to "rationalise" whatever grades I decide upon. Not only will Dean Fucaloro not be able to tell what I've done, but even you right-handed students won't be able to tell. (After all, I've been getting away with this for more than 25 years now!) Besides, I get so much desire-satisfaction from treating right-handers this way that it's easily worth the risk of getting caught and punished.'

'Well, you might be able to get away with mistreating right-handers, and it might be worth it to you to do it even if you were to be caught and punished, but, nevertheless, you still ought to grade right-handers by the agreed-upon criteria. Why? Because you ought to! For the sake of doing what you ought to do, you ought to do it!'

'What you are saying is that I ought for moral duty's sake, or categorically, rather than for the sake of satisfying a desire to stay out of trouble with Dean Fucaloro, or hypothetically, to grade right-handers by the college's agreed-upon standards. But I don't agree with you in believing that I ought categorically, for moral duty's sake, to do this. And how can I possibly do any action, including this one, categorically, rather than merely hypothetically, unless I *believe* that I ought categorically to do it? "Ought implies can", remember, and, since I can't possibly do the action categorically unless I *believe* that I ought categorically to do it, it can't be so that I ought categorically to grade right-handed students by these agreed-upon criteria. Sure, if I were to *believe* it to be my moral duty to grade right-handers in this way, then not only would it be possible for me to do it for moral duty's sake, but I would give myself the moral duty to do it. But, as it happens, I don't believe it to be my moral duty to do this, and therefore I can't possibly do it for moral duty's sake.'[1]

'Oh, but yes you can!' the students protest. 'It may not be possible for you to grade right-handers by the agreed-upon criteria for the sake of doing what you ought to do unless you *believe* that that is what you ought to do for the sake of doing what you ought to do, or, as you would say, unless you believe that you ought *categorically* to do it. We agree so far. But it *is* possible for you to *believe* (in agreement with us) that you ought for the sake of doing what you ought to do, categorically, to grade right-handers by the appropriate criteria, and, since this is so, it is also possible for you, for the sake of doing what you ought to do, categorically, to grade right-handers by these criteria. Moreover, even if you don't believe it, you ought whether you want to or not, for the sake of believing what you ought to believe, *to* believe it. No, your subjective beliefs won't get you off the hook. You are responsible *both* for the beliefs you hold *and* for the actions you do. You determine both by freely deciding. You are not a robot. You are a person, a being with the power of thinking (even if you don't develop and exercise this power!), and as such you are capable of deciding freely, that is, independently of causes as well as of whatever desires you may happen to have, both what propositions (including the proposition at issue here) to believe and what actions (including the one at issue here) to do on what motives or purposes!

'You've said on several occasions that Ted Bundy's actions –

raping and then killing, for the sake of his own desire-satisfaction, a large number of women – were morally evil even though Bundy himself did not believe it to be categorically imperative for him not to do them. You hold him to be responsible for, and so morally evil by virtue of, his *not believing* that raping and killing are categorically imperative for him not to do as well as his *doing* the acts of rape and killing themselves. The same consideration applies to you: just as Ted Bundy was not justified in *not* believing raping and killing for pleasure to be categorically imperative for him *not* to do, so you are not justified in *not* believing grading right-handers and left-handers by the agreed-upon criteria to be categorically imperative for you *to* do. No matter what or how strong your desires may be, you ought, for the sake of doing what you ought to do, categorically, to decide *both* theoretically to *believe* that you ought to grade right-handers and left-handers alike by the college's agreed-upon academic criteria *and*, consequently, practically to *do* it!'[2]

II

If I am *not* justified in *not* believing the proposition stating that I ought whether I want to or not to grade right-handers by the agreed-upon academic criteria and so ought whether I want to or not *to* believe it, *then*, certainly, I ought whether I want to or not actually to grade right-handers in this way rather than in ways that would satisfy my (not really, of course!) insatiable desire for revenge.[3] But *why* am I not justified in not believing this proposition? *Why* ought I, whether I want to or not, categorically, to *believe* that I ought whether I want to or not, categorically, to grade right-handers and left-handers alike by the college's agreed-upon academic criteria?

There exists an all-powerful and all-knowing creator of all things whose will is sovereign (rather than subject to a moral law), according to at least one version of traditional theism,[4] and, according to what Robert M. Adams refers to as the '*un*modified' Divine Command Theory,[5] I am not justified in not believing that I ought categorically to grade right-handers by the agreed-upon academic criteria if and only if this omnipotent, omniscient, sovereignly-willing creator commands me to grade right-handers by the agreed-upon criteria. If he commands me to do it, then I

ought for moral duty's sake both theoretically to *believe* I ought
for moral duty's sake to do it and practically to *do* it. 'According
to such a theory,' as Adams puts it, '[the omnipotent, omniscient,
sovereignly-willing creator's] commands are the standard, conformity to which constitutes the ethical validity of human social
requirements, and the correctness of one against another when
they disagree', so that 'it will be [this creator's] commands that
will ground obligation as such.'[6]

Assuming this omnipotent, omniscient, sovereignly-willing creator
to exist, does he command me to grade right-handed students by
the college's agreed-upon criteria? In commanding me to do this,
I have learned from Adams (if I have understood him correctly),
the omnipotent, omniscient, sovereignly-willing creator must give
me 'signs' by which, if I am 'sinless', I will be likely to recognise
his command. For 'one is not addressed by a divine command
that one does not recognise unless the relevant signs were intended by [the sovereignly-willing creator] to be such that *if one
were sinless*, one would *in all probability* recognise in them a divine command requiring at least what [he] meant to require'.[7]
But what if I am not sinless, and so am unable at all to recognise
in the 'signs' a divine command to grade right-handers by the
accepted criteria? Or what if I am sinless, but, against the 'probability', I nevertheless am unable to recognise the command? Do
I then *not* have the moral duty to grade right-handers by the accepted criteria? If, whether sinless or sinful, I am unable to recognise in the 'signs' that I am commanded to do this, then how
can it be categorically imperative for me to do it? After all, if I
cannot possibly *do* it for moral duty's sake (categorically) rather
than for the sake of satisfying some desire or other (hypothetically), then it cannot *be* my moral duty to do it. And, on the divine command theory (whether unmodified or modified), unless
I can believe, justifiably – by recognising it in the 'signs' – that
the sovereignly-willing creator commands me to do it, I cannot
possibly grade right-handers by the agreed-upon criteria for moral
duty's sake (categorically) rather than merely for the sake of satisfying a desire (hypothetically). How, then, I need to know, whether
I be sinless or sinful, am I to recognise the omnipotent, omniscient,
sovereignly-willing creator of all things to be commanding me to
follow this policy in my grading?[8] The facts that, on traditional
Christian doctrine, all of us are sinners and, second, that advocates of the Divine Command Theory disagree radically about

what the sovereignly-willing creator's commands are, for example, on the question of whether he commands us forcibly to prevent abortions from being performed, do not lead me to believe that I (or anyone else) can recognise either the 'signs' themselves or the commands expressed in them with any reasonable degree of reliability.[9]

Let's assume, though, that in some way or other I do recognise in a sign of some kind – and so am not justified in not believing – that the sovereignly-willing creator commands me to grade right-handers by the appropriate academic standards. This still does not show that I am not justified in not believing that I ought categorically to follow this policy in my grading. From the proposition 'Grading right-handers by the agreed-upon academic criteria is commanded by the omnipotent, omniscient, sovereignly-willing creator of all things', the proposition 'Grading right-handers by the agreed-upon academic criteria ought categorically to be done' does not logically validly follow. For there is an expression in the conclusion, namely, 'ought categorically to be done', that is not contained in the single premise. Consequently I can believe the premise and yet, without contradicting myself, deny the conclusion. At the very least, I must also not be justified in not believing another premise, namely, a premise stating that I ought categorically to do an action (or adopt a policy of action) *if and only if* the sovereignly-willing creator commands me to do it. Hence, *if* I am not justified in not believing *both* that he commands me to grade right-handers by the agreed-upon criteria *and* that an action is categorically imperative for me to do if and only if he commands me to do it, *then* I am also not justified in not believing that I ought categorically to grade right-handers by the agreed-upon academic criteria. Given that these 'ifs' are satisfied, then, I ought categorically both theoretically to *believe* that I ought categorically to grade right-handers by the agreed-upon criteria and practically to *do* it.

Unfortunately, however, that is not *all* that I am not justified in not believing theoretically and doing practically if I am not justified in not believing that an action is my moral duty to do if and only if doing it is commanded by the sovereignly-willing creator of all things. For if the omnipotent, omniscient creator of all things is *sovereignly*-willing rather than morally good, that is, if he wills however he wishes rather than in accordance with and for the sake of moral duties determined by a moral law that he does not have the power to change at will, then, contrary to what seems to me to be at all believable, he could will to command me to do virtually any action whatever. Not only could he command me to proceed with my intention to 'get even' with right-handers, for example, but, if he so willed, he could command all of us to practise gay-bashing,[10] say, or the subordination of women to men.[11] Hence if I were to believe, in agreement with this *un*modified Divine Command Theory, that I ought as a matter of moral duty to do whatever he commands me to do, then, as Immanuel Kant pointed out long ago, my decision so to believe 'would form the basis for a moral system which would be in direct opposition to morality'.[12]

Moreover, if I were to decide to believe that an action is my moral duty to do if and only if he sovereignly wills to command me to do it I would give myself a moral duty to decide both what to believe theoretically and what to do practically by obeying his commanding, and, as Paul Tillich points out, this too seems to be contrary to, rather than required by, what I can reasonably believe my moral duty really to be. If I 'understand the moral commandments as expressions of a divine will, which is sovereign and without criteria' and 'must be obeyed as it is given in revelation', Tillich explains,

> The question then is: Why should anyone obey the command-ments of this divine lawgiver? How are they distinguished from commands given by a human tyrant? He is stronger than I am. He can destroy me. But is not that destruction more to be feared which would follow the submission of one's personality center to a strange will? Would not this be just the denial of the moral imperative?[13]

Continuing Tillich's questioning mode, would not students be deciding and acting contrary to, rather than in accordance with, moral duty if they were to decide to believe and do whatever I, a full professor who sits on a prestigious endowed chair, tell them to believe and do simply because I tell them to believe and do it? Are not cult followers deciding to believe and do contrary to, rather than in accordance with, moral duty when, perhaps out of devotion to the 'cause', they decide to believe and do whatever their leader tells them to believe and do? Is not a person who, out of love, decides to make himself or herself into a submissive servant of whoever is the object of his or her love acting contrary to, rather than in accordance with, moral duty? Whether I do it out of a desire to express admiration of an authority, out of devotion to a cause, out of love for someone or something, or, *especially* – as the principle under consideration would require me to do – out of the motive of duty for duty's sake, and whether my 'heteronomous subjection of the will',[14] as Tillich calls it, is to a human commander or to an omnipotent, omniscient, sovereignly-willing creator of all things, my freely willed servility, my 'heteronomous subjection of the will', seems also (although perhaps not as obviously) to be, in Kant's words again, 'in direct opposition to morality'.

So, *unless* I am prepared to believe that it could be categorically imperative for me to engage in gay-bashing, to treat women as 'created *for* men', or to subject my decision-making about what to believe and what to do 'heteronomously' to someone or something external or 'strange' to me, I can*not* be justified in believing, as the *un*modified Divine Command Theory asserts, that an action (or policy of action), whether theoretical or practical, is categorically imperative for me to do (or policy to adopt) if and only if the assumed-to-exist omnipotent, omniscient, *sovereignly*-willing creator of all things commands me to do it. Hence, the fact, if it be such, that this sovereignly-willing creator commands me to grade right-handers by the college's established criteria really has (or should have) no bearing on the question of whether I ought categorically *both* to *believe* I ought categorically to do it *and* categorically to *do* it.

Basically, Adams agrees with these objections to the Divine Command Theory. Not only does he agree that, in his words, 'the more extreme forms of divine command theory . . . imply that if [the sovereignly-willing creator] commanded us, for example, to make it our chief end in life to inflict suffering on other human beings, for no other reason than that he commanded it, it would be *wrong* not to obey',[15] but – by judging an 'Autonomous Relief Worker [who] directs food to the poor, not just because he has been instructed to do so, but *primarily* because he cares about the needs of the poor' and 'would *disobey intructions* if they seemed to betray the humanitarian cause' to be morally superior to a 'Conscientiously Obedient Relief Worker' who distributes food to people who need it 'only because he has been instructed by his employers to do it, and believes unquestioningly that that morally obliges him to do it'[16] – Adams also shows that he agrees, at least in part, with Tillich's objection to the 'heteronomous subjection of the will' that is required by the unmodified Divine Command Theory.

These considerations do not lead Adams to reject the Divine Command Theory altogether, however, but only to 'modify' it so that it is no longer subject to these objections.

Suppose, still, that I recognise in the 'signs' that the assumed-to-exist omnipotent, omniscient, sovereignly-willing creator of all things commands me to grade right-handers by the proper academic criteria. Why, on this modified Divine Command Theory, ought I to believe that I ought as a matter of moral duty to do what he commands me to do and, therefore, as a matter of moral duty to grade right-handers by the proper academic criteria? 'Divine command metaethics is a type of social theory of the nature of obligation', Adams answers, and, 'according to social theories of the nature of obligation', he explains, 'having an obligation to do something consists in being required (in a certain way, under certain circumstances), by another person or group of persons, to do it.' Why, then, ought I to acknowledge the other person's requirement as an obligation? '[V]aluing one's social bonds gives one, under certain conditions, a reason to do what is required of one by one's associates or one's community (and thus to fulfill obligations, understood as social requirements).'[17] If I value my relationship with the person, then I should believe what he or she requires of me to be an obligation for me to do. And the same holds for requirements – commands, in this case – given by the omnipotent, omniscient, sovereignly-willing creator of all things. If I value my relationship with him, I then have a 'reason' for believing that I ought as a matter of moral obligation to do what he commands me to do.

I am justified in holding this belief only conditionally, however, according to Adams's modified Divine Command Theory, not unconditionally. For I should believe it only by virtue of my valuing my relationship with the creator, and my valuing my relationship with him is conditional not only upon his being the omnipotent, omniscient, sovereignly-willing creator of all things, but also upon his being loving and not commanding me to do actions that either are 'repulsive' to me, given my many 'subjective valuings',[18] or are in conflict with 'principles [I] *would* give [my]self if I were giving [my]self a moral law',[19] as they would be if, say, he were to command me to practise gay-bashing or to subordinate women to men. If on the other hand he were not loving but, instead, as Kant suggests he could be, 'vengeful' and 'lust[ing] for power',[20] then I would of course *not* value my relationship with him but would be alienated and so would have a reason *not* to consider myself to be morally obligated to obey his commands.

Hence, on the modified Divine Command Theory, if I understand it correctly, I ought only conditionally, not unconditionally, to believe that an action is my moral duty to do if and only if this sovereignly-willing creator commands me to do it. *Provided* that he is loving and does not command me to do anything that is repulsive to me or that I independently consider to be morally wrong for me to do, so that I value my relationship with him, *then* I ought as a matter of moral duty both to *believe* I ought to do and to *do* what he commands me to do. And of course, however disappointing it might be to me to discover this, his command to me to grade right-handers by the proper academic criteria is neither repulsive to me nor is it in conflict with what I independently deem to be morally wrong for me to do.[21] Consequently I ought to believe that I ought categorically to grade right-handers by the college's agreed-upon standards rather than by my desire for revenge. *If* these (and perhaps other) conditions are met, so that I *value* my relationship with this loving, sovereignly-willing creator, *then*, by virtue of this valuing, I have reason to believe that I ought as a matter of moral duty to do what he commands me to do, which, in this case, is to grade right-handers by the proper standards.

Now, let me say that, *if* I were to believe in the existence of an omnipotent, omniscient, *loving, sovereignly*-willing creator of all things who made his commands known to me and never commanded me to do any action that is either repulsive to my 'subjective valuings' or in conflict with 'principles [I] *would* give [my]self if I were giving [my]self a moral law', and *if* there were no other moral theory that more adequately explains why, even if I don't believe it, I am *not justified in not believing* that I ought categorically to grade right-handers by the proper academic criteria (or why, even if he didn't believe it, Ted Bundy was *not justified in not believing* that he ought categorically not to rape and kill for pleasure), *then* I would be a modified divine command theorist myself. I do not believe that such a being exists, however, and –

as I will explain momentarily – I *do* believe another moral theory better explains what needs to be explained.

In what ways is the modified Divine Command Theory lacking? It largely avoids Tillich's criticism that it would require 'heteronomous subjection of the will', I hope I have succeeded in showing, since it does not require total and unconditional surrender to the divine commands but allows me to retain not only my 'subjective valuings' but also even to refuse to obey divine commands if they command me to do what I independently believe to be my moral duty not to do. But it does not successfully avoid the objection that the divine commander could command me to do actions that are obviously my moral duty *not* to do. A *loving* commander would not command me to inflict suffering on others whenever I felt the inclination to do so, of course, but, in Adams's words, since 'very diverse preferences about what things are to be treated as personal rights seem compatible with love and certainly with deity', 'it seems only contingent that a loving [sovereignly-willing creator] does or would frown on increasing the happiness of other people by the painless and undetected killing of a person who wants to live but will almost certainly not live happily'.[22] Most importantly from my perspective, however, along with the difficulty of knowing *what* the commands are, the modified divine command theory is lacking because it does not succeed in showing why I am *not justified in not believing* that I ought as a matter of moral duty to do what the sovereignly-willing creator commands me to do. It shows that I ought to believe this *if* I value my relationship with him, to be sure, but it also allows that, if I *don't* value this relationship, then it is not so that I ought to believe that I ought as a matter of moral obligation to do what he commands me to do. And if it is not so that I ought to believe that I ought as a matter of moral duty to do what he commands, then – still assuming that he commands me to do so – it is also not the case that I ought to believe that I ought as a matter of moral duty to grade right-handers by the proper academic criteria. Strange as it may seem to say so, it would be only *hypothetically* imperative for me to believe that I ought *categorically* to do what he commands me to do.[23]

III

If I am *not* justified in *not* believing the proposition stating that I ought whether I want to or not to grade right-handers by the agreed-upon academic criteria (and so ought whether I want to or not *to* believe it), *then* I ought whether I want to or not actually to grade right-handers in this way rather than in a way that would satisfy my desire for revenge. But *am* I not justified in not believing this proposition? Ought I, whether I want to or not, categorically, to *believe* that I ought whether I want to or not, categorically, to grade right-handers and left-handers alike by the college's agreed-upon academic criteria?

What I do if I 'get even' with right-handers by grading them by exceptionally rigorous standards rather than by the college's agreed-upon standards is of course to prevent them from fulfilling, through their interaction with me, their own freely willed end (presumably, to have their work in the course evaluated accurately by me in accordance with the agreed-upon standards) and compel them, instead, to fulfil an end willed by me (namely, the satisfaction of my desire for revenge). Even though they are in fact free 'I's or persons, that is, beings with the power of thinking and therefore of freely willing ends or purposes, I treat them merely as means to the attainment of an end determined externally to them by me and therefore as unfree 'it's or things, that is, beings lacking the power of thinking and therefore having no power of freely willing ends of their own. If on the other hand I grade them by the agreed-upon standards (agreed upon implicity by me as a member of the faculty and by them as students who elect to enrol in the class), I do not treat them merely as means to my end. On the contrary, by promoting the fulfilment of their freely willed end I treat them as ends in themselves and therefore as free 'I's who freely will this as their end. And I ought categorically *not* to treat free 'I's merely as means to ends determined externally to them, and so as if they were unfree 'it's, and *to* treat them as ends in themselves, and so as free 'I's, because, I shall argue – with help especially from G. W. F. Hegel – I am *not justified in not believing* that I ought categorically to act only in ways that treat all free 'I's, *including first of all myself*, always as free 'I's, persons, and never as unfree 'it's, things.

Now, by way of preparing to explain why I am not justified in not believing that I ought categorically to act only in ways that treat *all* free 'I's always as free 'I's, persons, and never as unfree 'it's, things, let me explain at least briefly what it *means* for me to treat *myself* as an unfree 'it', to begin with, and then as a free 'I'.

As an 'I' or person, I am not the biological organism that you see before you, I need first to make clear. 'I am alive *in* this bodily organism which is my external existence',[24] to be sure, as Hegel puts it. Indeed, as an 'I' I depend upon it, especially upon the proper functioning (biological, electrical, chemical, and whatever) of my brain. But 'when I say "I," I *eo ipso* abandon all my particular characteristics, my disposition, natural endowment, knowledge, and age'.[25] For all of these – including even my desires, such as my desire to take revenge on right-handers – are *objects about which* I think and will and *from which* I therefore abstract myself. As an 'I', then, a person, I am that from which I can*not* abstract myself, namely, the *sub*ject or 'thinking power',[26] to use a term of Hegel's, whose activity the thinking is. As an 'I' I am thus, in Hegel's words still, 'the ultimate and unanalysable point of consciousness'[27] in relation to whom everything else is external. 'The ego is quite empty,' as Hegel puts it, 'a mere point, simple, yet active in this simplicity.'[28]

As an 'I', a 'thinking power', I am in fact free, moreover, at least negatively or contra-causally, in the degree to which my power of thinking is not merely potential but also actual. For by virtue of my power of thinking I am capable of willing or deciding what propositions to believe theoretically – and consequently also what actions to do or policies to adopt practically, since practical activity is done *on* theoretical beliefs – freely *from* causes that are external to me. My acts of will, my decisions, are not mere effects of preceding causes. As evidenced by the fact that I am capable of deciding what to believe (even if I don't!) by obeying the normative laws of deductive and inductive logic in my thinking, I am free in making – and therefore responsible for – my decisions about what to believe theoretically and what to do practically. I determine myself, that is, I determine my believings and doings, my 'content', by deciding freely. As a 'mere point' with the power of thinking, as Hegel explains, 'anyone can discover in himself the ability to abstract from everything whatever, and in the same way to determine himself, to posit any content in himself by his own effort'.[29,30]

What then does it mean for me to treat myself not *as* a free 'I' but, instead, as an *un*free 'it'? I treat myself as an unfree 'it' – I 'alienate' my freedom, and hence my personhood, from myself, in other words, and thereby to this extent transform myself into a thing – if, in my power of negative, contra-causal freedom, I freely decide to decide what to believe and what to do by subjecting my decision-making heteronomously to someone (or *some-*

thing, perhaps, such as a strong desire) external to me and there-fore *unfreely*, as I would do, for example, in Hegel's words, 'in ceding to someone else full power and authority to fix and pre-scribe what actions are to be done . . . or what duties are binding on [my] conscience or what religious truth is, &c.'[31] As a free 'I', I can freely will to will in obedience to an external of some kind and therefore *unfreely*, and to do so is to treat myself not as a free 'I' but, instead, as an unfree 'it'. I remain negatively, contra-causally free if I do this, to be sure, and so I am still responsible for the beliefs I hold and the actions I do. It is *my* free decision to determine my believings and doings by deciding submissively; my 'heteronomous subjection of [my] will' is by my own free act of will. I am nevertheless freely *unfree*, and so treat myself as an unfree 'it' rather than as a free 'I,' since my free decision is to decide what to believe and what to do unfreely by 'ceding' my decision-making heteronomously to someone (or something) ex-ternal to myself as the 'mere point' with the power of thinking and willing.

By way of contrast, therefore, it should be clear that I treat myself as a free 'I' rather than as an unfree 'it' if, in my power of negative, contra-causal freedom, I freely decide to decide what to believe and what to do by *not* subjecting my decision-making heteronomously to anything whatever that is external and, in-stead, subjecting it *autonomously* only to myself, that is, by obey-ing only my own 'I'. 'The will [that is, the 'I'] is free', as Hegel says, 'only when it does not will anything alien, extrinsic, foreign to itself (for as long as it does so, it is dependent), but wills itself alone – wills the will.'[32] I treat myself as a free 'I' if and only if, in my negative, contra-causal freedom, I freely decide to decide what to believe and what to do autonomously by obeying myself as 'I' and therefore freely.

This is not to say that I treat myself as a free 'I' if I freely decide to believe and do whatever I may *want* to believe and do, I hasten to emphasise. For my wants or desires are *ex*ternal rather than *in*ternal to me as 'I', and therefore I freely decide to decide *un*freely – and so treat myself as an unfree 'it' – if I freely decide to decide what to believe and do as I *want* to. On the contrary, I freely will to will in subjection only to myself as 'I' – I 'will the will', and thereby treat myself as a free 'I' – only if and to the extent that I freely will to will 'what is rational'.[33] I freely decide to decide freely if and to the extent that I freely decide to decide what propositions to believe theoretically and what actions to do practically by thinking in obedience to 'the necessary forms and self-determinations of thought' – 'pure reason'[34] – namely, the principles of deductive and inductive logic. For as person or 'I', remember, I *am* the 'mere point' who thinks, the 'thinking power', and since, in Hegel's words, 'in logic a thought is understood to include nothing else but what depends on thinking and what thinking has brought into existence',[35] I therefore obey myself as 'I' – and so treat myself as a free 'I' rather than as an unfree 'it' – if and only if I decide what to believe and what to do by deliberating logically validly.

So why *ought* I *categorically* to treat myself always as a free 'I' and never as an unfree 'it'? Because I am *not justified in not believing* that I ought categorically to do so. *Why* am I not justified in not believing this? Because to treat myself as a free 'I' is freely to decide what to believe and what to do *freely* by thinking logically validly, and I can *deny* that I ought categorically to decide what propositions to believe – and therefore also what practical actions to do – by deliberating logically validly (rather than by subjecting my deliberating and deciding heteronomously to something external, by doing which I would then treat myself as an unfree 'it') only by presupposing and so *affirming* at the same time that I ought categorically *to* do so. Since by believing any proposition whatever I presuppose that I am justified in deciding to do so by deliberating logically validly, I contradict and thus refute myself if I deny rather than affirm that I ought categorically to decide what to believe by deliberating logically validly. Hence I *cannot be justified in not believing* that I ought categorically to treat myself always as a free 'I' (by believing and doing autonomously, that is, as logically valid thinking requires) and never as an unfree 'it' (by believing and doing in heteronomous subjection to something external).[36]

Now, if I am not justified in not believing that I ought categorically to treat myself always as a free 'I', by believing as logically valid thinking requires, and never as an unfree 'it', by subjecting my believing heteronomously to an Other of some kind, then I am also not justified in not believing, in words borrowed from Immanuel Kant this time, that 'I ought never to act except in such a way *that I can also will that my maxim should become a universal law*'.[37] For unless there should happen to be relevant differences between myself and other 'I's or between my circumstances and theirs, I must believe that, *if* I believe that other 'I's ought categorically always to act toward me in a certain way, then – since otherwise I contradict myself – I ought categorically always to act toward them in this same way. Or, in other words, since otherwise I believe the self-contradictory proposition that the same action both *is* and *is not* categorically imperative to do, I am not justified in not believing, as Hegel puts it, that 'what is one man's duty ought also to be another's'[38] and, consequently, that I have the same moral duty to other 'I's that I believe them to have to me. And I in fact do – and necessarily so – believe that other 'I's ought categorically always to treat me in a certain way. Specifically, I *cannot not* believe that other 'I's ought categorically to treat me always as a free 'I' and never as an unfree 'it', and therefore I *cannot be justified in not believing* that I ought categorically to treat other 'I's always as free 'I's and never as unfree 'it's. Logically valid thinking requires me to believe that I ought categorically, in Hegel's words, to 'behave towards others in a manner that is universally valid, recognizing them – as [I] will others to recognize me – as free, as persons'.[39]

So, as it turns out, the students are correct in believing that, *whether I believe it or not*, I ought categorically to grade right-handed students by the college's agreed-upon standards rather than on the basis of my desire to 'get even' with right-handers. For since I am *not justified in not believing* that I ought categorically to treat other 'I's always as free 'I's and never as unfree 'it's, and since I treat right-handers as unfree 'it's rather than as free 'I's if I treat them merely as means to the satisfaction of my desire for revenge and as free 'I's only if I grade them by the agreed-upon criteria, I therefore *am not justified in not believing* that I ought categorically to grade right-handers by these criteria.

IV

'One of the reasons, surely, why divine command theories of ethics have appealed to some theologians,' Adams comments by way of characterising the *unmodified* divine command theory, 'is that such theories seem especially congruous with *the religious demand that God be the object of our highest allegiance*.'[40] Although it is not Adams's intention, let me take 'the religious demand that God be the object of our highest allegiance' as the criterion for determining *what* God is. 'God', then, let me say, is not a proper name, comparable to Yahweh, Baal, and the like, but is instead a title for *whatever it is* that *should be* 'the object of our highest allegiance'. To determine what is God is thus to determine what it is to which we ought, whether we want to or not, to be ultimately allegiant.

Now, if God is that to which we ought to be ultimately allegiant, there is a clear connection between God and moral duty. If I (or any 'I') am justified in believing something to be God, then I contradict myself unless I also believe that I ought as a matter of moral duty to do whatever ultimate allegiance to this something requires me to do, and, conversely, if I am justified in believing that I ought as a matter of moral duty to do whatever ultimate allegiance to it requires me to do, then I contradict myself unless I also believe it to be God. By the same token, however, the reverse also holds. If I am justified in believing it is not the case that I ought as a matter of moral duty to do what ultimate allegiance to it requires me to do, or, even more, if I am justified in believing that I ought as a matter of moral duty *not* to do what ultimate allegiance to it would require me to do, then I must also believe that it is *not* God.[41]

And by this reasoning, *both* for me *and* (if I read him correctly) for Adams, the omnipotent, omniscient, sovereignly-willing-and-commanding creator of all things is *not* God. That is, he is *not* that to which I (or any other 'I') ought to be ultimately allegiant.

'If our supreme commitment in life is to doing what is right just because it is right, and if what is right is right just because [the sovereignly-willing creator] wills or commands it, then', according to Adams, 'surely our highest allegiance is to [the sovereignly-willing creator].' That is, he would be God. 'But the modified divine command theory seems not to have this advantage', he continues,

> For the modified divine command theorist is forced to admit, as we have seen, that he has reasons for his adherence to a divine command ethics, and that his having these reasons implies that there are some things which he values independently of his beliefs about [the sovereignly-willing creator's] commands. It is therefore not correct to say of him that he is committed to doing the will of [the sovereignly-willing creator] *just* because it is the will of [this sovereignly-willing creator]. Indeed it appears that there are certain logically possible situations in which

his present attitudes would not commit him to obey [this creator's] commands (for instance, if [he] commanded cruelty for its own sake). This may even suggest that he values some things, not just independently of [the sovereignly-willing creator's] commands, but more than [his] commands.[42]

And so, if by 'God' we mean whatever it is to which we ought to be ultimately allegiant, then, judged from the perspective of Adams's modified divine command theory, the assumed-to-exist omnipotent, omniscient, sovereignly-willing creator of all things is not and cannot be God.

Similarly, from the perspective of my own semi-Hegelian, semi-Tillichian ethical theory, this assumed-to-exist omnipotent, omniscient, sovereignly-willing creator of all things cannot be God. Since ultimate allegiance to *anything whatever* that is external to me as an 'I' entails *freely* deciding to decide what to believe theoretically and what to do practically *unfreely*, that is, by a 'heteronomous subjection of the will', and so treating myself as an unfree 'it' rather than as a free 'I', I (and all other 'I's) ought as a matter of moral duty *not* to be ultimately allegiant to this sovereignly-willing creator.

Now if God cannot be anything whatever that is external, what then *is* God? God can only be whatever it is to which I express ultimate allegiance simultaneously with acting morally *good*ly, that is, simultaneously with acting both in accordance with and for the sake of my self-imposed fundamental moral duty to treat all free 'I's, bearers of spirit, including first of all myself, always as free 'I's, bearers of spirit, and never as unfree 'it's. And this something is not *a* being that would of necessity be external to me, but, rather, being-itself, the power of being that I (and all other 'I's) actualise within myself if and in so far as I develop and express myself as a freely free 'I' by obeying this moral law. 'God is being-itself',[43] as Tillich puts it in a now familiar formula, in the sense of 'the power of being in everything that is',[44] and since – which I fear I won't be able to explain here – being-itself's inner aim or *telos* is to become actual as spirit, *free* being, I express ultimate allegiance to it simultaneously with acting in accordance with and for the sake of my self-imposed moral duty to become and be freely free, *rationally* free, in my willing (which of course requires me, in turn, to treat other 'I's always as free 'I's and never as unfree 'it's).

Notes

1. Moral obligation carries *two* requirements. It requires me – and anyone else, needless to say – not only to do (or not do) an action but also to do it for moral duty's sake, that is, categorically, rather than for the sake of satisfying a desire I may happen to have, that is, hypothetically. But since I cannot be required to do what I cannot possibly do, and since I cannot possibly will it as my purpose to do an action for moral duty's sake, or categorically, unless I *believe* the action to be my moral duty to do, it cannot *be* my moral duty to do it – it cannot *be* categorically imperative for me to do it – unless I *believe* it to be. Hence moral duties, categorical imperatives, to do (or not do) actions (or to adopt or reject policies of action) can only be *self*-imposed. If I *believe* an action to be categorically imperative for me to do, then – provided, of course, that I am justified in my decision to hold the belief! – the action *is* categorically imperative for me to do. (*Believing* it to be my duty to do by no means guarantees that I actually will *do* it, though. I may still decide to act for the sake of satisfying my desire rather than for the sake of duty.)

2. To say that I am free to decide what propositions to believe with what degree of confidence, etc., is not to say that I can decide freely to believe, for example, that there are seven dogs at home waiting for me to feed and play with them, for in this case the evidence is overwhelming that there are 27, not seven! Instead, it is to say that my decision to believe (or withhold belief, or disbelieve, or simply ignore) a proposition is not merely an effect of preceding causes. I may well be *influenced* by factors external to me as a deliberating and deciding self, a thinking and willing 'I', of course, such as by my genetic code, my brain chemistry, my gender, my rearing – including perhaps even my toilet training – and the like, and, especially, by my existing beliefs and my desires. I am nevertheless free in the sense that, even if I don't develop and use it, I have the power to decide (or will) what to believe by deliberating (thinking) in submission to the rules of deductive and inductive logic, and, by virtue of this freedom, this power to decide independently of causes, I am responsible – morally, at least in the case at hand – for the beliefs I hold (just as Ted Bundy was responsible for the belief he *failed* to hold.) After all, are not all of us participating in this conference for the purpose of deciding what we should (whether we want to or not) believe about moral duty and God?

3. However tiresome and awkward the expression '*not* justified in *not* believing' may be, I'm afraid you'll just have to bear with me. To show simply that I am justified in believing, rather than that I am *not* justified in *not* believing, is not strong enough to show that I ought whether I want to or not, categorically, to believe a proposition. To say, for example, that, *had he thought of it and had he chosen to do so*, Ted Bundy would have been justified in believing that he ought categorically not to engage in raping and killing for pleasure does not suffice to show that he ought whether he wanted to or

not *to* have thought of it and *to* have chosen to believe it. In order to show this it is necessary to show that, *whatever* his thoughts and decisions may actually have been, he was *not* justified in *not* believing that he ought categorically not to engage in the practices of raping and killing for pleasure.

4. I do not mean to give a complete list of this creator's characteristics, needless to say. Mainly, I mean here to draw a contrast between an omnipotent and omniscient creator whose will is *sovereign* with one whose will is *subject to a moral law* that is independent of and prior to his will. For if his will is subject to a moral law, then it is this law, not his commanding *per se*, that determines what I ought categorically to do. I use this abstract description rather than the title 'God', moreover, in order to keep open the questions of *whether* this omnipotent, omniscient, sovereignly-willing creator *is* God, and, more fundamentally, of *what* really *is* God. *If* I (and everyone else) ought *fundamentally* categorically to do what the sovereignly-willing creator commands me to do, *then* he is God, I would say, but, on the other hand, *if* I (and everyone else) am not obliged categorically to obey his commands, or, more strongly, if I ought categorically *not* to obey but to *defy* his commands, *then* he is not God. God, then, it seems to me, can only be whatever it is, if anything, that I (and everyone else) ought *fundamentally* categorically to serve or submit to. Since an omnipotent, omniscient, sovereignly-willing and commanding being is stereotypically masculine, I also use masculine pronouns in referring to him.

5. 'A Modified Divine Command Theory of Ethical Wrongness', in Gene Outka and John P. Reeder, Jr. (eds), *Religion and Morality* (Garden City, NJ: Doubleday, 1973), pp. 318–47. Reprinted in Robert M. Adams, *The Virtue of Faith* (New York: Oxford University Press, 1987), pp. 97–122. Even though I am using some of Adams's words to characterise the *un*modified Divine Command Theory, he himself rejects this theory in favour of a *modified* Divine Command Theory. His main reasons for rejecting the *un*modified and proposing the *modified* Divine Command Theory will be explained in a moment.

6. 'The Concept of a Divine Command', this volume , pp. 59–60.

7. Ibid., p. 79 (my italics). I must confess that, prior to reading Adams's essay for this conference, and not being an advocate of any form of divine command theory of moral duty myself, I was unaware of the special problems there are with understanding what a divine command is. I of course understand what I mean when I command my dogs not to behave in a certain way, say, not to take tidbits of food off the dining table. In commanding them, if I may paraphrase Adams's characterisation of Paul Grice's analysis, I utter 'No! Stay off the table!' with the intention of impelling the dogs not to take tidbits off the table, and to have as their motive for not taking the tidbits their recognition of this intention in my utterance. Not only do not all of the 27 dogs always do what I command them to do, however, but, in addition, not all of them always understand what I am commanding them to do. And this latter could not be so if I

were, as the creator is presumed to be, omnipotent and omniscient. For if I were omniscient, I would know that not all of the dogs would understand what I was commanding them to do, and, if I were omnipotent, I would see to it, at the very least, that all of them did understand what I was commanding them to do – even if I were to leave them at liberty to disobey my command. As omnipotent and omniscient, my intention, Adams persuades me, must be, not to impel the dogs to stay off the table motivated by their understanding of my command, but, instead, simply to command them, by signs I give them (including waving a plastic baseball bat as well as saying 'No!'), to stay off the table.

8. Although he has not proposed systematic answers to this question, Adams indicates that 'scriptures and natural ethical inclinations are obvious candidates' for 'what signs are or could be used by [the sovereignly-willing creator] in this way' ('The Concept of a Divine Command', p. 79). In the case at hand, 'natural ethical inclinations' surely won't help, however. For if I had a 'natural ethical inclination' to grade right-handers by the agreed-upon criteria, or even a 'natural ethical inclination' to *believe* that I ought to grade right-handers in this way, then I wouldn't be in the process of asking *why* I ought categorically so to grade right-handers. What about scriptures, in particular, the Bible? There are no scripturally-revealed commands specifically about how I ought to grade right-handed students, as far as I know, but there may be scripturally-revealed general rules that would apply. One possibility, students often suggest, is the Ninth Commandment, 'Neither shall you bear false witness against your neighbour' (Deut. 5:20), since giving grades to students other than what they have earned as measured by the agreed-upon criteria can be thought of as a form of bearing false witness. But when they read further, 'You shall walk in all the way which the Lord your God has commanded you, that you may live, and that it may go well with you, and that you may live long in the land which you shall possess' (Deut. 5:33), they learn that this command expresses only a hypothetical, not a categorical, imperative, since it permits me to grade however I want to, provided that I am willing to forego living well and long in the promised land. A more promising scripturally-revealed command might be, 'As you wish that men would do to you, do so to them' (Luke 6:31). Since otherwise I would be doing to right-handers what I do not want them to do to me, I ought categorically to grade right-handers by the agreed-upon academic criteria. There is a serious objection to this Golden Rule, however, I should mention. As the late Procter Thomson, who was for many years Professor of Economics here at Claremont McKenna College, expressed it (possibly borrowing from George Bernard Shaw): 'Miss Jones is a *very* attractive woman. Ought I, as a matter of moral duty, categorically, to do to her what I want her to do to me?' In a word, the difficulty with the Golden Rule – unless we are very careful about how we interpret it – is that it makes our duties toward others depend upon the wants that we ourselves happen to have.

9. To me, these observations pose the unanswerable question of why an *omnipotent*, omniscient, sovereignly-willing creator does not do a better job at making his commands known to all of us, sinners and sinless alike, who are subject to them.

10. 'If a man lies with a male as with a woman, both of them have committed an abomination; they shall be put to death, their blood is upon them' (Leviticus 5:13).

11. '[A] man ought not to cover his head, since he is the image and glory of God; but woman is the glory of man. (For man was not made from woman, but woman from man. Neither was man created for woman, but woman for man)' (1 Corinthians 11:7–9).

12. *Groundwork of the Metaphysic of Morals*, trans. H. J. Paton (New York: Harper Torchbooks, 1964), p. 111.

13. P. Tillich, *Love, Power, and Justice* (New York: Oxford University Press, 1954), p. 76.

14. P. Tillich, *Systematic Theology*, 3 Vols (Chicago: University of Chicago Press, 1951–63), Vol. I, p. 127.

15. R.M. Adams, 'Moral Arguments for Theistic Belief', in C. F. Delaney, (ed.), *Rationality and Religious Belief* (Notre Dame, IN: University of Notre Dame Press, 1979). Reprinted in Robert M. Adams, *The Virtue of Faith*, p. 147.

16. 'Autonomy and Theological Ethics', *Religious Studies*, 1979, Vol. 15. Reprinted in *The Virtue of Faith*, p. 125. My italics.

17. 'Divine Commands and the Social Nature of Obligation', *Faith and Philosophy*, July 1987, vol. 4, no. 3, p. 264.

18. Ibid., p. 273.

19. 'Autonomy and Theological Ethics', *The Virtue of Faith*, p. 126.

20. *Groundwork of the Metaphysic of Morals*, p. 111.

21. My supposed (not really, let me repeat!) belief about grading right-handers is not that grading right-handers by the proper criteria is morally *wrong* to do, remember. Rather, it is only that I don't believe it to be my moral duty to do.

22. Adams, 'Moral Arguments for Theistic Belief', *The Virtue of Faith*, p. 149.

23. Having developed his modified Divine Command Theory over the years since 1979, Adams has made several arguments in addition to the 'social theory', referred to above, concerning why I should believe that I ought as a matter of moral duty to obey the commands of a loving omnipotent, omniscient commander. If I read them correctly, however, it seems to me that all of these arguments imply that I need motives, based upon other values I have, for doing so, such that, lacking these motives, I do *not* have a 'reason' for believing myself to be morally obligated by his commands.

24. G.W.F. Hegel, *Philosophy of Right*, trans. T. M. Knox (Oxford: Clarendon Press, 1962), para. 46, p. 43.

25. Ibid., para. 4, Addition, p. 226.

26. *Logic*, trans. William Wallace (Oxford: Clarendon Press, 1975), para. 28, p. 49.

27. Ibid., para. 24, p. 38.

28. *Philosophy of Right*, para. 4, Addition, p. 226.

29. Ibid., para. 4, p. 21.
30. Now, a word in passing about the 27 dogs: they, too, I am convinced, have purposes or ends, but they do not will these *freely*. They are conscious and, if given a choice, they usually will choose a piece of steak over, say, a carrot (although they'll eat the carrot if they can't get the steak). Moreover, they seem to have great enough power of thinking to be able, at least to some degree (and some have more ability than others, the Afghan hound more than the Doberman, I think), to determine how best to achieve their ends; they can adapt means to ends. What they can*not* do, however, as far as I can tell, and what beings who really do have the power of thinking – 'spiritual' beings, that is, such as we humans and perhaps Klingons (*Star Trek*) and wookies (*Star Wars*) – *can* do, is to will their ends *freely*. Dogs' ends are determined by their desires, whereas we thinking beings are at least capable of thinking about our desires and deciding freely, independently of them, which if any to pursue. Hegel puts it correctly, I believe, as follows: 'An animal too has impulses, desires, inclinations, but it has no [free] will and must obey its impulse if nothing external deters it. Man, however, the wholly undetermined, stands above his impulses and may make them his own, put them in himself as his own. An impulse is something natural, but to put it into my ego depends on my will which thus cannot fall back on the plea that the impulse has its basis in nature' (*Philosophy of Right*, para. 11, Addition, p. 229).
31. *Philosophy of Right*, para. 66, p. 53.
32. G.W.F. Hegel, *The Philosophy of History*, trans. J. Sibree (New York: Dover Publications, 1956), p. 442.
33. *Philosophy of Right*, para. 15, Addition, p. 230.
34. G.W.F. Hegel, *Science of Logic*, trans. A. V. Miller (London: George Allen & Unwin, 1969), p. 50.
35. Hegel, *Logic*, para. 24, p. 39.
36. This is what underlies Tillich's criticism of the divine command theory referred to earlier. I ought categorically *not* to submit categorically 'to an external will imposed upon [me], an arbitrary law laid down by a heavenly tyrant' (*Morality and Beyond* (New York: Harper & Row, 1963), p. 24) because to do so is to 'destroy' myself as a free 'I' by alienating my freedom from me. 'That in man which makes him a person [is] his rational, responsible, deciding center' (*Biblical Religion and the Search for Ultimate Reality* (Chicago: University of Chicago Press, 1955), p. 32), and it is precisely my free 'deciding center' that I transform into an unfree 'it' if I submit. The decision – or 'leap of faith' – by which I submit is itself a free decision for which I am therefore responsible. I am 'free in the moment of [my] leap', as Tillich says, but my free decision is in this case a decision to submit and thus 'involves the sacrifice of [my] freedom' ('The Person in a Technical Society', in Gibson Winter (ed.), *Social Ethics: Issues in Ethics and Society* (New York: Harper & Row, 1968), p. 122) and so my self-transformation into an unfree 'it'.

37. Kant, *Groundwork of the Metaphysic of Morals*, p. 70.

38. Hegel, *Philosophy of Right*, para. 261, p. 161.

39. G.W.F. Hegel, *Philosophy of Mind*, trans. William Wallace and A. V. Miller (Oxford: Clarendon Press, 1971), para. 432, p. 172. Translation slightly revised by me. Hegel objects to Kant's principle of universalisability, to be sure. 'The proposition: "Act as if the maxim of thine action could be laid down as a universal principle", would be admirable if we already had determinate principles of conduct. That is to say, to demand of a principle that it shall be able to serve in addition as a determinant of universal legislation is to presuppose that it already has a content. Given the content, then of course the application of the principle would be a simple matter. In Kant's case, however,' according to Hegel, 'the principle itself is still not available and his criterion of non-contradiction is productive of nothing, since where there is nothing, there can be no contradiction either' (*Philosophy of Right*, para. 135, Addition, p. 254). We *do* provide a content, however, by believing, as we necessarily do, that others ought as a matter of moral duty to treat us always as free 'I's and never as unfree 'it's.

40. Adams, 'A Modified Divine Command Theory of Ethical Wrongness', *The Virtue of Faith*, p. 111 (My italics).

41. This does not obtain if, as does my colleague Stephen T. Davis in his exceptionally informative and well-argued *Logic and the Nature of God* (Grand Rapids, MI: William B. Eerdmans Publishing Co., 1983), we conceive God to be what is 'supremely worthy of worship' rather than as that to which we ought to be ultimately allegiant. Two first-year students from Chicago in my Concepts of God class, Brian Mikes and Anand Subramanian, made this vividly clear to me. 'What is supremely worthy of worship, or admiration', they contended, 'is Michael Jordan [the recently-retired star basketball player with the Chicago Bulls], but it does not occur to us to believe either that we ought to be ultimately allegiant to him or as a matter of moral duty to do whatever he might tell us to do.' I agree with Davis in believing that a being who is supremely worthy of worship would have to be morally good, and hence subject to a moral law that he does not have power to repeal or change at will, rather than totally sovereign. See his *Logic and the Nature of God*, especially Chapter 6.

42. Adams, 'A Modified Divine Command Theory of Ethical Wrongness', *The Virtue of Faith*, p. 111.

43. Tillich, *Systematic Theology*, vol. I, p. 237.

44. Tillich, *Love, Power and Justice*, p. 110.

Part III
The Problem of Evil

5

Evil and the God-Who-Does-Nothing-In-Particular

MARILYN McCORD ADAMS

I EVIL AND THE GOD WHO DOES ONE THING

In his 1986 Bampton Lectures, Maurice Wiles recognises *moral* problems, about 'the character of God' among others, surrounding traditionally typical claims about divine action in the world. Many – to Wiles's mind – theologically naive statements make God the direct and deliberate agent of things it would be immoral for us to do (for example, striking York Minster with lightning in retribution for the putative heresies of the Bishop of Durham; given the ability to benefit all, arbitrarily rescuing only some of equally deserving victims).[1] The issue of how divine agency is related to 'the confused pattern of evil and good in human history'[2] is raised at a more general level by the problem of evil, which argues for the logical incompatibility of 'God exists and is omniscient, omnipotent, and perfectly good' with 'evils exist', on the ground that an all-powerful being would be able to prevent or eliminate any and every evil, an omniscient being would know all about them, and a perfectly good being would want to prevent or eliminate them all if it could.[3]

Metaphysical Ultimacy

Wiles refuses to travel the broad road to resolution opened by denying divine omnipotence. (After all, inevitable weakness or inability always excuse!) On the contrary, his *systematic* commitment to God's 'metaphysical ultimacy'[4] drives him to insist, against Charles Hartshorne, that God has the power to function as absolute controller,[5] with patristic theologians that God cannot be

'affected by forces or events which come entirely from outside
the sphere of his own influence',[6] and against Rudolf Bultmann
and other neo-Kantians that it makes sense to speak of divine
power to intervene.[7] Wiles even remains agnostic about claims of
natural or metaphysical necessity advanced by free will approaches
to explain 'what' omnipotence is not the power to actualise.[8]

Science and Freedom

Nevertheless, Wiles has bound himself to honour additional *systematic* commitments to the integrity of science and the radical[9]
freedom of human beings. Because science has been such a remarkable vehicle for 'advances in knowledge', he issues a methodological maxim against obstructing its progress with the rock
(stumbling-block?) of authority.[10] And he extends the same privi-
lege to the academic discipline of history.[11] Again, Wiles understands human freedom and creativity, and non-manipulative loving
relationships to lie at the heart of divine purposes in creation.[12]
Important for present purposes, he deems a high doctrine of created freedom necessary to distance God from natural evils, from
sin,[13] and from creaturely indifference to God.[14] Further, Wiles
regards human freedom as incompatible with physical determinism.[15] (It is not clear to what extent Wiles recognises his endorsement of the latter as systematically driven as opposed to given in
experience, that other arbiter to which (together with science)
theology must answer.[16] To be sure, *experience* reveals our practice of holding one another morally accountable, and some moral
theories make axiomatic the thesis that contra-causal freedom is
presupposed for moral responsibility. But the metaphysics of
voluntary action is not a datum, but a matter of philosophical
interpretation.)

Radical Self-Restraint

At any rate, Wiles concludes that respect for science and human
freedom dictate a radical doctrine of divine self-restraint,[17] according to which a God with power to intervene and manipulate
rests content with a single continuous creative act of bringing the
whole world into being[18] and performs no particular acts in relation to creation.[19] Attempting to disambiguate his claim by distinguishing it from traditional and contemporary competitors, Wiles

explains (i) that God creates things with their natures and powers *ex nihilo*;[20] (ii) that in doing so God adopts a single unifying intention for creation;[21] and (iii) that the latter involves created natures being 'set loose' to 'do their own thing' without *any* active divine interference.[22] He admits that only differences in metaphor separate his position from the deists' where God's relation to the physical world is concerned.[23] As for human free agents, Wiles offers the 'working model' of God as author of an improvised drama

> in which the actors are each given the basic character of the person he or she is to represent and the general setting in which their interaction is to be worked out but in which they are left free to determine experimentally how the drama is to develop. In the process of getting deeper into their parts and discovering their reactions to one another in the given situation they may be led on to enact the kind of drama which the author had always intended and already envisaged in principle though not in detail. The resultant drama would be both the author's and the actors', though we would be more ready to speak of the author as agent of the drama as a whole than as agent of any of the individual speeches or incidents within it.[24]

Thus, for Wiles, divine power remains omnipotent in scope, but divine policy is one of radical non-interference.

Particular Providence: A Problem of Evil?

Wiles seems convinced that *any* belief in particular divine providence would carry the additional *moral* disadvantage of exacerbating the problem of evil. His implicit assumption is that *fairness* would require an omnipotent, omniscient agent to treat like cases alike and so forbid 'occasional' divine intervention to prevent or eliminate evils sometimes and not at others;[25] a sense of moral proportion, to make preventing the worst the top priority for action. But we know *from experience* that natural and moral evils – even of horrendous proportions – exist and so are not always barred. Thus, experience and morals join science in concluding against any particular providence in nature. Similarly, particular providence in human relations would confront us with the embarrassing 'fairness' question of why God converts some and not others.[26]

Again, although Wiles admits that the same occurrence may some-times have more than one explanation – for example, 'one in terms of observed physical phenomena and the other in terms of an intended human action' or different accounts 'from different scien-tific disciplines' – he finds problems 'in our attempts to describe how those different accounts are related to one another'.[27] He rejects Austin Farrer's willingness to live with 'our ignorance of "the modality of divine action"', because the ancient and honourable dispute about the logical compossibility of divine providence with human free will raises the spectre of a 'wholly unacceptable' 'ma-nipulative' divine 'control of human action'.[28]

Impossible Theodicy

Despite Wiles's attachment to a high doctrine of created freedom, he renders a negative verdict on both Augustinian and Irenaean free will approaches to theodicy (that is, attempts to give mor-ally sufficient *reasons why* God permits evils in the amounts and of the kinds and with the distribution found in this world). First, the traditional doctrine of the fall and original sin cannot explain the origin of evil, because it contradicts the deliverances of sci-ence to suppose it is historically true.[29] Second, he finds philo-sophically undecidable key questions about whether actual moral and natural evils are metaphysically necessary for human free-dom (as Irenaeus, John Hick,[30] and Richard Swinburne[31] hold) or whether it is logically possible for God to make free creatures who never sin (as John Mackie contended).[32] Third, Wiles feels that actual evils such as Auschwitz and Hiroshima are 'too great' to be wholly explained by such rationales.[33]

Origins versus Overcoming

Accordingly, Wiles sides with those (such as Irenaeus and Hick) who locate the significance of evil, not in its origins, but in its overcoming. Since Wiles's God has more power than process the-ology allots, it is even more important for divine moral credi-bility that God suffers at the hands of the creatures to whom He has given such free rein.[34] Yet, Christian faith promises more than divine participation in the costs; it understands 'the cross and resurrection' as 'a composite unity' and insists on divine victory.[35] For Wiles the insufficiency of real and present satisfactions to defeat 'the sheer brutality of some forms of suffering' constitutes a transcendental argument for 'some future fulfilment of the more transcendent kind that has characterized Christian faith'.[36] And he joins his voice with Origen's in insisting that 'Christ remains on the cross as long as one sinner remains in hell', until all human suffering has been redeemed.[37]

Free Will and Fulfilment: Active Creatures, Passive God?

Nevertheless, reverting to his respect for human incompatibilist freedom, Wiles insists that the resolution of the divine plot, the fulfilment of God's purpose for the world of eliciting 'a fullness of personal life through the exercise of freedom',[38] is to be accomplished apart from any particular divine providence.[39] To be sure, God is ever-present, and all humans made in God's image possess some 'capacity to attain, however incompletely, some awareness' of God and God's 'intention'. But the exercise of that power is entirely up to created free choice. In Wiles's estimation,

> Such recognition, and very partial realization, of God's purpose as the world has seen in the past have been primarily forwarded by those who have used their God-given potential to open themselves to and identify their own goals with what they have grasped of the will of God. In the language of process theology they have responded to the lure of the divine love available to them.[40]

Wiles's is not the 'God who has' one and only one 'plan for your life', but rather One whose purposes can be instantiated by a wide variety of created choice patterns. Those who continually seek God's will become aware of divine presence, but – given divine existence and presence and God's creative act of sustaining creatures and their powers in being – the rest of the labour belongs to free human beings.[41]

II SOTERIOLOGICAL STRATEGY: CLARIFICATIONS AND COMPLICATIONS

Wiles's Bampton Lectures offer a soteriological sketch of considerable sensitivity. Because that genre afforded limited space, however,

I will develop my assessment and critique at first by way of some clarifying amplifications.

Free Will and the Origins of Evil

Methodologically, I join his rejection of the Augustinian account of the origin of evil, on historical grounds. I would go further and insist on the bankruptcy of free will approaches as a means of shifting responsibility off God on to someone else. Among human agents, the fact that an action of agent B intervenes between the action of agent A and some consequence C is often sufficient to remove from agent A any or primary praise or blame for C. But even here, the *Novus Actus Interveniens* principle applies on the assumption that the 'new' agents are fully competent, or at least competent to the degree required for moral responsibility. It 'cuts' proportionately 'less ice' where agent A is a normal adult and agent B is an infant, toddler, schoolchild, etc. Suppose, for example, that an adult placed a two- or three-year-old in a room filled with gas that was safe to breathe but explosive when ignited. Suppose that in the room there was a stove furnished with brightly coloured knobs within the child's reach. The adult warns the child not to touch the knobs and then leaves, whereupon the child turns the knobs, lights the stove, and blows itself up. Even though the child is a personal agent, who *knew* that it wasn't supposed to play with the knobs, this does nothing to remove the lion's share of responsibility for the child's death from the adult who 'set up' the situation. The child's agency isn't fully developed enough to be entrusted with decisions where 'the stakes are so high'. Rather it is the job of adults, to the degree that they can, so to orchestrate the environment of choice situations that children can 'learn by doing' without serious danger to anyone's life or limb. Even into late adolescence, the law holds parents primarily responsible for the choices of their offspring. Analogously, according to the traditional doctrine of the fall, God created Eden *ex nihilo*, structured in such a way that if angels and humans always obeyed, utopia would persist, but if any disobeyed, evils would ensue in the amounts and of the kinds and with the distributions we now experience. My claim is that the general ontological gap between the infinite and eternal and the finite and temporal manifests itself in a disproportion between divine and created personal agency that is incommensurately greater than that between human infants and adults. Thus, even if disobedient created choice triggered the fall of creation, God would remain fully *responsible* for created ruin. Blame, of course, is another matter, depending in part on the agent's obligations (if any) and wider intentions and capacities for defeating evil with good.[42]

Horrors at the Heart

Again, Wiles gets to the heart of the problem when he identifies Auschwitz and Hiroshima as representative of the class of evils on which traditional Free Will and Big Picture theodicies founder. Presumably, in saying that such evils are 'too great', he does not have in mind merely what we might call their 'extensive' quantity (for example, the statistical frequency with which they occur, although in fact such atrocities have been all too characteristic throughout human history), but rather the *intensity*. Elsewhere,[43] I have tried to articulate this intuition by identifying the class of horrendous evils as evils participation in which (either as victim or perpetrator) constitutes *prima facie* reason to doubt whether the participant's life can (given their inclusion in it) be a great good to him/her on the whole. *Paradigm horrors* include the following: the rape of a woman and axeing off of her arms, psychophysical torture whose ultimate goal is the disintegration of personality, betrayal of one's deepest loyalties, cannibalising one's own offspring, child abuse of the sort described by Ivan Karamazov, child pornography, parental incest, slow death by starvation, participation in the Nazi death camps, the explosion of nuclear bombs over populated areas, having to choose which of one's children shall live and which be executed by terrorists, being the accidental and/or unwitting agent of the disfigurement or death of those one loves best. Such evils constitute *reason* to doubt whether the participants' life can be worth living, precisely because it is so difficult humanly to conceive how such evils could be overcome. My own view is that horrendous evils exhibit such a disproportion to any and every package of created goods that only appropriate relation to the incommensurate goodness of God could overwhelm them.

Moreover, this criterion for horrendous evils is meant to be *objective* but relative to individuals. Habitual complainers skilled in making the worst of a good situation prove individuals not to be incorrigible experts on what would ruin the positive meaning of their lives. Curmudgeons show it not to be a matter of what people sincerely say. Nevertheless, nature and experience endow people with different strengths; one bears easily what crushes another. Certainly, the individual's own estimate is a major piece of evidence as to whether his/her life has been a great good for him/her on the whole.

Evils No Match for God!

Likewise, Wiles is on target with his insistence that Christian religion promises divine *victory* over evils. In his famous article 'The Defeat of Good and Evil', Roderick Chisholm attempted to lend precision to this idea by contrasting the relation of *balancing off* (which occurs when the opposing values of mutually exclusive parts of a whole partially or totally cancel each other out) with that *defeat* (which cannot occur by the mere addition to the whole of a new part of opposing value, but involves some 'organic unity' among the values of parts and wholes, as when the positive aesthetic value of a whole painting defeats the ugliness of a small colour patch).[44] Likewise, it is helpful to distinguish two salient contexts of balancing off or defeat: one global (which depends upon the value relations of evils to the history of the world as a whole), and the other the whole course of the individual's life.[45]

Not only do horrendous evils seem *prima facie* to *balance off*, indeed *engulf* any positive value in the participant's life with which they are not organically connected; they also reach deep into the individual's meaning-making structures, threatening to *defeat* the positive significance of his/her life. Perhaps for this reason, Wiles concludes that mere apocalyptic reversals serving up pie in the sky by and by, will not be victory enough.[46] Rather, as I have insisted, God will have been good to each created participant in horrors, only if He endows such participation with *positive meaning* via organic relation to some great enough good within the context of that individual's life!

Symbolic versus Concrete Values Distinguished

One further distinction is worthwhile – namely, that between (what I will call) 'symbolic' and 'concrete' balancing off or defeat. Briefly, symbolic value is the value a thing has by virtue of what it symbolises. The signification-relation may be natural (intense pain is a natural sign of physiological damage or malfunction; physical malformation, that one is not a paradigm instance of one's kind; martyrdom to the death, the enormous worth of the object of loyalty), or conventional (beach-wear at an announced black-tie dinner is a sign of contempt for the hostess; driving a Mercedes, a sign either of actual high social status or 'yuppification'; smoking Marlboro's, of rugged virility). Any given action or event, condition or state of affairs may have multiple, sometimes contradictory dimensions of symbolic value (for example, Christian religion sees the cross of Christ, intended as a symbol of shame and degradation by the Roman government, as transformed by God's intentions into a sign of glory). With this we contrast, in a 'rough and ready' manner, 'concrete' value for persons, which has to do with pleasure and pain, with health, wealth, and material well-being.

Relations between symbolic and concrete values are complex. Physical assault has the negative symbolic value of insult by virtue of the negative concrete value of its aptitude to produce bodily harm, while inappropriate dress or using the wrong fork at dinner are usually concretely neutral, and acquire negative force only within a system of etiquette. Likewise, a person whose concrete welfare (because of fatal cancer, or a death-sentence from the courts) is ruined may nevertheless show great dignity, while others may enjoy great material wealth indifferent to their state of social disgrace. Even those who lack concrete resources may confer symbolic goods on one another through expressions of appreciation, praise, or treating one another as persons rather than things. Conversely, those whose material needs are guaranteed may still confer benefit on one another through such exchanges. Yet, it was the systematic attempt to degrade prisoners to a bestial level that made the concrete deprivations of Nazi concentration camps so horrendous.[47]

Symbolic Conquest

With symbolic and concrete values thus not completely congruent, evils can be balanced off or defeated along the one dimension and not the other. It is plausible, for example, to suppose that since God is a good incommensurate with any creature, any relation of honouring or being honoured by God confers incommensurate symbolic value on a creature – symbolic worth sufficient to *balance off* any and all of its concrete or symbolic ills,

even participation in horrors. Thus, Christians with a high doctrine of eucharistic presence tell how God immeasurably honours
communicants, whether by 'coming under their roofs' bodily under
the form of bread and wine or by raising faithful hearts to spiritual communion in heaven. Again, while denying individuals post-
mortem experience and satisfaction, Hartshorne reassures us that
the omniscient God will pay each and every life the compliment
of eternal aesthetic appreciation. Stoics who – like Wiles – deny
particular providence still find in us humans the capacity to endow concrete ruin with great significance by humbling and sub-
mitting ourselves to the natural order and praising its and our
Maker. Similarly, religious martyrs transform their tortured deaths
from degrading occasions of victimisation into acts of worship
by offering themselves in sacrifice to God.

Other accounts relate God to created suffering in such a way
as to afford symbolic *defeat*. Thus, *pace* Wiles, process theologians
who deny the divine power to bring concrete relief can insist that
God honours created suffering by identifying with it (pan-en-
theistically, by being the One in Whom all created suffering occurs). Similarly, Chalcedonian Christians can maintain that the
divine Word's suffering in the human nature of Christ crucified
opens a dimension of meaning for created participants in horrors
via the window of sympathetic identification with the passion of
Christ. Fellow travellers with Wiles could go further, advertising
Christ crucified as an outward and visible sign of agony in the
divine nature, of literal compassion in the inner life of God. Christian mysticism could take another step, identifying created suffering with actual occasions of union with the divine life. While
insisting – contrary to process theology – that God could have
existed without any creatures at all, Christians might still maintain that God *literally* feels or experiences the *same* pain or agony
that we feel, or that what creatures experience as pain or agony
are literally visions into the inner life of God. Outdistancing the
Stoics, Christian theologians could consistently claim that the *facts*
of such identification and/or intimacy, *whether or not they are recognised by the created participant in horrors, constitute* an immeasurable honour and endow the worst that creatures can suffer, be,
or do with great positive meaning, and defeat both the concrete
and symbolic negative value of such conditions by integrating
them into their relationship with God, which is of immeasurable
symbolic value.

For my part, I agree with Wiles that God's suffering with us – in both natures – is an essential ingredient in an adequate Christian response to horrendous evils. For believers, it helps to shore up divine credibility against Job's suspicion that God demands more of His creatures than He is willing to go through Himself! For those with eyes to see, it affords the conscious consolation of divine honour in the midst of concrete ruin. Perhaps I part company with Wiles by insisting that God's participation in horrors in Christ's human nature, along with commiseration in the divine nature, are *sufficient for symbolic defeat* of horrors whether or not the created person recognises this. In any event, so far as I can see, such symbolic defeat is possible for Wiles's God-Who-*does*-nothing-in-particular. The above accounts require particular participation in horrors by Christ in His human nature; some posit particular *sufferings* in the divine nature, while not even that is necessary for the view that *our* sufferings are visions into the inner life of God.

Concrete Hopes

Nevertheless, however much I insist on the centrality of symbolic values to both the problem of evil and its solutions, I fully concur with Wiles that Christian religion has typically gone beyond Stoicism to promise not only symbolic defeat of evils, but also unmixed concrete well-being. For untold thousands, the ante-mortem balance of concrete goods over ills remains decidedly unfavourable: some experience lives of unrelieved misery; many find bad times decidedly outnumber the good; more still find the concrete pleasures and comforts of divine love psycho-spiritually inaccessible. Nor, as Wiles notes, can these unhappy states be plausibly 'chalked up' to commensurate faults of the agent's own. Even mortal happiness is tainted by temporality. No arena of post-mortem satisfaction is required for symbolic defeat (as Hartshorne notes). But Christian religion usually advertises divine goodness to created persons as guaranteeing them lives that are great goods to them on the whole and in the end – along concrete as well as symbolic value-dimensions. If symbolic defeat of horrors is to be achieved via integration into the creature's relationship with God, Christian religion has preached how 'the sufferings of this present life' will resolve into incomparable joys of recognised beatific intimacy with a Heavenly Lover. Thus, I agree with Wiles that the

Christian hope requires life after death in an environment where such concrete fulfilments can be enjoyed.

Particular Providence: Systematic Liability or Necessity?

Precisely because I share so many of Wiles's soteriological intuitions, I am puzzled by his dismissal of particular divine providence.

1. If we focus our systematic attention narrowly on the problem of evil, I see little to be gained. Wiles claims a moral advantage in saying that God-does-nothing-in-particular as opposed to intervening sometimes but not always, to avert trivial but not horrendous evils. My own view is not that the doing/allowing distinction is irrelevant to divine action – after all, it paints a different picture of divine character to say (with Leibniz) that the Holocaust is something God directly and deliberately wills, than to concede (with free will approaches) that it occurs by divine permission. Nevertheless, permission of horrors by a God with power to prevent them constitutes such a powerful objection to divine goodness as to require a lengthy soteriological story, one that resolves tragedy into not only symbolic but concrete defeat.

Again, worries about fairness reflect an assumption of scarcity, the dubious judgment that if God will not provide enough special help to go around, better an even-handed deprivation for everyone! But once it is granted that divine goodness to created persons involves guaranteeing *incommensurate* concrete and symbolic good to each, fairness principles lose all but their short-run bite. No one will get *more* than anyone else; those whose gratification is delayed would not have received *more* had they escaped ante-mortem participation in horrors. The symbolic defeat of the latter is contemporaneous with its occurrence; only the recognition of its integration into an unending relation of beatific intimacy with God and concrete defeat are postponed. Once surrounded by heavenly bliss, none will complain about 'twinkling of an eye' procrastination or begrudge another the particular divine interventions in his/her life. Nor do I come to this conclusion by underestimating the negative value of horrors. Like Wiles, I try everywhere and always to rivet attention on them.[48] My intention is rather to draw out some implications of the *incommensurate* goodness of God!

2. Further, in my judgement, Wiles's concession that divine goodness to created persons requires the concrete defeat of hor-

rendous evils within the context of the individual participant's life serves to ground not only a transcendental argument for post-mortem fulfilment, but also an inference to the necessity of particular divine providence. Wiles's vision of a God-Who-does-nothing-in-particular, Who entrusts fulfilment of His purpose to creatures whose powers have been endowed for that end, sounds an untimely echo of liberal theology's optimism. Twentieth-century experience mocks any hope that we humans might bring in the Kingdom by freely choosing our way into greater awareness of and alignment with God's will. On the contrary, our nature and environment are such as to make us radically vulnerable to horrors.[49] Moreover, human agency is easily broken beyond any non-miraculous possibility of repair – whether by child abuse, the horrors of war, or brain chemistry – setting up psycho-spiritual dynamics that destroy and pervert relations with other human beings, and distort and obscure any awareness of God. And the latter damage frequently falls on individuals quite apart from any commensurate fault of their own. I submit that the scope God has already allowed creatures 'to do their own thing' has made a mess far too big for human beings to clean up all by ourselves (although it will be our vocation to make some contribution). Given our record to date, for God to continue a radical non-interference policy would be to turn the alleged divine aim at loving and creative relationships from an intention to a pious hope or idle wish. If Wiles's God is like Origen's, restless so long as a single soul remains in such hellish misalignment, He is doomed to frustration unless He quits sitting on the heavenly side-lines and gets into the act Himself!

III PARTICULAR PROVIDENCE VERSUS CREATED FREE WILL

Solving the problem of evil was not the only systematic desideratum motivating Wiles to reject particular divine providence. He also saw no way to reconcile it with his high doctrine of human freedom. Two points require examination here: (i) if particular divine providence were incompossible with incompatibilist free will for creatures, why is it so obvious that the former rather than the latter has to go? (ii) is particular divine providence really inconsistent with the phenomena of human voluntary action?

Incompatibilist Freedom – a Moral Requirement?

The strength of Wiles's attachment to a doctrine of incompatibilist free will is difficult to square with his methodological respect for science and experience. For Wiles himself privileges *biology*'s theory of the evolution of the human species over the traditional Augustinian doctrine of the fall. And *experience* bombards us with the fact that we humans are *personal animals*, beings whose agency is tied to an animal life-cycle. Developmental psychology[50] teaches how we human beings start life ignorant, weak, and helpless, psychologically so lacking in a self-concept as to be incapable of choice. We learn to 'construct' a picture of the world, ourselves, and other people, and to become people capable of choice, only with difficulty over a long period of time and under the extensive influence of other non-ideal choosers. Further, human development is the interactive product of human nature and its environment, and from early on we humans are confronted with problems that we cannot adequately grasp or cope with, and in response to which we mount (without fully conscious calculation) inefficient adaptational strategies. Yet, the human psyche is habit-forming in such a way that these reactive patterns, based as they are on a child's inaccurate view of the world and its strategic options, become entrenched in the individual's personality. Typically they are unconsciously 'acted out' for years, causing much suffering to self and others before (if ever) they are recognised and undone through a difficult and painful process of therapy and/or spiritual formation. Having begun thus immature, we arrive at *adulthood* in a state of *impaired freedom*, as our childhood adaptational strategies continue to distort our perceptions and behaviour.[51]

If we begin with experience and do our action and moral theory from the ground up instead of the top down, morality might more plausibly strike us as a scheme devised among and for, *not ideal agents*, but *adults with impaired freedom*. Its modest goal is to regulate behaviour and attitudes, to produce and encourage habits that make possible social cohabitation and collaboration in the battle for survival against the hostile forces of nature. So long as developmental impairments fall within the wide tolerance of statistical normality, their existence does not excuse agents from discharging their moral obligations to other human beings or exempt them from blame when they fail to do so. Rather such cognitive and emotional defects are *compatible* with *moral responsibility*, and with *accountability to other humans* for one's choices and at least some of their consequences. It is thus appropriate for us to hold each other morally responsible when we break our promises, steal another's car, cause (through neglect or malice) serious bodily harm, use our power to deprive large groups of people of the means of survival, and so on. It can also be appropriate, in the course of holding each other responsible and accountable, to attach rewards and sanctions to value and disapproved behaviour and attitudes, whether in the form of praise and blame, economic penalties or compensations, or deprivations of freedom. For we humans are not generally gifted with psychoanalytic and spiritual knowledge and insight, nor do we have the social technology required to take account of such 'normal' impairments in our methods of social organisation. Morality may be the best framework humans generally can master and/or apply on a large scale to promote friendly and curtail anti-social behaviour and attitudes.

On this 'empirical' view (which I favour), morality is robbed of its metaphysical and value-theory pretensions to network all and only ideal agents with incompatibilist freedom and to trump all other evaluative considerations where personal agents are concerned. It would follow further that the data of human moral practices are neutral vis-à-vis the truth of determinism (whether physical or theological).

Mismatched Agencies

However the debate about free will may go on the horizontal level where relations among human agents are at stake, the doctrine of particular divine providence shifts attention to the vertical connection between the creature and its Maker. Here my first point is that *the radical disproportion between divine and human agency prevents God from being a member of our moral community, enmeshed in our networks of rights and obligations.* Similarity in scope and power has not always been treated as *sufficient* for membership in the same moral community. In the patron/client system, one had also to belong to the same clan or village, literally to occupy a role in the same social entity, to be a contributor as well as a consumer within the group. Obligations didn't extend to outsiders, or if they did, they were attenuated in direct proportion to the degree of relationship. Modern moral theory encourages us to treat the whole human race as one community. D. Z. Phillips suggests the possibility that communication, playing the same language game, is criterial.[52] Perhaps animal rights activists would go further, insisting that dolphins, if as intelligent and 'personal' as some speculate, be included even though we do not in fact communicate with one another. My converse contention is that where agent-capacities are sufficiently incommensurate (as ours are with those of insects and worms and clams), the beings in question are not members of the same community: the insects, worms, and clams do not have rights against us, which we have correlative obligations to respect.

You may object that this has nothing to do with commensuration, but rather with the fact that insects, worms, and clams are not *personal* agents. My reply is that the gap between divine capacity for thought and choice, on the one hand, and human personal agency on the other is infinitely greater than that between us and these 'lower' animals. Thus, though we are persons in the image of God, we are such distant mirrors as not to have any rights against God. Likewise, as the great medieval Franciscans acknowledged, if God has any obligations, they are to Godself.

It follows that the existence of evil does not so much challenge divine *moral* goodness as raise questions about his intentions and policies in relation to us. Does God love us? Can God be counted upon to be good to each created person, make our lives deeply meaningful on the whole and in the end?

Agency-Obstructors versus Agency-Enablers?

My second principal point is that *where agencies are disproportionate, it is necessary to distinguish among the effects of the 'bigger' on the 'smaller' those that are agency-obstructing or manipulating from others that are agency-enabling or developing, that supply necessary pre-conditions for the 'smaller' agent to function at all.* Consider, for example, a mother's relation to her infant offspring. According to developmental psychologists, human infants can actualise their potentiality for personality only in a personal human environment. The infant organism is first enabled to organise the booming, buzzing confusion of its psychic field when it 'recognises', imprints on the mother's face. Particular nurturing acts of the care-taker – holding, singing, babbling, caressing, feeding, changing, rocking – all contribute to a hospitable environment which engenders the trust and confidence the infant needs to take the risks involved in development. Its wholesome progress through the stages to maturity presupposes not only the nurturing *presence* of adults but also a plethora of *particular acts*. My suggestion is that what the mother does by way of training and controlling the child in its earliest stages is agency-developing and enabling; it cannot count as manipulation until the child's agency is better formed.

The ontological gap between God and creatures means that however mature adult human agency may seem in relation to other human beings, it never gets beyond (up to?) the infantile stage in relation to the divine. Just as the mother's face and particular nurturing acts are enabling conditions of the infant's actually becoming a human person, so – Scripture and tradition suggest – the Holy Spirit of God is the personal environment that first pulls us into focus as spiritual beings capable of connecting with one another's spirits, even of romancing with God. Beyond that, the personal and nurturing presence of the Holy Spirit is a necessary enabling condition for drawing us into vocational focus, thereby constituting our agency as disciples.

Like Wiles, I am uncomfortable with the idea that God has 'one and only one plan for your life', principally because both metaphysics (in particular, the ontological size-gap) and experience (see the *Confessions* of St Augustine) furnish reason to doubt whether we are ever smart enough to identify such a plan with any accuracy. More likely, a God Who chose to create and form committed relationships with agents incommensurately smaller than Himself would need to be flexible and resourceful enough to integrate virtually any pattern of past created choices into a meaningful vocational whole. Wiles's image of God as author of an improvised drama suggests a similar fluidity of plot, but de-emphasises the vast gap between divine and created agent-size.

My contention is that once returned to the forefront, such ontological incommensuration combines with the mother–infant analogy to make room for particular divine providence without jeopardising the phenomena of created voluntary action. Just as developmental psychology understands the infant's emerging personality as an interactive product shaped by the characteristics and the many and varied responses of mother and child, so the formation of our identities as spiritual beings and disciples is a collaborative process involving give and take on both sides, but one in which the Holy Spirit functions as an agency-enabler and developer rather than an agency-obstructor or manipulator.

In his last lecture, Wiles takes a line from process theology and speaks of divine *presence* as luring us into alignment with God's unifying purpose for the universe without exercising any particular providence at all.[53] Of course, *for all we know*, divine being may be like a complex symphony or painting, so rich that – quite apart from God's *doing* anything in particular – our acts would open us up to some sort of implicit awareness of first one aspect and then another, each evoking novel responses which 'change our lives'. My counter-point is that *for all we know* this is not the case. Nothing in our spiritual *experience* requires us to say so. However defeasible,[54] Scripture and tradition pull in the opposite direction, as does my interactive developmental model which nevertheless preserves the phenomena of human voluntary action. If the doctrine of particular divine providence is to be rejected, some other motivation will have to be found.

IV PARTICULAR PROVIDENCE AND THE INTEGRITY OF SCIENCE[55]

Wiles finds such additional reason ready to hand, as close as his conviction that the doctrine of particular divine providence compromises the integrity of science. But this worry is polyvalent and tugs our intuitions about several distinct issues. The first concerns *the practice of science*. Against biblical literalists who advocate everything from the flatness of the earth to creationist science, Wiles wishes to guarantee to the sciences the *autonomy* to investigate their subject-matters by their own methods, to follow the disciplines regardless of the conclusions to which they lead. The second arises in relation to *the nature of scientific laws*: whether they are *universal generalisations or statistical*; and whether they are *comprehensive*, in the sense that there are laws to cover everything that happens within their domain. A third involves *the metaphysical interpretation of science*, whether it should be given a realist or instrumentalist or anti-realist construal.[56]

Straightforward contradictions will arise between science and theology only if both are given realist interpretations. Wiles seems to endorse scientific realism when he defends the autonomy of the sciences on the ground that it produces advances in *knowledge*.[57] Apparently giving theology a realist construal, Wiles rejects particular divine providence as a threat to science and thereby breaks ranks with Aquinas and many other traditional theologians who take realism about science and theology for granted but insist on a God-Who-does-something-in-particular. By contrast, instrumentalists or anti-realists about science might equally commend the autonomy of scientific investigation on pragmatic grounds and even – like Bishop Berkeley – combine this with realism about theology. Instrumentalists or anti-realists about both would see no cognitive conflict between these distinct domains.

Logically independent of these are the content questions. Wiles acknowledges that many scientists take, for example, the laws of physics to be statistical, and admits that this in itself opens the way for particular divine actions that don't contravene physical laws. Further, even where laws were understood to be universal generalisations, the notion of non-physical causes producing physical states would trespass on scientific turf only if one believed the science of physics to be complete and comprehensive, in such a way that the occurrence of *any and every* physical state is covered by some law(s) connecting physical states of its type with physical states of another type. Thus, a mind/body dualist who believed that movements of type *M* were invariably preceded by brain states of type *B* might nevertheless deny the existence of any invariable physical laws regarding the production of type *B* brain states and maintain that some type *B* brain states are caused by the mind's choice. Nor is Wiles himself in any position to insist on the comprehensiveness of physics, given his commitment to human incompatibilist freedom and the omnipresent phenomena of our voluntarily moving our own bodies. In any event, experience shows that no science has actually developed to the point of comprehensive coverage; nor does it obviously lie among the actual aims of science. Yet only if scientific laws were both universal generalisations and comprehensive would the contents of science rule out particular divine providence. And once again, an instrumentalist or anti-realist about science could live with this as well.

V CONCLUSION

Where evil is the problem, particular divine action is necessary, and ontological and value incommensuration key. If God does nothing in particular, Christian hope – that the sufferings of this present life will ever resolve into the glory of lives concretely beneficial and deeply meaningful for those who live them – is utterly unreasonable. Happily, this 'size-gap' between God and creatures combines with my developmental analogy to suggest how particular providence might function as agency-enabler and developer without jeopardy to human voluntary action. By nature, as a being a greater than which cannot be conceived, God is such a great Good that appropriate relationship to Him can not only balance off but defeat horrendous evils. Wiles's worry that particular divine providence might threaten science conflates many issues; most important in the end is the epistemological difficulty of accurately detecting the hand of God at work in one's life and in the world at large – a task for which Scripture and tradition have always advertised human reason as ill-equipped – and the metaphysical question of whether God *does* anything in particular at all!

Notes

1. Maurice F. Wiles, *God's Action in the World: The Bampton Lectures for 1986* (London: SCM Press, 1986), Lecture 1, pp. 1–2.
2. Ibid., p. 6.
3. Wiles gives focused attention to the problem of evil in his fourth lecture, 'Whence Comes Evil?', in *God's Action in the World*, pp. 39–53.
4. Wiles's inference to metaphysical ultimacy from the religious sense of God as 'final succour and absolute demand' (see *God's Action in the World*, Lecture 2, p. 16) is not obviously valid. As Wiles later notes, the latter notion implies that God can conquer evil, that eventually one's relation to God will be fully satisfying (see Lecture 5, pp. 50–1) – and these are arguably sufficient to ground the above-mentioned religious sense of God as 'final succour and absolute demand'.
5. Wiles, *God's Action in the World*, Lecture 2, pp. 16–20, 22–3.
6. Ibid., pp. 24–5.
7. Wiles, *God's Action in the World*, Lecture 3, pp. 31–2.
8. In particular, Wiles addresses the questions of whether 'the actuality, and not merely the possibility, of wrong choice is inherent in genuine freedom', of whether '[m]oral evil' is 'an indispensable ingredient in moral growth'; *or* whether 'there is no logical incoherence in the concept of God creating free beings who would always in practice freely choose the good' (*God's Action in the World*, Lecture 5, p. 46). Likewise, only a transcendental argument will permit us to assume that it is possible 'that personal life as we now know it can find its

fulfilment outside the physical finite world of our present experience' (Lecture 5, p. 52). Cf. Alvin Plantinga (in *The Nature of Necessity*, ch. IX (Oxford: Clarendon Press, 1974), pp. 164–93) whose free
will approach to the logical problem of evil relies on the allegation
that there are contingent states of affairs that even an omnipotent
God cannot create.

9. See *God's Action in the World*, Lecture 5, p. 26, where Wiles speaks
of 'the radical degree of freedom of action with which' 'human creation' has 'been endowed'.

10. Wiles, *God's Action in the World*, Lecture 1, p. 7.

11. Ibid., pp. 6, 8.

12. Wiles makes this point several times. (i) In Lecture 3, speaking of
God's intention in relation to creation, Wiles comments: 'if we are
right to speak of the world as a single intentional act at all, it seems
undeniable on any score that human consciousness and human loving
must be seen as vital elements in that intention' (*God's Action in the
World*, Lecture 3, p. 30). (ii) Again, in Lecture 5, he suggests that
we may speak 'provisionally' of God's unifying purpose in creation
'as maximizing the growth of personal freedom and creativity within
relationships of love both at the human level and between human
beings and God' (Lecture 5, p. 54). (iii) And in Lecture 5, he rejects
a literal appropriation of biblical language asserting God's providence in history as implying 'some hidden manipulation' of created
'deliberative processes', which 'leads us back to the all controlling
God who does not respect the freedom of the world he has created'
(Lecture 5, p. 62), whereas Wiles regards such 'manipulative control of human action' as 'wholly unacceptable' (Lecture 5, p. 63).

13. See Lecture 3, where Wiles rejects the potter–clay and world–soul
models of God/creature relations, on the ground 'that the self who
is claimed to find expression through them could not ... be the
God of Christian faith. Too much sin and evil would come within
those things that the model requires us to see as forms of God's
self-expression' (*God's Action in the World*, Lecture 3, p. 37). Cf. Lecture 2, p. 22.

14. See Lecture 6, where Wiles insists that 'the mystery of a genuinely
free human choice must not be eliminated' from the explanation of
why 'some people come to faith and some do not' (*God's Action in
the World*, Lecture 6, p. 78).

15. Thus, in Lecture 8, he refers to 'a false form of physical determinism according to which psychological change could only be brought
about by a prior modification of the brain circuits' (*God's Action in
the World*, Lecture 8, p. 100).

16. See Wiles, *God's Action in the World*, Lecture 1, p. 11.

17. See Wiles, *God's Action in the World*, Lecture 2, p. 25; Lecture 3, p.
38; Lecture 6, p. 80.

18. Thus, Wiles affirms 'that the primary usage for the idea of divine
action should be *in relation to the world as a whole rather than to
particular occurrences* within it' (*God's Action in the World*, Lecture 3,
p. 28) (my italics). Again, and apparently to his mind equivalently,

he maintains, 'for the theist who is necessarily committed to a unitary view of the world, the whole process of the bringing into being of the world, which is still going on, needs to be seen as *one action of God*' (p. 29) (my italics).

19. Working out this second conjunct is the principal burden of proof that he tries to discharge in Lectures 3, 5, and 6.
20. Wiles, *God's Action in the World*, Lecture 2, p. 16.
21. See *God's Action in the World*, Lecture 3, p. 28, where Wiles insists that 'an action always involves an intention and a goal' and that 'to call something an "act"' 'is to give a unity to what would otherwise appear only as random occurrences, and to do so by bringing them together as contributory to some overall intention'. Later he partially specifies the intention as involving 'human consciousness and human loving' 'as vital elements' and infers that 'purely physical occurrences ... provide the substructure that serves to make that intention, and therefore the one divine action possible' (Lecture 3, p. 30). Note how Wiles here assigns a means–end structure to divine intention, whereas earlier he insisted that 'it would be wrong to think of God as deliberating through choice' and suggested instead that divine creation and purpose might 'flow naturally from the kind of person' God is (Lecture 3, p. 27). Traditional adherents of divine immutability rejected any *temporal* process in divine willing, but many recognised a deliberative structure in God's reasons for acting while claiming that God grasped the calculation 'all at once'. It is not clear whether Wiles shares their hesitations about divine deliberation, or whether he has some alternative objection to God's acting for reasons as opposed to from spontaneous generosity.
22. Note that many traditional theologians thought it followed from divine simplicity that there could be only a *single* act on God's part, one that was metaphysically identical with the divine essence. Wiles's disagreement with them is not about the *unity* of the divine act, nor even about a willingness to describe its content as directed to the world *as a whole*, but rather about whether the intentional content of that act is fully or (to what extent) partially determinate – that is, whether God wills only the existence of things with their natural powers, or (*à la* Leibniz) a fully determinate world history, or something in between. In traditional language, Wiles seems to restrict God's willing in relation to creation to what was traditionally included in the *antecedent* divine will. See my *William Ockham*, ch. 28, section 3, pp. 1168–73.
23. Wiles, *God's Action in the World*, Lecture 3, p. 36: 'the difference between a deistic picture according to which the emergent properties of evolving matter are in some sense inherently programmed in advance and a theistic model according to which God is ever-present, ever-active creator, calling out those emergent properties *in via* is the difference between two alternative imageries, each of which has its own weaknesses rather than between two substantially conflicting claims'.

24. Ibid., p. 38.
25. See Wiles's opening list of naive examples of divine action in *God's Action in the World*, Lecture 1, pp. 1–2. See also his admission that 'even the possibility of miracle' which he allows 'raises acute problems for theodicy' and his approving account of Hebblethwaite's view that 'the direct intervention of God, however rare the occasions of it, would ... have disastrous implications for our understanding of the problem of evil' (Lecture 5, p. 67).
26. Wiles, *God's Action in the World*, Lecture 6, p. 78: 'Why is it that some people come to faith and some do not? The most we can claim so far is to have clarified some of the constituent elements that must have a place in any answer that might be put forward. In the first place the mystery of a genuinely human free choice must not be eliminated.'
27. Wiles, *God's Action in the World*, Lecture 5, p. 56; Lecture 8, p. 98; cf. Lecture 2, p. 16.
28. Wiles, *God's Action in the World*, Lecture 5, pp. 60–3.
29. Wiles, *God's Action in the World*, Lecture 4, pp. 42–3.
30. See John Hick, *Evil and the God of Love* (New York: Harper & Row, revised edn 1978) esp. pp. 255–61, 318–36.
31. See Richard Swinburne, *The Existence of God* (Oxford: Clarendon Press, 1979), chs 10–12; and 'Knowledge from Experience and the Problem of Evil', in William J. Abraham and Steven W. Holtzer (eds), *The Rationality of Religious Belief: Essays in Honour of Basil Mitchell* (Oxford: Clarendon Press, 1987), pp. 141–67.
32. Wiles, *God's Action in the World*, Lecture 4, pp. 46–7. Cf. J. L. Mackie, 'Evil and Omnipotence', *Mind*, 1955, vol. 64, pp. 200–12.
33. Wiles, *God's Action in the World*, Lecture 4, p. 48.
34. Thus, Wiles writes: 'If God is "responsible" for evil, in however modified a sense, because he has taken the risk of creating a world in which it was highly likely, or even logically bound, to emerge, then there are strong moral objections to any view of God which regards him as immune from the damaging consequences of that evil.' But he emphasises once again that the powers that act on God cannot come from outside the divine sphere of influence (*God's Action in the World*, Lecture 5, p. 49).
35. Wiles, *God's Action in the World*, Lecture 4, pp. 50–1.
36. Ibid., pp. 51–2.
37. Ibid., p. 52.
38. Wiles, *God's Action in the World*, Lecture 8, p. 108.
39. The defence of this claim is the main burden of Wiles's last three lectures (6–8).
40. Wiles, *God's Action in the World*, Lecture 8, p. 102.
41. Ibid., pp. 104–5.
42. I have used this example in other papers, first in 'Theodicy without Blame', *Philosophical Topics*, 1988, vol. XVI, pp. 215–45, as well as 'Chalcedonian Christology: A Christian Solution to the Problem of Evil', forthcoming in *Philosophy and Theological Discourse*, ed. Stephen T. Davis (London: Macmillan, 1996).

43. I first defined this category in 'Theodicy without Blame', and subsequently in 'Horrendous Evils and the Goodness of God', *Proceedings of the Aristotelian Society*, 1989, supp. vol. LXIII, pp. 299–310; reprinted in Marilyn McCord Adams and Robert Merrihew Adams (eds), *The Problem of Evil* (Oxford: Oxford University Press, 1990), pp. 209–21; and 'Chalcedonian Christology: A Christian Solution to the Problem of Evil'.

44. Roderick Chisholm, 'The Defeat of Good and Evil', revised and reprinted in Marilyn McCord Adams and Robert Merrihew Adams (eds), *The Problem of Evil* (Oxford: Oxford University Press, 1990), pp. 53–68. In my judgement Chisholm is wrong to make defeat and balancing off *exclusive* relations: for example, the ugliness of some square centimetres in a Monet painting might be both balanced off by a greater number of pretty square centimetres and defeated by the aesthetic value of the overall design of the painting of which they are integral parts.

45. I emphasize this distinction of contexts of defeat in 'Horrendous Evils and the Goodness of God', and again in 'Chalcedonian Christology: A Christian Solution to the Problem of Evil'.

46. I have argued that the soteriological plot line of apocalyptic theology is not subtle enough to defeat horrendous evils, in effect in 'Separation and Reversal in Luke–Acts', in Thomas Morris (ed.), *Philosophy and the Christian Faith* (Notre Dame University Press, 1988), pp. 92–117; and in 'Aesthetic Goodness as a Solution to the Problem of Evil', in Arvind Sharma (ed.) *God, Truth, and Reality: Essays in Honour of John Hick* (London: Macmillan, and New York: St Martin's Press, 1993), pp. 46–61.

47. I explore two categories of symbolic value in my paper 'Symbolic Value and the Problem of Evil: Honor and Shame', in Shlomo Biderman and Ben-Ami Scharfstein (eds), *The Interpretation of Religion* (Leiden: E. J. Brill, 1992), pp. 259–82. See 'Chalcedonian Christology: A Christian Solution to the Problem of Evil', and 'God and Evil: Polarities of a Problem', *Philosophical Studies*, 1993, vol. 69, pp. 39–58.

48. Especially in 'Theodicy without Blame', 'Horrendous Evils and the Goodness of God', and 'Chalcedonian Christology: A Christian Solution to the Problem of Evil'.

49. I elaborated this in 'Chalcedonian Christology: A Christian Solution to the Problem of Evil'.

50. What follows is a very abstract and generic sketch of human development from an interactionist point of view, of the sort exemplified by Sigmund Freud, Erik Erikson, Jean Piaget, and Lawrence Kohlberg. I do not here draw upon points that distinguish one thinker from another.

51. 'Inefficient adaptational strategies' is modern psychology's way of referring to what Augustine called 'ignorance' and 'difficulty'. He would probably accept my developmental story, so far as Adam's descendants are concerned, but seems to believe that had Adam been created immature, he could have passed through childhood in

perfect obedience and arrived at adulthood without attendant 'hang-ups'. From the viewpoint of psychological theory, this is difficult to conceive, given the role alienation plays in the child's conceiving of itself as a distinct self. The psychology of the 'unfallen' would have to deny that actually conflict of wills is metaphysically necessary to the child's differentiation.

52. D. Z. Phillips, *The Concept of Prayer* (New York: Schocken Books, 1966), ch. 3, pp. 43–50.

53. Wiles, *God's Action in the World*, Lecture 8, p. 102; cf. pp. 104–5.

54. See Wiles, *God's Action in the World*, Lecture 1, p. 7: even though a Christian 'may properly approach' Scripture 'with an *a priori* expectation in their favor', still Scripture and tradition 'can make no absolute claim on our acceptance'.

55. My ideas in this section have been shaped by discussions with Derk Pereboom and Robert Merrihew Adams, neither of whom should be blamed for my conclusions!

56. Defining the contrast between realist and anti-realist or instrumentalist positions has proved notoriously difficult. One common account makes realism the view that there is a fact of the matter prior to and independently of whatever human beings may individually or collectively think or believe, whereas anti-realists or instrumentalists deny this. As Geoffrey Sayre-McCord notes, it is difficult to apply such an explanation to the science of human psychology. He analyses realism as 'embracing just two theses: (1) the claims in question, when literally construed, are literally true or false (cognitivism), and (2) some are literally true' ('Introduction: The Many Moral Realisms', in Geoffrey Sayre-McCord (ed.), *Essays on Moral Realism* (Ithaca, NY: Cornell University Press, 1988), pp. 1–23; esp. p. 4). He further explains that realism can be contrasted with instrumentalism, in which case 'the central issue is whether the claims of the disputed class should be interpreted as having truth-values' and so given 'a cognitivist interpretation'; or with idealism in which case 'the issue is whether minds (or their contents) figure expressly in the truth-conditions for the claims in question' (ibid., p. 7). He adds that both realist and idealist embrace a cognitivist construal. Thus, where realism is contrasted with instrumentalism, Bishop Berkeley was a realist about tables and trees, but an instrumentalist about the theoretical entities of microphysics; where realism is opposed to idealism, Berkeley was an idealist about tables and trees.

57. Wiles, *God's Action in the World*, Lecture 1, p. 7.

6

Reply: Redeeming Sorrows

ROWAN WILLIAMS

There are two main areas where I find Professor McCord Adams's paper unsatisfactory in terms both of philosophical analysis and of moral adequacy to the question of suffering – especially the kind of suffering she describes as 'horrendous', suffering that gives reason to doubt whether the sufferer's life as a whole can be regarded as a 'good' for him or her. I shall concentrate on these two issues, rather than on the overall critique of Maurice Wiles, which is full of interest and deserves longer consideration in its own right: though some of what I want to say about divine action may prove to be pertinent to this subject. So I intend to look first at the whole matter of how evil, especially of the extreme kind discussed, might be understood as offset or defeated in the general economy of the universe; then at the concepts of divine action invoked to underpin the thesis of the paper.

'[H]orrendous evils exhibit such a disproportion to any and every package of created goods that only appropriate relation to the incommensurate goodness of God could overwhelm them' (p. 113). I take this to mean that there are evils such that, after enduring them, the sufferer's sense of worth and hope is so damaged that no particular experience of the finite world could restore it. And, as the argument develops, it seems that 'appropriate relation' to the divine goodness is to be conceived in two ways: from the perspective of the onlooker, such evil is defeated by being placed in a broader context, in which the divine self-identification with mortal suffering in the person of the incarnate Word demonstrates that God 'honours' the experience of any and all human suffering by being present in it; from the perspective of the sufferer (who may have no access to this perspective of 'symbolic defeat'), there must be a concrete defeat, consisting in a promised post-mortem beatitude, where the incalculable excess of divine goodness over any and all experience of pain obviates any concern over an uneven distribution of finite goods. The generosity of God is 'incommensurate' with the need or injury of a finite sufferer, and can therefore never fall short of the capacity to restore a full sense of worth and hope.

My first worry is over these notions of proportion and incommensurateness. In so far as they have a natural home, it is in the realm of a certain kind of aesthetics; and this tends to slant the way in which the issue is considered, privileging the observer's point of view. If we speak of 'proportion', we seem to be presupposing an ideal state of relation between elements of our experience: just so much of this, and no more. And this in turn implies that it would be sensible to speak of a proper or fitting quantity of suffering in a life, the sort of amount that could be offset without too much trouble and integrated within an overall story that came out well, that did not leave too many moral loose ends. Now I know that those who use the language of 'disproportion' here are not explicitly committed to anything quite so crude, and that their aim is to register the fact that there are kinds of suffering so intensely destructive that we cannot imagine a process whereby they could be healed and lived with. There is a difference between even the worst attack of toothache and the memory of twelve years of continuous sexual abuse as a child. But is the language of 'proportion' the right one for this distinction? That is to say, is the relation between destructive and constructive experiences properly conceived as one in which a certain quantity of the one balances a certain quantity of the other?

The situation is more complex, surely. As Professor McCord Adams recognises (again on p. 113), people respond in widely diverse ways to what happens to them: 'one bears easily what crushes another'. But this ought to suggest that we abandon the pseudo-aesthetic mode in talking about such matters. What makes an experience bearable for one person and the final and intolerable blow for another is, of course, in large measure what they have been made by previous experience. That is to say, we cannot take 'experiences' as psychological atoms that can be assessed on a scale of proportionateness to each other and to an imagined whole. There is, philosophically speaking, no such thing as 'an' experience, capable of being unproblematically isolated and assessed. Rather, our interaction with what we do not choose or control, our environment, develops and modifies what we sense and say of ourselves; and we do not know in advance what a new stage of this interaction will do to our linguistic and narrative construction of who we are. We do not know what it might be that would silence or paralyse the whole process of self-construction to the point where we had no desire or energy to continue to 'present' ourselves to ourselves. Nor can we easily say what could or would restore this. In small measure, most of us recognise the impossibility of correlating 'experiences' when we are in a state of extreme pain or unaffected delight. The Roman general at his triumph had his slave at his shoulder to whisper, 'Remember you are human', but it is hard to imagine what strictly affective difference this might make. And all this, I take it, is what Wittgenstein wanted to draw our attention to in saying that the world of the happy and that of the unhappy were not the same world.

This should in turn make us cautious about accepting too hastily the conclusion that no finite outcome could heal the effects of appalling injury. It must be emphasised that there is and can be no way of theorising this without blandness and dishonesty; but I am concerned that the notion of humanly unhealable hurts should not be used as a device to bring in the need for divine (unmediated?) consolation. Just as we cannot tell what experience of suffering or humiliation will destroy the hope of an apparently serene person (it may be something which, because of deeply buried personal history, has a significance utterly obscure to the observer, something that may look relatively slight to anyone other than the subject), so we cannot simply state that 'horrendous' evil resists all finite outcomes for good. Towards the end of *King Lear*, a play that deliberately invites us to look at extremes of suffering and the arbitrary way in which they are both inflicted and resolved or accepted, Lear imagines for a moment that his dead daughter is alive:

> She lives! if it be so,
> It is a chance which does redeem all sorrows
> That ever I have felt.

Leaving aside the (useless) question of whether Lear's experience counts as 'horrendous', the point is that the bare fact of Cordelia's survival is being regarded as an adequate element in healing a memory of acute suffering. The question of whether it is 'proportionate' to the suffering is not asked and could not be answered. But the way in which the whole matter is treated here should remind us of the incalculable elements in talking of injury and restoration. Let me take another example from the literary imagination: Robertson Davies' novel, *World of Wonders*, describes the life of a master conjuror, a man whose adult career has been a triumph of sophisticated illusion – the illusions of his trade, and the magnificent fiction of his professional autobiography and public persona. We are allowed to hear from him his true autobiography, as related to a group of friends and colleagues; and it is a record of the 'horrendous' that makes very painful reading indeed. He is abducted as a child from his village in rural Ontario by a drug-addicted paedophile who works in a travelling circus (the 'World of Wonders' of the title), and for the whole of his childhood and early adolescence is a virtual slave to his kidnapper; he is forced to spend endless hours imprisoned in a mechanical figure that is part of the circus entertainment, manipulating its works; he has no life outside the sad troupe of minor criminals and inadequates that make up the circus, and, of course, he continues to be routinely abused by his original captor. Now what could we say about a 'package of created goods' adequate to make of this a bearable story? The reader (and the listeners to the story in the book itself) will be inclined to say that this is a triumph of evil; but Davies does not let us get away with any simple moralisings. Magnus, the conjuror, has created a life that is for him worth living, as a result of a wide range of events, interior and exterior. Is he a 'whole' person? In a number of important ways, no. Yet it would make no sense to say that the appalling evil of his childhood experience could be touched only by the direct hand of God.

I do not quote these examples to imply that 'horrendous' evils needn't be as bad as they seem; far from it. My problem is with the calculus of good and bad experiences suggested by the language of proportion, a calculus that appears to be a long way from what happens in the ways people attempt to make sense of their lives. As I said earlier, such talk privileges the observer's standpoint, turning the question of how evil is to be lived with into the question of how a satisfactory object can be constructed. While there is a long tradition, going back at least to Augustine and Plotinus, of discussing the question of evil in aesthetic terms, we ought, I believe, to be suspicious of the whole discourse in so far as it makes the problem more mine than the sufferer's and misconceives

the nature of 'experiences'. I do not see how there can be a calculus of values for discrete experiences that would allow the
observer/theorist to assess the worthwhileness of a life as a whole;
and I do not believe that the subject whose suffering is under
discussion will naturally think in such terms. Even in aesthetics,
the language of balance or proportion is massively more complicated than the rather odd observation on appreciating a painting
in Professor McCord Adams's paper suggests. I can make no sense
whatever of the notion that we evaluate the overall aesthetic quality
of a work by balancing its 'ugly' and 'pretty' [*sic*] parts. Why
should we call an isolated square centimetre of a Monet painting
'ugly' (and what on earth are we doing looking at square centimetres, anyway)? What is it 'ugly' *as*? It isn't meant to be a painting
in its own right, and has no existence simply as a square centimetre in the abstract. By what imaginable criteria could we make
any aesthetic judgement at all about it, and why ever should we
want to? In fact, exactly the same problem arises here as with the
notion of discrete things called experiences; the inadequacy of
the language in the aesthetic sphere should already be alerting
us to the inadequacy of the whole of this sort of aesthetic analogy.

It will be clear by now that I am not happy with the idea of
'symbolic defeat', to the extent that it still stays with the observer's
perspective. If we look at what Professor McCord Adams says
about the symbolic defeat of evil by way of God's identification
with the experience of human suffering, we find this expressed
pretty clearly: the fact of God's presence in suffering, whether or
not the sufferer is (or could be?) aware of it, gives incalculable
meaning or positive value to suffering because it constitutes the
suffering in question integral to a relation with God. This is rather
sketchily put, but it deserves some unscrambling. I take it that
the point is something like this. God in Christ assumes not only
humanity in general but humanity specifically in its vulnerability.
Because the life of God incarnate is worked out, articulated, in a
human biography in which acute physical and mental suffering
occur, such suffering cannot be held to be of itself an absolute
obstacle to perfect and conscious union with God; indeed, it may
seem as part of the concrete working out of God's will, not in the
sense that God actively wills particular sufferings, but because
the way in which sufferings are endured becomes an aspect of
the way in which the love and generosity of God are made concrete and historical. So far, I shouldn't want to disagree. It is the

next stage that seems to me problematic. Here, it appears, we are invited to draw two doubtfully warranted conclusions. There is first the notion that God might be said 'literally' to experience whatever agonies human beings endure and, second, that the experience of pain can be a moment of identification with the 'inner life of God'. While these are only possible options for the theologian, as presented in Professor McCord Adams's paper, they are clearly meant to bear some apologetic weight. The first is puzzling on two counts: we need an extra argument to say that because God in some sense suffers in Jesus Christ, God suffers in (presumably) the same sense in every finite intelligent subject; and, following on from that, to say that God literally suffers everything that we suffer founders on some very obvious problems, such as the fact that God is not an historical or material agent. While we may say as much as we like about divine knowledge of and compassion for our pain, the one thing we cannot say without either trivialising our talk of God or departicularising our talk about human suffering is that God endures human pain exactly as any human subject does. I shall come back later to the wider question of how we should speak of divine action (and passion), but for now wish only to register a grave objection to the imprecisions and potential nonsense involved in taking these proposals as they stand.

As for the second conclusion, this also seems to founder on two serious obstacles. It risks (once again) treating experiences as isolable units: x has experience e, God also has experience e, therefore God and x share a single experience; for God, experience e is part of an indivisible life of bliss, so for x, experience e can also in principle be integrated into a life of bliss. This ignores the point made a little while back, about experience's location within an evolving story of self-awareness and self-presentation. It also leaves open the question of how the integration moves from being a potentiality to being a reality for the subject. Can the affirmation of the possibility alone of integration or the conferral of meaning serve even for the observer as an adequate account of the 'defeat' of an evil whose problematic nature lies precisely in the injury done to a subject? The added unclarity of saying that suffering can be ('literally' again) an insight into the inner life of God should be noted: is this claiming that suffering becomes intrinsic to being divine? That would be an eccentric conclusion, both in terms of the arguments actually presented here, and in terms of the ways in which classical Christology, up to the end of the Middle Ages, laboured to avoid any account of the union between God and humanity in Jesus that licensed a direct ascription of suffering to the divine person of the Word *qua* divine. But that is an issue that would lead us far afield. What remains obscure to me is how any of this argumentation justifies talking about symbolic defeat. The involvement of the incarnate Word in suffering, in traditional Christology, most emphatically allows us to say that it is possible to interpret one's suffering as not only compatible with but intrinsic to one's own unique living-out of the calling to realise God's likeness in the flesh. But this surely, as an interpretative resource, depends on acts of interpretation, themselves dependent for their specific possibility upon the history of the subject of suffering, the linguistic resources available, the images opened up by the tradition in which he or she lives, and so on. The passion of God incarnate is certainly a given for the Christian, a central point of reference and critique; among other things, it challenges any account of divine action that simply assimilates it to the supremely successful exercise of power as normally understood, and warns us that we shall find more to say about God by talking of vulnerability than by talking of the unqualified triumph of a sort of individual will over recalcitrant circumstances. But this is not to authorise fantasy about the 'feelings' or 'experiences' of God (it ought not to be necessary to underline the absurdity of this). Nor is it to produce a theory that allows us to believe that all forms of destructive evil will be 'overcome' simply in virtue of the direct proximity of the divine life to them. The passion of Christ, as an inexhaustible resource of possible meaning and healing, is one thing; I cannot see that it can be generalised into a universal principle that confers value on suffering irrespective of the sufferer's own account.

The discussion thus slips over into discussion of 'concrete defeat'. Once again, I want to distinguish two phases of the argument, the earlier of which I can understand, the latter I find unacceptable and doubtfully intelligible. For the subject, symbolic defeat is not enough; thus we must think of further concrete experiences that will restore the sense of worthwhileness to a scarred life. As we have seen, we should not leap to the conclusion that nothing but divine presence without mediation will do this job. But it is perhaps reasonable to say that, given an unlimited time scale, more and more possibilities arise for developments in what

I have called the self-awareness and self-presentation of a subject, such that there would at least be resource for healing. If theologians speak at this point of the significance of post-mortem existence, it is not to justify or explain suffering, but to try and imagine a context ample enough for the subject of profound injury to grow into a different kind of self-perception. Such contexts exist in our ordinary experience, in therapeutic relationships, new kinds of communal life, and the sheer unpredictable range of stimulus that might or might not effect a transformation. For those whose death cuts them off from any such possibilities, theology can only point to its fundamental belief in a God who is faithful and eternal, and say, 'if there is hope, it lies there'. If it knows its business, it will not want to go much further. But even if we allow such a minimal appeal to the post-mortem dimension, what we have to say is that the subject remains what he or she has become as a result of the experiences of this life; the possibilities that lie open are defined by a particular history – as they would be in a 'normal' therapeutic situation. Otherwise, we should have to suppose that the post-mortem identity had suddenly ceased to be the identity constructed by this history and no other. This would resolve the problematic nature of destructive evil by a kind of eschatological dissolution of the particular subject as such: in the light of eternity, the suffering of the abused child or the victim of torture is no more 'difficult' to heal than that of an academic who fails to get the job they wanted or a theatrical producer whose grant from the Arts Council has been halved.

I don't think this will do. What I am not clear about is whether this is what Professor McCord Adams is really proposing. I can see the point of saying that no one is going to 'grudge' the different length of time it has taken to arrive at 'concrete defeat' for different subjects, once we are all enjoying the beatific vision. But that is hardly the point. If the love of God is simply an overwhelming tide of 'positive experience' that can be guaranteed to swallow up any and all specific negative experiences, we are left with nothing to say about the particular ways in which suffering damages the self and the particular needs that are to be met in healing it. The 'indifference' of divine love is in danger of becoming an abstraction that ultimately devalues particular histories, and the promise of a specific healing or wiping away of tears is reduced to the promise of a maximally positive experience for all one day. And – to go back a little in the argument – this is also the ground for my unease with the idea that the resolution of earthly pains of a specially acute kind must lie in an unmediated experience of the divine love – as if the love of God could now be bestowed on an individual subject without the intervention of a 'world'; as if we could make sense of a notion of experience that bypassed the world – our entire environment, our history and language, our essential interconnectedness with other subjects. Here there raises its head the familiar spectre of a kind of philosophical ethos that regards the world as a regrettable barrier between the subject and truth.

But this brief evocation of post-mortem developments is, in Professor McCord Adams's essay, part of a justification for particular acts of (interventionist) divine providence. God, for reasons that are, I suppose, systematically inaccessible, elects to provide specific experiences of nurture or guidance for some finite subjects; and, because of the ultimate equivalence of everyone's experience of the divine love, there can be no place for resentment that one receives this and not another. In the long run, we all have the same guarantee. Is there, then, any rationale to the divine intervention? We can, it seems, answer this only in general terms, by way of an analysis of human moral agency, which brings out the character of such agency as exercised in 'impaired freedom'. There are no finite 'ideal agents', since we are all moulded by the experience and upbringing we have had: 'our childhood adaptational strategies continue to distort our perceptions and behaviour'. God's agency, in contrast, is incommensurably greater (I know this phraseology is problematic, and shall come back to it shortly); it cannot be in competition with ours, so that its presence never threatens our limited liberty. It thus makes sense to conceive God's agency as one that enables our own in whatever ways are appropriate – as a parent's agency enables an infant's.

There are welcome recognitions here, notably the more nuanced account of the evolution of a subject and the acknowledgment of incommensurability between divine and human action. However, the argument is developed in a way that actually undercuts these points, especially the latter. It appears that for some subjects the ordinary historical environment for human growth is inadequate: it must be supplemented by divine intervention. What Professor McCord Adams in particular does not make clear in her admirable evocation of the Holy Spirit as enabler of our Christian freedom is how we are to differentiate between the action of God's Spirit in the usual mediating forms in which Christians speak of it and special or additional actions intervening in the processes of the created order: the phraseology of this discussion suggests that part of the 'normal' process of the formation of Christian freedom in us is the presence of specific actions by God the Holy Spirit. So is the Spirit's action an emergency intervention or a normal interweaving of divine agency with the processes of human growth? A little earlier, we have had an appeal to the necessity of particular providence on the grounds that the world's condition is far too gravely askew for finite agency to be able to resolve its difficulties. 'The scope God has already allowed creatures "to do their own thing" has made a mess far too big for human beings to clean up all by ourselves (although it will be our vocation to make some contribution).' This might mean – as an orthodox theological commentator of a broadly Thomist orientation would probably say – that the predicament of fallen humanity is such that the incarnation is required to overcome the evil consequences of Adam's sin; the 'intervention' here would be God's assumption of human nature and the gift of the Holy Spirit in the fellowship of the Church, Christ's Body. But is this what is being said? It sounds more as if the world is in need of constant divine intervention, especially in a century as bad as ours. If we turn back to the later discussion of the role of the Holy Spirit as enabler, we are left rather in the dark as to whether we are to envisage a regular series of interventions rather than the somewhat different case of a particular worldly history (Israel, Jesus and the Church) being 'read' as communicating transformative divine action.

The difference is significant because it affects what we say about divine action; and, at long last, I shall turn to this second area of major unease with Professor McCord Adams's paper. What is disturbing in her account of providence is that it suggests that providential divine action has something of the nature of crisis management – that is, it is essentially reactive. It becomes more necessary the worse things get. The implication is that, as human history evolves, it is quite likely that we shall need increasing supplements of direct divine intervention to save us from even worse disasters than we currently experience. If I understand the drift of the argument correctly, the character of this intervention is to do with the fostering of holy lives, rather than with spectacular modifications in the course of historical events. But the difficulty remains that the world requires, increasingly, more than the 'natural' can provide. I shan't comment here on the strictly theological problems of a view that might imply that the work of Christ is inadequate to the task of renewing the world, or that God will always act to prevent a worst possible outcome of the consequences of human sin and irresponsibility. I prefer to concentrate now on the conceptual difficulties arising from the implied picture here of divine action. While we are told that this action is incommensurable with ours, the gist of the discussion in fact suggests that it is not strict incommensurability at all that is at issue, but incalculably large quantitative difference. The comparison of the distance between God's action and ours to that between parent's and infant's rather suggests as much; but the essential point is that God is conceived as reacting to a situation which we have to suppose God failed to provide for in advance. How else are we to read the curious statements about God stepping in 'after' we have been allowed a certain amount of exercise of our created liberty? We are, in fact, returned to the most crude and basic form of the protest to which theodicy seeks an answer: could God have made a better world? Is the divine action in creating somehow deficient or incompetent? If God has continually to intervene when created choices become (disproportionately?) destructive on a large scale, is the world as originally created incapable of realising the divine purpose? And if God is capable of the endless damage limitation apparently envisaged here, is God not capable of creating an environment where this sort of intervention is less necessary? And so on. But the deeper problem lies in the notion of God's action as resting on punctiliar decisions to step into a crisis, or to intensify our awareness of the 'personal environment' sustained by the Holy Spirit. And this leaves us with a God whose action is not really incommensurable in relation to ours, but very like ours in character, though utterly different in scope. It is action that has to weigh circumstances and assess the seriousness of situations, action involved in decision-making, conditioned by what it responds to.

There is a passage on p. 124 which highlights the problem. Maurice Wiles's suggestion is mentioned, that God's agency is exercised as a pervasive 'attracting' presence, not as a series of punctiliar determinations; and the response is that 'for all we know' this is not so, and that the Bible and the theological tradition tend to pull in another direction. This is a startling refusal to engage in any properly philosophical discussion of what is involved in saying that God acts. Plenty of theologians and philosophers have pointed out that, if God is conceived as acting in a punctiliar way, the divine action is determined by something other than itself; likewise if God is conceived as 'reacting' to anything. If either of these conceptualities gets a foothold in our thinking about God, we ascribe to God a context for God's action: God is (like us) an agent in an environment, who must 'negotiate' purposes and desires in relation to other agencies and presences. But God is not an item in any environment, and God's action has been held, in orthodox Christian thought, to be identical with God's being – that is, what God does is nothing other than God's being actively real. Nothing could add to or diminish this, because God does not belong in an environment where the divine life could be modified by anything else. God is the empowering source of anything other than God being real, that is, the ultimate 'activator' of all particular agency. This is the heart of Aquinas's doctrine of God, and it has been given eloquent restatement in David Burrell's remarkable monograph *Aquinas: God and Action*. Burrell is particularly good at showing how, in order to speak of God's causal relation to the universe, we do not need to imagine 'an' activity by which some change is effected: we need only point to the fact of dependence ('if it weren't for *a*, there wouldn't be *b*'; or 'the occurrence of *x* in *b* is the action of *a* in or on *b*').

This suggests that the discussion of divine action in both Wiles and Professor McCord Adams is misplaced. We do not have to choose between God acting primitively to create, then acting by suasion or attraction, on the one hand, and God acting to create and subsequently supplementing that action with new actions on the other. God is eternally and actively real – in classical Augustinian and Thomist terms, God is active in knowing and enjoying what it is to be God. In making the world, God neither performs a single and unrepeatable action, nor initiates a series of actions. All we can say is that it is the case that the range of possible ways in which God's being, knowing and loving might be reflected or 'imitated' by beings other than God (that is, beings whose action is not identical with their nature, but who realise or articulate what they are in processes) is actual. We might say that God 'decides' to create, if we like, but we'd better be aware that, while we have no other obvious way of saying that no one and nothing

'made' God create, we cannot attempt to understand this 'decision' as if it were a decision comparable to the ones we make –
at particular moments, faced with a range of options. And what
creation then means is that the single divine act on which everything depends activates a variety of patterns of action in the dif-
ferentiated and time-taking system that exists as other-than-God.

How, in such a perspective, do we talk about divine action or
particular providence? The answer can only be in terms of the
character of the finite system as a whole. If there are moments
when the act of God is recognised more plainly than it is in others,
or when the subject senses a closeness to the underlying act of
God that has the effect of prompting, warning, reassuring or
guiding, we are not to think of the fabric of the finite order being
interrupted, but rather of the world being such that, given certain configurations of finite agencies, the texture of the environment is more clearly transparent to the simple act of divine
self-communication. It is as if, to use a rather faulty metaphor,
the created order is a texture of uneven thickness. The flaw in
the metaphor is that it could be taken as meaning that the created environment is a kind of obstacle between the spiritual subject and God; and I have already noted the inadequacy of that
way of seeing things. But the basic model of a 'timelessly' or-
dered system, in which the more evident presence of the divine
action was not an intervention but the foreordained result of certain finite outcomes at least allows us to hold off the mythological notion of a God who reacts to circumstances. What I have in
mind is, of course, spelled out in one (memorable) way by Simone
Weil, for whom divine action is only perceptible when the ego
renounces or displaces itself. This is when grace occurs; not that
it can be produced by performing particular actions or acquiring
certain dispositions, because it is always and necessarily impossible to predict what exactly it would involve in any complex situation for divine action to be more effectively present; nor that the
divine activity can be counted on to 'tidy up' any moral loose
ends hanging around. Weil would indignantly reject any use of
this model of divine action for the production of a theodicy. But
she sees the point that, in a different idiom, is fundamental to
the classical doctrine of God: if God is not in an environment,
God's action can never have the form of an episode intruding
into the history of created causality or finite agency. It must not
be in competition for a shared logical space (and this is, I sup-

pose, why a theologian like Augustine can so firmly reject a view of miracle that regards it as a direct divine interruption of finite agency, as opposed to an extraordinary realisation of possibilities inherent in finite agency itself; but that is another matter).

This is what is involved in treating divine action as really 'incommensurable' with human (or finite in general). And this is why the alternatives of Wiles's austere limitation of divine action to the bare positing of the finite order and McCord Adams's commitment to the possibilities of multiple interventions represent a false dichotomy. It does not answer to say of the latter option that for all we know it may be the case. We have to do what the theologians of the tradition have always done: to take the undoubtedly punctiliar and anthropomorphic language of scripture and piety in talking of God's agency and ask how it can be read in the light of the doctrine of God to which the system of doctrinal and biblical speech overall points. Since there is at the heart of this speech a conviction that God is that on which every particular depends, the one who creates from nothing, the logic of our discourse about God's action must observe the constraints imposed by the implicit prohibition against describing God as an agent among others. And I hope this can be said without inviting the lazy response that this is an imposition of alien metaphysics on the personalist idiom of the Bible.

Where does this leave us as regards the problem with which we began in this paper? If God's action is strictly incommensurable with finite agency in the way I have argued, we have even less hope of deploying God as a 'balancing' factor in the aesthetic/moral equation that would allow us to judge the final worthwhileness of a sufferer's life. God is never going to be an element, a square centimetre, in any picture, not because God's agency is incalculably greater but because it simply cannot be fitted into the same space. To pursue the Christological issues raised here and elsewhere by Professor McCord Adams, it is like the concern of high scholasticism in particular that the presence of the Word as incarnate in Jesus should in no sense be conceived as 'competing' with the full created subjectivity or identity-as-subject of Jesus. We cannot say that, where 'packages of created goods' fail in the potentiality for healing the effects of unspeakable outrages, we can call on the infinite good of divine attention, involvement and beneficence to supply what is missing. It is simply not that sort of problem, and to treat it in such terms lands us, I have argued, with a dry and philosophically eccentric view of human experience and how identity is constructed by conscious subjects, and with a dubious doctrine of God's agency. I believe we should hold out for genuine incommensurables: the incommensurability of the worlds of the happy and the unhappy, and the incommensurability of God's agency and ours.

This leaves the question of the healing of outrages unresolved, of course. But I do not think that we can properly or intelligibly draw distinctions between evils that are in principle capable of resolution by way of created goods and evils that require nothing less than direct divine response. If my sub-Thomist analysis of divine action is correct, then in any imaginable created order the love of God is actively present in particular configurations of finite causes. In heaven, however we are going to understand that, we perceive (following the insight of a Bonaventure or a John of the Cross) not 'naked deity' but God in ourselves and in all things. Thus the problem of 'offsetting' appalling evil is no different in principle in this world and in the world to come; and the recognition of this, along with the difficulties raised for how we are to conceive the processes of 'self-awareness and self-presentation', should warn us off the whole project of looking for factors to balance and overcome negative experience. Human biography doesn't seem to work like that. The non-'horrendous' evil may be the final breaking point in a long history of the attrition of someone's sense of worth; and the apparently inadequate 'created good', the bare survival of a child, the acquisition of confidence, the triumph of will (deeply ambiguous as that is, as in Robertson Davies' story), will sustain a sense of worthwhileness, of life as a recognisable good. These matters are resistant to any kind of generalisation. But it is this resistance that relativises the whole issue of theodicy. So often, as we are all aware, the problem of theodicy is not experienced as such by those for whom, according to all the discussions, it ought to be an agonising primary question. That it is not a problem tells us nothing that makes it easier to reflect on the suffering of others; it doesn't even make it easier to think about or look at the suffering of those who don't find their suffering a problem. We are brought back constantly, in thinking about this, to the uncomfortable question of who theodicy is being done for.

So much of the language of Professor McCord Adams's treatment, which is far from insensitive to the gravity of the issues involved, like so much of the language of the whole tradition of theodicy, seems to presuppose that the purpose of theodicy is to make the world of human experience capable of being contemplated without despair. The trouble is that, if this really is the agenda, two seductions of the spirit will always haunt the enterprise: either there will be pressure to argue that the situation is not as bad as it seems, or there will be the urge to arrive at a perspective that is in principle not accessible to us, a position where we are not obliged – as here and now we are – to know suffering as unhealed and, often, humanly unhealable as far as we can see (it is always salutary to think of the quantity of human lives, in past ages and our own, totally without access to means of healing or sense-making). Perhaps it is time for philosophers of religion to look away from theodicy – not to appeal blandly to the mysterious purposes of God, not to appeal to any putative justification at all, but to put the question of how we remain faithful to *human* ways of seeing suffering, even and especially when we are thinking from a religious perspective. Part of the task of a good theology and of a candid religious philosophy is, I believe, to reacquaint us with our materiality and mortality. And part of that is the knowledge of suffering as without explanation or compensation – and also the knowledge, of course, that there are unpredictable, unsystematisable integrations of suffering into a biography in the experience of some. But this is to say, I think, that we should be worrying about seeing suffering always in its historical particularity: this, here, for this person, at this moment, with these memories. This might make us pause before ascribing all the world's pain 'literally' to God; for if God is compassionate towards the world, this is not self-pity, but the exercise of that radical love which is attention to the other in its difference, not its kinship; thus in its specificity within the world that is not-God. Being aware of this becomes a morally important matter in a context where love is always in danger of being redefined as natural solidarity (an aspect of this whole area that I have tried to address elsewhere).

In plain English, I suspect that it is more religiously imperative to be worried by evil than to put it into a satisfactory theoretical context, if only because such a worry keeps obstinately open the perspective of the sufferer, the subject, for whom this is never a question of aesthetics, however imaginatively and discriminatingly pursued. What might be called the 'mortal' knowledge of suffering, the knowledge of it as contingent and thus potentially unconsoled, matters not because our intellectual hubris needs bridling (though it doubtless does), but because it insists that certain things are known by 'testimony' – which means by converse, exchange, sociality, by attending to a perspective that is not and could never be one's own. Now in fact, as the philosopher ought to know, this is really an observation about knowledge as such; it is just that some kinds of knowing are less patient than others of reduction to the terms of the ego ambitious for self-sufficiency. And the pain of others is perhaps foremost among such items of knowledge. Thus my earlier insistence on the need to query the observer's perspective here is not just a piece of intellectual squeamishness. I want to insist on this as a condition for religious thinking of any sort, which, if it is serious in articulating the contemplative ideal which I think is fundamental to religious perception and talking, is bound to the task of attention to perspectives that remain irreducibly different – even if that difference entails a self-dispossession and recovery of the self through the other, as for Hegel (I am still convinced that Hegel is a basically Christian philosopher!). The suffering of an historically particular other must be a paradigm for the kind of knowledge that will not allow us to stop listening, because we cannot completely internalise or domesticate it. In that sense – and that alone? – knowing about suffering might be a way into knowing about God. But this has to go on avoiding the pietistic reduction of such a vision to the idea that suffering is a 'mystery' that teaches us humility, and also the fashionable but, I believe, deeply questionable notion that suffering offers access to the heart of a suffering God. The subject's account of their pain most basically reminds me that the world is a world of differences and so of converse and so of listening. If I learn this, I may have learned a bit of what classical theology wants to say about God – that it is impossible to give God an essential definition or to map God on a conceptual scheme, because what God is, the world isn't. And I shall not know God without acknowledging what my own knowledge is like, historical and situational; so that I know God as supremely what I must listen for and can never domesticate.

Even the best and subtlest of theodicies cannot but seem a strategy for evading most of this. 'Who is it for?' is a question very close to 'In whose presence is it done?' If the answer to that is, 'In the absence of the perspective of the sufferer as subject or narrator', how can it fail to evade – to evade not only humanity, but divinity as well?

Part IV
Religion and Moral Relativism

7

Relativism about Torture: Religious and Secular Responses

PHILIP L. QUINN*

Torture is wrong, we say. Do we mean that torture is always wrong? Some of us do. We do who honour Amnesty International because it acts on this moral judgement. Included in its mandate is a commitment 'to oppose the death penalty, torture, or other cruel, inhuman, or degrading treatment or punishment of all prisoners' and 'to oppose abuses by opposition groups – hostage taking, the torture and killings of prisoners, and other arbitrary killings'.[1] But there are hard cases to consider. Suppose the only way to find out where a bomb is located in an airplane, before it explodes and kills all on board, is to torture the terrorist who planted it. Does the prospect of saving many lives that would otherwise be lost render it morally permissible for security forces to torture the terrorist? Or suppose the terrorist would remain mute under torture but would crack if her child were tortured before her eyes. Would it be morally right for security forces to torture the terrorist's child? Respectable opinion divides on the answers to questions about such hard cases.

The shared morality of our society holds that torture is generally wrong. We would reject any ethical theory that told us that torture is not generally wrong. Most of us do not subscribe to those versions of utilitarianism according to which torture is morally right whenever the benefits to third parties equal or outweigh the harm to the victim. Our opposition to torture can be expressed in several moral vocabularies. Some speak of a right not to be tortured

---

* I dedicate this essay to Amnesty International and its supporters.

151

and a correlative duty not to torture. One might distinguish between the two hard cases I have mentioned by saying that the guilty terrorist has forfeited her right not to be tortured but her innocent child has not. Following W. D. Ross, one might say that the *prima facie* duty of the security force not to torture is overridden in the case of the terrorist but not in the case of her child. Those of us who think that torture is always wrong will have to say that the *prima facie* duty not to torture is never overridden.

I take it that this strong claim is not presently part of the common morality of our society. We agree that torture is generally wrong, but there are those among us who consider it right in at least some hard cases. Moreover, our society is haunted by the spectre of relativism of various sorts. We have to take seriously the possibility that, even if torture is always wrong in our society, it is sometimes or often right in other societies. We also have to listen to those who argue that, even if the belief that torture is always wrong can be justified to the members of our society, it cannot be justified to the members of other societies. So there is room to doubt that the judgement that torture is always wrong is part of a common morality of humanity, a morality that 'applies and can be justified to persons as such' or a set of moral judgements that 'not only apply, but could be justified, to persons in a variety of cultures'.[2] How can those of us who believe that torture is always wrong respond to the threat of relativism?

Some among those who think that torture is always wrong have religious commitments. They will be inclined to respond to relativism in religious terms. However there may be danger in doing so. As Robert M. Adams notes, 'one of the objections often raised against religious theories in ethics is that in a religiously pluralistic society they will be divisive, undermining the common, or shared, morality on which a society depends for its health'.[3] Ours is certainly a religiously pluralistic society, and the contemporary world as a whole manifests even more by way of religious pluralism than our society does. To the extent that this objection has merit, the appeal to religion to support the judgement that torture is always wrong is not only unlikely to succeed in justifying it to persons as such but is also likely to make disagreement over it more intractable. The prospects of such disagreement turning into conflict can be made to seem menacing. Criticising Basil Mitchell's attempt to provide a theological vindication of the 'traditional conscience', Jeffrey Stout writes: 'until theism proves able to gather a reasonably broad rational consensus around a specific conception of the good, an eventuality that now seems remote, we probably should not follow advice like Mitchell's. The risks of reviving religious conflict like that of early modern Europe are too great.'[4] So there is a real question about whether and, if so, how religion can help in formulating a cogent response to the relativist's challenge to the judgement that torture is always wrong.

This essay is devoted to discussing that question. It is divided into four sections. In the first, I spell out the relativist challenge in some detail. Next I present and criticise a particular religious response to the challenge. By way of contrast, I then discuss a recent secular response to the challenge and argue that it fares no better than the religious response. Finally I suggest a response that may allow us to make some progress towards justifying the judgement that torture is always wrong to rational animals or human persons as such.

I   RELATIVISM: METAPHYSICAL AND EPISTEMOLOGICAL

Like most 'isms', relativism is not a single, clearly defined doctrine or thesis. Relativistic claims can be spelled out in many ways. It is therefore incumbent on me to specify the conception of relativism with which I shall be working in this essay. I now turn to that task.

The first thing I need to do is to specify that to which other things are being relativised. There are several candidates to consider. One might relativise to individual persons, cultures, societies, ethnic groups, races, nations or states. When I am discussing metaphysical relativism, I find it natural to relativise to societies. When I am discussing epistemological relativism, I find it natural to relativise to individual persons. What are metaphysical and epistemological relativism?

Those of us who hold that torture is always wrong are absolutists of a sort. We think that the moral prohibition of torture is binding on absolutely everyone and at all times. Our opponents deny this. They think that the moral prohibition of torture does not bind some persons at some times. Metaphysical relativism is a philosophical theory or family of theories that would, if true, explain why our opponents are right. According to one member of that family, there is no such thing as the property of being wrong.

Wrongness is instead a relation between actions and the societies in which they occur. On this view, the judgement that torture is always wrong has to be understood as the claim that all acts of torture bear the wrongness relation to the societies in which they occur. Our opponents might concede that all acts of torture occurring in our society bear the wrongness relation to it, but they can add that some acts of torture occurring in other societies do not bear the wrongness relation to them. If they do say this, they can go on to claim that the prohibition of torture does not bind those who perform acts of torture that do not bear the wrongness relation to the societies other than our own in which they occur.

Of course our opponents would not have to appeal to metaphysical relativism if certain conditions were to obtain. Though this seems implausible, it might turn out that no act of torture occurring in our society maximises utility but some acts of torture occurring in other societies do maximise utility. In such circumstances, according to act utilitarianism, all acts of torture occurring in our society are wrong and some acts of torture occurring in other societies are not wrong. But it seems very likely that some acts of torture occurring in our society do maximise utility. So I think our opponents would do better to appeal to metaphysical relativism than to rely on act utilitarianism if what they want is a distinction between moral prohibitions that apply without exception in our society but do not apply without exception in other societies.

The relativity of epistemic justification is easy to prove by example. As I write these words, I am justified by my perceptual experience in believing that PQ now sees a red fire-plug on the lawn outside his office window. Since I am now alone in my office, I dare say that no one else, with the possible exception of an omniscient deity, is presently justified in believing that PQ now sees a red fire-plug on the lawn outside his office window. But complications arise once a couple of simple distinctions are made. One is a distinction between being justified in having a belief and justifying a belief. Being justified in having a belief is a state or condition; justifying a belief is an activity. As William P. Alston notes, 'the crucial difference between them is that while to justify a belief is to marshall considerations in its support, in order for me to *be* justified in believing that p it is not necessary that I have *done* anything by way of an argument for p or for my epistemic situation vis-à-vis p'.[5] Those of us who believe that torture is always wrong consider ourselves to be justified in having that belief. But we need not, and for charity's sake probably should not, deny that our opponents are also justified in believing that torture is not always wrong. After all, being justified is a contextual affair. As Jeffrey Stout puts it, being justified in believing something involves 'a relation among a person, a proposition, and an epistemic context'.[6] Epistemic relativism with respect to being justified seems close to being undeniable. But this having been acknowledged, it remains to be seen whether we can marshall arguments and evidence to justify our belief that torture is always wrong either to ourselves or to our opponents. And, of course, since turnabout is fair play, we need to remain open to the possibility that our opponents can justify their belief that torture is not always wrong either to themselves or to us.

This brings us to the distinction between a belief being justified for a person and a belief being justifiable for a person. It is a distinction between actuality and possibility of some sort. There are many mathematical theorems whose proofs I could understand if I studied them, though I have not up to now studied the proofs or had belief in those theorems justified for me some other way such as by the expert testimony of a mathematician. Belief in such theorems is presently not justified for me but is justifiable for me. No doubt there are mathematical proofs known to the experts that I am incapable of understanding. So there are mathematical beliefs that are justifiable by way of proof for others but are not justifiable by way of proof for me. For all I know, there are now or some day will be recondite beliefs in the sciences that are justifiable for others in some way but not justifiable for me in any way. A certain amount of epistemic relativism about justifiability also seems quite plausible. We would not find it particularly disturbing if it were restricted to esoteric domains of culture such as advanced mathematics or the most refined kinds of art appreciation. One can lead a good life that does not include them; they are, from an ethical point of view, optional activities.

But for almost all of us morality is not an optional activity, and this lends practical significance to the question of whether any moral beliefs at all are justifiable to mature human beings as such. We who hold that torture is always wrong might hope that this belief can be justified to a universal audience of all humankind. Those among our opponents who maintain that torture is generally but not always wrong might similarly hope that their belief can be justified by considerations that are decisive for all persons who encounter them. Applied to these two beliefs, epistemic relativism concerning justifiability yields the result that such hopes would be vain. Arguments and evidence sufficient to convince a universal audience that torture is always wrong seem not to be available in the historical record so far, and a pessimistic induction leads to the conclusion that they will not be forthcoming in the future. Of course this might be the result of nothing deeper than a contingent failure of human ingenuity. However it might turn out that, no matter how ingenious human beings prove to be, the judgement that torture is always wrong can be justified only to some individuals in our society and in others.

So relativism presents those of us who hold that torture is always wrong with two issues to worry about. The first is that, even if the judgement that torture is always wrong applies to everyone in our society, it may not apply to everyone in societies other than our own. The second is that, even if the belief that torture is always wrong can be justified to some individuals in both our society and others, it cannot be justified to all members of all societies, to rational animals as such. And torture is only a special case of a more general phenomenon. The relativistic worries are apt to arise whenever there are deep moral disagreements among apparently reasonable people. Abortion is another example that springs to mind.

Can anything be done to overcome relativism about the wrongness of torture? I explore this issue by discussing two arguments, one religious and the other secular, for the conclusion that torture is always wrong.

II A RELIGIOUS RESPONSE

Diverse religious traditions will provide the materials to mobilise a wide variety of considerations in support of the conclusion that torture is always wrong. What is more, there are within single religious traditions the resources to mount several distinct arguments for that conclusion. In order to keep my discussion fairly specific, I am going to consider only one such religious argument. It is an argument I expect to be looked on with sympathetic eyes

by theists who share the Hebrew Bible and are prepared to interpret it rather literally.

In the Hebrew Bible's first creation story we are told that God
said, 'Let us make man in our image, after our likeness.'[7] There
being no impediment to God's will in this matter, presumably
things transpired as God intended, and human beings were made
in the image and likeness of God. So let us consider the following argument:

1. Torture severely damages human beings.
2. All human beings are things made in the image and likeness
   of God.
3. Hence torture severely damages things made in the image and
   likeness of God.
4. Severely damaging things made in the image and likeness of
   God is always wrong.
5. Therefore torture is always wrong.

How does this argument fare as a response to our worries about
relativism?

The first thing to note is that it addresses the worry that the
moral prohibition of torture is exceptionless in some societies but
not in all. If displaying the image and likeness of God is the property whose possession makes the damage torture does wrong,
then the prohibition of torture protects all human beings in all
circumstances, because they all possess that property whenever
they exist. No human being in any society ever lacks the property of having been made in the divine image and likeness, on
this view, and so no human being may be tortured in any circumstances.

The argument is valid. I myself think all its premises are true,
and so I consider it a sound argument. Philosophers debate about
whether certain valid arguments transmit justification from their
premises to their conclusions, but there is no reason to doubt
that this argument would do so if its premises were justified.
Moreover, there are epistemic contexts in which all its premises
are justified for some people, and I think some theists are actually
in such epistemic contexts. So I am persuaded that this argument
can be used to justify its conclusion for some people. And this
might in some circumstances be of practical importance. Imagine

an inquisitor who has been taught that it is morally permissible to torture heretics until they recant and been provided with the consequentialist rationale that such torture is a legitimate means of securing the welfare of heretics in the afterlife. Upon being presented with this argument, the inquisitor might, with justification, undergo a change of mind, resolving henceforth to stick to persuasion and leave the rest to God's mercy.

But, of course, there are also epistemic contexts in which the argument's premises are not all justified to everybody, and many people are in such contexts. Hence the argument does not dispel our second relativistic worry. In particular, there are people who are justified in disbelieving the argument's assumption that all human beings are made in the image and likeness of God because they are justified in believing that there is no such being as God. And there is no reason to think that this assumption can be justified to all such people. Things might, for all we know, have been different. Natural theology might have been a resounding success long ago; we might have discovered a proof for the existence of God of such simplicity and force that no rational person who considered it could gainsay it. We might also have found a similar proof for the truth of the interpretation of the Hebrew Bible needed to support the argument's crucial religious assumption. But in fact we have no such proofs, and the prospects for finding such things are dim indeed. So it seems tolerably clear that the judgement that torture is always wrong cannot be justified to persons as such by this argument because its religious premise cannot be justified to all rational animals.

Although induction from a single case is a risky business, I would be willing to bet that a similar problem will arise for any attempt to use a religious argument to justify the conclusion that torture is always wrong to a universal audience. The argument will contain one or more theological premises. While some people may be justified in believing those premises, there will be no way to justify them to everyone. And so a religious argument seems most unlikely ever to eliminate relativism of justifiability concerning the judgement that torture is always wrong.

But perhaps this is an infirmity peculiar to religious argument. Because of their subject-matter, religious beliefs may be particularly ill-suited for justifiability to a universal audience. Maybe we would do better to rely exclusively on more widely shared secular beliefs in an attempt to justify the proposition that torture is always wrong to persons as such. At any rate, this possibility deserves some consideration.

III A SECULAR RESPONSE

The secular liberalism of the Enlightenment has been getting a bad press lately. A good deal of the criticism has focused on the liberal conception of the self. The litany of charges is by now quite familiar. Liberal selves are cultural constructions of modernity, and this fabrication has been discredited by postmodern deconstruction. Liberal selves are atomistic individuals perfectly contrived to fit into the ideology of competitive capitalism. The vaunted autonomy of the liberal self is an illusion which masks the realities of social and cultural determination. The alleged dignity of the liberal self is a religious mystification that saps the vitality of life and inhibits expression of the will to power. But such notions as individuality, autonomy and human dignity have heretofore played an important role in the liberal project of grounding claims for universal human rights. Rights are often said to be possessed by persons because of their dignity or in order to protect their autonomy. So if autonomy is illusory and dignity mere mystification, such things cannot be what is special about human persons in virtue of which they are bearers of rights, among them a right not to be tortured. This lends urgency to the question of whether universal human rights can be grounded in some other features of human persons, characteristics whose acknowledged reality survives the critique of Enlightenment liberalism. Supporters of Amnesty International should have a special interest in the answer to this question, and so it is fitting that the contributors to the first series of Oxford Amnesty Lectures were asked to address it. In the letter of invitation they were told: 'Our lecturers are being asked to consider the consequences of the deconstruction of the self for the liberal tradition. Does the self as construed by the liberal tradition still exist? If not, whose human rights are we defending?'[8] Behind such questions lies this challenge: find or construct a defensible alternative to the liberal self if it has been discredited and is now defunct.

In his Oxford Amnesty Lecture, Wayne Booth accepts this challenge. He rejects the conception of the self he finds in the writing of John Stuart Mill, particularly *On Liberty*. As Booth reads Mill, the Millian self is valuable primarily or exclusively for what is unique or different about it.[9] But there is not much that is unique about most human beings, and this makes it hard to defend Amnesty's judgement that torture is always wrong. As Booth puts it,

> It's not hard to see why Amnesty's program must be suspect if the victim's worth is to be found only in his or her individual uniqueness. Why should anyone worry if one such atomic isolate is harmed or destroyed, when there are plenty of other examplars left over – except, of course, for those individuals who happen to be really valuable because original? Why worry if a few of these atoms here and there are injured?[10]

According to Booth, there really are no such atomic isolates, and there never have been any.

The alternative conception of the self that he favours is derived from classical rhetoric and modern Western literature and criticism. On this conception, what is essential to the self is found 'in its freedom to pursue a story line, a life plot, a drama carved out of all the possibilities every society provides' (p. 89). Moreover, selves work out their life plots by incorporating into themselves other selves. As Booth puts it,

> our lives – even the drabbest of our lives – are narratable as *plot lines*, but the plots are plotted not just outside us but within us; my father and my mother are in me, encountering one another there; they meet there with my playmates from infancy, my schoolmates, my teachers, my various friends and enemies, my favorite literary characters and their authors, all of whom enter and some of whom remain forever (p. 90).

Metaphorically speaking, then, each self is a society of selves.

For Booth, two values attach to selves that are societies engaged in living out a dramatic story. First, there is a universal value shared by all human lives: 'all lives are inherently irreducibly valuable because the very possibility of enacting the human drama at all is laden with value' (p. 92). Second, there is a value not all human lives have to the same extent because some story lines are better than others, but each of us has possibilities for encountering and incorporating into our selves better selves that improve the narrative. Torture attacks both these values. As Booth sees it, if you decide to deny me (actually an 'us') the right to let my (our) dramatis personae 'determine' my (our) choices, you injure me (us) fully as much as if you (now also, of course, plural) cut off any act of absolute originality, because you see, for me (us), my (our) next steps are all part of a path that is inescapably a manifestation of the uniquely valuable lot of all persons: the plotting of a life story (p. 94).

And in light of his critique of the value of what is unique and different, he hastens to add that 'the value is here more in the freedom of the plotting than in the uniqueness' (p. 95). Of course, this addition is bound to raise doubts whether what Booth esteems about human selves is much different from what was prized in the liberal tradition stemming from Kant. At bottom, Booth values the freedom human selves have to plot their own life stories, narratives that may be improved by incorporating into the societies that selves are other, better selves. Kant valued the autonomy human selves have to legislate morality for themselves and freely to obey such self-legislation. It is not surprising that a literary critic and a moral philosopher should have somewhat different views of why human freedom is valuable. But it seems clear that Booth and Kant are united in valuing the freedom of each and every human being.[11]

Using Booth's literary conception of the self, we can construct an argument for the conclusion that torture is always wrong. It goes as follows:

6. Torture severely damages human beings.
7. All human beings are societies of selves capable of plotting the stories of their own lives.
8. Hence torture severely damages societies of selves capable of plotting the stories of their own lives.
9. Severely damaging societies of selves capable of plotting the stories of their own lives is always wrong.
10. Therefore torture is always wrong.

So here we have a secular argument parallel to the religious argument previously discussed. What are we to make of it?

It seems clear Booth thinks that being a society of selves capable of plotting the story of its own life is the property whose possession makes the damage torture does wrong. He says: 'to freeze me where I am, to cut off my possibility of encountering and imbibing better selves, indeed to impose on my drama the self I become under torture, is the ultimate offense' (p. 93). If so, the argument addresses the worry that the prohibition of torture is exceptionless in some but not all societies, provided that special cases of those who, like the severely retarded, lack the capability to plot and enact narratives are set aside. Normal humans in all societies are, in Booth's view, societies of selves capable of plotting the stories of their own lives, and so torture is the ultimate offence to normal humans in all societies.

This argument too is valid. I do not know whether it is a sound argument because I do not know what literal truth, if any, stands behind the metaphorical claim that human beings are societies of selves. Even if my parents, schoolmates, friends and colleagues enter into me in some sense, they do not feel physical pain when the torturer applies the thumbscrew to me. But I do not pretend to know that there are no literal truths that could be used to unpack the metaphor, and so I will not challenge the truth of any of the premises. I will also grant that the argument would transmit justification from its premises to its conclusion and that there are epistemic contexts in which all its premises are justified for some people. Perhaps Booth himself inhabits such a context. Hence I am prepared to admit that this argument can be used to justify its conclusion for some people.

Again the rub comes when one asks about justifiability to a universal audience. There are epistemic contexts in which the argument's premises are not all justified to everyone, and some people are in such contexts. Thus the argument fails to rid us of the second relativistic worry. In this instance, the premise some people are justified in rejecting is the moral assumption that severely damaging societies of selves capable of plotting the stories of their own lives is always wrong. Those who are justified in believing that torturing the terrorist in order to save the lives of the plane's crew and passengers is morally permissible, when the numbers are large enough, are justified in disbelieving the argument's moral premise.

Is there some argument that could be used to justify that premise to persons as such? Booth says things that suggest he wants to provide such an argument. In discussing the situation in which destroying one social self will save a fair number of others, he tells us that 'seeing the self as a society simply lifts us off the chart of consequentialism entirely' (p. 96). And he goes on to claim that 'the values of the social self are essentially non-consequentialist and non-calculable: they are "infinite", if you will' (p. 96). But when we look for argument to back such claims, we find Booth giving us only rhetorical questions. He concludes his case as follows:

> You can add and subtract lives only if lives are atomic isolates. But how can you add or subtract lives that indeterminately overlap untold other lives? If you can't specify a unit, how can you count? (p. 97)

To the last of these questions, the proper reply must surely be that we know perfectly well how to count. Whatever else may be true of human lives, they are in the first instance the lives of individual biological organisms, the lives of individual animals. The life of the individual human animal is an appropriate unit for counting. If you torture the terrorist, you inflict damage on the life of one human animal, the terrorist, but you save the lives of many human animals, the plane's crew and passengers, that would otherwise be destroyed. If you do not, you spare the life of one human animal from being damaged, but the price you pay is that you allow the lives of many human animals you could have saved to be destroyed. If it is wrong to torture the terrorist in such circumstances, this cannot be because there is a serious question or doubt about how to add or subtract lives. After all, each of the human animals that lives such a life in the case under consideration possesses the property to which Booth attributes value, the capability of freely plotting its own life.

There is one more arrow in Booth's quiver. He tells us that implicit in his account of the social self there is 'an argument that ought to work, if listened to, even with the most self-centered, non-altruistic of would-be torturers' (p. 97). What is this remarkable argument that would give us something to say to the torturer? It goes as follows:

> You – you loyalist torturer – are actually destroying your own self. Since selves overlap – not just metaphorically but literally – it is clear that you are destroying not just the life drama of the tortured one but of your own soul as well, including – and here is where your bosses come in – that part of their selves that results from their having taken in the willingness to torture, and to torture this particular victim (p. 97).

Echoing John Donne, Booth summarises the point that seems to him unmistakable in this way: 'Then do not send to ask whom the torturer is torturing: He is torturing thee' (p. 97).

I think there are two flaws in this argument. The first is that at this point in his discussion Booth has conveniently forgotten that his talk about selves as societies and overlap of selves is metaphorical rather than literal. Earlier in the discussion he had been quite explicit about this, saying 'we have to choose whatever *metaphor* [my emphasis] seems best to rival Mill's bumps and grinds of atomized units – a kind of *society*; a *field* of forces; a *colony*; a *chorus* of not necessarily harmonious voices; a manifold *project*; a *polyglossia* that is as much in us as in the world outside us' (p. 89). It is therefore inconsistent of Booth to claim later on that selves overlap literally and not just metaphorically.

But even if we grant that some literal sense can be given to Booth's talk about overlap of selves, his argument works only on utterly implausible assumptions about the extent to which there is overlap of selves. Perhaps there is something to be said for the Aristotelian idea that one's friend is an other self. We might put this in Booth's terms by saying that each of two friends is a member of the society that constitutes the other. And maybe this idea can sensibly be extended at least to the other people who are major characters in the narrative of one's life. But the bosses usually know better than to insist that anyone torture a friend or even an acquaintance. Often torturer and victim encounter one another as complete strangers. When this occurs, the torturer can set to work with great assurance that he is not a member yet of the society that makes up the victim's self and so is not engaged yet in destroying his own self. Of course the torturer may become a member of that society in due time; torturers have been known to achieve a peculiar sort of intimacy with their victims in some cases. However this only argues that the self-centred torturer ought to be careful to limit the amount of time spent on any one victim. The bosses can respond easily enough by employing more torturers and scheduling each for less time per victim. More generally, it is completely unrealistic to imagine that, in all human encounters in which cruelty is a possibility, there will be enough overlap of selves to justify refraining from action to a self-centred person contemplating cruel behaviour on the grounds that such behaviour is really self-destructive.

It thus seems to me that Booth's arguments fail to justify the questionable moral premise in the argument for the judgement that torture is always wrong. What is more, I know of no argument that is likely to succeed where Booth's arguments fail. So I think prospects are not good for finding an argument that could be used to justify that premise to a universal audience. In the end, then, our sample secular argument and our specimen religious argument are in the same boat: both fail to eliminate relativism with respect to justifiability of the conclusion that torture is always wrong.

There are plenty of other secular arguments for the conclusion that torture is always wrong, and I obviously have no way to prove that none of them could be used to justify that conclusion to persons as such. But I think I have reason enough to doubt that any secular argument is likely to perform this justificatory activity with success. Such arguments typically have premises drawn from some theory. In the case of the particular argument I have been examining, the theory in question is a theory of the self and so might be thought of as a metaphysical theory. In other cases that are easy to imagine, the theory from which premises are taken will be an ethical theory. But, as Robert M. Adams reminds us, 'nothing in the history of modern secular ethical theory gives reason to expect that general agreement on a single comprehensive ethical theory will ever be achieved – or that, if achieved, it would long endure in a climate of free inquiry'.[12] The same goes for the history of modern secular metaphysical theory, literary theory and theories in the humanities generally. It is logically possible that such lack of agreement, even when it is projected indefinitely into the future, is to be explained by something like a perverse tendency in humanists to be quarrelsome. But I think it more probable that the best explanation is that there is no way to justify comprehensive theories in the humanities to human beings as such. So I am convinced that chances are slim indeed that there is any secular argument that can be used to justify the judgement that torture is always wrong to all persons of good will. *A fortiori* I believe there is virtually no chance at all that there is such an argument that would work for the attentive, self-centred would-be torturer. And so it looks as though epistemic relativism with respect to justifiability concerning such propositions as torture is always wrong and abortion is always wrong, as well as some of their contraries, is here to stay. Many of those who are strongly convinced that torture is always wrong or that abortion is always wrong will be unhappy with this conclusion. But is there any alternative to resigning ourselves to living with it?

IV   WAYS OF MAKING PROGRESS: TWO SUGGESTIONS

Richard Rorty speaks for those who are resigned to being unable to refute the torturer or even the clever schoolyard bully. In an autobiographical passage, he says:

> Like a lot of other people who wind up teaching philosophy, I, too, got into the business because, having read some Plato, I thought I could use my budding dialectical talents to *demonstrate* that the bad guys were bad and the good guys good – to do to contemporary bad guys (for example, the bullies who used to beat me up in high school) what Socrates thought he was doing to Thrasymachus, Gorgias, and others. But, some twenty years back, I finally decided that this project was not going to pan out – that 'demonstration' was just not available in this area, that a theoretically sophisticated bully and I would always reach an argumentative standoff.[13]

Like Rorty's theoretically sophisticated bully, the theoretically sophisticated torturer cannot be refuted. Indeed, it seems highly unlikely that there is any argument that would serve to justify the judgement that torture is always wrong to the theoretically sophisticated torturer. Of course this does not mean we are left with nothing to say to the torturer. Following Rorty, we might try to make torture look bad by redescribing it, and this might serve to convert some people who believe that torture is not always wrong. More generally, we might appeal to vivid representations of torture in the arts to get people to appreciate how awful torture is and to persuade them to oppose it.

So, even if there is no single argument that can be used to justify the claim that torture is always wrong to a universal audience, there may be ways of persuading increasing numbers of people, in our society and in others, to believe that it is. My first suggestion is that those of us who believe that torture is always wrong should make use of some of these techniques of persuasion to convince others to share our view. In effect, I am proposing a campaign aimed at making the belief that torture is always wrong a part of the pre-theoretical common morality of our society and, eventually, of all human societies. In this regard, the moral education of our children is particularly important. We should try to get people to bring up their children persuaded that torture is always wrong. To be sure, this is a proposal that calls for delicacy in the implementation. Showing young children photographs of the worst victims of torture is almost certainly inappropriate: though it may produce in them a revulsion from torture, it is also apt to traumatise them. And as children mature, the boundary between moral education and indoctrination must increasingly be respected. It is hard to tell whether a campaign to make the belief that torture is always wrong a part of the common morality of our society has much chance of success. But surprising things have happened. I take it the belief that slavery is always wrong is now part of the common morality of our society. This was not the case as recently as a century and a half ago. There is therefore room for hope of success.

My second suggestion is that we explore another possibility for justifying the judgement that torture is always wrong to persons as such. I have argued that neither my specimen religious argument nor my specimen secular argument will by itself do the trick. Either of them will at most justify that judgement to some but not all rational animals. I have also urged that these conclusions can be generalised. I consider it most unlikely that there is an argument such that it can be used to justify the judgement in question to all persons. But even if I am right about this and there is no such argument, it does not follow that the judgement that torture is always wrong cannot be justified to all persons. This is because it does not follow that it is not the case that, for every person, there is some argument such that the judgement in question is justified to the person by the argument. The order of the quantifiers makes a big difference. In other words, the possibility of something like what John Rawls describes as an overlapping consensus on the proposition that torture is always wrong has not been ruled out by anything I have said so far.[14] We need to ask whether that proposition can be justified to some people by one argument, to others by another, and to all people by some argument or other.

What are the prospects for achieving an overlapping consensus on the proposition that torture is always wrong? I do not know. But it seems to me that the only realistic hope of justifying that proposition to persons as such or to persons in a variety of cultures depends on there being different arguments or, more generally, sets of considerations to do the justifying work for different folk. And I also think the conditions that render this the only realistic hope are likely to endure as long as freedom of inquiry and the kind of cultural diversity I prize persist. As I see it, then, the best shot those of us who believe that torture is always wrong have at bringing it about that this belief can be justified to persons as such (or, more modestly, to all reasonable people of good will) is to do what we can to make the judgement that torture is always wrong the object of an overlapping consensus, first locally, in our own society, and then globally, in all other human societies.

In this endeavour both religious and secular arguments would play essential roles. There are in our society, it seems to me, some people to whom the judgement that torture is always wrong could be justified only by considerations drawn from religious or theological ethics, and there are some people in our society to whom that judgement could be justified only by non-religious considerations or arguments. And when we expand our horizons to encompass the globe, we will want to acknowledge that there are many people in other societies to whom the judgement in question could be justified only by religious considerations rooted in traditions other than the theisms currently dominant here in the West. So the project of achieving overlapping consensus would also need to appeal to diverse religious arguments that can be mounted from within different religions.

It is only by way of making a contribution to an overlapping consensus on the judgement that torture is always wrong that religion could, in my view, help in overcoming relativism with respect to justifiability regarding that proposition. Where the great world religions do not overlap in belief, the disagreements are often if not always between people whose world-views are, as far as we can tell, approximately equal in epistemic justification. The same goes for many disagreements between adherents of religious world-views and proponents of some of the major secular alternatives. It is not realistic to expect overlapping consensus on an extensive body of theological, metaphysical or ethical theory. For the foreseeable future, humanistic theory will be an area in which there is no prospect, with respect to any particular theory, of there being, for each inquirer, some argument such that the argument can be used to justify the theory to the inquirer. Nor do I see much chance for overlapping consensus on such controverted moral claims as that abortion is always wrong or various of its contraries. Hence I am fairly confident that relativism with respect to being justified and with respect to justifiability will long continue to enjoy very wide scope in humanistic disciplines and in our moral lives. But I do entertain the modest hope that the domain of such relativism can be reduced somewhat by constructing, on a piecemeal basis, overlapping consensus on some fairly specific moral judgements about which there is presently disagreement. I would regard it as moral progress if the proposition that torture is always wrong were one such judgement. I think the chances of attaining overlapping consensus on this judgement are good enough to make the project of trying to achieve it worth engaging in.

Notes

1. 'Preface to the Oxford Amnesty Lectures', *Freedom and Interpretation: The Oxford Amnesty Lectures 1992*, Barbara Johnson (ed.) (New York: Basic Books/HarperCollins, 1993), pp. vii–viii.
2. Gene Outka and John P. Reeder, Jr, 'Introduction', *Prospects for a Common Morality*, Outka and Reeder (eds) (Princeton, NJ; Princeton University Press, 1993), pp. 3, 4.
3. Robert Merrihew Adams, 'Religious Ethics in a Pluralistic Society', *Prospects for a Common Morality*, Gene Outka and John P. Reeder, Jr (eds) (Princeton, NJ: Princeton University Press, 1993), p. 93.
4. Jeffrey Stout, *Ethics After Babel* (Boston, Mass.: Beacon Press, 1988), pp. 222–3.
5. William P. Alston, *Perceiving God* (Ithaca, NY, and London: Cornell University Press, 1991), p. 71.
6. Jeffrey Stout, 'On Having a Morality in Common', *Prospects for a Common Morality*, Gene Outka and John P. Reeder, Jr (eds) (Princeton, NJ: Princeton University Press, 1993), p. 220.
7. Genesis 1: 26.
8. Barbara Johnson, 'Introduction', *Freedom and Interpretation: The Oxford Amnesty Lectures 1992*, Johnson (ed.) (New York: Basic Books/HarperCollins, 1993), p. 2.
9. For a more generous and, I think, more accurate interpretation of Mill, see Charles Taylor, 'The Politics of Recognition', *Multiculturalism and 'The Politics of Recognition'*, Amy Gutmann (ed.) (Princeton, NJ: Princeton University Press, 1992), pp. 30–1.
10. Wayne C. Booth, 'Individualism and the Mystery of the Social Self, or, Does Amnesty Have a Leg to Stand On?', *Freedom and Interpretation:*

The Oxford Amnesty Lectures 1992, Barbara Johnson (ed.) (New York: Basic Books/HarperCollins, 1993), p. 87. Hereafter page references to this essay will be made parenthetically in the body of my text.

11. It also seems clear that Booth's view will encounter familiar difficulties when it comes to attributing value to all human beings. Severely retarded humans cannot do much by way of enacting dramatic stories, but surely the prohibition of torture protects them too. I will ignore this difficulty.

12. Adams, 'Religious Ethics', p. 97.

13. Richard Rorty, 'Truth and Freedom: A Reply to Thomas McCarthy', *Prospects for a Common Morality*, Gene Outka and John P. Reeder, Jr (eds) (Princeton, NJ: Princeton University Press, 1993), p. 282. This essay is reprinted from *Critical Inquiry*, 1990, vol. 16, pp. 633–43.

14. See, for example, John Rawls, 'Justice as Fairness: Political not Metaphysical', *Philosophy and Public Affairs*, 1985, vol. 14, pp. 223–51, for discussion of the prospects for an overlapping consensus about some aspects of justice in a pluralistic and democratic society. The hope is that groups which disagree in religious, metaphysical and other theoretical beliefs can share a political conception of justice, each group finding within its distinctive theoretical perspective grounds for endorsing the shared conception.

8

Reply: Ethical Universality and Ethical Relativism

JOSEPH RUNZO

In the epilogue of *Crime and Punishment*, Raskolnikov has a dream of a terrible new plague which affects the mind and will:

> Each thought that he alone had the truth ... They did not know how to judge and could not agree what to consider evil and what good; they did not know whom to blame, whom to justify ... They gathered together in armies against one another, but even on the march the armies would begin attacking each other, stabbing and cutting, biting and devouring each other ... The most ordinary trades were abandoned, because everyone proposed his own ideas, his own improvements, and they could not agree. Men met in groups, agreed on something, swore to keep together, but at once began on something quite different from what they had proposed. They accused one another, fought and killed each other ... All men and all things were involved in destruction.[1]

Civilised society deconstructs when it loses a perceived universality in values, especially ethical values. For civilisation depends on a vision both of the common good and of the good in common. Yet as the nineteenth century began to evince, and the twentieth century has come to embody, the civilising cohesiveness of a perceived ethical universality is increasingly subject to the stress of relativism.

The roots of relativism – anti-authoritarianism both secular and religious, the empowerment of traditionally disenfranchised groups, awareness and appreciation of human diversity, and in general an increasing tolerance – are forces to be lauded, not lamented.

How then can the plethora of relative human values be accounted
for without vitiating the universality of fundamental values inherent in the human condition? Specifically, how can the relative
and the universal be reconciled in ethics? I shall argue that some
ethical principles *are* universal, though morality is relative.

I

Religious tolerance of the dietary laws of others, tolerance of the
marital arrangements of variant cultures, tolerance of sexual differences, of gender differences, and so on, provides the underpinnings for relativism in ethics. Ethics is often about the good.
But it is also about very ugly things. And morally repugnant acts
raise particular problems for attempts to accommodate the relativistic element in morality. Consider rape, child abuse and torture. Here are strong candidates for universal moral prohibitions.
Tolerance is all well and good, but will not a relativistic tolerance lead to condoning the morally grotesque?

Torture is one of the most difficult cases for a relativist ethics.
Though the perpetrators of, for example, rape and child abuse
might think that their self-interest outweighs the interests of the
sufferer, it is hard to see how such a self-centred perspective will
stand up to moral scrutiny. Surely ethical egoism is merely self-
interested prudence, and not a normative moral position at all.
Surely rape and child abuse can never be morally justified. But
what about torture?

Consider the following scenario: a simple but well-meaning
minority resident of a major city knows when and where a gang
of political terrorists from the same minority plans to detonate a
bomb in a city centre high-rise, threatening thousands of lives.
The simpleton is not a member of the gang, but believes the gang's
assurances that no one will be harmed. Moreover, the simpleton's own life was saved by the gang, and the simpleton believes
in reciprocal loyalty to those who help others. The simpleton won't
talk to the police except to admit to knowing the gang's plans. Is
it morally permissible for the police to use torture if necessary to
extract the information needed to save thousands of lives?

Philip Quinn addresses the question of the morality of torture
in 'Relativism about Torture: Religious and Secular Responses'.
He argues that the *prima facie* duty not to torture is never over-

ridden, though this duty cannot be justified – at least currently – to all people. The question he raises is 'How can those of us who believe torture is always wrong respond to the threat of relativism?' I agree with Quinn about the universality of the moral wrongness of torture. But the 'threat of relativism' is ambiguous. It suggests a false dichotomy between ethical relativism and the universality of the moral prohibition on torture. Morality can be relative, yet torture universally wrong.

Claims to justify torture in certain circumstances are typically based on an appeal either to a greater good (saving many lives) or to a purported higher good (preservation of the group, the state, the ideology). The misuse of just such appeals to justify particular acts shows the bankruptcy of act-utilitarianism. More fundamentally, the problem with torture cannot be in the results produced by the individual act of torture, or in the particular reasons why it is done. Like murder, the problem with torture is torture itself. Trying to justify torture is analogous to employing the 'extraordinary man theory' that Raskolnikov propounds in *Crime and Punishment*.

Unlike the ordinary person, the 'extraordinary man' has the right to commit crimes if

> it is essential for the practical fulfillment of his idea (sometimes, perhaps, of benefit to the whole of humanity) . . . I maintain that if the discoveries of Kepler and Newton could not have been made known except by sacrificing the lives of one, a dozen, a hundred, or more men, Newton would have had the right, would indeed have been in duty bound . . . to *eliminate* the dozen or the hundred men for the sake of making his discoveries known to the whole of humanity . . . legislators and leaders of men, such as Lycurgus, Solon, Mahomet, Napoleon, and so on . . . did not stop short at bloodshed either, if that bloodshed were of use to their cause.[2]

In Dostoevsky's novel, we see the problem with the 'extraordinary man' theory when Raskolnikov uses it to justify his murder of the pawnbroker:

> on one side we have a stupid, senseless, worthless, spiteful, alien, horrid old woman, not simply useless but doing actual mischief . . . a hundred thousand good deeds could be done and

helped, on that old woman's money which will be buried in a
monastery! For one life thousands would be saved from corruption and decay. One death. And a hundred lives in exchange
– it's simply arithmetic.[3]

The reader is appropriately repulsed by both the morally repugnant murder of the pawnbroker and her sister, and the morally
repugnant theory. There *is* no reason which could justify murder. The moral prohibition against murder is universal. In this
respect torture is like murder.

Consider again the scenario of the simpleton and the terrorists.
Suppose the simpleton wasn't well-meaning but 'spiteful, horrid,
not simply useless but doing actual mischief'. Would this increase
the permissibility of torturing him to discover the terrorists' plans?
Absolutely not. The moral status of the simpleton doesn't have
anything to do with the moral status of the countenanced torture. Thus, David Little does not show why torture is wrong when
he argues against 'recreational or intimidational torture of children and other defenseless innocents' on the grounds that 'severe suffering for no good reason' is wrong.[4] Of course, inflicting
any kind of pain – for example, even the psychological pain caused
by lying – is wrong if done for *no* good reason. The hard cases
are when it seems as if there *is* a good reason to carry out torture. And the point about torture is *there could not be a good reason for torture*. This is the point that Quinn sees.

But it can be objected that if morality is relative, then the moral
prohibition on torture cannot be universal. If dietary laws, or
prohibitions on sexual preference, or marital alternatives within
one morality do not apply to another, then the prohibition on
torture within one moral code cannot be applied to others. Now,
in *Crime and Punishment*, Dostoevsky effectually suggests a turn
to religion to 'know how to judge and . . . agree what to consider
evil and what good'. Would an appeal to religion provide a justification of the universal moral wrongness of torture which could
overcome these relativistic forces?

II

Religion *was* once thought to be a bulwark against moral relativism. But with the secularisation of society and the consequent
division of morality into 'public' and 'private' (the latter the re-

ligious) spheres, and the acceptance of religious pluralism both within society and between societies, religion is now one more factor in the relativisation of societal norms. Even within a specific religious tradition, moral imperatives vary from cultural setting to cultural setting as well as varying over time. Some forms of African Christianity incorporate polygamy; Western Christianity condemns it. In the Hebrew scriptures, slavery is condoned, and in the Pauline epistles it is accepted; in contemporary Western Christianity it is condemned. Hence the notion of an 'appeal to religion' to justify universal moral principles is too general. At best, an appeal could be made to a particular form, or strand, of a religious tradition as practised in a specific time and place.

Furthermore, even if the relativising effect of different religious points of view could be neutralised, or the restrictions of a particular form of religion were at least acknowledged, this leaves several problems. Consider monotheism. Kant argues that one should trust one's sense of what is moral *before* trusting that a purported revelation from God is indeed a revelation from God. He argues that (1) it is impossible to have sufficient epistemic warrant for claims of revelation from the divine and (2) it is possible for every rational being to be epistemically warranted in the truth-claims of 'rational religion', where in 'rational religion' one first knows what one's moral obligations are, and then infers that those obligations are divine commands.[5] Elsewhere I have argued that Kant is mistaken about the first proposition, since theistic beliefs can be properly basic beliefs, and so not subject to the kinds of doubts they would be subject to if based on evidence.[6] But I think that this still leaves basic theistic belief on the *same* epistemic footing as basic moral belief, not epistemically *more* reliable than basic moral beliefs. So Kant is right in so far as religious belief does not provide a *more* epistemically reliable foundation on which to base moral belief.

Moreover, Kant is also right in so far as moral beliefs should sometimes properly override religious belief. We see the curious way in which a sympathetic view of religious motives can distort moral perception in the historian Henry Kamen's analysis of the use of torture during the Spanish Inquisition. After quoting several descriptions of torture from the period, he observes:

While these examples give us some insight into the agony of victims who underwent torture, it should be remembered that the hundreds of cases of people who overcame it demonstrate the relative mildness of inquisitorial procedure. A comparison with the deliberate cruelty and mutilation practised in ordinary secular courts of the time shows the Inquisition in a more favourable light than its detractors have cared to admit . . . the tribunal as a whole had no interest in cruelty and . . . attempted at all times to temper justice with merciful treatment.[7]

Apparently, because the inquisitors' intentions were good (that is, religious and did not involve cruelty for cruelty's sake) and the level of torture was less than that practised in civil courts, the use of torture was 'just'. But what has gone wrong here is not *why* people were tortured, as if there could be mitigating motives, but that people were tortured at all. There is no such thing as an 'acceptable' level of torture. And religious motives just make the use of torture all the more appalling.

Let us turn to a final problem with any attempt to base a universal prohibition on torture on religious considerations. Consider the Divine Command Theory of ethics.[8] William Frankena argues that:

> when one accepts a definition of any term that can be called ethical, one has already in effect accepted an ethical standard. For example, when one agrees to take 'right' to mean 'commanded by God,' and at the same time to use it as a key term in one's speech, thought, and action, this is tantamount to accepting the moral principle 'We ought to do what God commands' as a guide in life.
>
> . . . when a theological definition is offered us, we may always ask why we should adopt this definition, and to answer us the theologian in question must provide us with a justification of the corresponding moral principle. And the point is that he cannot claim that either it or the definition follows logically from any religious or theological belief (which is not itself a disguised ethical judgment).[9]

Put in Wittgensteinian terms, this is to say that once one accepts a religious definition of morality one has already accepted the relevant religious 'form of life'. Consequently, theological considerations cannot provide a convincing argument for those who are not committed to that religious form of life.

This is a point which Quinn skilfully articulates in 'Relativism about Torture'. He constructs sound arguments from religious premises, as well as sound arguments from secular moral premises, to the conclusion that torture is always wrong. But as he points out, though the arguments are sound, they will not justify the belief that torture is wrong to those who cannot accept the respective religious or secular premises.

The basic problem is that neither a normative ethical theory, nor meta-ethical definitions of object language moral terms like 'good' and 'right', could provide a universal justification for the moral prohibition on torture. As Quinn acknowledges, justification – both being justified and regarding justifiability – is contextual and subject to epistemological relativism.[10] To take one example, even if God exists, and even if some version of the Divine Command Theory of ethics accurately captures the relation of God in Godself to the world, vast numbers of people – for example, most of the world's 300 million Buddhists – are epistemically justified in not believing that God exists. So they are epistemically justified in disbelieving any argument for the prohibition of torture which is based on theological premises involving the Divine Command Theory.

Despite this conclusion, I think Quinn rightly sets out the task for those who believe that torture is always wrong: a prohibition on ever employing torture should be made part of the 'pre-theoretical common morality of society'. In US society this has been done for the prohibition on slavery. Could it similarly be done for torture, for all societies? The strongest case for a universal prohibition on torture could be made if we could identify a basis for this prohibition which supervenes normative moral codes. That is, could there be there a universal meta-ethical consideration that entails or at least supports a universal prohibition on torture?

IV

The hardest case to deal with in trying to promote a universal prohibition on torture would be the acceptance of cognitive relativism – the notion that truth (and value) are relative to the worldview of a society.[11] Since I have done so elsewhere, I will not argue for cognitive relativism here, except to indicate how its acceptance could be compatible with the preservation of ethical universals.

The rise of the notion of the inextricable historicity of everything human, the Quinian attack on the analytic/synthetic distinction, and the even more recent rise in the acceptance of a pluralistic society, lend support to relativistic conceptions, including relativistic conceptions of ethics. Importantly, developments in psychoanalytic theory break down the formerly rigid distinction between reason – the absolute – and emotion – the variant and relative. Indeed, psychological determinism may be far more intransigent than cultural determinism. If nothing else, certain types of formerly mysterious behaviour that once appeared to be wilful and morally wrong now appear to be genetically based. For instance, 49 per cent of children with one schizophrenic parent and 66 per cent of children of two schizophrenic parents are themselves either schizophrenic or schizoid. Genetically, a person may have a disposition to schizophrenia, becoming schizophrenic as a result of environmental factors, including parental behaviour. For there are not only public structures of sin in which we are enmeshed,[12] but private psychological structures of sin. For even the most elemental understanding of the insights of psychoanalytic theory gives new meaning not only to St Paul's lamentation, 'I do what I would not do, and do not do what I would do', but to the profound wisdom of the Hebraic notion that the iniquity of parents is 'visited on the children and the children's children, to the third and the fourth generation' (Exodus 34: 7, RSV). What sometimes formerly appeared to be morally culpable actions which people chose as fully rational beings now appear to have an important emotional and relativistic component.

All these factors taken together have tended to support ethical relativism. This can be expressed as radical relativism – the view that truth-claims, and values, and so judgements of truth and value, do not apply outside the society within which they are formulated.[13] In this vein, Richard Rorty regards morality as convention and concludes that even torture is not essentially wrong,[14] and Don Cupitt says

> *all* frames – whether we are talking about religion, morality, scientific theory, philosophy, logic or whatever – *all* frames are historical improvisations ... We make truth and we make values ... [Morality can now] be seen as our own continual creative production of new values.[15]

However, as Jeffrey Stout observes, this sort of relativism does not make disagreements about truth *intelligible*; it just erases, or attempts to erase, such disagreements.[16] But another sort of relativism – what I shall call cognitive and value relativism – does not fall to this sort of objection.

On cognitive and value relativism, truth and value are relative to a world-view. But to be viable, cognitive and value relativism must allow that world-views overlap. It would be self-stultifying to treat the ethical discourse of different world-views as mutually conceptually isolated. For the ethical person wants to hold the 'correct view' about the nature of morality. But as soon as someone holds that their view is 'correct', they are assuming some standard of judgement that others with other views could hold. The assumption is always that rational people who do not currently agree with one *could* come to agree with one's ethical views. Otherwise, one's ethical judgements would carry no public weight. And of course, in order for a judgement about another ethical view to be reasonable, or for there to be an actual dispute between different ethical views, the conceptual resources of the one view must overlap with a significant portion of the conceptual resources of the other view. Without this overlap of conceptual resources, there can be no conceptual identity across the world-views, and so there would not be reference to the *same* topic.[17]

Next, to see how truth could be relative, yet some truths universal, let us consider the truth-claims of geometry. Triangles are planar figures with three sides and three angles. Triangles have 180 interior degrees – in Euclidean geometry. But in Reimannian geometry they have more than 180 degrees. If you want to refer to triangles, you must refer to planar figures with three sides and three angles. This defines the subject-matter and is a universal truth. But depending on the system of geometry one wants to employ, triangles can be correctly described either as having exactly 180, or as having more than 180, interior degrees. (But notice, not both at once.) That is to say, it is *true within* Euclidian geometry that triangles have exactly 180 interior degrees, and it is *true within* Reimannian geometry that triangles may have less or more than 180 interior degrees.

There is a parallel in ethics. Moral values and moral truth-claims are relative to a particular morality – and more broadly relative to a socially constructed world-view. But variety presupposes commonality. And just as one does not have a scientific theory unless one takes a scientific point of view, nor a theology unless one takes a theistic point of view, one does not have a morality unless one takes the moral point of view. The point of commonality, and what is a universal moral value and entails universal moral truths, is the moral point of view.

V

What does it mean to take the moral point of view? Whatever else the moral point of view consists of, we can at least identify four characteristics: (1) taking others into account in one's actions *because* one respects them as persons; (2) the *willingness* to take into account how one's actions affect others by taking into account the good of everyone equally; (3) abiding by the principle of universalisability – that is, the willingness to treat one's own actions as morally laudable or permissible only if similar acts of others in comparable circumstances would be equally laudable or permissible, and to treat the actions of others as morally impermissible only if similar acts of one's own would be equally morally culpable; and (4) the willingness to be committed to some set of normative moral principles.[18]

Among the characteristics (1) to (4), (1) – taking others into account because one respects them as persons – is the salient and perhaps the seminal feature of taking the moral point of view. I will focus on (1) as a means of further elucidating the notion of the moral point of view.

Why one ought to take others into account because one respects them as persons is not significant for praxis; *that* one ought to so act is preeminently significant. For taking the moral point of view is an *ultima facie* obligation. Where does this obligation come from? This obligation is like the Kantian directive to 'always treat others as ends in themselves and not merely as means to an end'. But I am not suggesting that this obligation can be undergirded by a Kantian argument to the effect that this follows as an action guide if one wants to be happy and *rational*.

Moreover, I do not think that respect for others as persons amounts to the possession of moral *rights*. It seems to me that there are objections on both ethnocentric and egocentric grounds to conceiving of talk about rights as the most essential element of morality. To take the ethnocentric objection, the notion of inalienable moral rights is a Western European conception based on a conception of humans as a community of rational, autonomous individuals with competing interests which need to be adjudicated. In contrast, in Chinese society which has a Confucian basis for morality, the elemental moral notion isn't one of rights, but rather of one's *role* in society, a matter of obligations to the society and so to others. It is not that rights should not be an important moral category, or might not be among the best moral categories for articulating some moralities, but that the notion of rights does not supersede other moral notions like that of an obligation or role.

Rights talk is also egocentric, and if it is taken as *the* primary moral category, then it is egoistic. For a salient emphasis on one's rights presents a self-interested and self-centred conception of the self, and of society as a group of individuals each protecting their own self-interest, and each a victim of the greed of others. This is not to say that self-interest is immoral, just that it is not *the* essential generative principle of morality.

As Margaret Farley argues in 'Feminism and Universal Morality', while the defence of autonomy is important to ethics, 'relationality' is also important: 'the capacity for relationship is as significant a characteristic of human persons as the capacity for self-determination'.[19] Relationality is an inherent and defining characteristic of persons. As such, relationality is an essential generative principle of morality.

Relationality is encapsulated in (1): taking others into account in one's actions *because* one respects them as persons. This fundamental characteristic of the moral point of view is, in turn, encapsulated in the Golden Rule. John Hick argues persuasively,[20] I think, that this imperative to do unto others as you would have them do unto you is a universal moral principle found in all the world's great religious traditions, whether one considers the writings of the Confucian teacher Mencius, the Jain *Kritanga* Sutra, the Taoist *Thai Shang*, the Islamic *Hadith*, the *Talmud*, or the book of *Luke* (6: 31). This universality underlies the different moralities of the great religious traditions.

The fundamental characteristic of relationality of the moral point of view is, as I said, largely captured in the Kantian ideal of a kingdom of ends and the Kantian principle to always treat people as ends in themselves, and never as mere means to an end. Perhaps it is best captured, though, in Martin Buber's description of the 'I–thou' perspective: 'When I confront a human being as my

You and speak the basic word I–You to him, then he is no thing among things nor does he consist of things.'[21] Relating to persons is different in kind from treating something as an 'it', and as Buber insists, without treating things as 'it's' 'a human being cannot live. But whoever lives only with that is not human'.[22] For as Buber puts it:

> What has become an It is then taken as an It, experienced and used as an It, employed along with other things for the project of finding one's way in the world, and eventually for the project of 'conquering' the world.[23]

True, some people do treat others as only means to their own ends, as things to be manipulated, living a life diametrically opposed to the Golden Rule. Nero, the Roman emperor who killed his mother and poisoned his brother, comes to mind. If they are rational, perhaps such inhumane people are justified in not believing that one should so act as to respect others as persons. But then they are not part of the moral conversation, and not only cannot the *ultima facie* obligation of taking the moral point of view be justified to them, but their egocentric point of view is irrelevant to assessing the ultimacy of the obligation to be moral.

What then justifies this conclusion that one has an obligation to take others into account in one's actions *because* one respects them as persons? While most of ethics is not a matter of intuition, I think this *is* a matter of intuition. That is, I do not believe that an argument can be given for the obligatoriness of the moral point of view. I will return to this shortly. For whatever the basis upon which the moral point of view is accepted, the immediate question is how the moral point of view might justify the principle that torture is always wrong.

VI

The reason torture is always wrong is that torture inherently treats the person being tortured as an 'it'; torture is diametrically opposed to treating a person as a 'thou'. For torture can never be used as a means for treating persons as an end in themselves. By its very nature torture is done to someone for some *other* end, using the person as a means to one's own ends. Put in terms of the Golden Rule, no one except the masochistic would want torture done to them in turn, and even the masochistic would not want to be tortured for the sake of the ends of another. In short, torture is not wrong just because it violates some principle within morality. Rather, torture is wrong because it violates the moral point of view itself.

This parallels the reason why rape and child abuse are wrong. For they too are inherently opposed to treating a person as a 'thou', treating them for their own sake as ends in themselves. No self-aware rational person would want to be forced to have sex; no self-aware rational person would want to be abused as a child. That is, the moral point of view, whatever the concomitant normative moral theory, necessarily universally precludes torture (and rape and child abuse).

This can also be put in terms of two other features of the moral point of view: (2) taking the good of everyone equally into account and (3) accepting the universalisability of one's actions. Alan Donagan, in explicating Kant's ethics, says:

> No rational being may be *simply* a means to benefiting another, but every rational being is required, so far as it is in his or her power, to be a means for the good of others. Yet the benefits anyone confers on anyone else must be in a system of social relations in which those who confer them are ends equally with those on whom they are conferred.[24]

As Donagan notes, a clear case in which those who confer benefits are *not* equal with those upon whom they are conferred is slavery. Torture is always wrong because, like slavery, it is an extreme case of this principle that those 'conferring benefits' are not equal with those receiving the 'benefits'.

Moreover, we have a stronger obligation to try to take the moral point of view than to try to do good. Since torture (like rape and child abuse) is inherently opposed to taking the moral point of view, there is no good, either for oneself, or for society, or for some ideology, which would somehow 'outweigh' this evil. In this respect, the prohibition on torture serves as a negative criterion of what *does not count* as taking the moral point of view.

Now, David Little suggests, regarding the prohibition on torture, that to describe intuitions about prohibitions against torture as justified because they are instrumental toward some goal like preserving the species or maximizing pleasure or achieving some other idea of the good puts the cart before the horse. . . . On the contrary, ends, ideas of the good, and the like are themselves evaluated as to whether or not they condone violations of such a prohibition and whether or not they weaken commitment to it.[25]

However, the prohibition on torture (and rape and child abuse) is not simply part of the *via negativa* to the moral point of view. Rather, much like saying that triangles are not three-dimensional objects, or that mathematical addition is not about the manipulation of physical objects, is part of what the ideas of triangularity and addition mean, saying that torture is wrong is part of what it means to take the moral point of view.

So what then provides epistemic warrant for holding that the moral point of view entails taking others into account in one's actions because one respects them as persons? As I said above, I think that the recognition of the moral point of view is a matter of intuition.[26] And I think that humans have a disposition to recognise the moral point of view. However, one cannot recognise anything without the relevant conceptual resources. Therefore, one must develop a commitment to a rudimentary world-view, that is, reach the age of reason and become a moral agent (normally within a society of moral persons) such that the disposition to acquire the conceptual resources for the moral point of view can be actualised. Finally, one must make a faith commitment to take the moral point of view.

The conviction that one should act so as to respect others as persons, while it might be supported by reasons, is itself a basic belief, and in the right epistemic circumstances, a properly basic belief. That is, it is not based on other beliefs as reasons. Hence, belief in the moral point of view is, in this regard, like belief in God. Just as theistic experiences are made possible within a theistic world-view, the commitment of faith in the moral point of view makes possible an experience of acting from the moral point of view, which in turn produces further basic beliefs regarding the moral point of view. Consequently, one does not need evidence or proof for the obligation to take the moral point of view because, as a basic belief, there need not be any reasons.[27]

The situation is different with the prohibition on torture. I agree with Quinn that a set of overlapping arguments might be needed to support the prohibition on torture. If I am right about the connection between the moral point of view and the prohibition on torture, then various moral arguments, religious as well as secular, might be used to support this connection. Thus, there might be overlapping but different world-views which provide different supporting conceptions of why one should never employ torture if one is to act in a way that respects others as persons. Indeed, we would expect variant arguments to support the prohibition on torture even *within* any secular or religious tradition.

VI

How, then, does religion, or rather the object of religion – Ultimate Reality – relate to morality? As Buber says:

> The purpose of setting oneself apart is to experience and use, and the purpose of that is living – which means dying one long human life long.
> The purpose of relation is the relation itself – touching the You. For as soon as we touch a You we are touched by a breath of external life . . . the lines of relationships intersect in the Eternal You.[28]

One way to put this is to say that personhood, or personal relations, are part of the fundamental structure of the universe. And one reason to say this is that there is a personal being who is the Ultimate Reality. For then we ought to take the moral point of view because this reflects the image of God. Many will not be part of this conversation because they do not share this theistic metaphysics. This just means that as a justification for taking the moral point of view, or as a justification for the prohibition on torture, theistic considerations will not succeed in the public forum, except perhaps in a theocratic society. At best, theistic considerations would support the agreed-upon conclusions of a secular society. But that is all right. What matters for the ethical life is *taking* the moral point of view, not the underlying metaphysics one has.

Similarly, what will matter in the long run is that the prohibition on torture become part of the pre-theoretical common morality of society. What matters is that abstaining from torture, like abstaining from rape or child abuse, and like taking the moral point of view itself, is an *ultima facie* obligation. Morality is relative, yet the wrongness of torture is universal. For, most fundamentally, the obligation always to act in a way that respects others *because* they are persons is universal.

Notes

1. Fyodor Dostoevsky, *Crime and Punishment* (New York: Bantam, 1982), p. 469.
2. Dostoevsky, *Crime and Punishment*, p. 226.
3. Dostoevsky, *Crime and Punishment*, p. 58.
4. David Little, 'The Nature and Basis of Human Rights', in Gene Outka and John P. Reeder, Jr (eds), *Prospects for a Common Morality* (Princeton, NJ: Princeton University Press, 1993), p. 83.
5. Immanuel Kant, *Religion within the Limits of Reason Alone*, trans. Theodore M. Greene and Hoyt H. Hudson (New York: Harper & Row, 1960), pp. 142–3.
6. Joseph Runzo, 'Kant on Reason and Justified Belief in God', in *World Views and Perceiving God* (London: Macmillan; New York: St Martin's Press, 1993), pp. 97–114, reprinted from Philip J. Rossi and Michael Wreen (eds), *Kant's Philosophy of Religion Reconsidered* (Bloomington, Ind.: Indiana University Press, 1991), pp. 22–39.
7. Henry Kamen, *The Spanish Inquisition* (New York: New American Library, 1965), pp. 177–8.
8. For a sophisticated and subtle formulation of the Divine Command Theory, see Robert M. Adams's presentation of a 'modified divine command theory' in *The Virtue of Faith and Other Essays in Philosophical Theology* (Oxford: Oxford University Press, 1987), chs 7 and 9. Richard Mouw provides an insightful analysis of the manner in which divine command theory can be responsive to contemporary ethical issues in *The God Who Commands* (South Bend, Ind.: Notre Dame Press, 1990).
9. William K. Frankena, 'Is Morality Logically Dependent on Religion?', in Gene Outka and John P. Reeder, Jr (eds) *Religion and Morality* (Garden City, NY: Anchor Press/Doubleday, 1973), pp. 303–4.
10. Philip Quinn, 'Relativism about Torture: Religious and Secular Responses', this volume, pp. 155–6. Jeffrey Stout makes this same point in 'On Having a Morality in Common', in *Prospects for a Common Morality*, p. 220.
11. I define and defend cognitive relativism and value relativism in *Reason, Relativism and God*, (London: Macmillan 1986).
12. See John Langan, 'Personal Responsibility and the Common Good in John Paul II', in Joseph Runzo (ed.), *Ethics, Religion, and the Good*

Society: New Directions in a Pluralistic World (Louisville, Ky: Westminster/John Knox Press, 1992), pp. 132–47.

13. This could be formulated as either subjectivism or as cognitive relativism with the corollary of incommensurability between world-views. I argue against subjectivism in *Reason, Relativism and God*, ch. 2.

14. Little, 'The Nature and Basis of Human Rights', in *Prospects for a Common Morality*, p. 73.

15. Don Cupitt, *The New Christian Ethics* (London: SCM Press, 1988), pp. 3–4 and 126.

16. Stout, 'On Having a Morality in Common', in *Prospects for a Common Morality*, p. 227.

17. Dialogue between two world-views is possible as long as the possessor of each finds the relevant concepts of the other view intelligible, but not necessarily identical to her or his own.

18. Cf. Runzo, 'Ethics and the Challenge of Theological Non-Realism', in *Ethics, Religion, and the Good Society: New Directions in a Pluralistic World*, p. 90, n. 45.

19. Margaret Farley, 'Feminism and Universal Morality', in *Prospects for a Common Morality*, p. 182.

20. John Hick, 'The Universality of the Golden Rule', in *Ethics, Religion, and the Good Society*, p. 158.

21. Martin Buber, *I and Thou*, trans. Walter Kaufmann (New York: Scribner's, 1970), p. 59.

22. Ibid., p. 85.

23. Ibid., p. 91.

24. Alan Donagan, 'Common Morality and Kant's Enlightenment Project', in *Prospects for a Common Morality*, pp. 65–6.

25. David Little, 'The Nature and Basis of Human Rights', in *Prospects for a Common Morality*, p. 82.

26. By intuition I mean what G. E. Moore meant in *Principia Ethica* (Cambridge: Cambridge University Press, 1965), p. x: 'When I call ... propositions 'Intuitions', I mean *merely* to assert that they are incapable of proof; I imply nothing whatever as to the manner or origin of our cognition of them.'

27. I argue for the parallel idea that theistic beliefs can be basic beliefs in *World Views and Perceiving God* , ch. 6, pp. 115–41.

28. Buber, *I and Thou*, pp. 113 and 123.

Part V
Buddhism and Ethics

9

Ethics Post-Zen

JOHN V. CANFIELD*

In North America the transplanted Ch'an or Zen sect of Buddhism flourished largely – but certainly not wholly – under the influence of Japanese antecedents. The inevitable conflict between those and North American customs and attitudes placed a strain on Zen's Western practitioners. For example the Samurai boot-camp aura of the awesome Zen *sesshin*, or silent retreat, alienated some North Americans used to easier-going ways. Again, an 'I'm from Missouri' attitude here threatened certain doctrinaire, traditional Zen beliefs.

In response to those and other pressures, Western Zen began, in some instances, to evolve away from its Japanese prototype. In one case, well-known in Zen circles, and publicised in the recent book *Meetings with Remarkable Women*, an American Zen teacher, Toni Packer, has even renounced Buddhism and undertaken a practice that, while it has roots in Zen, is no longer Buddhistic. It is that *sort* of practice I want to consider in this paper. Since it has no name I will refer to it as the post-Zen position.

I should emphasise, however, that the 'post-Zen' I am interested in is a certain logically possible development out of Zen, whether or not any particular actual practice, such as the one just referred to, exemplifies it. My aim here belongs to philosophical anthropology (to adopt the name). I want to describe the salient features of that possible religious movement, and show how and why it departs from its Zen roots. Once its content is settled I shall discuss its connections with issues that fall under the heading of the ethical.

* I am indebted to comments by Radhi Hertzberger, to those by the participants at the Claremont Conference, to the critical remarks of Frank J. Hoffman, and, above all, to talks and comments by Toni Packer, some of whose ideas are, I am sure, reflected in this paper.

I PHILOSOPHICAL ANTHROPOLOGY

Part of the interest of the present study lies in seeing what that 'philosophical anthropology' I just mentioned amounts to, by seeing it at work. Like all meta-level concepts it must be explained finally in terms of examples. But discussing it briefly in general terms may help clarify what I am up to here.

A religion, like an army, is an ongoing institution; it survives the death of those who enact it, for the individual actors are replaced by others. It can change in many different ways over time, while remaining the same religion. Christianity, for example, evidently began as a small doomsday cult, a splinter group within Judaism. It survived the non-occurrence of the end of the world and, in the Roman church, for instance, accommodated that doctrinal element only as an event of some far distant future. Furthermore, subgroups within the religion may – in different times, in different places, or under different rules of conduct – behave in significantly different ways; compare, for example, the Inquisition with a monastic group given over to the contemplative life, to take just two instances from an enormous range of variety. In response to that variety, one task of philosophical anthropology is to describe sets of behaviours that constitute the enactment of the religion at a given time and place. What, in detail, would it have been like to believe such and such, or to belong *then and there* to the religion in question? An important part of the answer is to describe the context in which the belief flourishes, or in which the religion, or that part of it at that time, exists. For example, to understand belief in the pantheon of Voodoo deities, one would do well to observe first-hand the wondrous sight of people who, in the course of a Voodoo 'ceremony', are ridden or taken over by one of those gods. At a more abstract level a philosophical anthropology of religion will inquire into a given religion's methods of fixing belief. In addition, the way of looking at religion that I am advocating will sometimes invent or construct possible religious movements. Here I attempt to extend to a much more complicated case Wittgenstein's practice of constructing simple language-games, such as that of the tribe of builders whose only language uses the words 'slab', 'beam' and so on. Wittgenstein's construction is meant to stand as an object of comparison; we understand our own use of requests more clearly if we view them in relation to that simple, slab–beam model. In religion too one can construct relatively simple, logically possible models of some or another form of the religious life. To do so for the case of 'post-Zen' is my main aim in this paper. I want to establish a bench-mark, something against which other, actual forms of the religious life can be compared. The model religion I construct is intended in that way to help us understand its ancestral forms better – that is, the various Zen sects – and to increase our intellectual grasp of various sects that are beginning to evolve from Zen. Although my aim is thus to construct relevant details of a possible religious movement, in doing so I have drawn upon observations of the particular post-Zen school I mentioned above. But still, my remarks are not meant as descriptions, but rather as laying out, by fiat, a certain possibility, for the purpose indicated.

Turning to specifics, my approach is first to separate certain tenets of Zen into two classes: the dogmatic, and the broadly empirical, as I shall refer to them. To do that I must first explain my nomenclature. I shall discuss 'dogma' in terms of the more familiar example of Christianity. The 'broadly empirical' I shall approach through the *Tractatus*. Only then shall I return to the mysterious East.

II THE ATHEIST'S DILEMMA

The essential idea here is that a given question is tied internally to some mode of inquiry for generating and justifying its answer, or to some particular truth-criterion operating within a given framework of investigation. By extension, a given assertion is also so linked. Analogously, the question 'Do the interior angles of the triangle equal 180 degrees?' will get different answers depending on which system of geometry is presupposed; and an assertion about angularity is correspondingly relative to some such system.

Thus consider the question-token: 'Are humans the result of special creation, or of evolution from other life forms?' If this is considered as tied internally to modes of inquiry implicit in modern biology, it is a non-starter. In other terminology, it violates the rhetorical presuppositions of that science. Appeal to God's activities is not allowed within the explanatory framework of science in general. On the other hand if the sentence token is considered as tied internally to a mode of inquiry that allows the invocation of sacred texts to settle or even be relevant to such matters, then the answer will be different. Even if the creationist cites physical evidence in supporting his views, he still stands outside biology's intellectual framework, with its standards of evidence, and general presuppositions, and so fails to make real contact with that science.[1] The kind of point I am pushing is long familiar in discussions in the philosophy of religion, in the thesis, for example, that attempts to prove or dispute God's existence by appeal to science are wrong-headed; the issue addressed is being linked internally to the wrong answer-framework.

Assuming the internal link just discussed, we come upon the atheist's dilemma. Someone might object to my previous remarks, as follows. If the theist's views belong to a self-contained system, with its own modes of justification, and if they are thus immune from scientific criticism, why can we not imagine an atheistic counterpart? The atheist might thus consider his 'form of life' as incorporating its own mode of inquiry, and his conclusion that God does not exist as maintainable, without possibility of attack from within that system.

But this is impossible. The atheist wants to deny God's existence. That is, he wants to deny what the theist affirms. He must therefore as it were reach out into the theist's system of affirmations in order to make his denial. He thus faces a dilemma. One possibility is that his negative answer to the question 'Does God exist?' is not an answer to the same question the theist answers affirmatively – because it is not governed by the same truth-criteria, in which case one hesitates to call him an atheist. Or it is an answer to the same question, governed by the same criteria, in which case it is the wrong answer. For by the mode of setting the matter that is linked internally to the theist's question, the answer must be affirmative.

But why exactly? Here one must not oversimplify. To speak of something like the religious (Christian) language-game, as opposed to the scientific one, is to make such an oversimplification. Just as science contains myriad specific ways of fixing belief, to use Peirce's phrase, so does religion. One – very common – mode of fixing belief in the Christian tradition, and in religion in general, appeals to dogma. It is this mode that I wish to focus on, for the moment. In a paradigmatic case, something is true by dogma if its truth is affirmed – laid down – by some group empowered (or self-empowered) to decide such issues, and if the group then succeeds in establishing that affirmation among the religion's devotees, or a significant number of them. Commonly, the doctrinal assertion laid down by the authoritative body will be enforced upon the congregation, and those who refuse to mouth the assertion will be stigmatised as apostates.

For example, in 49 AD, sixteen years after the crucifixion of Jesus, his surviving followers, including Paul of Tarsus, Peter, Jesus' brother James, Barnabas, and various other apostles and elders met in the Council of Jerusalem to hammer out certain controversial issues of doctrine.[2] One result was to establish, by agreement of the participants, the important truth that circumcision is not necessary for salvation.

To take another example, in 1870 a council of bishops at Rome declared the doctrine of papal infallibility, giving the Pope the right to establish doctrinal truth concerning faith and morals. This was as it were the establishment of a meta-dogma giving the Pope single-handed authority to settle ground-level issues of doctrine. It is significant that members of the council who were unable to accept the council's declaration broke off to form their own sect, the 'Old Catholic Church'.[3]

The then reigning pope, Pius IX, had already been exercising the right or ability to decide religious doctrine by fiat. For instance in the papal bull *ineffabilis Deus* he had laid it down that the Blessed Virgin Mary was born free of original sin (a truth I myself first learned of in Sunday school).[4]

Dogma as explicitly established, as in these examples, has its roots in phenomena present in primitive tribes that lack any-thing like councils or tribunals governing accepted truth. People in those tribes will more less agree on certain major features of religion-like truth-systems. For example the Yanamamo conceive of the universe as a four-tiered world, with two levels above the one where they live, and one below. The immediately superior level is similar in its extent and nature to their native rain forest habitat. Those who die pass on to that world, where they continue to exist. The Yanamamo have a system governing what a tribesperson is to say about life after death. One learns what to say, by hearing what one's fellow tribe members say. This class of 'say so' truths seems to me to belong to the class of truths of dogma.

In the case of non-primitive religion as well, truths of dogma need not be set down explicitly by some council or official. They can grow and be established by religious tradition, and then inherited by pesent-day followers of the sect.

I do not assume that truths of dogma will not be supported by argument, or in some way justified. The rival parties at some church council will doubtless put forward various arguments for their position. They do not see themselves as merely making a fiat. Nevertheless, it is a truth of the logic of inquiry that the thesis that wins the day in the council takes on the status of official truth; it becomes a given that the thesis is true. One must affirm it, at risk of being a heretic. The council has established a fiat, whether it sees itself as doing so or not.

Dogma, as defined by those examples and remarks, governs the actions of the people who belong to a given 'congregation' or sub-group. But it is only their vocal actions (or acts of writing, etc.) that are in question – what they can say on a given subject. It is essential that no empirical criteria govern the truth of dogmatically sanctioned affirmations, nor any other criteria, such as purely exegetical ones. Appeals to sacred texts or to tradition may be made by contending parties when an item of dogma is being debated, by the members of a council, say. But in the paradigmatic case, once the dogma has been fixed, it must be affirmed by the congregation. It becomes, in some cases at least, a litmus test for being an accepted member of the congregation. And of course in many instances one's life may hang on the question of whether one is so accepted. Typically those who for one reason or another cannot make the affirmation may form a splinter group in which the opposing dogma holds sway, as in the case mentioned above of the 'Old Catholic Church'.

The class of truths of dogma is doubtless vague at the edges, but I hope my examples and remarks serve sufficiently to characterise it for present purposes.

The salient feature of dogma is that it is true by explicit or implicit fiat. I count as implicit fiat the case where one's religious beliefs, or one's beliefs that are closely related to religious questions, such as beliefs about the afterlife, are settled as it were by a historically fixed and inherited tribal consensus. Similarly, some rules of present-day chess are true by implicit fiat, in that they are inherited from the misty past – the basic rules governing how pieces move, and what counts as winning, for example – whereas a rule like one of those governing losing on time is the explicit result of modern-day fiat.

The curious effect of the salient feature in question is that a truth of dogma cannot be successfully denied. For the truth in question is internally linked to its mode of establishment; and by facts of the case and the mode of establishment in operation, it is true.

What then of the atheist? Does God exist? Well, it is true by fiat – dogmatically true – that the Pope is Christ on earth. And since the doctrine of the Trinity is also true, that means that God exists. The atheist, again, cannot answer 'No' to the question 'Does God exist?' without changing the rules governing the truth of such assertions, including this one from the catechism: 'God made us to know Him and love Him.'[5] And if he changes the rules of truth governing the question he changes the question. But it is the God talked about in the question that he wants to deny.

Good news and bad. Truth by fiat has the strength that it is undoubtedly *true* and the weakness that it is true by *fiat*.

But there are atheists! Is their view self-defeating? Strictly speaking, yes. But the atheist can take comfort in the fact that instead of trying *per impossible* to deny the existence of God, he can convert himself into a radical relativist, and point out that 'God exists' is true – at least for the subclass of cases where it is affirmed as dogma, or as a consequence of dogma – only by fiat.

This reminds me of the attitude of a clever child of 14 whom I once knew. Though raised inside a strict theistic religion, he had become an atheist, denying God's existence. His view was that 'God exists' is just something people say. Throughout human history, different peoples say different things.

Of course the inference from the dogma-relative nature of the truth of a proposition to its falsity is mistaken. Nevertheless, one who recognises that relativity may be emotionally unable to enter into the system operative in his neck of the woods (if he is unfortunate enough to live in a place where there is one system in control of everyone).

The following then appears to be the closest the atheist can get to stating his denial:

Religious truth [or at least dogmatic religious truth] is just something people affirm. Different groups of people in different times and at different places establish different such 'truths'. These do not really conflict, any more than seemingly rival theorems from different geometries really conflict. Only the person who is blind to the nature of dogmatic truth (that it is true by fiat) and who is ignorant of the wide variety of seemingly conflicting such religious truths can affirm one of them as *the* truth.

Myself, I believe they are all whistling in the dark, and refuse
to enter into any of those truth-systems. Take my 'God does
not exist' as short-hand for the above remarks.

One point in this position is false. Atheism is not the inevitable
result of relativism. The latter is misunderstood if it is taken to
imply that the relativist cannot accept as true – and as *the* truth –
the claims of a given system. A radical relativist might accept the
dogmatic claims of some particular sect as true. From the inside
they are true, and he may chose to stand, as it were, on the inside, and give allegiance to the religion, and not merely out of
expediency but from conviction. He may admit that what his religion affirms is true only by stipulation, but maintain that it is
the one correct stipulation.

Such allegiance may result from the fact that religion, besides
its dogmatic claims, has many facets a person may value, features such as providing a communal feeling among its members,
or, again, a sense of *us versus them*; its appeasement of deep-seated
anxiety over death; its abatement of profound feelings of guilt;
or aspects such as ritual, ceremony music, chanting, prayer, and
ecstasy.

III THE QUASI-EMPIRICAL

By way of objection to my previous remarks it might be pointed
out that there is an empirical or at least what one might call a
quasi-empirical way of understanding the question 'Does God
exist?' This way appeals to the mystical experience of God, as in
Meister Eckhart's 'The eye with which I see God is the eye with
which God sees me.' The answer to the question is yes if it is
attested to by the mystic's meeting with God. If 'Does God exist?'
(or any other religious question) is internally tied to the possibility
of such quasi-empirical proof, then it is not a dogmatic claim any
longer.

Here there is needed a close study in philosophical anthropology
to separate the kind of mysticism I have in mind from the much
more common, ecstatic experiences of being born again, and the
like; I confess that I am inclined to think of *such* 'experience of
God' as a mixture of dogma, hysteria and 'enthusiasm'.[6]

Given that separation, I grant the objection. The distinction it relies upon is central to my aim of plotting the transition between Zen and post-Zen.

Having laid out the first concept I shall use in describing that transition, I must now address the second, the idea of mystical or quasi-empirical truth.

Here I feel most at home in dropping religion altogether, for the nonce, and discussing the issue in terms of some remarks from the *Tractatus*. But since my eye is on the target of the Buddhistic 'mystical experience' I shall discuss Wittgenstein's views with the thought of applying them in an Eastern and not a Western direction. Thus if what I say should ring false as applied to the experience of a union with God, I shall not care.

There are two grounds, each necessary, for speaking of the mystical experience as quasi-empirical. First, it must be conceived of as involving no particular sensation or specific inner experience. Second, it must be conceived of as yet in some way making a difference, indeed an enormous difference, to the mystic. Both features are represented in the *Tractatus*. To begin with the second, Wittgenstein speaks of two different worlds, one of the happy, the other of the unhappy man (6.43c). But this is a transcendentally happy man, one who has solved the riddle of life (in a way) (6.521) and who views the world *sub specie aeterni*, or as a 'limited whole' (6.45a).

> Feeling the world as a limited whole – it is this that is mystical. (6.45b)

The possibility that is raised here, then, is that of undergoing an enormously significant transition, from that of 'unhappy' to that of transcendentally 'happy'. At the same time, the experience of one who 'feels the world as a limited whole' is not describable empirically. The facts of the world are as they are; and furthermore, they are contingent:

> All that happens and is the case is accidental. (6.41)

The mystical transition from unhappy (unenlightened) to happy (enlightened) does not occur as a result of experiencing some or another contingent fact, or from having some or another empirical sensation or contingent inner experience. Rather, in that transcendental moment,

[The world] becomes an altogether different world. It must, so to speak, wax and wane as a whole. (6.43)

That is, it changes, waxes or wanes as a whole, without any particular fact of the world changing. Again:

How things are in the world is a matter of complete indifference for what is higher. God does not reveal himself *in* the world. (6.432)

Taking the world as Wittgenstein describes it, I shall speak of the possibility of a mystical experience that is 'quasi-empirical', by which I mean that although it is not empirical, in that what the person undergoes cannot be described empirically, and in that the experience is not that of a change in facts, whether 'external' or 'internal', nevertheless it is an experience of some change, in that the world of that person has become in some unsayable way different, and significantly so – a difference that the person obviously takes as for the better.

Applying the point to the question of religious truth, it becomes clear that what is seemingly the same assertion, or some corresponding question, can be nevertheless ambiguous, since it can be taken as linked either to dogma, or to the possibility of such a quasi-empirical confirmation.

IV ZEN

Zen too has many aspects. For one thing it is an organised religion of long history, with corresponding economic and broadly political concerns. It owns and operates temples and shrines, for example. It has an extraordinarily rich literary and artistic past (which those who treat Zen as a fad from the 1960s seem unaware of). It has characteristic rituals, ceremonies, and institutions.

And it adheres to the same basic claims as do all forms of Buddhism. That is, it affirms the following:

- Universal causation
- The doctrine of karma
- Rebirth (as opposed to reincarnation)
- No-self
- The possibility of enlightenment

These claims are explicit or implicit in what is known of the Buddha's earliest teaching, and are common to Hinayana and Mahayana forms.

The first three are dogmatic claims. The practising Buddhist accepts them because they are central claims of the religion. They have neither empirical nor quasi-empirical implications. The radical relativist may refuse to affirm them, rejecting them from without as being true merely by fiat.

It is the post-Zen position that the latter two claims have a different logical status from the former three. They are quasi-empirical.

It is easy to accept the last of the doctrines as quasi-empirical. That there is such a thing as enlightenment can be put in Tractarian terms: the world can be taken as a limited whole; the world of the unhappy man can become the world of the happy man, without changing in any empirically discernible way.

The more difficult point is to conceive of the doctrine of no-self as quasi-empirical. Indeed, a central question for understanding the nature of the post-Zen position is to understand its version of the Buddhist doctrine of 'anatman' or no-self. I shall understand that question as follows: What *should* the post-Zennist say about the self?

V NO-SELF

To talk about the no-self one must first talk about the self. There are, I shall say, two levels of belief in self. One is theoretical, the other existential. The first is solely the product of theorists, whether philosophers, psychologists, sociologists, or whatever.

There are various and some very arcane theories of the self. But it seems to me that underlying and informing them is a certain primitive but highly plausible account of the self, one the person in the street will be readily moved to adopt. According to this basic Cartesian doctrine the self is the referent of 'I' (or in general of the first-person-singular pronoun), when 'I' is used in present-tense psychological affirmations such as 'I think...', 'I want...', 'I intend...' and so on.

The theoretical denial of the self also takes many forms. I would defend Wittgenstein's position on the issue. According to it, 'I' in such locutions as just indicated is not a referring expression. If that is so, the 'I' is a grammatical fiction, in the same league – to

trot out the example once again – as that Nobody whom the
messenger in *Through the Looking Glass* passed on the road. On
this view the self of the metaphysician is not denied; it is not
affirmed that there is no such self. Rather it is said that the metaphysician's view is nonsensical, the product of being misled by a
grammatical picture, namely the picture of the use of the 'I' in
question as being a referring one. I have argued for the Wittgensteinian view elsewhere, and now believe I can defend it in a
more convincing way, by reference to primitive or very early uses
of those first-person assertions. But my present interests lie some-
where else.

They lie with that second form of belief, the existential or gut-
level one. The difference between the two levels comes out clearly
in the case of those who deny the self on theoretical grounds,
believing for example that the self is in some way a fictional product
of our life in society. Such theorists may strongly deny the self,
while yet showing in their lives a very close attachment to self –
a gut-level acceptance of the enormous importance of that one
particular 'I'. For example, someone has defended the no-self
position in several publications; in opening a new book in his
field, he turns first to the index, to see if he is referred to. A
more serious example may be his unacknowledged, perhaps ve-
hemently denied, but none the less very real fear of death – of
the demise of that 'I'.

What is it then to have an existential belief in self, as opposed
to some merely theoretical one? I suggest it is to live in certain
ways that are, as one might say, self-involved.

I have discussed four such ways elsewhere; here I will merely
list the first three of them.[7] The first involves the coming to hold
an actual image of oneself as seen through the eyes of another,
together with one's reactions to having formed that image. The
point is discussed in a wonderful way in Kleist's parable 'The
Puppet Theatre' and it forms the heart of Charles Cooley's discussion of the 'looking-glass self'.[8] A second form arises from the
first by dropping the demand that the image in question be some
actual, existing image, such as a visual image of oneself. An
imageless belief that one is being seen by the other in a certain
way, and one's corresponding concern over that supposed fact,
will also count as existential belief in self. The third form I distinguish is that of maintaining a self-image; the belief in self is
manifested in – or comes down to – actions (perhaps subtly nuanced

actions) designed to maintain one's self-affirmation as, for example, a courageous person.

My present interest is in the forth form, that of self-reverie. One of the ways of living that should count as manifesting an existential belief in self can only be described by discussing what goes on in the agent's mind. I refer to the constant stream of I-centred thoughts that constantly occupy members of our species. These thoughts can be reasonable, rational, goal-directed and perspicuous, but often they are not. More typically they reflect the thinker's own inner dramatisation of his life, as hero or villain, victim or victimiser, lucky or hard done by, as one who should have done so and so and who might yet achieve such and such, and so on. In some people such thoughts become extremely obsessional and inescapable; and for everyone, thoughts can be painful.

I need a concrete example of the sort of thinking I have in mind, and shall resort to quoting myself quoting Marx – Groucho, that is.

MRS TEASDALE: I've taken the liberty of asking the Ambassador to come over here because we both felt that a friendly conference would settle everything peacefully. He'll be here any moment.

FIREFLY [*patting her hand*]: Mrs Teasdale, you did a noble deed! I'd be unworthy of the high trust that's been placed in me if I didn't do everything within my power to keep our beloved Fredonia at peace with the world. I'll be only too happy to meet Ambassador Trentino and offer him, on behalf of my country, the right hand of good fellowship [*Jovially*] And I feel sure that he will accept this gesture in the spirit in which it is offered ... But suppose he doesn't? A fine thing that'll be! I hold out my hand and he refuses to accept it! That'll add a lot to my prestige, won't it. [*He starts shouting indignantly.*] Me, the head of a country, snubbed by a foreign ambassador! Who does he think he is that he can come here and make a sap out me in front of all my people? Think of it! ... I hold out my hand and that hyena refuses to accept it! Why, the cheap, four-flushing swine! He'll never get away with it, I tell you!

MRS TEASDALE: Oh!

FIREFLY: He'll never get away with it!

[*At that moment,* TRENTINO *enters with a retinue of Sylvanian officers ...*]

FIREFLY: So! You refuse to shake hands with me, eh?
[*He slaps* TRENTINO *with his gloves. The music stops.* MRS TEASDALE *wails . . .*]

Taken as inner monologue, Firefly's words illustrate a common syndrome. In such a pattern of thought someone becomes angry (or whatever) at another in virtue of what the first person *imagines* the other to say. These imaginings need not be rational or realistic. The person enacts the other's response, and then reacts, in anger, or jealousy, or whatever, to that response, then in turn imagines or enacts his response to that, and so on.

One really does get angry in response to what one imagines the other to say, or in response to how one imagines the other to react. Apparently what happens is that the body responds, or begins to respond, as it would to an actual, non-imaginary situation in which one became angry. The bodily changes thus initiated work against the person's well-being. These thought processes can also affect one's real-life actions and reactions.

Our ordinary everyday lives abound in Groucho syndromes and similar self-involved patterns of fantasy.[9] The general point is this. Humans typically engage in self-reverie. They get caught up in a chain of I-thoughts, ones that will often circle back to consider the same point. These I-thoughts can manifest themselves in various observable ways, for example, in the distrustful or aloof attitude one might show to someone who has been figuring in one's I-thoughts in a certain negative way, or in one's actual, if muted, physiological – and hence theoretically 'observable' – reactions to some thought of insult or danger. The thus observable way of life I count as one of the most significant forms of existential belief in self.

The post-Zen denial of self must naturally be at the existential level, if it is to stand any chance of inheriting what is essential to its Buddhist prototype. Zen's claim that it is a doctrine beyond words is meant to emphasise its insistence on realising the Buddha's message in one's life – in one's manner of living. Post-Zen must carry on that concern with the adept's form of life, or else it would omit what is Zen's cardinal virtue. So now – from our meta-theoretical perspective – a problem corresponding to one discussed earlier arises. What does an existential denial of self come to?

My suggestion is this. To deny self at an existential level is to live in a manner manifesting a no-self way of life. To do that in turn is to live in one of two ways: either one lives free of any self-reverie – free of I-thoughts – or, if I-thoughts occur, they do not capture one. The first possibility is easier to discuss than the second.

On the first possibility, those recurring and in fact harmful thoughts disappear. One acts, as the Buddhists say, with an empty mind (a phrase that has got me in trouble before). On the second possibility, I-thoughts may cross the screen of one's mind, but one is not, so to speak, caught up in them. They appear to one perhaps as a phenomenon thrown up by the activity of the brain; they are observed, as one might neutrally observe clouds crossing the sky.

In either case, the no-self way of life must show itself. Imagine an unhealthy-looking, grim-faced person, slumped in his chair, nervously snapping a ball-point pen open and closed; a sudden noise and he gives a nervous start. And now we add: and this person's mind is free of all I-thoughts.

The problem would be that having his mind free of thoughts bought him nothing. If the life of the no-self person is indistinguishable from the life of everyman, in every detail except for the matter of verbal utterances, then the claim of no-self becomes uninteresting, at least from the point of view of a religion that is concerned with more than what people say, more than mere dogma.

On the other hand the realisation of no-self is supposed to be open to anyone, and we must not demand that it alter the broad outlines of what people do. Someone may like his job, his family and friends, and not want to alter his behaviour towards them.

So the life of the no-self person must change, and not change. The way out of that corner is to acknowledge that there are different levels of behaviour. Behaviours that are the same at one level of consideration may differ at another. My model for this is language. All the people of a country speak the same language, but different regional groups have different accents. And a given individual has his own particular way of speaking – his voice is recognisably his, and recognisably different from even those with the same regional accent. It is at, or close to, this third level, that of fine behaviour, that we must look for the difference between the self and the no-self life.

My postulation is that there is a difference at the level of fine behaviour – at the level, that is, of those subtle nuances of behaviour that mark us off from others, even others who do the things with the same regional accent, as it were.

But let me illustrate these levels. Going into a store and buying an apple is something people do from one end of the country to the other. Their large-scale behaviour, as we might call it, may well be identical: one goes in, looks over the apples, picks one up and examines it, takes it to the counter, and so on. Near an urban Zen centre I once observed a young man walk into a store and buy an apple, more or less in the way just described. But I could tell that he was a Zen student by his behaviour. He had caught, as it were, the regional style, tell-tale mannerisms of his fellow Zen students, which he had acquired in the same way Roderick Chisholm's graduate students once acquired his habit of raising his voice in a questioning intonation at the end of some philosophical assertion. I won't attempt to describe those middle-level Zen mannerisms, beyond saying that they involved a certain assumed bold and studied directness of action. As concerns that crucial third level of fine behaviour, I shall postulate that if the apple-buying student's Zen teacher – differing from the student, let us say, in being enlightened, and hence in leading a no-self life – had bought the apple, then although there would have been the same large-scale behaviour, and the same middle-level or 'regional style' behaviour, there would have been in principle a discernible difference in fine behaviour.

Again I cannot hope to describe the differences at that third level. I think I have observed them, no matter how confusedly. They seem to involve, on the part of the person observed, a certain effortless rapport with others and the world, with no or few defences in place, sympathetically open to what the other brings forward.

That there should be fine differences between one who is captured by self-reverie and one who is not seems plausible on the face of it, if, that is, one grants the assumption that the body can react to thoughts by releasing chemical messengers, by stress, and the like.[10] For instance, a person condemned to death may be in no danger at this given moment, but his mind may not allow him to forget his plight, and he may go over and over his bleak future in thought; and these thoughts may trigger inappropriate physiological reactions, as if to flee or fight, and those in turn may show themselves in his subtle or not so subtle *manner* of behaving – for instance in the way he raises a cup to his lips. His thoughts are painful, and he shows that in nuances of behaviour.

We must ask also after the meaning of the existential affirmation that 'The self does not exist', – as opposed to either a merely

theoretical or a merely dogmatic assertion of those words. That
is to say, how is the sentence so used? A crucial aspect of the use
of any expression is the context in which it is uttered and responded to. My previous discussion allows me to demarcate an
important element of that context. The speaker, let us say, once
manifested the fine behaviour typically associated with one given
over, as virtually all of us are, to self-reverie. But then a change
occurred, more or less permanent, let us assume, after which the
fine behaviour was of the type associated with someone lacking
or free of the baneful effects of self-reverie.

In *such* a context, I want to say, 'The self does not exist' is not
a description of anything; rather it is what Wittgenstein called an
Äusserung. An *Äusserung* is a certain speaking forth in a certain
context. For example a child utters the word 'book', thereby naming
the object the child intends to fetch; the *Äusserung* does not describe the child's inner state. What is the appropriate response of
the hearer, in our case? Well, there are apparently two possibilities.
If the hearer is similarly leading a no-self life, free of self-reverie,
and in some way taking the world as a limited whole, then his
response may be simply to acknowledge the speaker's words.
Affirmation and response mark a meeting of minds, a shared way
of life. If the hearer on the contrary is enmeshed in the coils of
samsara, then the speaker's utterance is presumably meant to appeal to the other in some such way as this: 'There is a better way
to live, if you could only stop chasing yourself down endless flights
of self-centred thoughts and see what is right before your eyes,
the world as it is.'

I would say in addition that other Buddhist and post-Buddhist
expressions of enlightenment are to be understood, meta-theoreti-
cally, in the same way. 'The oak tree in the garden', to take that
famous Zen 'description' of enlightenment, or 'the world as a limited whole' or 'there is no self' (existentially understood) all have
the same use. That use presupposes the 'context' I described above.
The mystics' denial of self and affirmation of enlightenment come
to the same thing.

VI POST-ZEN

Against the background of my previous remarks I shall sum up
the post-Zen position, as I wish to construct it. Concerning the
five Buddhist doctrines I have discussed, it treats the first three

as mere dogma, and does not affirm them. It does not stand within that scheme of merely verbal, system-certified affirmations. It does however affirm the last two doctrines, that of the possibility of enlightenment and the assertion of no-self. It treats both as quasi-empirical, in the sense indicated, and thus as existential in nature.

In fact it treats the realisation of no-self as identical to the realisation of 'the world as a limited whole' – or however else one wishes to characterise the 'mystical experience'. It advocates a way of life that manifests those twin realisations in fine behaviour congruent with the similar behaviour of the Zen masters. Theoretically it characterises belief in self as, in part, the acceptance of a grammatical fiction.

Of course there is much more to Zen than doctrines and fine behaviour. In keeping with their North American roots, post-Zen systems might eschew or significantly play down the ceremonial and ritualistic aspects of Zen. Also in keeping with home custom, the more blatantly militaristic-seeming features of Zen, such as its use of the *keisaku*, or stick, may disappear. On the other hand post-Zen would do well to keep some toned-down version of that central Zen institution, the silent retreat. In silence the mind becomes aware of being always caught up in self-reverie, and of the great power of those I-thoughts. In silence one may experience some taste of the freedom that comes when self-reverie dampens down, and one may even – so I am told – arrive at the happy person's view of the world as a limited whole.

VII   ETHICS

I shall make two points about the ethical implications of a post-Zen position. In philosophy ethics is usually taken as concerning what we might call mundane questions, such as a person's relations to others – what his moral obligations to them are, and so on. In Wittgenstein's 'Lecture on Ethics' the term was used in a different way. There the main question of ethics involved not the mundane but the transcendental – the mystical, one might say.

That view of ethics is sympathetic to a certain thesis common to contemplative strands in religion. It is the thesis, one might say, of the unhappiness of human life. The first of the Buddha's Four Noble Truths says that life – well, at least much of life – is suffering. His response to one who asked him certain metaphysical questions was that someone whose house is on fire, and whose children might burn, does not stop to ascertain what started the fire, how hot it is burning, and so on – rather he takes his children and runs from the house. The image shows the Buddha's view of human life: whether you know it or not, the house is on fire. The Christian mystic, as seeker, is haunted by the suffering of those around him, and desperate to find surcease in some direct knowledge of God. On this transcendental view of ethics, even if all our mundane questions of morality were answered, there would be left over the one, momentous problem, of finding a way out of the net, of dealing with the world seen on the black side of the mystic's vision, where life as ordinarily lived is a trap. It is obvious that ethics for that post-Zen view is paramountly transcendental, in the way indicated, and speaks above all to those who share the dark part of the vision of someone like Pascal, where the soul, before the great moment of union, is divided against itself.

But being 'transcendental' in that way does not make it supernatural. The particular post-Zen view I wish to construct, rather, is rooted in a naturalistic vision of the world, where the mundane facts of biology, anthropology and history are taken for granted. Humans are a species of animal, an especially clever one, but not one separated from the others by some unbridgeable Cartesian gap; and one that like all the rest is mortal.

Post-Zen also has implications for ethics as more traditionally conceived. One can't trust single-element answers to large questions, but at least *a* thing that seems to keep humans from acting decently towards other humans is our self-concern, especially when it is raised to a higher power by becoming a case of some or another us against them. It is an assumption of the thesis I have been developing here that a person who becomes free of self-reflective reverie will, by that very fact, become able more deeply and truly to perceive other humans. It is a further assumption that the person so freed will respond with compassion to others.

So I follow Hume in saying that our moral judgements are grounded ultimately in fellow-feeling. I just postulate the extra, 'mystical' element that one free of self-reverie will have more access to a naturally occurring feeling of compassion for others. Such a feeling is often buried, but it can be seen in operation in our species, at least in our better moments.

It might be objected against this view that the trivial change I imagine happening – the dropping of I-centred thoughts – could hardly be responsible for such a major change as a deepening of compassion. Again, it might be objected that lack of compassion has more than one source, as do misery and anxiety, so that none of these can be expected to disappear solely as a result of the imagined change in question.[11] First, it seems to me that these objections will appear especially strong to someone who has not become aware in a clear way of the hold that self-reverie has on one; a person who has felt its grip will be more likely to countenance the possibility that the objections are wrong. Second, my premise here is that the disappearance of self-reverie, or its losing its hold upon one, and the coming to see the world as a limited whole, come to the same thing. If that is so then both objections deny either the validity or the power of the mystic's beatific vision.

In these pages I have been describing a possible language-game that I am in no position to play. But the question of the truth or falsity of the mystic's *Äusserung* does seem to be what I have called a quasi-empirical question, and hence one that is open to 'experimentation' of a sort.

Notes

1. To take another, more controversial issue, questions in mathematics, such as 'Does "777" occur in the expansion of pi?' or 'Is Fermat's last theorem true?' were faulty in so far as they were not linked to some method for reaching and verifying an answer, and were thus not on all fours with questions that are so linked, such as, 'Does "777" occur in the first ten thousand numbers in the expansion of pi?' On the view I am presupposing here, recent success in answering the two questions just cited, such as the computer-generated expansion of pi that uncovered that series of 7s, involves an implicit stipulation of a method and presuppositions for getting a positive answer, where these partially fix the content of the question in one of several possible ways.
2. Paul Johnson, *A History of Christianity* (New York: Penguin, 1976), pp. 3–5.
3. Ibid., p. 394.
4. Ibid., p. 392.
5. Perhaps I should give an example from the Protestant side of the ledger. In effect Calvin made it true by proclamation that Satan and the devils 'can neither conceive any evil nor, when they have conceived it, contrive to do it, nor having contrived it lift even a little finger to execute it, save in so far as God commands them' (quoted by Johnson, p. 287). That being the case, God exists.

6. One observable difference between the two would lie in their ante-cedents. The mystical experience is typically preceded by a long period of questing, under the guidance of some spiritual teacher. The various forms of this could be delineated. Antecedents to the experience of being born again would typically differ, I think.

7. See John Canfield, *The Looking-Glass Self* (New York: Praeger, 1990), pp. 171–212.

8. Heinrich von Kleist, 'On the Marionette Theatre', translated by Cherna Murray, *Life and Letters Today*, 1937, vol. 16, pp. 101–8; Charles Cooley, *Human Nature and the Social Order* (New York: Scribner's, 1902).

9. The previous three paragraphs are taken from *The Looking-Glass Self*, p. 189.

10. This is a point Toni Packer makes in lectures.

11. Robert C. Coburn argued that way, I believe, in his review of my book *The Looking-Glass Self* (*The Philosophical Review*, Jan. 1993, vol. 102, no. 1, p. 131).

10

Reply: Before 'Post-Zen': A Discussion of Buddhist Ethics

FRANK J. HOFFMAN

It is one of the main contentions of this paper that Buddhist ethics remains just as it was before, after one has considered Professor Canfield's talk about 'post-Zen', and that what is called 'post-Zen' has little or nothing to do with Buddhism as such. Although I have tried to interpret Canfield's paper sympathetically, on the basis of the draft received for comment I do not believe that he has shown either that what is called 'post-Zen' has importance for the interpretation of the historical development of Buddhist ethics in particular, or that an increase in conceptual clarity about any significant philosophical thesis results from considering what he has said so far.

In the first section of this paper I partially summarise Canfield's paper and raise questions about some of its main points. In the second section I present some ideas about Buddhist ethics. It is necessary to do this second task so that it will become clear just why what Canfield calls 'post-Zen' has little or nothing to do with Buddhism *per se*. In the third section of the present paper I conclude with some philosophical reflections.

I   RESTATEMENT AND ANALYSIS

1. Canfield says he is interested in 'a certain logically possible development out of Zen'. This is an odd way to put it, since the statement of the meaning of 'logical possibility' (that is, statement *s* is logically possible if and only if it contains no self-contradiction)

is inimical to the overall Zen perspective, replete as Zen is with paradoxes and even the use of contradiction to a spiritual purpose.

2. Canfield claims: 'My aim here belongs to philosophical anthropology (to adopt the name). I want to describe the salient features of that possible religious movement, and show how and why it departs from its Zen roots.' Has he sufficiently clarified in the next section what this means? We *already* have the term in use as 'philosophy of man'. Does the older use equate with Canfield's? What sort of thought-experiment is Canfield conducting here? How can one judge thought-experiments in Canfield's employment – by their usefulness or what?

Examples are, Canfield claims, the way to explain it 'finally' (whatever that would be like), but general features of philosophical anthropology (herein afterwards 'PA') will be mentioned.

(a) PA treats religions as multi-person organisms.

(b) At a more abstract level PA will inquire into a given religion's methods of fixing belief.

(c) PA will sometimes invent or construct possible religious movements.

(d) Here, for example, Canfield says he attempts to extend Wittgenstein's practice of constructing simple language-games (such as the tribe of builders) 'to a much more complicated case'. About this point, I would like to ask: is it *one* case, many sorts of cases, or perhaps a muddle? Really, is there anything in particular that can be picked out by the use of the expression 'ethics post-Zen'? If so, would that phenomenon have a distinctive relationship with Zen (and hence justify the appellation 'post-Zen') or could it be arrived at by other avenues such as, for example, the 'death of God theology'?

(e) With PA one can establish a 'bench-mark' – 'something against which other, actual forms of the religious life, can be compared', Canfield claims, so that the 'model religion' constructed 'help[s] us understand its ancestral forms better'. But if it doesn't exist, how can it have 'ancestral forms' – is there an atemporal sense of the term 'ancestral' that does not do violence to the concept? Also, what is a 'bench-mark' in Canfield's philosophical employment of the term – a criterion? If so, let's say so. In addition, one meaning of 'bench-mark' has to do with measuring position and altitude, whereas another has

to do with measuring quality or value. Which sort, the descriptive or the normative, is at work in Canfield's shop?[1] As
for understanding 'ancestral forms', is it the ancestral forms
of religion or specifically of Zen that are supposed to be
unearthed?

(f) Canfield thinks that there is a particular Zen 'school' which
provides a backdrop against which he can articulate the details of a possible religious movement. It is not at all clear
that there is any such 'school'. He gives us only the briefest
clue, by mentioning 'an American Zen teacher, Toni Packer',
who 'has even renounced Buddhism and undertaken a practice that, while it has roots in Zen, is no longer Buddhistic'.

(g) In addition to the conceptual issue of whether one can make
good sense of 'ancestral' without temporal reference, another
conceptual issue which arises here is whether there could be
a Zen school which is not Buddhistic. It might be argued that
Zen is by definition one of the Mahayana Buddhist schools,
so that this is not 'logically possible'. If there is no such Zen
school, then there seems to be no basis on which to proceed
with Professor Canfield's line of thought after the first page
of his paper. So far as I can see, the precise relationship between Toni Packer's 'post-Zen' practice (or even her *sort* of
practice) and Zen is not clarified in Canfield's exposition.

3. Turning to specifics Canfield attempts to separate 'certain tenets
of Zen into two classes: the dogmatic, and the broadly empirical'.

The distinction is worked out in Section II, 'The Atheist's Dilemma'. The 'essential idea' is that questions are tied to particular modes of inquiry or truth criteria, and that some questions
are 'true by dogma'. Although 'truths of dogma' may be sometimes argued for or justified (since proponents do not see themselves as merely making a fiat), 'it is a truth of the logic of inquiry,
that the thesis that wins the day in the council takes on the status
of official truth'. In the case of dogma, neither empirical nor exegetical criteria 'govern the truth of dogmatically sanctioned
affirmations'. As a result, 'a truth of dogma cannot be successfully denied' since its truth is linked to its mode of establishment.

This would appear to rule out *change* in dogmas. How is religious change to come about if, indeed, 'truths of dogma' cannot
be 'successfully denied'? Also, Canfield's method of description
borrows an exclusivist understanding and emphasis on credal

formulae which are inimical to most of the ways in which East Asians, say, think about religious matters in inclusivist terms.

4. Regarding 'blind to the nature of dogmatic truth', the problem remains whether one should call this 'truth' at all.

5. Regarding Canfield's idea of 'the closest the atheist can get to stating his denial', it seems that if a fiat is a performative, it could be replied to by the atheist with yet another performative, rather than with a statement. For, as Sutherland shows, there are other forms atheism can take than propositional belief.[2] Canfield does not consider such possibilities for denial that are expressed in other than propositional form, and these happen to be ways of expression characteristic of Zen masters.

6. Canfield holds that atheism is not the only possible consequence of relativism, for a relativist may choose to stand on the inside and give allegiance to a particular religion maintaining that, although the tenets of the religion are true by stipulation, they happen to be 'the one correct stipulation'. Part of this strikes me as right: atheism is not the only possible consequence of relativism.[3] (To extrapolate, a relativist might just as easily be a conventionalist as an anarchist.)

But the stimulating issue here is whether there can there be any criteria for adjudicating disputes about what is to count as the one correct stipulation? Perhaps there is an incoherence in the very idea of 'the one correct stipulation' – an incoherence which would vitiate (as senseless rather than as simply mistaken) the whole characterisation of the atheist's position on Canfield's account of it.

7. In Section III, 'The Quasi-Empirical', Canfield defends himself against the rebuttal that there is 'an empirical or at least what one might call a quasi-empirical way of understanding the question "Does God exist?"'

(a) He replies with a distinction to separate his kind of mysticism from 'the much more common, ecstatic experiences of being born again, and the like'.
(b) He holds that quasi-empirical religious experience is possible, by which is meant: the world of the mystic has changed for

the better as the mystic sees it, even though no empirical change has occurred nor any change of external or internal facts.

A question to be raised at this point is whether and if so how and to what extent Canfield's position here is like John Wisdom's position in the widely anthologised article, 'Gods'?

8. In Section IV, 'Zen', he says that there are five basic claims common to all forms of Buddhism: universal causation, the doctrine of karma, rebirth (as opposed to transmigration), no-self, and the possibility of enlightenment.

(a) The resultant essentialisation of Buddhism does not do justice to the complex historical development of Buddhism, and consequently will not work to the consensual satisfaction of scholars of Buddhism. It ignores developments such as the Daruma School (discussed below in Section II of my paper), as well as the point that how the claims are to be construed in a particular context shapes what the claims mean.

(b) Canfield thinks that it is simply a correct descriptive point that the first three claims of the five above are dogmatic. But here nothing can be said generally like this that is not a scholar's abstract creation. The history of Buddhism is too convoluted for such a simplistic ossification to be accurate.

(c) Canfield says that 'the post-Zen position' holds that the last two claims (no-self; possibility of enlightenment) are empirical.

But since rebirth and enlightenment are co-relative concepts in Buddhism, it is logically odd that the possibility is even entertained that one might have an entirely different status from the other – one as dogmatic and the other as empirical. For whatever precise formulation of rebirth and enlightenment is articulated, in general the statement of the rebirth doctrine makes necessary reference to the enlightenment doctrine, and vice versa. From the insider's perspective of religious practice which is necessary to state the doctrines, rebirth is hopefully *towards* enlightenment, and enlightenment is *from* the round of rebirth. Since each is thus necessary to characterise the other, these concepts must have a life in the same sort of system of concepts.

(d) Canfield asserts that whereas the possibility of enlightenment is easy to understand as quasi-empirical, by reference to the

Tractatus idea that the world can be taken as a limited whole, the world of the unhappy person can become the world of the happy person without any empirically discernible change taking place. I want to ask: why not use 'experiential' rather than 'quasi-empirical' here, since 'experiential' is less likely to be misleading?[4]

(e) Canfield has greatest difficulty conceiving of no-self as a quasi-empirical doctrine. This becomes 'a central question for understanding the nature of the post-Zen position'.

9. In Section V, 'No-Self', Canfield asserts that to talk about no-self one must first talk about self. He distinguishes two levels, theoretical and existential.

(a) Since 'I' is not a referring expression (Wittgenstein), the metaphysician's view of self is shown as nonsensical rather than being denied. This seems right: the meaningfulness of an assertion being a prior concern than its truth or falsity, meaningless statements cannot be judged to be false.

(b) But the existential form of belief in self is more pertinent to this paper. To have an existential belief in self is to live in ways that are self-involved. The one of the four which he concentrates on is self-reverie.

(c) The 'post-Zen' denial of self must be at the existential level, 'if it is to stand any chance of inheriting what is essential to its Buddhist prototype'.[5] This existential level difference is either that 'one lives free of any self-reverie' or that 'if I-thoughts occur, they do not capture one'. Levels of behaviour are distinguished, such that it is possible to see a no-self way of life as identical to the enlightened life: 'the mystics['] denial of self and affirmation of enlightenment come to the same thing'.

Again, is there anything 'essential to the Buddhist prototype'? Canfield seems to be thinking of Buddhism as some sort of monolithic whole – with an 'essence' – when it is, in fact, more like a convoluted, ever-expanding structure (compare Wittgenstein's use of 'medieval city' in reference to language). Also, the fact that the expressions 'no-self way of life' and 'enlightened way of life' may refer to the same thing does not mean that there is no difference at all between these doctrines, any more than that beliefs about the 'morning star' and the 'evening star' are identical beliefs.

(d) 'To deny self at an existential level is to live in a manner manifesting a no-self way of life' – this is one of Canfield's most important insights. It is not original with him, however, and is evident in quotations which may be gleaned from Wittgensteinian philosophers of religion such as D. Z. Phillips (for example, in *Death and Immortality*) and S. R. Sutherland (for example, in *God, Jesus, and Belief*). Immortality is discussed further in Section III of my paper below.

10. In Section VI, 'Post-Zen', Canfield sums up his construal of 'the post-Zen position'. It treats universal causation, the doctrine of karma, and rebirth (as opposed to transmigration) 'as dogma, and does not affirm them'. It does affirm no-self and the possibility of enlightenment as 'quasi-empirical' and existential in nature. '[P]ost-Zen systems might eschew or significantly play down the ceremonial and ritualistic aspects of Zen'.[6]

Professor Canfield does not seem to see, however, that rebirth and enlightenment are co-relative concepts, and that (as argued above) such a position as he attributes to post-Zen is logically incoherent because it would affirm one co-relative concept (enlightenment) and not assent to the other (rebirth). The post-Zen position does not affirm rebirth, for 'it treats the first three as mere dogma, and does not affirm them'.

To explain, Canfield's view is that for the post-Zen person no-self and the possibility of enlightenment 'have a different logical status from the former three' (that is, from universal causation, the doctrine of karma, and rebirth). In Canfield's construction of the post-Zen position, of the five claims considered essential to Buddhism only no-self and the possibility of enlightenment are, in Canfield's terms, 'quasi-empirical', while the other three are regarded by Buddhist believers as 'true by fiat'. The implication is that a post-Zen person would be able to embrace the possibility of enlightenment while regarding rebirth as 'mere dogma', as just one of the things Buddhists say about Buddhism. What Canfield does not seem to recognise is that drawing out this implication shows that, and how, the post-Zen position constructed by Canfield is logically incoherent.

11. In Section VII, 'Ethics', Canfield makes two points about the ethical implications of 'a post-Zen position'. First, post-Zen ethics has to do with ethics in a 'transcendental' (Wittgenstein) sense;

second, post-Zen ethics has implications for ethics in a traditional sense in militating against a sort of self-concern which becomes 'us versus them'. This position is supposed to result in a deepening of compassion. Although Canfield has described a 'possible language game that I [Canfield] am in no position to play', he believes he has shown that there is a quasi-empirical issue open to a sort of 'experimentation'. A question to ask here is whether quasi-empirical religious experience is different from any other kind of religious experience?

The move from no-self to compassion is not especially clear in Canfield's exposition. It is also a strange use of the term 'experimentation' to employ it here – as if Zen adepts were analytically going about in white lab coats, rather than revealing the spontaneity of being through everyday actions of mindfulness and compassion as have many of the world's great artists, but rather few of its scientists.

Overall, I would like to ask: has Professor Canfield really shown 'how and why' the 'possible religious movement' called 'post-Zen' departs from its 'Zen roots'? I do not see how Canfield's paper amounts to either a contribution towards a better understanding of the development of Buddhist ethics or a contribution towards greater clarity on any conceptual issue.

II

In this section of the paper Buddhist ethics is discussed.[7] Although such a rudimentary discussion may be judged to be insufficiently precise from this or that text-specialist point of view within Buddhology, I trust that it will be illuminating enough to reinforce my argument that Canfield's 'post-Zen' construction has little or nothing to do with Buddhism.

It might be thought that it is inappropriate for me to raise considerations about actual Buddhist belief and practice, since Canfield says that he is constructing a 'logically possible development out of Zen, whether or not any particular actual practice ... exemplifies it'. My justification for making points about what Buddhists actually believe is that Canfield himself includes a brief section (IV, 'Zen') which purports to describe some of the 'many aspects' of Zen, and, indeed, the 'basic claims' of 'all forms of Buddhism'. Since Canfield himself thinks, in at least one place in the paper,

that considerations of what Buddhists in fact believe are relevant
to his overall project, I hope I shall not be regarded as disgressing
in introducing the following material.

Preliminary Considerations

Buddhism is not a credal religion. That is to say, even for initia-
tion as a monk or nun (let alone for the layman) there is no 'litmus
test' of reciting propositions believed, such as the ones in Canfield's
list of five. When Western Christians study Buddhism they sometimes study texts with a view to finding (read: constructing) a
creed, because on mainstream accounts Christianity is itself a credal
religion.

There is no central authority comparable to the Pope in Roman
Catholicism who legislates *ex cathedra* ('from the chair' of Peter)
and is traditionally regarded as infallible in matters of faith and
morals. If, for example, the Dalai Lama is able to unite Buddhists
on some occasions in cooperative activities, that is because of the
moral force of his personality as leader of Tibetan Buddhists seen
against the dual background of the well-known persecution of
the Tibetan Buddhist Church by mainland Chinese communist
authorities and the authority accorded to Buddhism by the Tibetan
people. As a pan-Asian phenomenon, Buddhism has no central
organisation. Consequently, despite the occasional council, there
is no overall pan-Asian method of doctrinal enforcement.

This does not mean that there is no rough and ready way to
make an in-group/out-group distinction between who is Buddhist
and who is not. If you ask Buddhists about this, then although
you may get different answers some commonalities remain. One
pattern that recurs is to say that becoming a Buddhist is a matter
of 'taking the three refuges': I believe in the Buddha, Doctrine,
and Order. But here there is no 'litmus test' that would apply
across all Buddhist contexts as to how the doctrines are to be
construed and exactly which are to be believed, for that is a matter of sectarian tradition and individual faith.

Minimally, and in some countries such as Japan, for example,
Buddhism might be a matter of temple registration such that being a Buddhist is decided by whether one's family is registered
at a temple and pays to support it. If one accepts the responsibility (normally attributed to the eldest son) of maintaining a
butsudan taken over from the household of the preceding genera-

tion, then one's being a Buddhist in this cultural way is reinforced even in the absence of doctrinal beliefs.

One may be Buddhist in this cultural way, while maintaining
relationships with other religious structures. Since Buddhism is
not a credal religion, in Japan, for example, one may maintain a
Shinto shrine (*kamidana*), a Buddhist altar (*butsudan*), and attend
Baptist Church on Sunday. Since overall the Japanese are not
exclusivist but inclusivist in religious orientation, the general tendency is to see no contradiction in being a Shinto–Buddhist–Baptist.

Recitation of the *pātimokkha* indicating the ethical norms may
be regarded as another thing that Buddhist practitioners may look
to in order to make the in-group/out-group distinction: a Buddhist is one who walks the Buddhist ethical path or *marga*.

Historical Counter-evidence

Since it will not be possible to summarise 'Buddhist ethics'
altogether in one part of a paper alone, I will call attention to
what Heinrich Doumoulin in the West and others previously in
Japan have called 'the Daruma School' of Japanese Zen Buddhism.
Doing so will help to counteract Canfield's tendency to 'essentialise
Buddhism' in five claims. As a proviso at the outset of this section, I would like to clarify that the discussion of the Daruma
School which follows is offered as one possible avenue from which
to argue against Canfield's position and not the only such road.
Consequently, even if the discussion of the Daruma School below
is deemed by some to be insufficient historical counter-evidence,
it does not follow that Canfield's position is correct.

One authoritative text for understanding the Daruma School
has three sections.[8] These concern, first, the 'historical succession
of generations similar to that found in the Zen chronicles', second, 'the doctrine of the unity of all things', and, third, 'the effi-
cacy of the school at work through the recitation of magical formulas
and the carrying out of esoteric rites'.[9] These sections provide, in
reverse order, the miracle, mystery, and authority which, in
Dostoevsky's 'Grand Inquisitor' section of *The Brothers Karamazov*,
characterises one form that Christianity might take.

But both are criticised: just as this is depicted as a degenerate
form of Christianity in contrast to that of the Christ who had
come to make people free – to give them a radical, for some intolerable, freedom – so too the Daruma School is criticised for

deviating from the path of the Buddha by influential figures in the development of Buddhism.[10]

What is interesting about the juxtaposition of the Daruma School with Canfield's idea of 'post-Zen' is that if we take the historical Daruma School and compare it with Canfield's 'post-Zen' in a narrow sense where this refers to Toni Packer's sort of practice, then some illuminating similarities and differences can be seen.

First, both are 'heretical' as judged by mainstream Buddhists. In Packer's case, she seems to readily accept the role of a 'non-guru guru' in the style of Krishnamurti. Her practice therefore seen from her point of view does not require validation from some external source such as Buddha or Buddhism, while it nevertheless retains the roots of practice in Buddhism.[11] The Daruma School, however, did not voluntarily embark on a side-path from Buddhism: its thought and ways were just not accepted by the collective judgement of mainstream Buddhist tradition as Buddhist. Thus, the 'intentional heresy' and 'unwitting heresy' do not amount to the same thing.

Second, one of the considerations which apparently motivated Toni Packer to depart from the role of a specifically Buddhist teacher has to do with sloughing off the socially defined role of one who performs ceremonies.[12] This is in marked contrast to the Daruma School, which emphasises the importance of esoteric rituals. Overall, without miracles or esoteric ceremonies, without deep, doctrinal mysteries requiring a rational intellect for their resolution, and without authority or lineage, Toni Packer's practice breaks – not only with the main points of one main text of the Daruma School – but with Buddhism as historically understood altogether, leaving an impression of 'clear water flowing quietly over rocks'.[13]

Having become too Zen for Zen as institution, has she willingly become a heretic? This is an interesting issue. Many religious reformers have been judged to be heretics in a similar way, but that does not make them wrong unless one makes the assumption that the future must resemble the past. In the present context the main point is that 'the trappings of religion' – such as miracle, mystery and authority – are very much in evidence in even one of the schools of the Zen Buddhist tradition often regarded as heretical (the Daruma School), whereas precisely these trappings are spurned by Toni Packer's practice.

It might be argued that just as there is a way of being Buddhist which is not un-Christian, there is a way of being as Toni Packer is which is not un-Buddhist. It is just that she wishes to disassociate herself from the trappings of Buddhism in order to affirm the spirit of Zen in a new way. On this view, has she gone beyond Buddhism to form a new group called 'post-Zen'? No: she is showing the spirit of Zen in a new way. It seems to me that in mentioning Toni Packer, Canfield raises an interesting issue about whether Packer is to be regarded as heretical or as continuous with tradition. A similar question could be raised about the authenticity of the Daruma School.

Third, a basic idea of the Daruma School, the idea of the identity of mind and Buddha and the unity of all, is not even mentioned in Canfield's five claims which he thinks give us the essence of Buddhism. (We should beware of the 'craving for generality', noted by Wittgenstein, to articulate an essence of a phenomenon.) Doumoulin mentions the term *jishin sokubutsu* (the doctrine of the unity of all things) as the Daruma School's idea on this point.[14]

The upshot of this discussion is that, first, it cannot be maintained that 'post-Zen' has been with us all the while in the form of heretical schools like the Daruma School, for the differences between them are too great. Second, Canfield's essentialisation of Buddhism in five claims can be shown to be inadequate by reference to schools of Buddhism such as the Daruma School which articulate Buddhism differently.

To paraphrase a comment by Zen teacher Dai-en Bennage, from a Zen view we in the West are not yet at Zen, so there is no sense in talking about 'post-Zen'. As Shundo Aoyama writes:

> Zen Master Kosho Ushiyama said, 'The original way needs nothing to be added, nor is it clogged up. It perfectly suffices in itself. Because human beings have the ability to think, they always want to add something, and soon everything gets clogged up.' Civilization today is clogged up as a result of the human desire to add more and more.[15]

Talk about 'post-Zen' with reference to Toni Packer's practice obscures the fact that her practice could be regarded as one of the possible ways of being Buddhist in America today. In any case, there is a difficult issue of interpretation here which the nomenclature of 'post-Zen' glosses over without contributing to any deep understanding of the phenomenon.

Ethical Schemas in Buddhism

No account of Buddhist ethics would be even roughly right without mention of the existence of traditional ethical schemas such as the Four Noble Truths and the Eight-fold Noble Path. In America, because of the association in the popular imagination of Buddhism and counter-cultural movements of the 1960s and 1970s and the writings of Alan Watts *et al.*, it is sometimes thought that Buddhism's 'freedom' is just a word for 'nothing left to lose' and that the idea of Buddhism overall is just that of a 'do your own thing' notion. But the counter-culture was not exactly an 'experiment', although it was experiential: as D. Z. Phillips observes in another context, 'waking to another shaky day is not to wake to an experimental one'.[16]

Even a cursory view of Zen training in monasteries (if not the Zen teacher's swift wack of a *keisaku* in the *dojo!*) will be enough to disabuse anyone of the above misinterpretation of Buddhism. The Four Noble Truths and the Eight-fold Noble Path should be mentioned as main examples of such schemas, although whether these schemas are to be emphasised (and if so, which points in particular) is a matter of individual faith and sectarian tradition within Buddhism.[17]

III

In concluding this paper I would like to address some philosophical issues which arise out of reading Professor Canfield's stimulating paper.[18]

Endless Life and Eternal Life

Much of my own work occurs on the interface between philosophy of religion and Buddhology.[19] Despite the fact that he speaks of theism, *mutatis mutandis*, in D. Z. Phillips's work, *Death and Immortality*, there are seminal passages for the interpretation of 'immortality' and 'enlightenment' in Buddhism.

In effect, in one such passage Phillips claims that living the ethical life is living the divine life in the here and now, and put in this way there is no reason in principle why this account cannot be extended to cover non-theistic religions (such as Theravada

Buddhism for example).[20] In another passage from the same work the applicability of Phillips's account to Buddhist ethics is very striking. There, speaking of various possible meanings of 'immortality', Phillips comments: 'immortality might mean the kind of moral attitudes I have been trying to outline in this chapter. Eternal life would mean living and dying in a way which could not be rendered pointless by death.'[21]

I take it that living in such a way as not to have the value of one's activity be contingent upon chance or change, loss or gain, praise or blame, is living the ethical life in the here and now. To do so is to give life an *in itself* ethical dimension. This is *eternal life* without the supposition of *endless life*. Both of these views are species of *immortality belief*, but they are very different in kind.

The endless-life view of immortality is specifically rejected in Buddhism with the setting aside of the *ātman* (viewed as a permanent, blissful, centre of consciousness). Buddhism teaches the *anātman* doctrine (literally, 'no soul'; more liberally, 'non-substantiality'). Buddhism therefore rejects immortality in one specific sense, that of 'endless life'.

In another sense, however, *amata* (literally, 'not mortal'; more liberally, 'the deathless') is predicated of *nibbāna* or enlightenment (Sanskrit *nirvāna*).[22] There are two main senses of the term for 'enlightenment' (Pali *nibbāna* or Sanskrit *nirvāna*).

In the first sense, *nibbāna saupādisesa* (*nibbāna* with the Five Aggregates[23] of bodymind intact), enlightenment may be understood as an event in life. For example, the episode styled the 'eureka' or enlightenment experience of the historical Siddhartha Gotama Sakyamuni Buddha under the *ficus religiosus*, the *bodhi* tree, on the banks of the River Neranjara just before he embarked on his teaching career as a 'fully enlightened Buddha' (*samyak-sambuddha*), counts as an *instance* of enlightenment which can possibly be instanciated by others who take the necessary time and effort.

In the second sense, *nibbāna anupādisesa* (*nibbāna* without bodymind), enlightenment in the case of the *Tathāgata* ('enlightened saint') is not an event *in* life, but the *boundary* (in contradistinction to empirical line drawn) between *samsāra* (the realm of birth, death, and rebirth) and what is *parinibbāna* ('final enlightenment') and not *samsāra*.[24] One might picture this generic archetypal experience as instanciated by 'the Buddha' reclining after having eaten poisoned food, but this is a depiction of what leads up to *parinibbāna*, not *parinibbāna* itself. For 'final enlightenment' there is no picture. One cannot (logically) go beyond all things to think the other side of the limit and then describe what that would be like.

A careful reading of the relevant passage in Pali context[25] by anyone aware of the above distinction in contemporary philosophy of religion between 'endless life' and 'eternal life' would reveal something interesting. For one would see that the import of the Buddhist idea of *amata*, 'the deathless', may be elucidated as an 'eternal life' view of immortality (in the sense of living the divine life in the here and now) rather than an 'endless life' view of immortality (as continuing to exist 'in' *nirvāṇa* after becoming a *Tathāgata* ('liberated saint').

So there is a lot more to an enlightened way of life in Buddhism than conquering 'self-reverie'. Enlightenment *in* life is a matter of loosening the grip that passion, hatred, and confusion (*raga, dosa,* and *moha*) have on one's life; that may include, but is not limited to, the sort of self-reverie Canfield discusses.

It should also be noted that reverie need not be the sort of *self*-reverie which Canfield finds pernicious: if mind is Buddha and Buddha is mind, reverie is no less a part of the here and now than any perception of waters quietly flowing over rocks. The possibilities of reverie should not go unnoticed lest one issue a blanket condemnation of it. I say this because unless one says more about self-reverie than Canfield does in his paper, the danger is that one may overgeneralise and miss the phenomenon in its full range. Reverie might, for example, hurl one into a possible future of selflessly saving all sentient beings through good works and/or meditation. It is easy to imagine a disconsolate Prince Siddhartha behind the palace walls after contemplating the Four Sights[26] and prior to the Great Renunciation as engaged in reverie about becoming a world-renouncer. Although the dynamic that Canfield unfolds may be the more typical one, there is nothing about reverie *per se* that necessitates it being always *self*-reverie in a self-aggrandising way.

Understanding the Buddhist doctrines, including *anatta* (no-self), does not make a person Buddhist. Knowledge is not virtue, nor is it necessary to assume that scholars of Buddhism themselves necessarily exemplify virtue.[27] Canfield's jabs at scholars who study 'no-self' yet are very attached to self as indicated by specific behaviours are amusing, but it is dubious that anyone thoughtful would believe that there is a necessary relationship between studying 'no-self' and living a no-self way of life anyway.

The Grip of General Speculative Theories

Buddhism opposes *prapañca* ('craving') and, in one sense of 'view'
or *diṭṭhi* (that is, where *diṭṭhi* is used in the sense of 'speculative
view'), opposes 'speculative views'. *Diṭṭhi* is not used in some
one way in early Indian Buddhism, and there is no blanket condemnation of views as such.[28] Even in Zen, there is to be 'no
reliance on words or letters' (*Platform Sutra*), but that is a far cry
from 'no words or letters' *simpliciter*.

Nevertheless, it is the expressed intention (even if not always
the practical result) of Buddhist doctrine to steer clear of the sort
of theorising which is controversial and not based in one's own
experience. Hence the Buddhist inclination is to shy away from
what pioneering Pali text translator Isaline Blew Horner frequently
called 'wordy warfare'.

But what then of the Buddhist ethical schemas (such as the
Four Noble Truths and the Eight-fold Noble Path)? These are not
part of some overarching ethical theory, but rather path-orienting
statements and specific rules for being on the path respectively.
Attempts to construct an 'ethical theory' in early Buddhism would
be inconsistent with the Buddha's salvific aim, for such theories
would be non-demonstrable, disputatious, and themselves sources
of attachment. However much some scholars would like it to be
otherwise, the plain fact is that there is no general *principle* (comparable to the 'categorical imperative' of Kant or the 'principle of
utility' of Mill) consistently endorsed in Buddhism which would
provide the backbone of an ethics as a branch of philosophy.

Rather than seeing this as a *limitation* of Buddhist perspective,
it might be seen as eminently sensible. For if D. Z. Phillips is
right, philosophers should give up the quest to answer the wrong-
headed question, 'what is the nature of the good life?'[29] Doing so
would not necessarily represent a retreat into nihilism, but rather
a clear-headed recognition that the relation between belief and
practice is not that between rational justification and subsequent
action.

Notes

1. See Stewart R. Sutherland, *God, Jesus and Belief* (Oxford: Basil Blackwell, 1984), p. 110. It is interesting to contrast Canfield's view with that of Sutherland, who argues for a view *sub specie aeternitatis* construed as 'regulative' rather than a 'benchmark' thus:

   As More sits in the tower waiting to be executed or as Jesus turns his face towards Jerusalem and execution, what distinguishes them from the fanatical or the insane is the possibility of self-questioning: only the madman excludes *even the possibility* that he might be deluded. Self-questioning requires a perspective other than one's own. Neither Rich nor the disciples could provide that alternative perspective: the argument with them was already over; their values had been found wanting. The only possible perspective which will in the end satisfy the logical demands of the situation is that of a transcendent order of values. Such values are reflected in 'God will know it' and in the idea of 'thy will'.

   However, such values, as eternal, cannot be presented to us as a set of benchmarks against which we measure our own values and those of others. The role of the conception of the view *sub specie aeternitatis* is not descriptive: it is, in Kant's term, 'regulative'. And its regulative role will be quite adequate for our purposes. What More or Jesus require is the idea simply of an order against which their judgements will be assessed.

2. Stewart R. Sutherland, *Atheism and the Rejection of God* (Oxford: Basil Blackwell, 1977).

3. Here I intentionally set aside the issue of whether and how one might distinguish between *sorts* of relativism (such as descriptive, normative, and meta-ethical), and the issue of how (if at all) such nicer distinctions might affect the present discussion. It is clear that relativism is not all of a piece.

4. In the world of Buddhist scholarship, K. N. Upadhyaya and D. J. Kalupahana represent divergent tendencies on this point. Upadhyaya (in *Early Buddhism and the Bhagavadgita*) inclines toward 'experientialism' and David J. Kalupahana (in *Buddhist Philosophy* and elsewhere) inclines toward 'empiricism'.

5. Here I would simply observe that it has not yet been demonstrated that there is any connection between Buddhism and what Canfield calls 'post-Zen' so as to justify the language of 'prototype'.

6. I find Professor Canfield's expression 'post-Zen systems' intriguing. What sort of 'system' – system of thought? Does Toni Packer, for example, offer a new 'system of thought'? What is crucial about Zen is precisely that it cannot be rendered as a 'system of thought', so that any juxtaposition on the same continuum of Zen and subsequent 'systems of thought' involves in fact a radical discontinuity under the guise of continuity.

7. My own understanding of ethics in Buddhism is informed mainly by stimulating teachers who introduced me to Theravada sources (Professor Chung-yuan Chang). Since Professor Canfield uses the

Japanese term 'Zen' in his exposition, I have endeavoured to check my understanding to include Japanese perspectives. In this regard, I am indebted to some conversations with Rev. P. Dai-en Bennage (Mt Equity Zendo, Muncy, Pa) and Professor William R. LaFleur (University of Pennsylvania). Those mentioned are not listed as necessarily approving the ideas expressed in this paper, and responsibility for the exposition rests with myself alone.

8. That is, the *Jōtōshōgakuron*. See Heinrich Doumoulin, *Zen Buddhism: A History*, Vol. 2, *Japan* (New York: Macmillan; London: Collier/ Macmillan, 1990), p. 11.

9. Doumoulin, *Zen Buddhism: A History*, Vol. 2, p. 11.

10. For example, the Daruma School was criticised by Dogen. See Doumoulin, *Zen Buddhism: A History*, Vol. 2, pp. 69–71.

11. I am indebted to Lelia Calder of Swarthmore College for a conversation about this point pertaining to Toni Packer's practice.

12. See the chapter on Toni Packer in Lenore Friedman, *Meetings With Remarkable Women* (Boston and London: Shambala, 1987).

13. Lenore Friedman, *Meetings With Remarkable Women* (Boston and London: Shambala, 1987) p. 64. Regarding (a) miracle, (b) mystery, and (c) authority we find Packer taking the views as explicated by Friedman that: (a) one does not need to be caught up in the psychological entrapment of awe of 'enclosures', which have been conducive to 'projection, propitiation, worship, magic, and ceremony' in assuaging fears of evil and violence (p. 60); (b) there is no mysterious doctrine to be fathomed – 'This center was not formed to enshrine a creed, or the creed of *no* creed. Not the idea of anything nor the idea of nothing. When there is nothing there is no need for any belief' (p. 60); and that there is no need to be in an authoritative lineage with Roshi Philip Kapleau (p. 39) or to support the custom of use of the authoritative vest (*rakusu*) as a sartorial mark of advanced student status (p. 50), or emblems of enforcement of dharmic authority such as the *keisaku* or hitting stick in meditation practice (p. 48). Practising Buddhists who are not scholars would anyway be aware of the *keisaku* as 'a light flat stick, representing the sword of Manjusri, used by a senior monk in the Zendo (q.v.) to rouse monks falling asleep or, at invitation, to smack shoulder muscles grown stiff from sitting' from practice or from Christmas Humphrey's *A Popular Dictionary of Buddhism* (London: Curzon Press, 1975), pp. 107–8.

14. Doumoulin, *Zen Buddhism*, Vol. 2, p. 11.

15. Shundo Aoyama, *Zen Seeds: Reflections of a Female Priest* (Tokyo: Kosei Publishing Co., 1990). First English edition translated by P. Daien Bennage.

In considering the possibility that Zen may be *passé* and post-Zen the wave of future 'systems', it seems that Professor Canfield needs to cover himself against possible replies by Zen teachers to the effect that his paper smacks of Western arrogance in presupposing that Toni Packer's sort of practice represents the future. One Zen teacher has suggested to me that Canfield's paper might be

regarded as presuming a special knowledge of a future development at a time when Zen teachers are just making small inroads
into the American religious scene. It is also likely that they would
regard the whole exercise of writing the paper as 'intellectual dodgem
cars' with no real conviction.

16. D. Z. Phillips, *Interventions in Ethics* (Albany: State University of
New York Press, 1992), p. 99.

17. A ready reference of recent date setting forth Buddhist ethical schemas
in a clear manner, which is not tradition-specific but pan-Asian and
to some extent philosophically constructive is Damien Keown, *The
Nature of Buddhist Ethics* (New York: St Martin's Press, 1992).

18. It was a pleasure to see that Professor Canfield also draws inspiration from the work of Ludwig Wittgenstein. Alan P. F. Sell, *Philosophy of Religion (1875–1980)* (London: Methuen; New York: Croom
Helm, 1988) describes the intellectual milieu of British philosophy
of religion in which I worked on Buddhism in the late 1970s and
until 1981 at the University of London, King's College at the
'Language School'. The influence of Wittgenstein was felt in both
the Philosophy Department under Professor Peter Winch and with
(Visiting) Professor Norman Malcolm, as well as in the Department
of the History and Philosophy of Religion, where I worked under
Professor Stewart R. Sutherland. Chris Gudmunsen, my predeces-
sor in the Tutorial Studentship in the Philosophy of Religion, did
an interpretation of *Abhidhamma* Buddhism under the title *Wittgenstein
and Buddhism*. The influence of Wittgensteinian philosophy of religion is particularly evident in Chapter 6, 'The Deathless (*Amata*)'
in my *Rationality and Mind in Early Buddhism* (Delhi: Motilal
Banarsidass, 1987).

19. Compare, for example, Stewart R. Sutherland, 'What Happens After
Death?' in *Scottish Journal of Theology*, December 1969, vol. 22, no. 4,
and Hoffman, *Rationality and Mind in Early Buddhism*, pp. 114–18.

20. D. Z. Phillips, *Death and Immortality* (London: Macmillan, 1970), p. 38.
Here Phillips observes that profit has nothing to do with the love
of God, and that immortality 'has to do, not with its existence after
death and all the consequences that is supposed to carry with it,
but with his [that is, the person who loves God] participation in
God's life, in his contemplation of divine love'.

21. Phillips, *Death and Immortality*, p. 50.

22. Hoffman, *Rationality and Mind in Early Buddhism*, pp. 103–18.

23. The five Aggregates (or *pañca khandha* in Pali) are often translated
as form, feeling, sensations, dispositions, and consciousness.

24. From a scholarly point of view, the vexed question of Buddhist *nirvaṇa*
comes up pointedly here. (How I frame the *nirvaṇa* doctrine draws
from the lectures and published works of David J. Kalupahana. See
also Richard Gombrich, *Precept and Practice* (Oxford: Clarendon Press,
1971) and, for a detailed discussion, see Guy Welbon, *Buddhist Nir-
vana and Its Western Interpreters* (Chicago: University of Chicago Press,
1968). It seems to me unreasonable to insist that the large-scale distinction between *nibbāna saupādisesa and nibbāna anupādisesa* can be

refuted by one or even a few isolated textual passages. It is supported by a mass of textual evidence articulated by Kalupahana, and as Gombrich observes, the weight of continuing Sinhalese tradition speaks for it.

25. See Hoffman, *Rationality and Mind in Early Buddhism*, p. 105 for the Pali text and English translation.

26. Namely, old person, sick person, dead person, and wandering recluse.

27. In this connection it is interesting to consider Tom Kasulis's paper on hypocrisy: 'Hypocrisy in the Self-understanding of Religion', in James Kellenberger (ed.), *Inter-religious Models and Criteria* (London: Macmillan, 1993), pp. 151–65.

28. David Kalupahana has sometimes spoken as though *diṭṭhi* is a technical term meaning specifically 'speculative view', and that Buddhists are opposed to *diṭṭhi*. But *diṭṭhi* is used in a variety of ways, and that Buddhists are not altogether opposed to views is evident in the concept of 'right view' in the Eight-fold Noble Path.

29. See especially the essay, 'What Can We Expect from Ethics?', in D. Z. Phillips, *Interventions in Ethics* (Albany, NY: SUNY Press, 1992), and specifically p. 103 therein.

Part VI
Atheism, Morality and Religion

11

Atheism and Morality

R. W. BEARDSMORE

Norman Malcolm once observed that, in Western academic philosophy, religious belief is commonly regarded as unreasonable and is viewed with condescension or even contempt. Malcolm himself did not, of course, take this view, but it is one which will be familiar to most philosophers, even if they do not themselves hold it. Nor need Malcolm's observation be restricted only to the realm of academic philosophy. For there are many atheists who, rightly or wrongly, seeing themselves as untouched by philosophy, would nevertheless subscribe to the view that religious belief is of its very nature confused or in some way intellectually inadequate. So, I had better start by saying that, though an atheist, I do not number myself among them. It is not, however, my aim in this paper to defend religion against such attacks but rather to turn my attention to an analogous attitude amongst those who would count themselves religious believers. And once again, this attitude is not one which is restricted to academic philosophers, but finds its counterpart amongst the general populace. It is moreover, like the view which Malcolm castigates, often marked by condescension, or even contempt, attitudes which are, by contrast, directed in this case towards the atheist. I have in mind the view that atheism is unreasonable, or in some way intellectually inadequate, because it is incapable of doing justice to the role that moral considerations play in our lives, or to put it rather more bluntly, but also rather more elegantly, because if God did not exist, then everything would be permitted.

As might be expected such a view is capable of more and less refined forms, of greater and lesser philosophical sophistication. And it is not, I suppose, surprising that the level of subtlety will to some extent depend on whether the proponent is or is not versed in the refinements of philosophical discussion. Recently my local daily tabloid contained for some while a debate on its letters page concerning the effects in Welsh society, and in Swansea in particular, of an alleged decline in religious belief. The general theme of many of these letters seemed to be that increased lawlessness and lack of respect for the lives and property of others could be directly attributed to a decline in the belief in a God who punishes transgressors. It was not, of course, difficult to detect in those who wrote in this way a genuine sense of injustice at the failure of earthly authorities to punish the morally or legally culpable, at the spectacle of the unjust prospering. Still, it does not require someone particularly well-versed in philosophy to see that it does no favours to God to portray Him as a sort of court of higher appeal charged with the task of punishing those whom the earthly authorities fail to convict. Nor, and perhaps more importantly from the point of view of the atheist, does it do any favours to morality to present it as a form of human practice whose value (and perhaps whose sense) lies in its enabling those who adhere to it to escape punishment, or more succinctly, to present morality as something whose value lies in its being to the advantage of the just.

It should not, however, be thought that it is only outside the realms of academic philosophy that such attempts to found morality on religious belief are prevalent. For the belief that morality requires justification in religious terms if it is to be taken seriously is to be found in the writings of academic philosophers themselves. Consider the following passage:

> Religious morality and Christian morality in particular may have its difficulties, but religious apologists argue that secular morality has still greater difficulties ... It leads, they claim, to ethical scepticism, nihilism, or at best to pure conventionalism. Such apologists could point out that if we look at morality with the cold eye of the anthropologist, we will find morality to be nothing more than the conflicting mores of the various tribes spread around the globe. If we look at ethics from a purely secular view, we will discover that it is constituted by tribal conventions, conventions which we are free to reject if we are sufficiently free from ethnocentricity. We can continue to act in accordance with them or we can reject them and adopt a different set of conventions.[1]

Nielsen himself does not find this alleged feature of secular moralities, that they may be rejected or adopted at will, problematic. For on his view, the alternative, namely that moral rules are in some sense determined by God's word, is merely a psychological prop, which the believer could, if he or she considered the matter rationally, do without. Nevertheless there are those religious believers who, sharing Nielsen's view of the alternatives, find in it a compelling reason to think of morality as God's gift. Thus Leszek Kolakowski, in his book *Religion*,[2] attempts to convince us that any serious concern for morality is parasitic on religion, by suggesting that unless moral laws are seen as having a religious source, unless the virtues are seen as God's gifts, then the only alternative is what he calls Promethean humanism. But his description of Promethean humanism as the view that 'people are entirely free in stating the criteria of good and evil',[3] that is to say, the view that people are free to choose what moral standards they wish to adopt, makes it clear that his view of the alternatives facing us is much the same as that of Nielsen. For both, religion is thought of as an attempt to found morality on something not dependent on choice, namely the divine will, and for both the alternative is the sort of conventionalism which makes our moral allegiances simply a matter of choice. The difference is simply that for Kolakowski the element of choice is seen as rendering morality arbitrary or futile, whereas for Nielsen the seriousness of morality lies precisely in the element of choice.

What is, however, not clear is why both Kolakowski and Nielsen should share the assumption that they do. Why should it be held that our moral values must be either the product of religion or the product of an apparently arbitrary choice? And it is difficult to escape the conclusion that this view is the result of a simple equivocation. A clue as to the nature of this equivocation is given by Nielsen's description of morality as simply a set of different conventions. For the word 'convention' *is* used most naturally to identify what is the product of human choice and often to describe cases where it does not much matter what choice people make, so long as (within a certain context) they make the same choice. Unlike in most other countries, the convention in Britain is that one drives on the left. There are different conventions, precisely because in different countries different decisions have been taken. And it would, at least in principle, be possible for these decisions to be reversed, as was indeed once the case in

Sweden. It is a convention of association football that the ball is not handled except by the goalkeeper. But this convention was challenged, if the (probably apocryphal) story is true, by a pupil at Rugby School who picked up the ball and ran with it. The result was that a decision to change the convention was taken in the game now known as Rugby football. But the possibility in these cases of deciding which convention to adopt is a function not of the fact that there are *different* conventions, but of the fact that they are different *conventions*. And it is only if we think of different ideas about what matters morally as conventions that it will seem to follow that there is a choice between them – that whatever values we adhere to, we do so because we have chosen. For the mere fact that in other places and in other societies people think differently has *in itself* no tendency to show that each of us must choose between these alternatives. Perhaps my children are important to me, so that in a whole range of situations, I shall regard myself as facing obligations to protect them, help further their careers, help them out of financial difficulties. And perhaps there are societies where they think differently about their children, for instance, societies in which female offspring are sometimes left to die, or where children are sometimes sold into slavery. But what of it? The fact that there are alternative ways of regarding one's children does nothing to show that these are alternatives for me or that I reached the values which I possess by selecting them from among a range of alternatives. Yet for Nielsen and Kolakowski the possibility of alternative values is held to entail just this conclusion.

Perhaps then the argument by which Kolakowski reaches his conclusions regarding atheistic morality will not bear examination. For there is no reason to accept Nielsen's view that, unless we hold a religious morality and think of our duties and obligations as deriving their authority from God's word, we shall be forced to the sort of conventionalist conception of morality which Nielsen advocates, but which Kolakowski sees as incompatible with moral seriousness. Still it does not follow that Kolakowski's conclusion that genuine morality is religious morality is false. For it may be that although there is no incoherence in the idea of an atheistic morality, as a matter of fact certain central features of our morality *do* derive from a religious background which we once shared. The point is developed by Elizabeth Anscombe in a well-known passage from her article 'Modern Moral Philosophy', where she argues that it is only because Christianity involved a law conception of ethics and because of the dominance of Christianity for many centuries, that 'the concepts of being bound, permitted or excused became deeply embedded in our language and thought'. She goes on:

> Naturally it is not possible to have such a conception unless you believe in God as a law-giver; like Jews, Stoics and Christians. But if such a conception is dominant for many centuries, and then is given up, it is a natural result that the concepts of 'obligation', of being bound or required as by a law, should remain though they had lost their root; and if the word 'ought' has become invested in certain contexts with the sense of 'obligation', it too will remain to be spoken with a special emphasis and a special feeling in these contexts ... The situation, if I am right, was the interesting one of the survival of a concept outside the framework of thought that made it a really intelligible one.[4]

Though Anscombe may appear to be resting her case on an assertion of historical fact, there is nevertheless a concealed assumption in her argument, which gives it whatever appearance of plausibility it may have. For, as has been pointed out by others, Anscombe seems to take it largely for granted that if a concept has outlived the practices or ways of thinking in which it originally had its sense, then in so far as it is still used it will have no sense. Since the notions of being obliged or permitted had their source in a religious context, where they were equated with what is obliged or permitted by a divine will, then they must lose their sense in a society where no such equation can be made.

But why should it be thought that it is only God's will which can intelligibly be said to place obligations on me? Certainly in a society in which religious belief is taken for granted, it is likely that people will see their obligations in this way, though it is not, I should have thought, more than likely, since there seems no reason why, for example, a man might not see obligations as arising from a love forbidden by his religion – say, the love of one man for another, or the love of a priest for a nun. Be that as it may, at least in a society where religious belief is losing its hold, why should it not be the case that institutions other than the church are thought of as imposing limits on what is or is not permitted? Suppose for instance that as a member of a trade union, I feel that I have an obligation to respect a picket-line, or that as a doctor I feel myself bound to respond to an emergency call in the middle of the night. Why should it be said that in these cases my reference to what I ought to do has a 'mere mesmeric force'? True, in such cases what obliges me cannot be said to be the will of God, but this does not mean that there can be no answer to the question 'What obliges me?' What obliges the trade unionist to observe the picket-line is simply his membership of a trade union. What obliges the doctor to answer the emergency call is the rules of his profession. In what way can these ways of speaking be said to lack sense?

No doubt such an answer would not satisfy Anscombe. And it might be thought that in one rather important respect it ignores what is central to her argument. For, it may be said, Anscombe does not claim that *any* sense of 'obligation' has, and must have, its basis in divine law, but only that what she calls the 'special moral sense' or sometimes the 'absolute' sense must do so. And, so the argument might go, this is borne out by the points which have been made so far. For though membership of a trade union may well carry with it the obligation to respect picket-lines, though doctors may have various professional obligations, these cannot be thought to be absolutely binding, since it is always possible for the trade unionist to resign from membership, possible for the doctor to find another profession. By contrast, where an obligation is thought of as the will of God, then there can be no question of the believer choosing to avoid it.

Unfortunately, if the argument is developed in this way, it quickly becomes apparent that it is merely a variant of the line of reasoning which has already been detected in the writings of Nielsen and Kolakowski, and rests on the same assumption. For again, why should the fact that there is an alternative to membership of a trade union, namely, resigning one's membership, be thought to show that this is an alternative for any particular trade unionist? Indeed, in so far as it is implied that the mere existence of an alternative way of life is sufficient to rob obligations of their absolute character, then the conclusion should be drawn that, even for the devout religious believer, God's commands do not possess the status of absolute obligations. For there is certainly an alternative to religious belief, namely atheism. The absolute nature of God's commands for the religious believer stems not from a denial of the possibility of atheism. It stems rather from the rec-ognition that such a way of life is not for that person a possibility.

If what I have said so far is correct, then it may seem that any attempt to show that morality can have no rationale in independence of religion, or that the latter is in some way dependent on the former is, regardless of whether it is presented as the consequence of historical research or as a consequence of conceptual analysis, merely the result of confusion. But perhaps this conclusion is premature. For might it not be argued that what undermines the positions of writers like Kolakowski and Anscombe is not the form of the arguments that they use, but rather their generality? Perhaps then it is the case that though there is no way of showing that morality as a whole is dependent on religion, there are nevertheless at least some central features of a religious morality for which there is no counterpart in the lives of atheists. Or to put the matter more circumspectly, might it not be argued that in so far as these features are to be found in the lives of atheists, their presence there is to be explained (at least historically) by the role which religion once played in the life of our society, a role which is the heritage of both believers and atheists? And here a remark quoted earlier from Kolakowski's book may be thought to point in the right direction. For there I mentioned Kolakowski's conception of the virtues as a gift from God. This view, as we saw, cannot be defended, at least in so far as it is intended to depict the role played by moral considerations in the life of atheists as well as believers. But perhaps, it may be suggested, the notion that certain aspects of our lives, or even our lives themselves, are gifts, together with the allied notions of gratitude and ingratitude, will serve as candidates for moral concepts, which, though they may play a role in the life of the atheist, can do so only in so far as the atheist shares with the religious believer a common historical background, a background in which religion played a central part. So that to the extent that we detect these ways of speaking in the atheist's vocabulary, this indicates at least one respect in which this vocabulary is parasitic on religion, or perhaps, as some might put it, indicates a religious element in that vocabulary. It is to this claim that I shall devote the remainder of my paper.

In Chapter 12 of his book *Good and Evil: An Absolute Conception*, Rai Gaita begins a discussion of the phenomenon of gratitude for life with a quotation from Pablo Casals in which the cellist describes the way in which he begins his daily routine. Casals describes this routine as 'mechanical', but he goes on:

> that is not the only meaning it has for me. It is a discovery of the world of which I have the joy of being a part. It fills me with awareness of the wonder of life, with a feeling of the incredible marvel of being a human being . . . I do not think that a day has passed in my life in which I have failed to look with fresh amazement at the miracle of nature.[5]

Gaita speaks later of Casals' words as being 'in the accent of gratitude'[6] and connects this with seeing life as a gift. Those who are inclined to speak in such terms, he tells us, see a certain kind of unity in their lives, such that they think in terms of the purposes for which they were given life and may see suicide as a species of ingratitude. He mentions in this connection a letter from Mozart to Padre Martini in which the composer speaks of our obligation 'to compel ourselves industriously to enlighten one another by means of reasoning and to apply ourselves to carry forward the sciences and the arts'.[7]

Gaita notes that someone who speaks in these ways, of life as a gift, or of gratitude and ingratitude, need not speak of the gift as God's gift. Nevertheless, he goes on:

> The person who speaks of life as a gift but who cannot speak of it as God's gift might say that to be religious in the 'strict sense' is to be able to speak of God and to speak His name in prayer. That does not mean that if someone is not religious in the strict sense, then they are not religious at all, or that they are religious in a waffly sense. If such a person may be said to speak of an implicit recognition, or love of, God, then they speak religiously even if they would only shrug their shoulders at such a claim. There are first- and third-person asymmetries here.[8]

I take Gaita's final remark to indicate that it is possible to speak of people as religious, even where they would not characterise their own lives in this way, and this I should not wish to deny. On the other hand there are also indications in this passage that he thinks that it is possible to say of anyone who speaks of life as a gift, that they are religious, at least in some sense, that they 'speak out of an implicit recognition, or love of God'. But whether or not Gaita would regard himself as committed to this conclusion, it is certainly common enough.

But is Gaita mistaken in supposing that to think of life as a gift is to think (in at least *some* sense of 'religious') in religious terms? For if he is, then, for the atheist, who is it who is thought of as making the gift? To whom is the atheist grateful? Consider the following passage from the autobiography of the country singer Hank Williams Jr. Williams is convalescing from a near-fatal climbing accident in Montana.

> It's September, and there's winter definitely in the air. Sometimes, I sit outside in the chill and stare into the wilderness, and my mind floats back up to the mountain. Sometimes I relive every minute, step by step. I feel myself falling, know that I'm dying. I spend hours on the side of the mountain, drifting between death and life and finally choosing the latter. I know I'm a different person now, and the task seems to be integrating the new person into the old life. I decide though, what I will *not* do. I will not testify and explain how I've found Jesus . . . that wasn't the lesson of the mountain. I spend a lot of time thinking of that lesson, which is so simple I can't imagine having not learned it a long time ago – if you're going to live, live. Just live your life to the best of your abilities.[9]

Though Williams later comes to speak as a religious believer, as someone who has found God, there is no sign that religious belief played a very profound role in his life, and almost none in the view of life presented in the passage that I have quoted. Nevertheless, just as Gaita says of the passage from Pablo Casals that it is in the accent of gratitude, one might well say the same of the passage quoted above. Williams's life has been spared, and his gratitude for this gift of life carries with it certain responsibilities and consequences. He knows that as a result of what has happened to him, his life will be different, that it must be lived in a different way.

But even if someone who lacks any religious belief *is* inclined to speak in these ways, this may not seem to remove the difficulties. For who has spared him? To whom does he have the responsibility to change his life? To whom does he owe gratitude? Who gave the gift of life? And it may seem that the only possible answer in these cases is precisely the answer which the atheist cannot give. For the atheist cannot say that God gave him the gift of life, that he is grateful to God, that God spared him, and so on. So must we not conclude that if the atheist is inclined to speak in these ways, this inclination can be explained only as the vestige of a religious faith, a religious faith which, because of his heritage, he is unable to expunge from his vocabulary? Otherwise, it may be argued, such phrases can have no meaning for the unbeliever.

But in what way can they be said to have no meaning? If an atheist, having been unexpectedly saved from death, speaks of life as a gift, why can this have no meaning unless he speaks of the gift as a gift from God? One answer to this question is to appeal to what is often nowadays referred to as the grammar of statements like 'I was given . . .' or 'I am grateful'. It is a point of grammar, so it will be said, that a gift must have a giver, that when one is grateful, then one is grateful to someone. And arguments of this form have a long tradition. They were, for example, used by Cardinal Newman to show that certain features of the way we all employ the notion of conscience proved a belief in God:

> If, as is the case, we feel responsibility, are ashamed, are frightened, at transgressing the voice of conscience, this implies that there is One to whom we are responsible, before whom we are ashamed, whose claim upon us we fear.[10]

Indeed, it might well be thought that in arguing that the presence in our lives of the notion of moral obligation implies the notion of a divine will which obliges us, Anscombe is using yet another variant of the argument.

In examining such arguments it is important to distinguish the philosopher's use of the term 'grammar' from its use by, say, English teachers or linguists. For in the latter sense a sentence which has no clear meaning may well be grammatically in order. It will be in order so long as it obeys certain rules of grammar, which are at least in principle capable of being enumerated. So in this sense 'She was grateful to the kitchen sink' or 'Julius Caesar gave Hank Williams Jr the gift of life' are grammatically in order, since they break none of these rules, even though in most contexts such remarks would be quite incomprehensible. But, in the sense in which philosophers speak of 'grammar' or 'logical grammar', where this is a criterion of sense, it is a mistake to suppose that what is grammatically sound, what makes sense, is determined by some set of rules. For despite what generations of philosophers may have thought, nothing general can be said here. To determine whether some claim or other makes sense we have to look at the context in which it is used, to see whether or not it has a role to play there. Thus, though it may seem plausible to suppose that there are some general rules, such as 'a statement having the form "p and not-p" never makes sense', we are inclined to assent to this claim simply because we tend to call to mind contexts in which such a statement *would* be rejected as nonsensical. In a given context, for example where the police are interrogating a suspect, it may be clear that the suspect's propensity to claim at one time that on the night in question he was in bed with his wife, and at another (for example, when faced with his wife's denial of this alibi) that he was drinking at the pub with his friends, will be taken to show that he is contradicting himself and so talking nonsense. Here there is no lack of clarity about the context (his interrogators have seen to that) and in *that* context his words do not make sense. Or again, I may be inclined to say that *any* sentence of the form 'x and y are feeling the same pain' contains a grammatical confusion, because I have in mind the incomprehension which I should feel if someone were to complain that I had given them my pain or stolen their pain from them, and forget that perfectly ordinary situation in which someone says to me, 'Oh yes, I know *that* pain. I've had it many times. It's called angina.' In these, as in all other cases, the logical grammar of a proposition is determined not by abstract rules, but by looking at what is done with the proposition in a range of particular cases.

When, however, it is claimed that life can be regarded as a gift only where someone is thought of as the donor, or that one can be grateful only for what someone has given one, the superficial plausibility which such remarks may seem to have when considered in the abstract is merely an illusion. It stems from having derived a rule from certain contexts, for instance, the way in which children think of Christmas presents (as gifts from someone, for example their parents, or Santa Claus) or in which religious believers think of their lives (as gifts from God), and from then trying to impose this rule on the way in which atheists may talk of their lives.

If, however, we look at the role which the notion of a gift (and the allied notions of gratitude, ingratitude, and so on) may have in the life of an atheist, then where is the puzzle? Hank Williams is in a situation in which he might be expected to die – in fact he lies in the snow for some hours, his skull so badly crushed that his brain is exposed. But he does not die. Someone, not a religious believer, speaks here of the gift of life. Why is this so puzzling, so unnatural? Like other gifts, it is something which he had no right to expect. It was not something due to him. It was something desirable. (You do not normally refer to the gift of a bad cold, even if someone gave it you). Like other gifts, it is not something to which one would normally remain indifferent, without people thinking of this as ingratitude. Nor is Williams indifferent. He speaks of the changes in his life, the responsibilities which the gift brings with it. And it is, of course, important that Williams does not think of his life as something which was saved by his own efforts, by a supreme act of will-power, for instance. For something is not normally a gift, if I have earned it. But it is by no means obvious that any of these features is essential if we are to speak of something of a gift. True they could not *all* be absent and it still be natural to speak in this way. In an unpublished paper,[11] Rush Rhees remarks that very often talk of gratitude for one's life is hypocrisy and illustrates the point with a passage from Flannery O'Connor's short story *Revelation*:

> 'If it's one thing I am', Mrs Turpin said with feeling, 'it's grateful. When I think who all I could have been besides myself and what all I got, a little of everything, and a good disposition besides, I feel just like shouting, "Thank you, Jesus, for making everything the way it is! It could have been different!"'

Mrs Turpin's avowals of gratitude are fraudulent because her attitudes towards her own life and character have, despite what she says, *none* of the features of one's attitude towards a gift, except that she speaks of a donor. In truth she sees the circumstances of her life as a matter for pride. But still it does not follow from this that there is some *one* essential feature which makes it appropriate to regard something as a gift. So, given what I have said about the way in which someone might view a miraculous escape from death as a gift of life, why insist that unless they are willing to identify someone as the giver, then they are speaking in a confused fashion? Why insist on any one feature? We speak of the bees as giving honey, and this is not thought to be unnatural, even though it might well be pointed out that we take the honey from them.

If what we have in these examples is a perfectly natural way of talking, a natural sort of reaction to certain sorts of good fortune, then there seems no reason to explain it as a variety of, or vestigial form of, the various ways in which believers may thank God for the gift of life. For in general some feature of our lives requires explanation only where it is in some way puzzling. The point was made forcefully, and on many different occasions, by the writer G. K. Chesterton. Observing, for instance, that in many different societies human beings express their sense of inferiority to others or their reverence for them by bowing, anthropologists had constructed elaborate explanations to explain the prevalence of this practice. Chesterton's response was to question the necessity for such explanations. Why, he asked, exclude the possibility that human beings bow to those they regard as superior simply because it is a perfectly natural thing to do?

It is by no means clear to me why this should not be an equally adequate explanation of the phenomenon which I have been discussing during the latter part of this paper. Reacting to a piece of good fortune or a natural blessing with gratitude seems, looked at in one way, simply a natural response. Of course, like many other responses it may play a different role, or even be expressed in different forms of human practice. In *Zettel*, section 540, Wittgenstein remarks: 'It is a primitive reaction to tend, to treat, the part that hurts when someone else is in pain, and not merely when oneself is.'[12] He might also have drawn attention to the fact that it is a natural human response to turn away from suffering, to avert one's gaze. But though both of these reactions are natural, they occupy a different place in different human practices. In particular, the former is emphasised to the detriment of the latter in Christianity, in for example the story of the Good Samaritan, whereas in many non-religious contexts it will be the latter which is encouraged to the detriment of the former ('Charity begins at home', 'Look after number one', etc.). In a similar way the natural tendency to react to a piece of good fortune as a gift, that is to say with gratitude, is counterbalanced by the equally natural tendency to curse the day one was born in the face of certain forms of extreme suffering, or perhaps to meet the suffering with resignation as does Hank Williams when he discovers that his looks have been destroyed by his fall on the mountain.

In an atheistic morality, these reactions simply coexist. By contrast, within Christian morality the response of gratitude is extended to both good and bad fortune. Thus, Herman Lange, a Catholic chaplain, hearing that he has been condemned by a Nazi court to death by beheading, writes the following words in his prison cell:

> For, after all, death means homecoming. The gift we thereupon receive is so unimaginably great that all human joys pale beside it, and the bitterness of death as such – however, sinister it appear to our human nature – is completely conquered by it.[13]

Clearly the conception of life, *whatever evils it may bring*, as a gift is a conception for which there is no counterpart in an atheistic morality. And nothing that I have said should be taken to deny that there exist such differences between religion and atheism. I have simply tried to argue that the atheistic conception of life as a gift cannot be convicted of incoherence just because the atheist is unable to identify the donor of the gift. Indeed, if it were thought to be philosophically legitimate for the religious believer to employ such arguments, it might well be countered by the atheist that, since it is normally a feature of a gift that it must be something desirable, then it is the religious notion of a gift from God which is unintelligible, since it drops one feature central to the atheist's account of a gift. But, for the reasons which I indicated at the beginning of this paper, and in view of many of the things which I have been emphasising throughout, it should be apparent that neither form of attack gets much sympathy from me.

Notes

1. Kai Nielsen, *Ethics Without God* (London: Pemberton Books, 1973), p. 48.
2. Leszek Kolakowski, *Religion* (New York: Oxford University Press 1982).
3. Ibid., p. 201.
4. G. E. M. Anscombe, 'Modern Moral Philosophy', in *The Collected Papers of G. E. M. Anscombe*, Vol. III (Oxford: Basil Blackwell, 1981), p. 30.
5. Pablo Casals, quoted in R. Gaita, *Good and Evil: An Absolute Conception* (London: Macmillan, 1991), pp. 214–15.
6. Ibid., p. 223.

7. Quoted in Gaita, *Good and Evil*, p. 219.

8. Gaita, *Good and Evil*, p. 225.

9. Hank Williams Jr *Living Proof*, (New York: Dell/James A. Bryans, 1983) pp. 130–1.

10. John Newman, *The Grammar of Assent*, ed. C. F. Harrold (Oxford: Oxford University Press, 1947), p. 83.

11. Rush Rhees, 'Gratitude and Ingratitude for Existence'. I am grateful to Professor D. Z. Phillips for drawing my attention to the relevance of this discussion.

12. L. Wittgenstein, *Zettel* (Oxford: Basil Blackwell), section 540.

13. Quoted in T. Huddlestone, *Dying We Live* (London: Fontana Books, 1965), p. 88.

12

Reply: Nietzsche, Kierkegaard and Anscombe on Moral Unintelligibility

JAMES CONANT*

There are two ways in which philosophers have tended to approach the question of how atheism and morality bear on one another: (1) by asking, broadly, whether morality *in toto* presupposes religious belief, and (2) by asking, more narrowly, whether the demise of religious belief has corroded *certain* features of morality. It is worth distinguishing these two ways of approaching the question. For even if one takes it to be obvious that atheism and morality are broadly compatible, that can still leave open whether certain features of our moral inheritance are at peril. Nietzsche, Kierkegaard and Anscombe are three philosophers who approach the question in the second way and all three advance some version of the following thesis: in the wake of the demise of a Christian tradition of religious thought and practice, we are left with certain concepts which continue to appear – but which no longer are – intelligible.

My ultimate aim in this paper is neither to defend nor to attack the *specific* charges of moral unintelligibility which figure in the writings of Nietzsche, Kierkegaard and Anscombe, but simply to

* This paper began life under the title 'Atheism and Morality: Reply to Beardsmore' as a contribution to a symposium on 'Atheism and Morality'. The symposium was part of the Fifteenth Annual Claremont Philosophy of Religion Conference, on 'Religion and Morality', hosted by the Claremont Graduate School and organised by D. Z. Phillips. I am indebted to questions raised by participants at the conference – especially R. W. Beardsmore and Raimond Gaita – and to comments on an earlier draft by Cora Diamond, Martin Stone and Lisa Van Alstyne. This paper is also indebted in more diffuse but no less substantial ways to the writings of Stanley Cavell and Cora Diamond.

clarify their logical structure in order to make clear what, in each instance, *would* count as a successful rebuttal of such a charge.[1] I hope thereby to shed some light on a widely misunderstood line of thought that runs throughout the work of this trio of provocative – and otherwise, in many respects, remarkably different – thinkers.

These three philosophers seem to be open to the following objection. They want to single out some particular (moral) concept presently in currency and mount a critique of it – a critique which purports to show the concept to be unintelligible. Yet in order to convince us that that particular concept is unintelligible, it would appear that these authors first need to make out *which* concept they have in mind. But if they can succeed in making this out, then – so the objection goes – they have undermined their own claim. For them to be able to single out the concept (which is to serve as the target of their critique) as *this* rather than some other concept, mustn't the concept at issue be at least a minimally intelligible one? If they can make out which concept is at issue, then they may go on to show that that concept (or any statement in which it occurs) is somehow incoherent, incredible, or otherwise flawed, but they are no longer in a position to claim that the concept in question is unintelligible. For that would amount to showing that there is *no* concept at issue, and hence nothing for their critique to be a critique of.

This objection harbours an important point (to which I will return): a point about the self-undermining nature of the charge – a charge that Nietzsche, Kierkegaard and Anscombe each appears to be concerned to level – that someone is not just *saying* something unintelligible, but employing a particular concept outside the conditions which allow for its intelligibility. I will be concerned to argue that it is a misunderstanding to think that this point represents an objection to the charge of unintelligibility which is levelled in the writings of these three philosophers. But, before turning to consider why, I will first explore a related objection advanced by R. W. Beardsmore in his stimulating paper 'Atheism and Morality'.[2]

I BEARDSMORE ON ATHEISM AND MORALITY

Why atheism today? – God has been thoroughly refuted ... [Yet] it seems to me that the religious instinct is in the process of growing powerfully – but the theistic satisfaction it now refuses with deep suspicion.

                                                    Friedrich Nietzsche[3]

Beardsmore wants to show that we can be atheists and hang on to morality, too. In so far as his aim is to secure the thesis that we can be atheists and still make perfectly good sense of a great deal of our moral discourse, I am in agreement with him. In so far as his thesis is that the intelligibility of none of the central moral concepts of Western culture depend[4] on a prior tradition of religious thought and practice, I am not in agreement with him. I will call the former 'the unexciting thesis' and the latter 'the interesting thesis'. Beardsmore seems to slide back and forth between them. He begins his paper by circumscribing the category of views he wishes to criticise as follows:

> I have in mind the view that atheism is unreasonable, or in some way intellectually inadequate, because it is incapable of doing justice to the role that moral considerations play in our lives, or to put it rather more bluntly, but also more elegantly, because if God did not exist, then everything would be permitted.[5]

Initially we are told that the target of the paper is the view that atheism is not capable of 'doing justice to the role that moral considerations play in our lives'. Does this mean that Beardsmore is concerned to criticise only those views according to which atheism is unable to do justice to the role *any* moral considerations play in our lives? Apparently not, for later on he makes it clear that it suffices to place a view within his target-range if it involves the more modest claim that '*certain* central features of our morality ... derive from a religious background' (my emphasis).[6] An effective criticism of this latter claim would be of considerable philosophical interest since it plays an important role in the writings of the three philosophers with whom this paper is concerned. But nothing in the thought of any of these three thinkers is felicitously paraphrased by the blunt and elegant formula which Beardsmore borrows from Ivan Karamazov: 'if God did not exist, then *everything* would be permitted'. (Ivan's worry is that once a religious framework is no longer in place *no* feature of morality will survive.)

The three thinkers with whom this essay is concerned are all only too aware that the subtraction of a belief in God from our system of beliefs can appear (as it does to Beardsmore) to be without consequence for our moral thought or practice. Their question is not: does the absence of a belief in God *appear to us* to affect the kinds of moral thought available to us? (They assume that, on the whole, it appears not to: that is what each of them – each in a very different way – takes to be the problem.) Their question rather is: does the disappearance of God, *despite* its apparent lack of consequence, in some way (presently invisible to us) determine the sorts of shape our moral thought can, in His absence, intelligibly assume?

To assuage a worry of this sort one needs to do more than just show that Ivan's inference (from God's non-existence to everything being permitted) involves a *non sequitur*. Thus Beardsmore's way, in the above passage, of 'more bluntly, but also rather more elegantly' reformulating the import of the views he wishes to criticise does not merely reformulate, but actually significantly narrows, the range of views which fall under the scope of his criticisms. The blunt and elegant reformulation lends his discussion the appearance of offering a criticism which applies equally to an Ivan Karamazov and an Elizabeth Anscombe – to the antitheses of both the unexciting thesis and the interesting thesis. What we need to see more clearly is how very different an Elizabeth Anscombe is from an Ivan Karamazov. I will therefore, first, briefly indicate why I think the unexciting thesis both true and unexciting. I will then outline the form which the antithesis of Beardsmore's interesting thesis takes in the thought of Nietzsche, Kierkegaard and Anscombe, and explain why I think Beardsmore's arguments against it fail to engage it.

II KARAMAZOV, NIELSEN AND KOLAKOWSKI

As soon as men have all of them denied God ... everyone will begin anew ... [E]veryone who recognizes the truth even now may legitimately order his life as he pleases, on the new principles. In that sense, 'all things are lawful' for him.

Ivan Karamazov[7]

Ivan Karamazov's view of the relation between religion and morality is clear enough: to deny God is to eradicate the distinction between those things which are permitted and those which are not. Dostoevsky's aim in vividly depicting the character of Ivan in *The Brothers Karamazov* is in part to make explicit what he takes to be the implicit nihilism of his contemporaries – to make explicit the degree to which the modern atheist has deprived himself of a basis for any coherent conception of moral obligation.[8] A rigorous and honest atheist should, Dostoevsky thinks, acknowledge that he is no longer *bound* by moral principles (though he can, of course, continue to conform his behaviour to their requirements 'as he pleases'). Beardsmore begins his paper by criticising two philosophers – Kai Nielsen (an atheist) and Leszek Kolakowski (a theist) – whose views belong to Ivan Karamazov's end of the spectrum of possible views concerning the relation between atheism and morality.[9]

Nielsen's aim is to argue against the claim that atheism undermines morality. This would appear sharply to distinguish him from someone like Dostoevsky (who was concerned precisely to uphold such a claim). According to Beardsmore, Nielsen arrives at his conclusion by way of an argument which turns on the assumption that morality rests on conventions which we are free to accept or reject as we choose. Beardsmore quotes the following lines from Nielsen:

> If we look at morality with the cold eye of the anthropologist, we will find morality to be nothing more than the conflicting mores of the various tribes spread around the globe. If we look at ethics from a purely secular view, we will discover that it is constituted by tribal conventions, conventions which we are free to reject ... We can continue to act in accordance with them or we can reject them and adopt a different set of conventions.[10]

According to Beardsmore, Nielsen seeks to argue against the claim that 'if God did not exist, then everything would be permitted' by arguing that what is (or is not) permitted does not depend on God's existence but rather on a set of social conventions which any individual with capacity for critical reflection is free to either accept or reject. Now the fact that someone who does not believe in God (as Nielsen avowedly does not) is inclined to conclude that what is permitted is ultimately a matter of individual choice would hardly come as news to Dostoevsky. Indeed, there is much in the thought that Nielsen (as summarised by Beardsmore) is a version of the sort of urbane, complacent atheist whose implicit nihilism Dostoevsky sought to expose. Though Nielsen wishes to question the relevance of the antecedent (concerning God's existence) to the consequent (concerning what is permitted) in Ivan's famous conditional, he still ends up in much the same place as Ivan. For he is willing to affirm something very close to the conclusion of Ivan's worry. He is willing to affirm that, in principle, just about anything *could* be permitted (it simply depends upon what 'conventions' you choose to follow).

It is the possibility of the existence of a divine law-giver which, for Ivan, introduces the possibility of genuinely distinguishing between what is permitted and what merely appears ('from a purely secular view') to be permitted. For Nielsen, there is nothing left to play this role and thus it is a contingent (partly sociological, partly psychological) matter what, for a given individual, is and is not permitted – one which could, in principle, be revised through an act of choice. Thus, according to Nielsen, something is only morally prohibited for me, in so far as I choose to accept a set of conventions which stipulate that matters of the relevant sort are prohibited. The fundamental resemblance between Nielsen and Ivan lies in the fact that they both want to go on speaking of what is and is not 'lawful', even though they urge upon us a conception according to which, in reality, nothing is any longer prohibited. They both employ a quasi-legal terminology of 'permission' and 'prohibition' as if it retained its original force, while having detached it from the framework of conceptual connections in which it is at home – a framework in which it only makes sense to speak of a person as prohibited from doing something if the prohibition has its source in something other than that person's choice to refrain from doing it.

Kolakowski wants to employ a variant of Ivan's reasoning – in much the same spirit as Dostoevsky himself – to mount a *reductio ad absurdum* of atheism. Kolakowski revises Ivan's conditional by substituting a version of Nielsen's conclusion as consequent, but takes Nielsen's *modus ponens* as his *modus tollens*: it's absurd to think that what is (and what is not) morally permitted is a matter of mere convention, therefore God exists. Kolakowski's reasoning parallels that of Ivan and Nielsen in that he agrees with them that without God we are free to decide for ourselves what is right and what is wrong:

This is the sense in which the saying 'if there is no God, every-thing is permissible' seems right to me ... [A]n imperative demanding that I be guided only by norms which I might wish to be universal has itself no logical or psychological founda-tion; I can reject it without falling into contradiction, and I may admit it as a supreme guideline only by virtue of an arbitrary decision unless it appears within the context of religious wor-ship ... When Pierre Bayle argued that morality does not de-pend on religion ... he pointed out that atheists are capable of achieving the highest moral standard ... That is obviously true as far as it goes, but this matter-of-fact argument leaves the question of validity intact ... A Christian apologist may admit the facts and still consistently argue ... that atheists owe their virtues to a religious tradition they have managed partially to preserve in spite of their false philosophy.[11]

Beardsmore is surely right to think that the alternatives repre-sent by Nielsen, on the one hand, and Kolakowski, on the other, present us with a specious dilemma: either our moral values are fixed by divine decree or they are the result of individual choice. A multitude of assumptions need to be in place before such a dilemma even begins to seem to exhaust our philosophical alter-natives – in particular, assumptions which position the concept of choice (in relation to our moral emotions, convictions and ac-tions) so as to leave no adequate foothold for the concept of moral *judgement*. To mention only four such assumptions:

1. There is the assumption that everything which forms part of our cultural inheritance is a 'convention' – something which we can, without further ado, simply choose to accept or reject. (Can we simply *choose* when and where we feel horror or shame or awe? Can we just choose what we are to count as meretric-ious or courageous or cruel?)
2. There is the assumption that – in the absence of an overarching sovereign or divine law-giver – in so far as our moral choices are constrained, the source of that constraint is to be expli-cated in causal rather than normative terms (in terms of socio-logical or psychological forces, rather than rational demands, to which we are subject).
3. There is the assumption that if we look at ethics 'from a purely secular view', we will discover that what is right is ultimately

'constituted' by what people in 'our tribe' think is right. (It is thus simply assumed that any view which is 'purely secular' no longer has the available resources to distinguish between what our tribe *thinks* is right and what *is* right.)

4. There is the assumption that if an individual is faced with a moral dilemma – circumstances in which he is torn as to what he ought to do, or in which he and someone whom he regards as fully reasonable (and perhaps even admirable) respectfully disagree about what one ought to do – then he arrives at his course of action by simply 'choosing' between two conflicting 'valuations'. (A soldier who on conscientious grounds disobeys a commanding officer – whom he respects and admires – may be described as 'choosing to disobey', but does he therefore *choose* to be in moral disagreement with his commander?)

I draw attention to these four assumptions (which are shared by Nielsen and Kolakowski) only to bring out some of the many steps which need to be taken before one can move at all easily from rejection of the claim that 'what is right and what is wrong is determined by God's commands' to acceptance of the claim that 'what is right and what is wrong is constituted by conventions we are free to accept or reject'.[12]

Once we put aside these ways of thinking about what the immediate ethical costs of atheism might be, where does that leave the views of philosophers – such as Nietzsche or Kierkegaard or Anscombe – who think that it is, nonetheless, the case that (to quote Beardsmore) 'certain central features of morality *do* derive from a religious background which we once all shared'? Beardsmore seems to think that it is a short step from the sorts of considerations which impugn the views of a Nielsen or a Kolakowski to those that would allow us to dismiss the views of an Anscombe. It is at this point that Beardsmore's paper seems to me to move much too quickly.

III NIETZSCHE

'Do we hear nothing as yet of the noise of the gravediggers who are burying God? Do we smell nothing as yet of the divine decomposition? Gods, too, decompose. God is dead. God remains dead. And we

have killed him . . . There has never been a greater deed; and whoever is born after us for the sake of this deed he will belong to a higher history than all history hitherto.' Here the madman fell silent and looked again at his listeners; and they, too, were silent and started at him in astonishment. At last he threw his lantern on the ground, and it broke into pieces and went out. 'I have come too early,' he said then; 'my time is not yet. This tremendous event is still on its way, still wandering; it has not yet reached the ears of men. Lightening and thunder require time; the light of the stars requires time; deeds, though done, still require time to be seen and heard. This deed is still more distant from them than the most distant stars – and yet they have done it themselves.'

Friedrich Nietzsche[13]

A feature of Beardsmore's paper worth pausing over is its tacit suggestion that the thesis in question – that certain central features of morality derive from a religious tradition we once all shared – is one which necessarily is more attractive to someone who seeks to enter the theistic side of a quarrel between theism and atheism. One need only briefly consider the example of Nietzsche in order to realise that the thesis in question can function as a double-edged sword in that quarrel. Nietzsche's interest in such a thesis is as an instrument of moral reform. Nietzsche's way of disenchanting his reader with certain features of traditional morality – and of calling for a 'transvaluation' of those values – is to underscore the manner in which those values depend upon a now (as he was fond of putting it) 'bankrupt' tradition of religious thought. Nietzsche sees Christianity as providing a foundation for the relevant features of traditional morality in at least three different ways: (1) intellectual, (2) practical, and (3) physiological. I will say a little about each.

For Nietzsche, first Judaism and then Christianity provided an intellectual foundation for morality by articulating a theological framework in which one could make sense of the idea that certain moral principles are absolutely binding. His paradigm of such principles are the Ten Commandments. Nietzsche argues that it is only against the background of a conception of moral principles as expressions of the will of God that one is in a position to make sense of the idea that such principles are universally binding. Nietzsche, however, unlike Ivan Karamazov, does not hold that the present intellectual bankruptcy of the Christian conception of an absolute moral order entails that one is now no longer bound by moral principles. Nietzsche has a name for such a view: nihilism. It represents a position which he predicts will become dominant in Western culture and which he views as both philosophically and ethically pernicious. Nietzsche describes nihilism as 'the sickness of our times', Christianity as 'the poison which brings on the sickness', and 'the task of the philosopher of the future' as one of providing 'the antidote'. Ivan Karamazov could serve as the prototype of the open-eyed nihilist.[14] Although Ivan is no longer able to believe in God, he knows that he is consumed by nostalgia for Him – and it is this piece of self-knowledge which distinguishes him from what Nietzsche likes to call 'the typical English moral philosopher' (that is, the typical urbane atheist). Nihilism is Nietzsche's name for the condition of melancholia we enter into when we are unable properly to mourn the death of God. Nietzsche's aim is to try to keep his reader from lapsing, out of a disappointment with the loss of the God of Christianity, into a refusal to countenance anything less than a surrogate deity as a possible source of value. He sees his readers as prone to recoil, out of the disillusionment brought on by the collapse of a highly specific, culturally entrenched metaphysical conception of the nature of value into its metaphysical mirror-image: a nihilistic conception of the nature of value – a conception which drains all values of their prescriptive force.

Christianity, however, according to Nietzsche, is not necessarily – and was not always – poison. It was, under earlier historical and cultural conditions, an important instrument in the development of civilisation and the enhancement of human potential:

> This fact can never be sufficiently pondered: Christianity is the religion of antiquity grown old; the presupposition of its existence is an ancient culture now degenerated ... The Christianity of that culture ... is now a balm only for someone who wanders through those past centuries as an historian ... Otherwise ... Christianity is poison.[15]

Nietzsche says here that a particular culture – a particular way of life – is a presupposition of the existence of Christianity. His point here and elsewhere does not rest on the twofold claim (commonly attributed to him) (1) that it is only possible to hold certain beliefs at certain times (though surely that is true) and (2) that since the culture of antiquity has crumbled it is now no longer really possible to believe in God (which is surely false). Nietzsche's point here, rather, rests on the following thought: Christianity forms an integral part of a particular conception of how to live, one which grew up under particular historical and cultural circumstances, and is not properly comprehended when conceived apart from those circumstances. The point is directed against an alternative way of conceiving of Christianity: namely, merely as a system of *beliefs* – and thus in complete abstraction from the *practice* of a particular way of life:

> It is false to the point of absurdity to see in a 'belief', perchance the belief in a redemption through Christ, the distinguishing characteristic of the Christian: only Christian *practice*, a life such as he who died on the cross *lived*, is Christian... Not a belief but a doing, above all a *not*-doing of many things, a different *being*... States of consciousness, beliefs of any kind, holding something to be true for example... are a matter of complete indifference... To reduce being a Christian, Christianness, to a holding something to be true, to a mere phenomenality of consciousness, means to negate Christianness.[16]

Nietzsche's point is, first, one about what Christianity is, and, second, one about the conditions of the meaningfulness of a great many of our moral (and not only moral[17]) concepts: (1) what it is to be a Christian is to live a certain sort of life (modelled on the one that he who died on the cross lived), and (2) the meaning of those moral concepts which Christianity has bequeathed to us is internal to their application within the context of such a life.[18]

'It is false to the point of absurdity', Nietzsche says, to conceive of what it is to be a Christian in the manner in which philosophers tend to: to see the distinguishing characteristic of the Christian as a matter of an individual's adherence to a particular belief. Thus Nietzsche, as we shall see, agrees with Kierkegaard on the following grammatical point: only an individual engaged in a life of Christian practice is a Christian. But Nietzsche identifies such a practice with 'above all a *not*-doing of many things'. Christianity means, for Nietzsche, above all a life of *ascetic* practice – a life in which the individual goes to war against all his natural instincts: a life in which the individual first disciplines, then masters and ultimately transforms himself through the discipline, mastery and transformation of his desires.[19] Christianity's glorious legacy to modern man, in Nietzsche's eyes, lies in its refinement of the discipline of *askesis*: 'the labour performed by man on himself' through which he learns to attain forms of 'mastery over himself'.[20] Christianity's inglorious legacy is nihilism – a nihilism brought on by the fact that the transformative potential of its values has been exhausted: what began as a call for a heroic effort of voluntary restraint is now culturally transmitted as a form of second nature. This is what Nietzsche means by his extraordinary claim that the ascetic ideal has brought about not only a philosophical and psychological but also a *physiological* metamorphosis of the human animal. An individual is Christian, for Nietzsche, to the extent that he exhibits what Nietzsche will hyperbolically refer to as a 'certain organization of instinct'.[21] Nietzsche sees most of us today as morally mutilated half-Christians. Christianity has left its mark on each of us through its having forged a certain relation between intellect and instinct, through its having determined what now seems to us a *natural* configuration of thought and desire. A responsible critique of Christianity, on Nietzsche's view, owes us not only a critique of that configuration, but also a vision of an alternative one – a vision of how we should seek to shape ourselves, of what sorts of beings we should strive to become.

Just as Nietzsche thinks 'it is false to the point of absurdity to see in a "belief" . . . the distinguishing characteristic of Christianity', so he also thinks it is false to the point of absurdity to see any honest attempt to repudiate Christianity as having no implications for our ways of living and being. Nietzsche thinks that there may be a sense in which many of us are now able to decide not to believe in God, but he does not think we can just *decide* not to be shaped by Christian values. He does not think that ceasing to be a Christian is a matter of merely changing one's beliefs, but rather of changing one's self. (It is precisely this practical task of transforming ourselves, divesting ourselves of the ways in which Christianity has shaped us, that Nietzsche wishes to recommend to us.[22]) Hence the overcoming of Christianity for Nietzsche lies not in the disappearance of a certain belief, but in a radical transformation of human existence into an existence no longer informed by Christian practice – no longer shaped by a Christian conception of what is valuable. It is a transformation that Nietzsche thinks is well under way but only half-completed; and here lies the source, he thinks, of our present awkward relation to our values. Each one of our evaluative concepts is internally related to, and often presupposes, a great many of the others; yet some are evidently obsolete, others indispensable – and, finally, some are of the sort which interest Kierkegaard and Anscombe as well: they appear indispensable but are in fact obsolete.

In Nietzsche's parable of the madman – which forms the epigraph to this section of the paper – we are told that the audience the madman addresses is comprised of 'many of those who did not believe in God'.[23] What those who do not believe in God do not know – and as yet, according to the madman, are unable to understand – is that God does not all of a sudden, at some point, simply cease to exist. Rather, God *dies,* and his death is a slow business. The madman sees the unfolding of the death of God where his audience sees only the onward march of progress and enlightenment.[24] The madman seems mad, provoking the laughter of those who do not believe in God, in his frantic insistence that we should prepare ourselves for the repercussions of this event – the death of God – which is now unfolding. Yet the time will come when even the most urbane of atheists will be able to smell the divine decomposition. The stench is not yet overpowering and so, at present, those who do not believe in God are able to imagine that the death of God marks nothing more than a change in what people should now 'believe'. One should now subtract the belief in God from one's body of beliefs; and this subtraction is something sophisticated people (who have long since ceased going to church) can effect without otherwise unduly upsetting how they live or what they value. The madman, on the other hand, thinks this tremendous event – the death of God – is still on its way. It will have arrived, not when people no longer believe in God, but when people realise that they are no longer able to make sense of many of the values in accordance with which they presently imagine they live. The process of divine decomposition is one in which many of the words which name the old values are gradually drained of their original meaning.

The most paradoxical aspect of the madman's message – that this event has already happened and yet is still on its way – forms a bond between Nietzsche's thought and that of both Kierkegaard and Anscombe. All three see us as prone to illusions of intelligibility when we draw upon moral and religious vocabulary. The fact that our moral discourse does not *seem to us* to lack intelligibility (and hence the fact that the question of its intelligibility does not seem in any way tied to questions concerning the vitality of Christian modes of thought and practice) is not to be taken as a reliable index of when, and in what sort of ways, we are presently able to make moral sense.

IV KIERKEGAARD

If then, according to our assumption, the greater number of people in Christendom only imagine themselves to be Christians, in what categories do they live? They live in aesthetic, or, at the most in aesthetic–ethical categories.

Supposing then that a religious writer has become profoundly attentive to this illusion, Christendom, and has resolved to attack it with all the might at his disposal – what then is he to do? First and foremost, no impatience. If he becomes impatient, he will rush headlong against it and accomplish nothing. A direct attack only strengthens a person in his illusion, and at the same time embitters him. There is nothing that requires such gentle handling as an illusion, if one wishes to dispel it. If anything prompts the prospective captive to set his will in opposition, all is lost.

Søren Kierkegaard[25]

Kierkegaard, in contrast to Nietzsche, does not think that atheism – or at least what we are apt to think of as atheism – is even a necessary, let alone a first step in the advent of a condition in which the greater part of society begins to hallucinate sense when they (apparently) employ moral or religious vocabulary. His name for the first and decisive step in the onset of such a hallucinatory condition is *Christendom*.

Kierkegaard is, however, in agreement with Nietzsche on the following point: Christianity is not a matter of simply believing that certain things are true; it is a matter of living in a certain sort of way. (Nietzsche's and Kierkegaard's most profound disagreement concerns whether we should seek to abandon or to return to such a way of living.) For Kierkegaard, as for Nietzsche, to see whether someone is a Christian is not merely a matter of finding out what sorts of propositions he assents to or what sorts of beliefs he has (or what sorts of justifications he is prepared to supply for those propositions or beliefs), but rather also a matter of looking to the way in which his conception of himsef as a Christian informs his life.[26] Almost everyone in the Denmark of Kierkegaard's day thought of himself as a Christian, yet Kierkegaard thought almost no one was. He thought most of his countrymen suffered from the illusion that they were Christians. The main source of this illusion, he says, is the confusion of objective and subjective categories.[27] Whether one is a Christian or not is now established with reference to certain 'objective' features of one's life (whether one goes to church on Sundays, or has been baptised, or lives in a Christian country and has Christian parents, etc.) regardless of how one comports oneself with respect to those features of one's life.[28] In this respect, Kierkegaard's view of the problem is diametrically opposed to Nietzsche's: Nietzsche wants to show his purportedly atheistic readers that they *are* still at bottom Christians, Kierkegaard wants to show his purportedly Christian readers that they are *not* Christians.

Kierkegaard does not take himself to be differing with his countrymen simply over what the word 'Christian' means. His claim is that by their own lights – if they reflect upon what it means for someone to become a Christian and if they also reflect upon their lives and get into focus how much of a claim Christianity actually exacts upon them – they will be able to see that they are not Christians.[29] They are tempted into various (what Kierkegaard calls 'categorical') confusions in order to disguise this fact from themselves. But, if provided with a perspicuous overview of the category of the religious, he thinks, they themselves will be in a position to acknowledge their confusions as confusions. If pressed to reflect upon their lives, Kierkegaard thinks his readers can be brought to see that they would be at a loss to say what licenses the claim that they are Christians.

Kierkegaard is a particularly provocative author to consider in the context of worrying (as Beardsmore invites us to) whether 'a religious background' is a necessary condition for the intelligibility of certain concepts. What the example of Kierkegaard shows is that even if we confine ourselves to the relatively uncontroversial thesis that 'a religious background' is a necessary condition for the employment of certain *religious* concepts, it will still by no means always be clear when the appropriate background is (or is not) in place. It is not something which can be determined by simply looking at the sort of vocabulary people employ.

Kierkegaard's aim is to bring his readers to see that (if they reflect carefully upon what they want to mean when they say of themselves that they are Christians) they do not mean by their words what they want to. What they want to mean is at odds with what they say. They have an incoherent desire with respect to their words – and, in particular, with respect to the word 'Christian'. They want to use the word in its religious sense and, at the same time, use the word in such a way that it has application to their present lives. It is not that they mean something determinate but somehow flawed by the word. It is rather, according to Kierkegaard, that they mean it incoherently: their use of the word hovers indeterminately between aesthetic and religious categories without respecting the conditions for the application of either. (As we shall see, there is an affinity here between Kierkegaard's and Anscombe's respective conceptions of what is – and what is not – involved in the sorts of illusions of intelligibility which they seek to expose.)

Kierkegaard thinks there are a great many words which have a specifically religious meaning – words such as belief, authority, obedience, revelation, prayer, silence, awe, wonder, miracle, apostle, and so forth. These same words, however, can be used in contexts in which they take on a different meaning. These same words can be used to express different concepts – concepts which do not have a religious import. Kierkegaard's interest therefore is not merely in what *words* his readers employ, but in what *concepts* those words express. The problem is that it is not always easy to command a clear view of when a word is being used to express a religious concept. Kierkegaard's way of referring to the sort of confusion we enter into in such cases (when we take ourselves to be employing an ethical or religious concept, but no ethical or religious sense can be made of our use of a word) is to say that we have fallen into 'a confusion of the categories'. His name for the procedure he employs for unravelling such confusions is 'qualitative dialectic'.[30] A 'dialectical' examination of a concept shows how the meaning of the concept undergoes a shift – and therefore, properly speaking, what concept it is that shifts – as the context in which it is employed changes. Qualitative dialectic is the study of the decisive (or qualitative) shifts to which the meaning of a word is subject as its employment shifts from an aesthetic to an ethical to a religious context. A religious concept, Kierkegaard thinks, is only able to have its sense within the context of a certain sort of life. Sometimes therefore Kierkegaard (or one of his pseudonymous authors) will want to paint a particularly vivid picture of what a Christian life would look like: a life that can only be understood in terms of – that is, one which is lived in – Christian categories. The point is to contrast that life with the life of a reader who imagines himself to be a Christian.[31] It is only in that other life, Kierkegaard wants to show, that 'the Christian categories have their full, mutually implicating meaning, and apart from it they may have any or none'.[32]

Kierkegaard's contemporaries are able to deceive themselves into thinking they are Christians because in the course of their lives they frequently employ religious vocabulary. The question Kierkegaard wishes them to focus on is not whether they think they have a use for such vocabulary, but rather *how* they use it. Only if their life as a whole has a certain shape – only if, as he likes to say, it is one which 'is lived in religious categories' – does that vocabulary, as they employ it, have a properly religious meaning.[33] What he suspects about the lives of most of his contemporaries is that the religious words which they wish to call upon either have come to assume an entirely different (non-religious) meaning – or, in many cases, no longer have any meaning whatsoever. The attraction to the use of such words is often tied, he thinks, to the user's wish to sustain for himself the illusion of being a Christian. Kierkegaard's sense of the difficulty of his project is thus tied to the suspicion that his reader may have deeply entrenched motives – motives which he conceals from himself – for not wishing to clarify for himself what it is that he means when he employs religious vocabulary. Those who live in Christendom are deeply attached to the idea that Christian concepts do indeed have application to their lives. For it is through the illusion that those concepts apply to their lives that they are able to imagine that their lives retain a religious dimension. Kierkegaard suspects that all this 'religious dimension' comes to in the end is a mere outward appearance – an aura – of solemnity, piety and profundity. Kierkegaard sees his contemporaries as thus wanting to be able to hold on to certain features of the concepts of Christianity while dispensing with all the others. On the one hand, they want their religious vocabulary to have application to a certain sort of life (one which was exemplified by him who died on the cross), while, on the other hand, they want it to apply to a very different sort of life (namely, that of someone who thinks of religion only when he goes to church on Sundays). They wish to call upon religious words in order to invest their lives with an aspect of depth and significance, without otherwise reflecting upon (let alone striving for) the sort of life in which a religious concept would have its point. They thereby, in the end, succeed in reducing ther religious vocabulary to one which is able to convey a certain aura – and nothing more.

V CONCEPTS AND WORDS

This word 'ought' . . . [has] become a word of mere mesmeric force . . . a word containing no intelligible thought: a word retaining the suggestion of force, and apt to have a strong psychological effect, but which no longer signifies a real concept at all.

Elizabeth Anscombe[34]

In the previous brief overview of Kierkegaard's critique of Christendom, we uncovered four further moments which are common to the thought of Nietzsche, Kierkegaard, and (as we shall see) Anscombe: (1) an illusion of sense results when we seek to hold on to certain features of a concept while (unwittingly) jettisoning others; (2) the attraction to certain forms of moral (and religious) confusion is tied to a desire to evade certain moral (or religious) demands; (3) we attempt to retain those features of a moral (or religious) concept which confer on our lives the appearance of being in accordance with those moral (or religious) demands, while wishing not to be in any other way (theoretically or practically) inconvenienced by our attachment to those features of the concept; and thus it comes to pass that (4) certain stretches of our moral (or religious) discourse continue to retain an aura of evaluative force while having been drained of sense.

Neither Nietzsche's nor Kierkegaard's point is one about whether certain pieces of vocabulary have to be discarded. Their point is about what sort of concepts we are (presently) able to express with that vocabulary. Theirs is not a point therefore about what sort of *words* we have at our disposal, but about what sort of *use* we are able to make of those words – what concepts those words express. Indeed, Nietzsche's point is often that the old words can only make sense for us now in so far as they make a new and different (what he calls 'transvalued') kind of sense. Kierkegaard's point is often that, if we wish to avoid certain forms of confusion, we must clearly distinguish between different (religious, ethical and aesthetic) concepts that are all expressed by the same word. In each of these cases, Nietzsche and Kierkegaard do not seek to prohibit us from using a certain word, but only to illuminate (1) the conditions under which that word expresses a particular concept and (2) the way in which our contemporary employment of that word fails to express that concept.

The same is true of the argument Anscombe puts forward in 'Modern Moral Philosophy'.[35] The point of that famous but widely misunderstood article is not that we must jettison a certain part of our moral vocabulary (because it is now impossible to make sense of those ways of speaking); but rather that there are certain ways in which we are no longer able to make sense with those words.[36] It is not that there is nothing that those words can now mean, but that there are certain ways in which we are now no longer able to mean them. Beardsmore misses this point. He thinks that Anscombe's argument commits her to the claim that it is now impossible to make any sense at all of talk 'of being bound, permitted or excused'.

Anscombe does, in setting up her argument, say the following:

> In consequence of the dominance of Christianity for many centuries, the concepts of being bound, permitted, or excused became deeply embedded in our language and thought.[37]

Her point is not, however, that – given the demise of a divine law conception of ethics – it is no longer possible to make sense of these ways of talking; it is not about the *words* 'bound', 'permitted' or 'excused'. Her point is about certain concepts and what happens when we now try to avail ourselves of them. The following two facts serve as the point of departure for her discussion: (a) that certain modern moral philosophers have found it difficult to uncover *any content at all* in talk of what one 'morally ought' to do, and (b) that they have gone on to try to rescue such ways of talking by attempting to find 'an alternative (very fishy) content' for the concept in order to retain the psychological force of the word.[38] Part of what allows Beardsmore (and not only Beardsmore) to mistake Anscombe's point for one about words (rather than concepts) is that he does not appreciate the extent to which what occasions Anscombe's historical speculations is precisely this feature of modern moral philosophy – namely, that 'our present-day ethicists' have been unable to discern any content in the very notion of moral obligation that *they themselves* wish to employ. One of Anscombe's aims, in her famous article, is to offer a diagnosis of how modern moral philosophy came to find itself at these particular crossroads.[39]

VI BEARDSMORE ON ANSCOMBE

Anscombe seems to take it largely for granted that if a concept has outlived the practices or ways of thinking in which it originally had its sense, then in so far as it is still used it will have no sense.

R. W. Beardsmore

Though he speaks, following Anscombe, of a *concept* which 'has outlived the practices or ways of thinking in which it originally had its sense', Beardsmore takes Anscombe to be saying that we should abandon certain ways of speaking because *those ways of speaking* prevent us from making sense. He finds this claim in a passage of Anscombe's which he quotes as follows:

> Naturally it is not possible to have such a conception unless you believe in God as a law-giver; like Jews, Stoics and Christians. But if such a conception is dominant for many centuries, and then is given up, it is a natural result that the concepts of 'obligation', of being bound or required by a law, should remain though they had lost their root; and if the word 'ought' has become invested in certain contexts with the sense of 'obligation', it too will remain to be spoken with a special emphasis and a special feeling in these contexts ... The situation, if I am right, was the interesting one of the survival of a concept outside the framework of thought that made it a really intelligible one.[40]

From now on I will refer to this as the focal passage. The passage is a puzzling one. If one tries to understand it apart from the role it plays within the essay as a whole, one is bound to misunderstand it. Anscombe speaks here of 'the survival of a concept' when (for reasons she herself helps to make clear) it seems at best peculiar to speak of what has survived as a 'concept'. Beardsmore takes this passage to imply that there is something which would count for Anscombe as *using* a concept outside the framework of thought which makes it a really intelligible one. Once one attributes this thesis to her, one is forced to read her – when she speaks of 'the survival of a concept outside the framework of thought that made it a really intelligible one' – as making either an incoherent point about the survival of a concept or a perfectly coherent but self-evidently false point about the survival of a term.

Beardsmore's full comment on the focal passage runs as follows:

> Though Anscombe may appear to be resting her case on an assertion of historical fact, there is nevertheless a concealed assumption in her argument, which gives it whatever appearance of plausibility it may have. For as has been pointed out by others, Anscombe seems to take it largely for granted that if a concept has outlived the practices or ways of thinking in which it originally had its sense, then in so far as it is still used it will have no sense. Since the notions of being obliged or permitted had their source in a religious context, where they were equated with what is obliged or permitted by a divine will, then they must lose their sense in a society where no such equation is made.

I'm not sure who the 'others' are that Beardsmore has in mind, but here is Peter Winch:

> It clearly does not *follow* from the alleged disappearance of circumstances which once gave a certain intelligibility to a linguistic usage that such a usage now has *no* intelligibility. The most we can conclude is that it now has to be understood rather *differently*. Whether it means anything, and if so what, can only be determined by an examination of its present use.[41]

Now this point strikes me as correct, but it is one that Anscombe can perfectly well take in her stride. (I hasten to add that Winch does not take it to constitute on its own an argument against Anscombe. He offers it merely as 'a preliminary point'.[42] Beardsmore, however, seems to think that something like Winch's 'preliminary point' suffices to dispose of Anscombe's claims. Hence he goes on to offer a series of examples of secular uses of various moral terms by way of an answer to the following rhetorical question: 'in a society where religious belief is losing its hold, why should it not be the case that institutions other than the church are thought of as imposing limits on what is or is not permitted?' Beardsmore writes:

> Suppose for instance that as a member of a trade union, I feel that I have an obligation to respect a picket-line, or that as a doctor I feel myself bound to respond to an emergency call in the middle of the night. Why should it be said that in these cases my reference to what I ought to do has a 'mere mesmeric force'? True, in such cases what obliges me cannot be said to be the will of God, but this does not mean that there can be no answer to the question 'What obliges me?' What obliges the trade unionist to observe the picket-line is simply his membership in a trade union. What obliges the doctor to answer the emergency call is the rules of his profession. In what way can these ways of speaking be said to lack sense?[43]

Beardsmore wants to point out that there are contexts in which it makes perfectly good sense to say someone is 'obliged' to do something. He takes this to dispose of the claim Anscombe makes in the focal passage. This argument only has force, however, if Anscombe is indeed making the sort of broad claim about the possibility of the continued meaningful employment of certain words (such as 'obliged') which Beardsmore attributes to her. What we need to see is whether such an interpretation of Anscombe fits what she says either in the immediate vicinity of the focal passage or anywhere else.

Let us first consider the immediate vicinity of the focal passage. In the first sentence of the portion of the focal passage omitted by Beardsmore, Anscombe writes: 'It is as if the notion "criminal" were to remain when criminal law and criminal courts had been abolished and forgotten.' To explore Anscombe's point here, let us imagine a future utopia which is utopian in two respects: (1) everyone shares a common ideal of community and a common conception of the virtues of a citizen which flow from that ideal, and (2) everyone acts in conformity with the virtues of a citizen so conceived. Hence in this society there is no longer any need for either law courts or a body of positive law. To citizens of this future utopia, the concept of crime (in the sense of a violation of a positive criminal code) – like that of ritual human sacrifice – seems a remote and barbaric feature of primitive civilisations. Such words as 'prison', 'police' and 'felony' (along with the concepts those words once expressed) have long since fallen into disuse. However, the word – but not the concept – *criminal* survives. In this future utopia, people continue to use the word 'criminal' in ways which resemble some of our present figurative uses of the word (uses which for us are parasitic upon, and grasped through, a prior understanding of the *concept* of criminal as one which is logically related to notions which articulate what is involved in the breaking and enforcing of criminal laws). In this future utopia, people might speak of the omissions or commissions of umpires, journalists, editors and philosophical commentators as 'criminal'. Anscombe's claim is not that people in such a future utopia will not be able to make any sense of such uses of the word.[44] Her point is just that there is a concept – which we at present have – which they can no longer mean when they use that word to describe their contemporaries. For there is no sense to be made of meaning *that* concept apart from its relation to the set of practices and institutions in which it has its life – apart, that is, from its relation to a nexus of other specifically *legal* concepts (such as infringement, *mens rea*, culpability, punishment and so forth).

Anscombe further imagines that the citizens of this utopia lead themselves into confusion through an incoherent desire to employ the word 'criminal' so that it continues to have the same force (of violating a legal prohibition) that it did back in the days when it was still possible to think of someone as violating the law. They want the word both to express a concept which applies to their lives (as lived within their utopian society) and to retain the same prescriptive force it had when it was applied (back in the old days) to individuals who had committed a crime. The citizens of this utopian society thus manifest a sort of incoherent desire with respect to the word 'criminal' similar to that which Kierkegaard discovered among the citizens of Christendom with respect to the word 'Christian': they want the word both to express a concept which applies to their lives as they presently lead them and to retain a feature of a concept the intelligibility of which requires that it does not so apply.[45]

Let us now consider the remainder of the missing portion of the focal passage:

A Hume discovering this situation might conclude that there was some special sentiment, expressed by 'criminal', which alone gave the word its sense. So Hume discovered the situation in which the notion of 'obligation' survived, and the word 'ought' was invested with that peculiar force having which it is said to be used in a 'moral' sense, but in which the belief in divine law had long since been abandoned: for it was substantially given up among the Protestants at the time of the Reformation. The situation, if I am right, is the interesting one of the survival of a concept outside the framework of thought that made it a really intelligible one.[46]

We resemble the citizens of the future utopia (sketched above) in that we live – so Anscombe claims – in a time when certain legal concepts no longer have application.[47] We, too, are often drawn to continue to employ certain bits of vocabulary which were once expressive of legal concepts (and which, when they were employed within a legal framework of thought, carried prescriptive force). And we, too, lead ourselves into confusion through an equally incoherent desire to employ these bits of vocabulary (such as 'obliged' or 'ought' or 'morally wrong') so that they continue to have the same force (of violating an absolute prohibition) that they did back in the old days (when it was still possible to think of someone as disobeying God's commandment).[48] The point of the focal passage therefore is about the conditions of intelligibly applying certain concepts – that is, that we fail to make sense when we attempt to use certain words ('obliged', 'ought') in a very particular way: such that they retain some but not other features of a concept which has its life only within a 'law conception of ethics'.[49]

We are now in a position to outline the general structure of Anscombe's argument and why it is that Beardsmore's objection fails to make contact with it. Anscombe's claim about a certain contemporary pseudo-notion of 'moral obligation' can be broken down into two parts: (1) the pseudo-notion shares some of the features of the notion of obligation which figures in a law conception of ethics, yet (2) it lacks the requisite relation to the framework of thought essential to the intelligibility of a concept with those features. There are thus two possible ways to criticise Anscombe.[50] One can challenge the first or the second half of her claim. (1) One can concede that there *is* a notion of 'moral obligation' presently in currency which has the features she says it does; and then one can try to show that it is not a pseudo-notion (but rather a perfectly coherent concept of moral obligation). Alternatively, (2) one can try to show that there is *no such notion* (that is, no notion with *those* features) to be found in modern moral philosophy. But one cannot dispute Anscombe's claim in the manner Beardsmore (and not only Beardsmore) attempts, ignoring both *which* pseudo-notions she thinks have only 'a mere mesmeric force' and *why* she thinks so.[51] One has not entered an objection to Anscombe's view, if all one does is identify some contemporary moral notion which is both perfectly intelligible and which happens to be expressed by the same word as the pseudo-notion in question.

Let us now restore the sentence (also omitted by Beardsmore) which immediately precedes, and with which Anscombe introduces, the focal passage:

> To have a *law* conception of ethics is to hold that what is needed for conformity with the virtues failure in which is the mark of being bad *qua* man (and not merely, say *qua* craftsmen or logician) – that what is needed for *this*, is required by divine law.[52]

That is the conception Anscombe says it is not possible to have 'unless you believe in God as a law-giver'. It is *a* conception of 'what is needed for conformity with the virtues' ('failure in which is the mark of being bad' *qua* human being). It is, however, for Anscombe, by no means the only available conception of what is needed for conformity with the virtues. The whole point of her paper was to suggest that modern moral philosophy might free itself of certain confusions if it returned to an Aristotelian conception of what is needed for conformity with the virtues. So far was she from suggesting what Beardsmore takes her to be saying – that is, that non-believers can never make sense of what they mean when they say that someone 'ought' to do something – that she proposes an alternative way of understanding what might be meant by 'ought': we should understand what is meant in each such case with reference to the genus of some particular virtue ('truthfulness', 'chastity', 'justice').[53] The justification of a moral claim about someone's behaviour, on this (Aristotelian) conception, rests on a conformity or lack of conformity with some particular virtue. Such a justification does not require us to invoke some prior overarching notion of what one 'morally ought to do'.[54] It is only this latter overarching notion (and not the entire fabric of our moral discourse) that Anscombe sees as an interesting case of 'the survival of a concept outside the framework of thought that made it a really intelligible one'. She traces this latter notion to a particular conception of ethics: one in which the prescriptive force of a moral claim depends exclusively on its relation to a set of overarching moral laws – it is this framework of thought which she thinks has not survived.[55]

Beardsmore is not entirely unaware of the fact that Anscombe's thesis is a more nuanced one than his first round of arguments against her allows. He realises that her argument has something to do with what is peculiar to a divine law conception of ethics. He therefore attempts to present her with a dilemma: either (a) she thinks that secular uses of locutions such as 'bound', 'permitted' or 'excused' are ways of speaking which lack sense (in which case his first round of arguments comes into play), or (b) she thinks that, even if such locutions do not strictly speaking lack sense, they nonetheless – in the absence of a belief in a divine law-giver – are unable sufficiently to bind, permit or excuse (in which case his second round of arguments comes into play).

The second horn of the dilemma (with which Beardsmore confronts Anscombe) rests on the assumption that Anscombe will find any notion of obligation other than that provided by a divine law conception defective, on the grounds that what is prescribed on such a conception will fail to be absolutely binding.[56] What escapes Beardsmore is that Anscombe contributes her remarks about the character of obligations prescribed by divine law not in order to champion theism,[57] but rather to illuminate the logical differences between a law conception of ethics and alternative conceptions.[58] Beardsmore assumes that Anscombe's aim in drawing attention to what is peculiar to the modal concepts which figure in a divine law conception of ethics is to disenchant us with secular ethics. He combines that mistaken assumption with two further misunderstandings. The first of these has to do with how Anscombe's argument bears on a more general quarrel between a theist and an atheist. Anscombe, in adumbrating a law conception of ethics, is concerned with someone who has a very particular conception of the place occupied by God in an account of the source of moral obligation. The opposition that she is concerned with is not one that pits the Christian believer against the non-believer.[59] Second, Beardsmore introduces his own proposal concerning what the notion of 'the absolute nature of God's commands' really comes to for a religious believer: a religious believer recognises God's commands as 'absolute' because he recognises that a certain sort of life – and no other way of life – is the life for him.[60] But this notion of 'absolute obligation' fails to mark what Anscombe was after in her discussion of divine law ethics: namely, a distinctive logical feature of one particular conception of ethics which distinguishes it from other conceptions of ethics held by both believers and non-believers.[61] The second horn of the dilemma (with which Beardsmore confronts Anscombe) thus fails to engage her thought for the same reason that the first horn does: because it fails to get hold of her central contention (that there is a *particular* concept of moral obligation the intelligibility of which depends on a *particular* conception of ethics).

VII   HOW CAN A CONCEPT SURVIVE THE CONDITIONS OF ITS INTELLIGIBILITY?

How is it that one can, as it were, see a meaning that is no meaning?

Elizabeth Anscombe[62]

The views of Nietzsche, Kierkegaard and Anscombe have the following three features in common. First of all, these thinkers are, as we have seen, interested in cases in which we continue to employ certain words but are no longer able to use them to express the concepts which those words formerly expressed. Second, they attribute this loss of concepts to the loss of a religious framework in which those concepts formerly had their life. Third, they see us, when we call upon these words, as prone to hallucinate a meaning where there is none. It is, I think, the difficult and paradoxical character of this third feature of their views which leads to a misunderstanding of each of the first two features. This, in turn, occasions the sort of wholesale misunderstanding of their claims that one finds in Beardsmore (and others).

The misunderstanding is a natural one. These authors seek to direct our attention to cases in which a particular concept apparently lives on in the absence of the framework of thought essential to its intelligibility. But one might well ask: how are we to make sense of the idea of the survival of a concept outside the framework in which it has its life? (If it can only have its life within *that* home, and it is now outside it, then why isn't it dead?) Anscombe flaunts this paradox, in the final sentence of the focal passage, when she writes: 'The situation, if I am right, is the interesting one of the survival of a concept outside the framework of thought that made it a really intelligible one.' If we take to heart what is said in the last half of this sentence (that the intelligibility of the concept in question depends on that framework of thought), then we will be unable to take to heart what is said in the first half (we will be unable to identify a concept which is an instance of 'the interesting situation'). Anscombe's sentence, when we try to understand it, comes apart on us. If we try to imagine such a concept, we end up identifying something which either (1) is a concept or (2) is not a concept. If (1), then it must be possible to *intelligibly* make out which concept is at issue; but in that case what we have is not an instance of 'the interesting situation'. If (2), then what is at issue is at most something which can be *mistaken* for a concept; but in that case what we have is not an instance of 'the survival of a concept'. Thus there are questions that Anscombe's discussion naturally invites – questions such as: 'Precisely *which* concept of "moral obligation' is she objecting to?', or: 'How does she know the modern concept is the *same* as the one which figures in a divine law conception?' – which it cannot answer without undermining its own thesis. It may be thought that this points to an incoherence in Anscombe's thought to which she herself is oblivious. But that would be to mistake a transitional feature of her method for her conclusion.

It is natural to read Anscombe's argument as if what she were saying is that there is a particular concept of moral obligation which is logically flawed for such-and-such reasons. If *that* were what she were saying, then she could identify which concept is flawed but she would have to back off from her strong charge of unintelligibility. In an article entitled 'The Reality of the Past', Anscombe provides a detailed discussion of the method which underlies such a charge. She offers the following example:

Suppose that a child wanted a cake that it had eaten. That it cannot have it again is a mere physical fact. But suppose that it wanted a bang it had heard, that is, that actual individual bang . . .

If a bang were made in response to this request and satisfied it, then this would show that 'A' was not being used as the proper name of a bang ... That 'A' is the proper name of a bang means that we do not speak of getting A again. 'Getting A again' is an expression similar to ones which have use in other contexts, as when 'A' is the name of a cake. When we transfer it to this context we do not transfer its use; for to describe its use we should have to describe in what circumstance we should say we had got A again, as we could do if 'A' were the name of a cake. But though we do not transfer its use we think we transfer some meaning and so we think that what is meant is something impossible.[63]

The case resembles the one discussed in 'Modern Moral Philosophy'. Both are cases in which we transfer an expression from one context to another without transferring its use, and in which 'though we do not transfer its use we think we transfer some meaning'. This leads us in both cases to want to identify the case as one in which what is meant is something logically flawed, something impossible – in the one case, something which possesses some but lacks other logical features of a proper name of an event; in the other case, something with some but not other logical features of a particular prescriptive concept. But each of these characterisations of the use of the transferred expression is unstable in the way in which we saw that the final sentence of the focal passage is unstable.[64] The (logically flawed) meaning which we believe we perceive in each of these cases is, in the end, to be recognised as a mere illusion of meaning. Anscombe makes this point explicit in 'The Reality of the Past'; the discussion continues:

We think we cannot imagine getting A again because of the essential character of what is denoted by the name. But the real reason is that 'getting A again' is an expression for which we have yet to invent a use in this context; so far no use for it exists. This doesn't seem enough, however: we think we *could* not give it a use – meaning that we could not give it the use it has in other contexts, the use that the form of expression suggests or reminds us of ... The senselessness seems to consist in the fact that we have no use for this combination of words. But it follows from this that the only sense that can be made of the philosophical assertion that the past cannot change is that to speak of a change in the past is to produce an expression for which no use exists and which therefore has *no* sense.[65]

What Anscombe says here applies to her discussion in 'Modern Moral Philosophy'. Anscombe's objection to the locution of 'moral obligation' as it figures in modern moral philosophy is not that it expresses a logically incoherent concept, but rather that it simply fails to express any concept whatsoever. When we transfer this expression outside a law conception of ethics we 'produce an expression for which no use exists and which therefore has *no* sense'.[66]

The initial realisation, however, that our words do not quite mean what we want them to say does not dissipate their appearance of sense. They retain (what Anscombe calls in 'Modern Moral Philosophy') a certain 'atmosphere of meaning'. What happens in such cases, according to Anscombe, when we attempt to transfer the meaning of an expression but the use does not transfer, is that an *appearance* of meaning is engendered – an apparent meaning which, upon reflection, we perceive not to be a legitimate meaning but which we nonetheless take to be some sort of meaning. Thus, in 'The Reality of the Past', she goes on to say:

> It remains true, nevertheless, that an idea of a change in the past retains an apparent meaning which is one of the sources of perplexity. For this appearance is such that one wishes to say that one can see that it is somehow not a *legitimate* meaning, and because of this one seems to be saying something positive in saying that the past cannot change. This might be expressed by saying that 'a change in the past' is an expression that *could* not be given a sense, meaning that the vague sense that one perceives in it could not be embodied in a use – as if one could understand the sense that it could not be given.[67]

What emerges clearly here is that Beardsmore's characterisation of Anscombe's thesis is a characterisation of something which figures in her discussion (of cases of appearances of intelligibility), but not as her thesis. Rather, it forms one of the threads of the fabric of confusion she wishes to unravel. Beardsmore thinks that Anscombe's view is that certain expressions (such as 'moral obligation') are ones 'that *could* not be given a sense'. If such expressions were *per impossibile* examples of the use of concepts outside the framework of thought which makes them really intelligible, then they would have an, as it were, impossible sense – they would combine logically incompatible features. But to think this is not only to fail to appreciate the instability of the final sentence of the focal passage, it is to fail to appreciate the entire method of elucidation which it subserves. To regard such expressions in this way is to be drawn in to the appearance of meaning which they engender – an appearance which Anscombe ultimately seeks to explode.

We can see more clearly now why Anscombe's thesis must be understood to be about the impossibility of intelligibly using certain concepts rather than about the impossibility of intelligibly using certain words. When she charges certain uses of the expression 'moral obligation' with unintelligibility, she is not claiming that these expressions have an, as it were, incoherent sense. Her charge – like Nietzsche's and Kierkegaard's – is not directed at the words, but at the user: in such cases, it is *we* who have failed to mean something by them. Her thesis, *pace* Beardsmore, is not that these words cannot be given a sense but that we have failed to give them one. But how are we to square this with her apparent eagerness to encourage us to exclude or discard certain expressions from the language? At one point she writes: 'It may be possible, if we are resolute, to discard the term "morally ought".'[68] Elsewhere she writes:

> It might remain to look for 'norms' in human virtues . . . But in *this* sense, 'norm' has ceased to be roughly equivalent to 'law'. In *this* sense the notion of a 'norm' brings us nearer to an Aristotelian than a law conception of ethics. There is, I think, no harm in that; but if someone looked in this direction to give 'norm' a sense, then he ought to recognize what has happened to the term 'norm', which he wanted to mean 'law' – without bringing God in: it has ceased to mean 'law' at all; and *so* the expressions 'moral obligation', 'the moral ought', and 'duty' are best put on the Index, if he can manage it.[69]

How are we to hear this call to put certain expressions on the Index? Such remarks can appear to confirm the impression that Anscombe thinks these expressions have an impermissible sense – that the problem lies with the flawed concepts these words seek

to express. But this would be a misunderstanding of the philosophical method she means to employ and which she takes herself to have learned from Dr Wittgenstein.[70] Elsewhere she writes:

> Wittgenstein said that when we call something senseless it is
> not as it were its sense that is senseless, but a form of words is
> being excluded from the language ... But the argument for 'ex-
> cluding this form of words from the language' is apparently
> an argument that 'its sense is senseless' ... The result of the
> argument, if it is successful, is that we no longer want to say
> [what we thought we wanted to say] ... Hence Wittgenstein's
> talk of 'therapies'. The 'exclusion from the language' is done
> not by legislation but by persuasion. The 'sense that is sense-
> less' is the *type* of sense that our expressions suggest.[71]

An argument for excluding a particular expression from the
language (for example 'moral obligation') will, at first, have the
appearance of being an argument that the sense of the expression is senseless. But this appearance is itself to be overcome.
What at first appears to be an argument about the incoherent
sense of certain words turns out to be one about our incoherent
relation to the words. The result of the argument, if it is successful,
is not that we take the expression to have a different sort of sense
(that is, a flawed one) than we had originally imagined, but that
we no longer want to call upon the expression at all; there is no
longer anything we want to say with it. But not because we are
in any way (logically) barred from using this form of words. 'The
"exclusion from the language" is done not by legislation but by
persuasion.' Anscombe seeks to persuade us to avoid the expression in question because we are evidently tempted to mistake
certain combinations of words (in which the expression in question figures without a sense) for meaningful propositions – because we are prone to see a meaning where there is no meaning.

VIII NIETZSCHE, KIERKEGAARD AND ANSCOMBE

*A farther proceeding in philosophy doth bring the mind back again
to confront religion.*

                                                    Francis Bacon[72]

In the preceding pages I have, on the whole, refrained from re-
marking upon the many significant differences between the views
of Nietzsche, Kierkegaard and Anscombe. My aim has been to
highlight a thesis they hold in common. All three are interested
in how the possibility of certain sorts of thoughts depends upon
the presence of a religious background. All three direct our attention
to cases in which – in the absence of the relevant background –
we continue to employ certain words but not the concepts which
those words once expressed. Each of these philosophers offers a
different analysis of what constitutes the relevant background:
Nietzsche understands it, in the first instance, as a historical and
cultural configuration, Kierkegaard as an individual's way of life,
Anscombe as a framework of thought.[73] Their respective analyses
of the problem of moral unintelligibility consequently overlap and
diverge in various ways.

In answer to the question 'Which moral concepts can our words
express?', Anscombe directs our attention to the conception of
ethics to which we subscribe; whereas Nietzsche and Kierkegaard
direct our attention to how it is that we live. In answer to the
question 'What religious background do we overlook?', Kierkegaard
wants to show us that a religious background we think is there
is not (we imagine it is flourishing when it is dead); whereas
Nietzsche and Anscombe want to show us that a religious background we think is not there *is* (we know that it is dead but not
that it continues to haunt us). In answer to the question 'How is
it that we are subject to illusions of moral intelligibility?', Nietzsche
directs our attention to the general way in which the meaning of
a moral concept presupposes a whole set of historical and cultural circumstances; whereas Kierkegaard and Anscombe direct
our attention to the local ways in which the meaning of a word
changes as its use shifts, and how we imagine we transfer the
meaning when we have failed to transfer the use.

Each of these differences between one of these philosophers
and the other two is a function of more fundamental differences
in their respective philosophical ambitions. Anscombe's aim, in
the first instance, is to clarify a logical confusion; Nietzsche's and
Kierkegaard's to clarify an existential one.[74] Kierkegaard seeks to
show his contemporaries that they are much further from Christianity than they imagine; Nietzsche and Anscombe seek to show
theirs that they are not quite as far from it as they imagine. Finally,
Nietzsche is only secondarily interested in our confusions concerning what we mean by our words (he thinks we have other

confusions of the soul which are far more profound); while Kierkegaard and Anscombe think some of our most profound confusions of soul show themselves in – and can be revealed to us through an attention to – our confusions concerning what we mean (and fail to mean) by our words.

Notes

1. Part of the point of this paper is that such a defence or attack is of necessity an arduous task. Given the premise (which it is the burden of this paper to establish) that there is no *a priori* incoherence to the sort of charge of unintelligibility which these philosophers are concerned to level, then the task is arduous for two reasons: (1) a rebuttal or a defence of such a charge requires considerable attention to the ways in which those who are the target of the charge actually talk and think, and (2) each individual charge must be examined separately and on its own merits.
2. It should be noted that the objection in question forms only a small part of the business of Beardsmore's contribution to this symposium. It should also be noted that the objection in question – though articulated in a helpfully explicit and succinct manner by Beardsmore – is one which lingers either in the background or the foreground of much of the secondary literature which takes the trouble to address the views of any one of these three philosophers on the disappearance of moral or religious concepts.
3. F. Nietzsche, *Beyond Good and Evil*, §53, trans. W. Kaufmann (New York: Vintage, 1966), p. 66.
4. The dependence which is at issue here is a conceptual one – whether the *meaning* of certain concepts depends upon a religious framework. It is no part of Beardsmore's business to deny a historical claim to the effect that many of our moral concepts first evolved within a religious context.
5. Beardsmore's paper is also in this volume. All subsequent quotations from Beardsmore are from this paper.
6. This formulation occurs as part of Beardsmore's summary of Anscombe's position.
7. Fyodor Dostoevsky, *The Brothers Karamazov*, (Constance Garnett translation), (New York: Macmillan, 1912).
8. Dostoevsky writes in his *Notebooks*:
   Ivan is profound, he isn't one of the contemporary atheists who merely show the narrowness of their world-view and the dullness of their dull little capacities in their disbelief... Nihilism has appeared among us because at bottom *we are all nihilists*. It is only the new, original form of its appearance which scares us. (*The Norton Critical Edition of The Brothers Karamazov*, ed. Ralph Matlaw (Norton, 1976), p. 769).
9. Beardsmore then tries to go on and show that Anscombe is vulnerable to the same arguments as Nielsen and Kolakowski.

10. Kai Nielsen, *Ethics Without God* (London: Pemberton, 1973), p. 48. Beardsmore quotes these lines out of context. Only after writing this paper did I succeed in laying hold of a copy of Nielsen's book. The context (of the lines Beardsmore quotes) is one in which Nielsen is taking up an adversarial point of view. He begins by directing an objection against himself; he then 'concedes' to his theistic interlocutor that as long as we restrict ourselves to an overly pared-down conception of morality (one from which we only 'look at morality with the cold eye of an anthropologist') we place ourselves in a dialectically vulnerable position ('theologians are then in a position to press home a powerful dialectical point' concerning 'the true nature of such conventionalism' (p. 48)). Beardsmore seems to think that Nielsen himself is prepared to bite the conventionalist bullet. But Nielsen's proximate aim in these pages is to 'make apparent the dialectic of the problem' (p. 50). It is not at all clear to me that Nielsen means his reader to identify the dialectically vulnerable position with his own (though where Nielsen does mean to end up on this issue is not easy to make out). I suspect that, in attributing a conventionalist account of moral obligation to Nielsen, Beardsmore has mistaken Nielsen's exposition of a particular stage of (what Nielsen calls) 'the dialectic between the theist and the atheist' for an exposition of Nielsen's own views. All subsequent references to Nielsen in this paper should accordingly be read as references to Nielsen as read by Beardsmore.

11. Leszek Kolakowski, *Religion* (New York: Oxford University Press 1982), pp. 189, 191–2.

12. It is worth noting that yet further philosophical assumptions are required before it seems to be self-evidently the case (as it does to Kolakowski) that the prescriptive force of the requirements of morality is somehow specially tied to the availability of a divine law-giver in a manner in which that of other sorts of normative requirements are not. Descartes thought that the necessity of the laws of logic and arithmetic was to be accounted for by the fact that God willed those laws to be among the basic principles of reason which governed our thought. However, a contemporary refusal to appeal to God in one's account of logical or mathematical necessity hardly, in and of itself, commits one to the claim that 'what is and what is not a correct logical inference (or a valid mathematical proof) is simply constituted by conventions we are free to accept or reject'. In the absence of considerable additional philosophical argument, the claim that 'if God did not exist, everything would be permitted' is no more evidently true in ethics than it is in mathematics. (This is not to deny that there are, of course, those who will wish to attempt to furnish a conventionalist account of the nature of logical or mathematical necessity.)

13. F. Nietzsche, *The Gay Science*, §125, trans. W. Kaufmann (New York: Vintage, 1974), pp. 181–2.

14. Indeed, as the remarks (quoted in note 8) from his *Notebooks* indicate, this is precisely how Dostoevsky himself conceived of Ivan.

15. F. Nietzsche, *Menschliches, Allzumenschliches II* (Leipzig: A Kroner, 1925) (*Human, All Too Human, Part II*), §224 (my translation).

16. F. Nietzsche, *The Anti-Christ*, §39, trans. R. J. Hollingdale (Harmondsworth: Penguin, 1968), p. 151.

17. Thus Nietzsche will include much of the philosophical terminology of the ancients and the medievals within the scope of his analysis. Nietzsche's point is meant to cut in both historical directions: not only do certain words fail to express certain concepts because those concepts depend upon 'an ancient culture now degenerated', but other concepts depend upon a very different and much more recent culture – one whose fundamental presuppositions fail to cohere with those of antiquity. Hence Nietzsche's suspicion of any philosopher who combines a sympathy for Christian modes of thought with a fondness for the fashionable philosophical concepts of his day – such as (Hegel's favourite) *Geist*: 'Our whole concept, our cultural concept, "spirit" had no meaning whatever in the world Jesus lived in' (*The Anti-Christ*, p. 141).

18. In making this sort of point, one of Nietzsche's favourite examples of a moral concept that depends on a Christian way of life is the concept of *chastity*.

19. Nietzsche sees Christianity – in its waging of a war against the natural desires and instincts of the human animal – as further extending and radicalising an asceticism already present in both Jewish and Hellenistic thought and practice. One should be clear, however, about how complex and nuanced Nietzsche's attitude is towards this historical development. For he thinks it is through such forms of violence against one's animal nature – in particular, those forms of violence voluntarily inflicted by an individual on himself – that a deepening of the human being, a dilation of the human self, was achieved. Thus, however harmful Nietzsche finds the ascetic ideal in its present form, he thinks that it is only through its tyranny that the human animal first became *interesting*:

> All instincts that do not discharge themselves outwardly *turn inward* – this is what I call the *internalization* of man: thus it was that man first developed what was later called his 'soul'. The entire inner world, originally as thin as if it were stretched between two membranes, expanded and extended itself, acquired depth, breadth, and height, in the same measure as outward discharge was *inhibited* . . .
>
> [I]t was on the soil of this *essentially dangerous* form of human existence, the priestly form, that man first became *an interesting animal* . . . only here did the human soul in a higher sense acquire *depth* and become *evil* – and these are the two basic respects in which man has hitherto been superior to the beasts! (*On the Genealogy of Morals*; in *On the Genealogy of Morals and Ecce Homo*, trans. W. Kaufmann (New York: Vintage, 1989), pp. 33, 84).

20. Nietzsche, *On the Genealogy of Morals*, pp. 59–60.

21. A parallel point holds for Nietzsche's conception of what an atheist

is – that is, someone who has truly overcome Christianity. Being an atheist is not being someone who has arrived at a certain intellectual 'result' or 'conclusion' but a way of being which a person inhabits 'as a matter of course' and 'from instinct' (see *Ecce Homo*, p. 236). Thus, as we have seen (in *Beyond Good and Evil*, §53), Nietzsche will often refer to those who take themselves to be atheists as still unwittingly dominated by 'the religious instinct'.

22. I explore this region of Nietzsche's thought in my 'Nietzsche's Perfectionism', in R. Schacht (ed.), *Nietzsche as Educator* (London: Routledge, forthcoming).

23. The parable begins:

> Have you not heard of that madman who lit the lantern in the bright morning hours, ran to the marketplace, and cried incessantly: 'I seek God! I seek God!' – As many of those who did not believe in God were standing around just then, he provoked much laughter). (Nietzsche, *The Gay Science*, §125, pp. 181–2)

24. 'The death of God' is Nietzsche's name for a crisis into which our civilisation is in the process of being plunged. Thus in so far as it names an event it is one which will take centuries to transpire.

25. S. Kierkegaard, *The Point of View for My Work as An Author*, trans. W. Lowrie (New York: Harper, 1972), p. 25.

26. It is against the background of this sort of issue (concerning what sort of life the person who calls himself a Christian leads) that one should understand Kierkegaard's incessant remarks about how Christianity is not a doctrine. The connection between these two topics is explicit in the following passage:

> Christianity is not a doctrine ... Christianity is a message about existence ... If Christianity (precisely because it is not a doctrine) is not reduplicated in the life of the person expounding it, then he does not expound Christianity, for Christianity is a message about living and can only be expounded by being realized in men's lives (*The Diary of Søren Kierkegaard*, ed. P. Rohde (New York: Citadel, 1960), p. 117).

27. Some comment on Kierkegaard's confusing philosophical terminology is appropriate here. The categories, for Kierkegaard, have to do with the relation between a subject and an object. A category is objective if what matters is the object, subjective if what matters is the relation to the object. The aesthetic is the category of objectivity, the mode of disengaged reflection; whereas the ethical and the religious are the categories of subjectivity, modes of relation which turn on the character of one's concern. The category of the aesthetic is one in which one relates oneself to an object so that the accent of one's concern falls on the object and not on one's relation to it. This contrasts with the category of the ethical where one's relation to the object is 'interested' and the category of the religious where the relation is one of 'infinite interest'. A relation is 'interested', for Kierkegaard, if it is tied to the task of forming one's self (into the sort of person one wishes to become) or leading one's life (in accordance with one's conception of what is valuable). Thus,

Kierkegaard says, a relation is objective if the accent falls on the *what*, subjective if the accent falls on the *how*. These are not, as such, terms of praise or blame. Kierkegaard's criticisms are never directed at some mode of thought which properly belongs to one of the categories, but at a mode of thought that involves what he calls a 'confusion of the categories'.

Kierkegaard's writings have been subjected to catastrophic mis-understandings because commentators have failed to realise that the terms 'the objective' and 'the subjective' represent pieces of ter-minology for distinguishing the relative priority of subject and ob-ject within each of the categories. Virtually all of the secondary literature on Kierkegaard assumes that the terms 'subjective' and 'objective' have roughly the meaning in Kierkegaard's work that they have in traditional epistemological discussions which distinguish between objective and (merely) subjective forms of knowledge. The objective in this sense is that which can be intersubjectively known, the subjective that which can only be known by me. This leads to the unhappy assumption that when Kierkegaard characterises the categories of the ethical and the religious as 'subjective', he means that they concern a kind of truth which is (epistemically) private and hence incommunicable. This misunderstanding is reinforced by a failure to attend to the authorial strategy of Kierkegaard's pseu-donymous works. (See my 'Kierkegaard, Wittgenstein and Nonsense', in Ted Cohen, Paul Guyer and Hilary Putnam (eds), *Pursuits of Reason* (Lubbock Tx.: Texas Tech University Press, 1992).)

28. The question of whether one has been baptised or not (or lives in a Christian country, etc.) counts as an 'objective' matter for Kierkegaard because it does not have to do in the relevant way with what kind of person one strives to be or what sorts of values inform one's life – the character of one's concern with such a fact (in this case, a fact about oneself) and the manner in which that concern reflects itself in one's life are not pertinent to determining whether the bare fact obtains or not. Whether one has faith in God (that is, whether one is a Christian) is not a fact that does or does not obtain regardless of who one is and how one lives. It is, according to Kierkegaard, something which involves an essential reference to the character of the subject's concern and hence is (according to this terminology) not an objective but a subjective matter. A community of pseudo-Christians – who sustain their belief in their own Christianity through a purely 'objective' understanding of what it is to be a Christian – is what Kierkegaard means by his term 'Christendom'. Christen-dom is the illusion of a flourishing Christian community.

29. He claims that all his reader requires in order to be able to arrive at this discovery is 'some capacity for observation' (*The Point of View for My Work as An Author*, p. 22).

30. I attempt below a brief description of Kierkegaard's conception of qualitative dialectic. I go into these matters in more detail in my 'Putting Two and Two Together: Kierkegaard, Wittgenstein and the Point of View for their Work as Authors', in Timothy Tessin and

Mario von der Ruhr (eds), *Philosophy and the Grammar of Religious Belief* (London & New York: Macmillan St Martin's Press, 1995).

31. We can now give a slightly more precise definition of 'Christendom'. It refers to the illusion which results when it comes to pass that the majority of people who employ an ostensibly Christian vocabulary use it to describe lives lived in aesthetic (or at most aesthetic–ethical) categories. As the epigraph to this section of the paper indicates, Kierkegaard's aim is to dispel this illusion.

32. I am quoting here from Stanley Cavell, 'Kierkegaard *On Authority and Revelation*', in *Must We Mean What We Say?* (Cambridge University Press, 1976), p. 170. The preceding discussion is indebted to this article.

33. This raises the question whether someone who does not lead a religious life can understand a religious concept. The problem does not differ in principle from that of the anthropologist who attempts to understand an ethical or religious concept belonging to a different culture. One can be said to grasp such a concept to the extent that one can imaginatively project oneself into the sort of life in which it has its point, sympathetically enter into the interests of those who employ the concept, and thereby comprehend its use.

34. G. E. M. Anscombe, 'Modern Moral Philosophy', in *Ethics, Religion and Politics: Collected Philosophical Papers, Vol. III* (Minneapolis, MN.: University of Minnesota Press, 1981), p. 32.

35. Thus in the epigraph to this section of the paper Anscombe is concerned with whether a particular word still *signifies a real concept*.

36. I am here in agreement with Cora Diamond's article 'The Dog that Gave Himself the Moral Law' (in *Midwest Studies in Philosophy*, Vol. XIII, eds. French, Uehling and Wettstein (Notre Dame IN.: Notre Dame University Press, 1988)) where she argues that Anscombe's argument 'must be understood to be about the survival of concepts or notions, not about the survival of words or expressions' (p. 161).

37. Anscombe, 'Modern Moral Philosophy', p. 30.

38. Anscombe applauds 'Hume and our present-day ethicists' for showing that the relevant notion is without content, but she chides our present-day ethicists for attempting to retain the psychological force of the term:

> I should judge that Hume and our present-day ethicists had done a considerable service by showing that no content could be found in the notion 'morally ought'; if it were not that the latter philosophers try to find an alternative (very fishy) content and to retain the psychological force of the term. It would be most reasonable to drop it. It has no reasonable sense outside a law conception of ethics; they are not going to maintain such a conception; and you can do ethics without it, as is shown by the example of Aristotle ('Modern Moral Philosophy', p. 32).

Anscombe distinguishes here – as she does throughout the paper – between the *notion* (what I have been calling the concept) 'morally ought' and the *term* (what I have been calling the word). But she may appear not to honour that distinction in so far as she speaks of something's being a notion while maintaining that it has no content. I take it that she courts this confusion intentionally (for reasons taken up in the penultimate section of this paper).

39. I will not in this paper attempt to explore the details of that diagnosis.
40. Anscombe, 'Modern Moral Philosophy', pp. 30–1.
41. Peter Winch, 'Who is my Neighbour?', in *Trying to Make Sense* (Oxford: Blackwell, 1987), p. 160.
42. Winch's own argument against Anscombe turns on the claim that one can already find in the New Testament a conception of moral obligation which does not presuppose the notion of divine law. He also appears to think that this point is connected to an internal tension in Anscombe's own views. Winch elaborates his disagreement with Anscombe through a discussion of the parable of the Samaritan:

> Jesus tells the parable ... in a way which presupposes that the moral modality to which the Samaritan responded would have a force for the parable's hearers *independently* of their commitment to any particular theological belief ... According to Miss Anscombe, the intelligibility of the obligation to help the injured traveller to which the Samaritan responded depends on accepting that it is a divine law that one should act thus. I think, on the contrary, that the concept of a divine law can itself only develop on the basis of our response to such modalities ('Who is my Neighbor?', p. 161).

Anscombe, however, would be happy to agree that the 'ought' in 'one ought to help an injured traveller' could have (and, indeed, should have) had a force for the parable's hearers independently of their commitment to any particular theological belief. What she would deny is that a *Christian* understanding of why one ought to render aid to an injured traveller (that is, the understanding that Jesus accepted and was concerned to teach) is one which is really intelligible apart from a conception of divine law. (Though she would presumably agree with Winch that Jesus' understanding of divine law differed significantly in certain respects from that of the Pharisees.) Thus Winch is in disagreement with Anscombe only if he wishes to claim that Jesus, (or, more generally, a Christian) understanding of why one ought to render aid to an injured traveller is one which can be fully grasped 'independently of a commitment to any particular theological belief'.

It is also not clear that Winch's point in the last sentence of the passage quoted above really expresses a disagreement with Anscombe. As Winch is aware, elsewhere Anscombe herself is concerned to insist that our modal and deontic concepts can only develop against the background of certain responses:

> God himself can make no promises to man except in a human language ... What we have to attend to is the use of modals. Through this, we shall find that not only promises, but also rules and rights, are in essence *created* and not merely captured or expressed by the grammar of our languages ... [Y]ou are told

you 'can't' do something you plainly *can*, as comes out in the fact that you sometimes *do*. At the beginning, the adults will physically stop the child from doing what they say he 'can't' do. With one set of circumstances this business is part of the build-up of the concept of a rule; with another, of a piece of etiquette; with another, of a promise; in another, of an act of sacrilege or impiety; with another, of a right. It is part of human intelligence to be able to learn the responses to ... modals without which they wouldn't exist as linguistic instruments and without which these things: rules, etiquette, rights, infringements, promises, pieties, impieties would not exist either ('Rules, Rights and Promises', in *Ethics, Religion and Politics*, pp. 99–101).
Winch takes this 'later work' of Anscombe's 'to undermine her earlier views about the moral "ought" but without explicit recognition on her part that this is so' ('Who is my Neighbor?', p. 162). Anscombe's later work only undermines her earlier article if the following two claims are in tension with one another: (1) to identify *which* (modal) concept a particular concept is, we need to examine its role within the framework of thought which makes it a really intelligible one, and (2) the acquisition of certain modal concepts presupposes the *prior* acquisition of certain other more primitive modal concepts (and the correlative development of the capacities for response upon which those concepts rest). 'Modern Moral Philosophy' is concerned only with (1), but nothing in that article is incompatible with (2). I take it that Anscombe holds both (a) that in order to acquire the concept of moral obligation which figures in a law conception of ethics we must first have learned to respond to various non-legal modals, and (b) the content of the concept which figures in a law conception of ethics cannot be analysed in terms of such modals.

43. Beardsmore's examples here are rather slippery since they are poised between ethical and non-ethical conceptions of what one 'ought' to do. If what 'obliges' the doctor to answer the call is, as Beardsmore has it, 'the rules of his profession' (and what obliges the trade unionist is the rules of his union) then we are not obviously on ethical ground; any more than we would be if we were to say to someone: 'Your king is in check, you are obliged to move it.' In these cases it is appropriate to invoke the (philosophically dangerous) language of being 'obliged' since there are rules that lay down what one is obliged to do and what one is prohibited from doing. If, on the other hand, we consider the doctor who fails to make the call as deficient in certain virtues (both charity and prudence come to mind!) and the trade unionist who crosses the picket-line as deficient in others (above all, fidelity, both to a cause and to his friends), then we are on moral ground when we say of either one that he did not do as he 'ought' to have done. But in the latter sort of case, what is gained by insisting on the language of (the doctor's or the trade unionist's) being 'obliged' to act in certain ways? What Beardsmore has given us is a pair of cases about which it seems right to say

that the individual in question is both 'obliged' to do something and furthermore he really 'ought' to do the thing he is obliged to do. (There are cases – think of doctors in Nazi Germany – where the two will not coincide. In such cases, we want what a person ought to do to trump what he is obliged to do. Anscombe's point is that it is only in the context of a law conception of ethics that we have a coherent notion of a source of obligation which always trumps.) I think Beardsmore is probably confused as to which of these two kinds of examples – a moral or a non-moral one – he is after. Neither example, properly described, is a problem for Anscombe. She is happy to allow talk of what is 'obliged' where there are rules or laws which prescribe what is permitted and prohibited; and she is equally happy to allow talk of what the virtuous person 'ought' to do. What she is suspicious of is our wanting to characterise cases of the latter sort as cases of 'obligation' (in the absence of any notion of a law or rule which obliges us): not because it is impossible to assign the *word* 'obligation' a sense in such a context, but because she thinks one is apt to become confused – as, I believe, Beardsmore in this very passage has become confused – about what it is one wants to say.

44. Indeed, she need not deny that they may happily continue to use the word in many contexts which resemble those in which we now employ the word figuratively. If they are, as assumed, ignorant of the strange legal institutions of their barbaric ancestors, then we can imagine that this word for them will perhaps no longer be inflected figuratively. What was once its figurative meaning will simply become its literal meaning and so they will mean something like 'outrageous' or 'reckless' or 'irresponsible' by the word. But even to imagine this is still to imagine a scenario according to which the literal meaning of the word – and hence the concept which that word expresses – has changed.

45. A citizen of this future utopia is presumably interested in calling someone other than himself 'criminal'. The analogy between the citizens of this future utopia and those of Christendom thus has its limits. One feature of a Kierkegaardian diagnosis of the investment in such forms of confusion does not extend to this case: the citizens of the future utopia are not attracted to this confusion because they are deeply attached to the thought that they themselves lead lives which are steeped in crime!

46. Anscombe, 'Modern Moral Philosophy', pp. 30–1.

47. This formulation is misleading in two ways. It might be less confusing to characterise the concept of moral obligation the intelligibility of which is at issue here for Anscombe as an *ethical* (rather than as a 'legal') concept – albeit a quasi-legal ethical concept – in order to clearly distinguish it from a secular legal concept. Second, I take it that Anscombe's view (although she does not say so in the article) is that it is only *most of us* late moderns who lead lives in which the relevant quasi-legal concepts are unable to gain a foothold; thus her argument is not meant to rule out the possibility that cer-

tain individual Jewish or Catholic believers may continue to have a
use for these concepts.

48. The parallel between Anscombe's point about modern moral philosophy and Kierkegaard's about Christendom is quite far-reaching.
Kierkegaard says of his contemporaries that (1) they detach the word
'Christian' from its relation to a family of other concepts (whose
content is tied to their application within the context of certain practices), and (2) they nonetheless seek to retain the aura of the word
after having drained it of its meaning. Anscombe can be seen to be
making both of these points in the following passage:

> All the atmosphere of the term ['morally wrong'] is retained while
> its substance is guaranteed quite null. Now let us remember that
> 'morally wrong' is the term which is the heir of the notion 'il-
> licit', or 'what there is an obligation *not* to do'; which belongs in
> a divine law theory of ethics ... And it is because 'morally wrong'
> is the heir of this concept, but an heir that is cut off from the
> family of concepts from which it sprang, that 'morally wrong'
> *both* goes beyond the mere factual description 'unjust' *and* seems
> to have no discernible content except a certain compelling force ...
> But actually this notion of obligation is a notion which only op-
> erates in the context of law. And I should be inclined to congratu-
> late the present-day moral philosophers on depriving 'morally
> ought' of its now delusive appearance of content, if only they
> did not manifest a detestable desire to retain the atmosphere of
> the term ('Modern Moral Philosophy', pp. 40–1).

49. Thus Anscombe's aim is much less general than is often supposed:
it is only to show that *particular* locutions (such as 'moral obligation', 'moral ought') – in so far as they are now used apart from a
certain framework of thought – continue to retain a certain atmosphere without having a meaning. Anscombe does not think all our
moral concepts are in trouble. It is thus a mistake to identify
Anscombe's thesis with that of other authors – who have been influenced by her and with whom she is now often grouped together
(such as Alasdair MacIntyre) – who argue that the possibility of
coherent moral thinking *as a whole* depends on a background we
have lost. If Anscombe held (as is sometimes presumed) that all of
our secular moral thought is unintelligible then her view would be
that every moral concept is in trouble. This would leave no foothold for the sort of argument that Anscombe actually does make –
one which requires that we be able to identify how a particular
concept fails to cohere with the rest of our moral thought.

50. This point is brought out very nicely in Cora Diamond's article ('The
Dog that Gave Himself the Moral Law') and the present discussion
is indebted to it.

51. I remind the reader that the aim of this paper is neither to defend
nor to attack Anscombe's claim, but simply to clarify how that claim
can and cannot be disputed. If I were to undertake such a dispute,
I would want to go after the first half of her claim. I would want to
draw upon the tradition of thought about the normativity of juridi-

cal and moral concepts which has its origins in Kant and Hegel. This would require taking issue with Anscombe's cursory dismissal of Kant's conception of the moral law (as a law one gives oneself) as 'absurd' ('Modern Moral Philosophy', p. 27).

52. Anscombe, 'Modern Moral Philosophy', p. 30.

53. Thus she proposes that we 'discard the term "morally ought", and simply return to the ordinary "ought"' (ibid., p. 41). She goes on to remark that 'the ordinary "ought" ... is such an extremely frequent term of human language that it is difficult to imagine getting on without it' (ibid.).

54. Thus Anscombe writes:

> It would be a great improvement if, instead of 'morally wrong', one always named a genus such as 'untruthful', 'unchaste', 'unjust'. We should no longer ask whether doing something was 'wrong', passing directly from some description of an action to this notion; we should ask whether, e.g., it was unjust; and the answer would sometimes be clear at once ('Modern Moral Philosophy', pp. 32–3).

Her point here is not that we should no longer ask 'is doing such-and-such wrong?' because the word 'wrong' is necessarily meaningless and to be avoided at all costs, but rather that we should no longer – when uttering these words – take ourselves to be asking a *certain sort of question*: one which would allow us to explicate the content of what we are asking in such a way as to isolate a notion of what it is for something to be 'morally wrong' which has prescriptive force independently of the particular virtue to which the action in question fails to conform.

55. On a law conception of ethics, it suffices to make a particular action right or wrong if – independently of any further reasons for thinking it good or bad – it is the sort of action which has been (divinely) commanded or prohibited. That is why Anscombe says that on a law conception of ethics it really does *add* something to a description of a particular unjust act (in a way that it does not in the absence of such a conception) to say of it that it is 'morally wrong':

> In a divine law theory of ethics ... it really does add something to the description 'unjust' to say there is an obligation not to do it; for what obliges is the divine law – as rules oblige in a game. So if the divine law obliges not to commit injustice by forbidding injustice, it really does add something to the description 'unjust' to say there is an obligation not to do it. And it is because 'morally wrong' is the heir of this concept, but an heir that is cut off from the family of concepts from which it sprang, that 'morally wrong' *both* goes beyond the mere factual description 'unjust' *and* seems to have no discernible content except a certain compelling force, which I should call purely psychological ('Modern Moral Philosophy', p. 41).

This is connected to a further feature of what makes Anscombe (in the absence of a divine law-giver) so nervous about an overarching quasi-legal notion of moral obligation:

If someone really thinks, *in advance*, that it is open to question whether such an action as procuring the judicial execution of the innocent should be quite excluded from consideration – I do not want to argue with him; he shows a corrupt mind (Ibid., p. 40).

Anscombe sees recent attempts to reinfuse an emphatic 'moral ought' with content – to supply an alternative source of overarching moral justification – as a temptation to moral rationalisation (and ultimately moral lunacy) in so far as it encourages us repeatedly to ponder whether something we otherwise have every reason to think morally abominable might not nonetheless be (given our alternative conception of the overarching source of moral justification) something which we 'morally ought' to do.

56. In this connection, Beardsmore writes:

> Anscombe does not claim that *any* sense of 'obligation' has, and must have, its basis in divine law, but only that what she calls the 'special moral sense' or sometimes the 'absolute' sense must do so ... Though membership in a trade union may well carry with it the obligation to respect the picket-lines, though doctors may have various professional obligations, these cannot be thought to be absolutely binding, since it is always possible for the trade unionist to resign from membership, possible for the doctor to find another profession. By contrast, where an obligation is thought of as the will of God, then there can be no question of the believer choosing to avoid it.

Beardsmore goes on to differ with Anscombe over why it is that for the religious believer God's commands 'possess the status of absolute obligations'. His differences with her here, again, rest on misunderstandings. Anscombe herself, as far as I know, never actually employs the locution 'absolute obligation'. She does distinguish between conditional and unconditional obligations, as well as between what is intrinsically unjust and what is unjust given particular circumstances. The intelligibility of neither of these distinctions, however, rests for her upon a notion of divine law. Neither of these distinctions therefore marks the sort of distinction between 'absolute' and 'non-absolute' obligations which Beardsmore reads into Anscombe.

Beardsmore (in his remarks quoted above) runs together a happy and an unhappy point: (a) only when employed in the context of a law conception of ethics does the term 'obligation' acquire a special moral sense, (b) what makes an obligation the sort which only God can prescribe is whether or not one can choose to avoid it. Beardsmore conflates these two points into a single notion of 'absolute obligation' which he attributes to Anscombe.

As to (a), though Anscombe would agree with it, she would not take it to imply that the term 'obligation' is deprived of modal force when employed in secular contexts (nor would she take it in such contexts to be necessarily conditional on roles of which one can divest oneself). The passage from 'Modern Moral Philosophy' which Beardsmore appears to have in mind (in his remarks quoted above) is the following:

The terms 'should' or 'ought' or 'needs' ... have acquired a special so-called 'moral' sense – i.e. a sense in which they imply some absolute verdict (like one of guilty/not guilty on a man) on what is described in the 'ought' sentences used in certain types of context ...

The ordinary (and quite indispensable) terms 'should', 'needs', 'ought', 'must' acquired this special sense by being equated in the relevant contexts with 'is obliged', or 'is bound', or 'is required to', in the sense in which one can be obliged or bound by law, or something can be required by law (pp. 29–30).

Anscombe's point here is not that the terms 'is obliged', or 'is bound', or 'is required to' only have genuine modal force given a conception of divine law. It is rather that a non-legal modal vocabulary ('should', 'ought', 'needs', 'must') acquires the modal force of terms such as 'is obliged', or 'is bound', or 'is required to' – and thus acquires a special moral sense (the sense in which one can be obliged or bound by law) – when it is employed in the context of a law conception of ethics; and only when it is employed in the sense in which something is required by law can this vocabulary be understood to imply an 'absolute' verdict (as opposed merely to retaining an empty atmosphere as of a verdict). So understood, Anscombe does not take (a) (as Beardsmore assumes) to impugn conceptions of ethics other than a divine law conception. She would take (a) merely to express a logical point concerning the difference between the prescriptive force of divine law and the prescriptive force the word 'ought' carries on a conception of ethics which is not a law conception. In particular, she would not take (a) to impugn an Aristotelian conception of ethics.

As to (b), it is not always the case that a status which incurs an obligation can be peeled off through an act of choice (as membership in a trade union can). But perhaps Beardsmore thinks that Anscombe is confused about this and that she thus holds that one can escape all obligations except divinely decreed ones by divesting oneself of membership in the sorts of status which incur them. However, as far as I can see, nothing Anscombe says in 'Modern Moral Philosophy' invites the attribution of such a view to her. Moreover, she explicitly repudiates such a view in 'On the Source of the Authority of the State' (in *Ethics, Religion and Politics*) where she contrasts one's obligations to a club (from which one can – and, in some cases, should – resign) and one's obligations to a government which exercises legitimate civil authority (from which one neither can nor should resign).

57. It is safe to say that many of the misunderstandings to which Anscombe's 'Modern Moral Philosophy' has been subjected are due to her readers drawing on their independent knowledge of her religious convictions and her explicitly apologetic religious writings. Readers therefore assume that they already know roughly what she *must* be saying in this article, too. In short, they fail to appreciate the extent to which the article undertakes a tactical (as it were, nonpartisan) intervention in the discourse of modern moral philosophy.

Not only does Anscombe not urge a divine law conception on her reader, she urges an alternative (Aristotelian) view – no doubt, in part, because she is confident that the majority of her readers (as she says) 'are not going to maintain such a [divine law] conception and you can do ethics without it' (p. 32).

58. It further escapes Beardsmore that her aim in exploring these differences is to bring out how a particular logical feature attributed to 'moral ought' (possessing overriding prescriptive force) is internally related to other features of a law conception of ethics.

59. Beardsmore's way of reconstructing Anscombe's concern would sort both the Stoic (who she thinks does have a law conception of ethics) and the Protestant (who she thinks doesn't) incorrectly for her purposes.

60. Beardsmore introduces his way of understanding 'absolute obligation' as an improvement over what he takes to be Anscombe's. He writes:

[I]n so far as it is implied that the mere existence of an alternative way of life is sufficient to rob obligations of their absolute character, then the conclusion should be drawn that, even for the devout religious believer, God's commands do not possess the status of absolute obligations. For there is certainly an alternative to religious belief, namely atheism ... [But the] absolute nature of God's commands for the religious believer stems not from a denial of the possibility of atheism. It stems rather from the recognition that such a way of life is not for that person a possibility.

This passage is concerned to contrast two ways of understanding the idea of an 'absolute obligation' (neither of which have anything to do with the logical features of a law conception of ethics to which Anscombe wished to direct attention). The misunderstandings discussed in note 56 lead Beardsmore to assume that Anscombe must be after the first of these. It is for this reason that he concludes that – if she chooses the second horn of the dilemma he outlines – her position will turn out to be 'merely a variant of the line of reasoning which has already been detected in the writings of Nielsen and Kolakowski'. Beardsmore's reason for proposing an alternative way of understanding 'absolute obligation' is in part, I take it, to avoid having his criticisms of Anscombe commit him to the view that all religious believers are as confused as he takes her to be.

61. What Beardsmore proposes isn't a distinctive feature of any conception of ethics. In Beardsmore's watered-down sense of what it is for something to be 'absolutely obligatory', even someone with an Aristotelian conception of what one 'ought' to do (such as the one that Anscombe urges on us) can acknowledge that it is 'absolutely obligatory' for a virtuous person not to act unjustly.

62. G. E. M. Anscombe, 'The Reality of the Past', in *Metaphysics and the Philosophy of Mind: Collected Papers*, Vol. III (Minneapolis, MIN.: University of Minnesota Press, 1981), p. 113.

63. Ibid., pp. 113–4.

64. These characterisations of the cases participate in the very confusions which they ultimately seek to illuminate. They are thus transitional ways of speaking that are, in the end, to be thrown away along with the confusions to which they are directed. Anscombe's method here resembles that of Kierkegaard. As Kierkegaard puts the point when explaining his own method: 'One does not begin *directly* with the matter that one wants to communicate, but begins by accepting the other man's illusion as good money' (*The Point of View for my Work as an Author*, p. 40).

65. Anscombe, 'The Reality of the Past', pp. 114–5.

66. This is why it is important to her argument in 'Modern Moral Philosophy' to begin with those modern moral philosophers who find it difficult to uncover *any content at all* in talk of what one 'morally ought' to do and yet wish to retain the term as one which expresses a prescriptive force. They serve as part of her evidence that at least some of us have logically incoherent desires with respect to this particular form of words.

67. Anscombe, 'The Reality of the Past', p. 115.

68. Anscombe, 'Modern Moral Philosophy', p. 41.

69. Ibid., p. 38.

70. The example and accompanying discussion quoted above from 'The Reality of the Past' is accompanied by the following footnote:

> In this example I have repeated some remarks made by Dr. Wittgenstein in discussion. Everywhere in this paper I have imitated his ideas and methods of discussion . . . [I]ts value depends . . . on my capacity to understand and use Dr. Wittgenstein's work (p. 114n).

71. G. E. M. Anscombe, *Intention* (Oxford: Blackwell, 1957), §18, p. 27. Anscombe in this passage is quoting §500 of her own translation of Wittgenstein's *Philosophical Investigations* (Oxford: Blackwell, 1953):

> When a sentence is called senseless, it is not as it were its sense that is senseless. But a combination of words is being excluded from the language, withdrawn from circulation.

The preceding section (§499) begins as follows:

> To say 'This combination of words makes no sense' excludes it from the sphere of language and thereby bounds the domain of language. But when one draws a boundary it may be for various kinds of reason.

This raises the question: what are Wittgenstein's reasons for proposing that we exclude particular combinations of words from the language? In the *Philosophical Grammar* (Oxford: Blackwell, 1974), we find this:

> How strange that one should be able to say that such and such a state of affairs is inconceivable! If we regard a thought as an accompaniment going with an expression, the words in the statement that specify the inconceivable state of affairs must be unaccompanied. So what sort of sense is it to have? Unless it says these words are senseless. But it isn't as it were their sense that is senseless; they are to be excluded from our language as if they

were some arbitrary noise, and the reason for their *explicit* exclusion can only be that *we are tempted* to confuse them with a proposition of our language (p. 130; I have amended the translation).
I take it that Anscombe's reasons for proposing that we explicitly exclude an expression from the language are the same as Wittgenstein's – not because it is as it were the sense of the expression which is senseless, but because '*we are tempted* to confuse' sentences in which it figures senselessly with meaningful propositions of our language.

Anscombe takes Wittgenstein's repudiation of the idea that certain propositions could express an inconceivable state of affairs (a senseless sense) to be a distinctive feature of his *later* thought. She takes early Wittgenstein to have endorsed the idea that certain (pseudo-) propositions have an inexpressible (because nonsensical) sense:

> [A]n important part is played in the *Tractatus*, by the things which, though they cannot be 'said', are yet 'shown' or 'displayed'. That is to say: it would be right to call them 'true' if, *per impossibile*, they could be said; in fact they cannot be called true, since they cannot be said, that 'can be shown', or 'are exhibited', in the propositions saying the various things that can be said (*An Introduction to Wittgenstein's Tractatus* (Philadelphia, PA: University of Pennsylvania Press, 1971), p. 162).

I take issue with this way of aligning Wittgenstein's early and later thought in 'The Search for Logically Alien Thought' (*Philosophical Topics*, vol. 20, no. 1).

72. *Philosophical Works of Francis Bacon* (London: Routledge, 1905), p. 45.
73. I include the hedge 'in the first instance' in order to avoid overstating the differences between their respective analyses. The emphasis in each falls in a different place; but the feature each of them harps on is present, in some way, in the analyses offered by the other two.
74. Without the qualifying phrase ('in the first instance') this would once again be an overstatement of their differences. For Nietzsche and Kierkegaard, our existential confusions are tied to conceptual ones. (Hence, for example, Kierkegaard's abiding concern with what he calls 'dialectical' or 'logical' problems – problems which arise from a failure to command a clear view of the categories.) For Anscombe, bad moral philosophy does not only corrupt how we think. (Hence, for example, for Anscombe bad moral philosophy – by encouraging us to leave open to question what would otherwise not be left open to question – leads us to tolerate and perhaps commit evil. Hence also, in particular, the connection between the thesis of the focal passage and the third thesis of her article as developed in the closing paragraphs: namely, the manner in which modern moral philosophy encourages one to take as open to question 'whether such a procedure as the judicial punishment of the innocent may not in some circumstances be the "right" one to adopt' (p. 42).)

Part VII
Voices in Dicussion

13

Voices in Discussion

D. Z. PHILLIPS

The essays in the collection do not indicate, of course, the discussions they occasioned. The following is based on notes I took throughout the conference, together with comments some participants presented me with on the day. The latter have been incorporated into the discussion. For the most part, however, the reactions to the conference discussions are mine. They do not claim to summarise different points of view in a way which would always satisfy their proponents. That is one reason why I have not attributed the various voices to specific participants in the conference. Where points were repeated at different times I have not hesitated to bring them together in a single 'voice' where I thought this to be stylistically or philosophically advantageous. Nevertheless, the different voices are meant, hopefully, to capture the character of the philosophical exchanges which took place. Some of the participants modified or extended their papers before publication. The discussion which follows takes no account of these further developments.

Voice A
When we think of the moral relations in which we stand to each other we tend to look for some facts, usually abstract facts, on which such relations can be based or by which they can be justified. But moral values reveal, not a reality of fact, but a reality of meaning. I'd like to try to bring out what that claim involves. An affective response, such as remorse, reveals something to both agent and spectator. A person comes to realise, in remorse, the evil he has been involved in and the preciousness of the human beings he has harmed. Remorse is constitutive of what it is to come to such realisations. This does not mean that our emphasis on affective responses allows us to say anything we like. On the

301

contrary, we have critical concepts in terms of which we can criticise our responses. For example, we may call some responses senti-mental. When a philosopher equates not contributing to Oxfam with murder, he robs us of the serious appreciations which en-able us to make responsible judgements.

I'm not really satisfied with the word 'preciousness' to convey what it is to respect human beings. I think it is captured better by the term 'sacred'. I realise that this has a religious origin, but I believe it can stand independently of this religious context in the moral significance it comes to have. It is misleading, how-ever, to say that we respond to human beings *because* they are sacred. Rather, what is meant by their sacredness is shown *in* this response. So much of contemporary moral philosophy fails to capture this sense of the sacred. It cannot be captured by utili-tarianism or Kant's notion of human beings as ends in themselves. Recognition of the sacred is, at the same time, a recognition of the mystery of other human beings. This appeal to mystery is not an explanation of any kind. You may ask me whether this mystery is on a different plane from mundane phenomena. The answer is: 'Yes and no'. No, if you think the different plane is a metaphysical realm to which I am appealing as a grounding for the sacred. Yes, if mystery shows how a place can be given to the sacred in our relations with others.

Voice B
I agree with you that the search for a metaphysical realm which somehow justifies our relations to others is idle. This does not mean that human life is relegated to mere appearance. I agree with you, too, that what is revealed in our relations is consti-tuted by our reactions. A 'higher' reality is forever beyond us.

Voice A
I'm not sure I understand you. You seem to be saying that it does not make sense to speak of a higher reality, but when you say it is forever beyond us, you seem to be referring to the very thing you say is unintelligible.

Voice B
I am equally puzzled by some of the things you say about a higher reality. I am not asking you to be more of a realist, but your references to religion puzzle me. Doesn't religion involve an ap-

peal to a radical transcendence? But for you, the sacred, the mystery of other human beings, are on a continuum with the development of a way of life. This reference to human conditions cannot be changed. That being so, any religion which claims to be a transhistorical reality will have to be demythologised.

Voice A

All I can say is that here is a phenomenon which we want to speak of in this way, in terms of mystery and the sacred. But we do not do so 'because' of anything. We simply react to others in this way. I have tried to show how reactions such as remorse are revelatory.

Voice B

But what is revealed? Surely, nothing beyond our culture and history. Once you start talking of revealing what is 'deeper', aren't you attempting to approach a transcendent being – at least, isn't that what the religious impulse involves?

Voice A

The metaphysical transcendent is meant to underwrite our reactions, but is discontinuous with what proceeds it. That is why it invites accusations of cliché. We have a rich vocabulary of criticism to draw on.

Voice B

I think matters are more complex. When you talk of transposing a concept from one context to another, of letting the sacred stand independently of a religious context, I think we become so used to talking of religion that we simply do not notice the metaphysical implications of our talk. Those implications cannot be transposed.

Voice A

What I am saying is that a certain kind of love goes hand in hand with a sense of mystery and the sacred. If you ask me why, I can only offer you the example. I would try to show you a compassion which shows no condescension to the afflicted; a compassion which Aristotle could make no sense of. I have to admit that for two thousand years this compassion has been and is conveyed by means of religion. I don't know what more to say. When I say that the compassion of the saints make possible this sense of the sacred, I'm contrasting it with various ethical theories which fail to capture it.

Voice B

It seems to me that the reference to mystery ducks the issue of transposition of concepts. Tillich spoke of mystery in relation to God, but admitted that by 'God' he did not mean what others meant. Is mystery an appeal to a single reality? But I am not advocating dropping the term. I admit that talk of mystery captures human worth in a way in which prosaic speech cannot. We create better than we know. We are always going beyond what we can articulate because our concepts are inadequate.

Voice C

Why do we need to bring in the notion of the sacred? Why not be content with saying that I felt remorse because I harmed a human being? What is added by speaking of the sacred?

Voice A

The appeal to 'the human' does not ground the remorse or sense of the sacred. Of course, there isn't simply one conception of remorse. When we say we feel remorse, don't add *because* he is a human being. We react as we do. Humans are not sacred in order that we may respond. The sense of the sacred shows itself in this response. But saying 'That's a human being' would not always capture this sense.

Voice D

While not denying the importance of the responses you have been talking of, I think that we have to account for the fact that, for many people, these responses to the sacred are responses to what they see as commands. I do not see how this can be accounted for satisfactorily without appeal to a Divine Command Theory. Such a theory does not commit us to any particular theory of revelation, but it does commit us to a belief in revelation in general. This is nothing less than taking the image of God seriously; God speaking to us – taking that seriously.

Voice E

If I had a theological belief, it would be a modified Divine Command Theory, but I simply do not think it works. I think that certain aspects of Kant's moral theory have given us the answer to the questions you raise.

Voice D

All I can say is that if I did not have a theological belief I would embrace a Kantian theory, but I simply do not think that works. Let me explain why I think a meta-theory is necessary. I believe that there is such a thing as practical rationality and irrationality. But it is useless for the purposes of theory, since it presupposes the factors one ought to be sensitive to. It is these ethical facts that need explanation.

As far as the epistemology of morals is concerned, we can do no better than appeal to W. P. Alston's concept of doxastic practice. We learn concepts as we grow up. I agree that they are the foundation of our ethical concepts, shaped in no small measure by our affective responses. This may happen in a religious form of life in which the religious and the ethical are intertwined. These facts are prior to any ethical theory. They are refined, but not replaced by theory.

I do not say that there are *compelling* reasons to doubt our practices. We find it reasonable, in a broad sense, to trust our reactions, but this trust involves faith. But this is not to deny that there are some grounds for doubting the soundness of our practices. So how does Divine Command Theory bear on all this? It is not the starting point. It is a theory about facts already believed in. The theory pertains only to one branch of moral facts, the one which has to do with obligation. So our first knowledge need not be theological. If we didn't first believe in ethical facts we would have no use for a Divine Command Theory. So ethical facts may be more deeply embedded than theory. That torture is wrong is more deeply held than any theoretical belief. But, of course, if you hold the theory it will have some ethical implications.

The God who asks something of us is the object of the highest allegiance, a perfect object. My belief may not be in the object of highest allegiance. Divine Command Theory is meant to apply to theists and non-theists alike. This effects what we take to be the character of the revelation in divine commands. If we take 'command' seriously, we must say that we are confronted by a form of communication, not a mere wishing. This implies that they are commands to all people. It implies a doctrine of general revelation.

Given all this, what is it for God to command, and what is the content of the command? What God commands is what God intends to command. But God's command cannot be issued to a person unless that person perceives the obligation, or is not at fault for not doing so.

I think that this opens the door to historical relativity. So the command of God may not be accessible and the people therefore are under no obligation. There is a relativity of obligation, but no relativity of value. For example, no command was issued with respect to slavery, and the people who practised it were therefore not under an obligation. Nevertheless, we can still say that the practice of slavery is a great evil.

Voice E
I still do not see why we need anything like a Divine Command Theory. I think that what I ought to do is independent of my beliefs, including religious belief. A murderer or a rapist may not believe that what they have done is wrong. They cannot have a duty to believe this, but not matter what they believe it is categorically the case that they should not do what they did. You, on the other hand, seem to want to make it a categorical matter that we should hold beliefs which, as far as I can see, there is no justification for holding. We couldn't say, categorically, that all people are not justified in not holding your modified Divine Command Theory. The basis of moral obligation must be something which shows every person that they are not justified in not accepting it. I do not see how your theory has that status. The theory we are led to accept, as a result of logical reflection, is one which involves a categorical moral imperative. We are certainly not prepared to surrender the issue of what to accept to the commands of an external commander. We cannot surrender that to a strange will. We ought to look for a law which is internal to our own thinking.

I think that we have such a law and it tells me how to treat other people. It sets purposes for us. I want others to treat me as a free being. I am guilty of a contradiction if I do not treat them in the same way. But when I turn to your Divine Command Theory, I do not see that it shows why I ought to behave in this way. On the contrary, it asks me to behave in a way which treats me as though I were an unfree agent.

Voice D
I admit that Divine Command Theory does not have resources within it to answer doubters. But, then, I do not think it is accepted on the basis of logic alone. This is because I do not believe that obligation constitutes the whole of ethics. There are also questions of value. In this context, I would argue for something akin to a Platonic conception of value, although I think that Plato thought that the object of highest value could be something less personal than God.

Voice B
We are obviously back at the question which worried the ancients: is the good because God wills it, or does God will it because it is good? I don't feel any pull at all towards the former.

Voice D
I want to say that we obey because God commands it, but not that it is good *because* God commands it. The only grounding of value is found in God, but the grounding is not the command. I am suggesting that there must be a natural transition from value to objectivity, the kind of transition Utilitarianism failed to provide.

Voice F
We have to recognise that many people are not interested in observing certain moral requirements. They are not interested. What is one to say to them? Surely it is questions such as these which drive one towards the need for objectivity. That is what the meta-ethical theory seeks to provide whether it succeeds in doing so or not.

Voice E
I applaud that desire for objectivity. I simply do not see how it can be grounded in an appeal to an alien will. Surely, we ought to be grounding it in the autonomous conscience.

Voice D
Why say that submission to God is submission to an alien will, or that it threatens one's autonomy? Do I feel threatened when I submit to the experts in physics, even though I have not worked these matters out for myself? Doesn't this seem the natural thing

to do? Why should it not be the same with God if you recognise God as the highest source of value?

Voice E
I agree that Divine Command Theory in the way you present it does not involve unthinking submission, but then it seems that if value is not grounded in a command, we do, after all, have to reach an independent judgement about what things are good.

Voice D
There are different cases here. Sometimes, as the result of an independent judgement, we may conclude that what is said to be God's command is not God's command. At other times, despite a person's judgements to the contrary, we might think it made sense to coerce an individual to conform with what is good or, at least, not to do the evil contemplated.

Voice B
That does lead one to wonder what role Divine Command Theory plays. At what level does it operate? Does it enable us to say whether or not God did command Abraham to sacrifice his son? Does the theory account or leave room for the particular? And once we get to the particular, the need for such a theory seems problematic. Why can't I say an action is vile and leave it like that? Why do I need the ultimate appeal to God? This seems even more obvious if we think of the obligations which arise from the institutions to which we belong, or the games we happen to be playing. If God is to be brought in at this level of particularity, you seem to need an anthropomorphic conception of God. On the other hand, how far can you go down the road of demythologising God without the notion losing its sense?

Voice D
The possibility of understanding a particular vocation in theological terms is one of the strengths of Divine Command Theory, despite obvious dangers. As to obligations in a game, references to what is personal cannot be eliminated. What would the rules matter apart from the other people playing the game?

Voice C

What you say does not apply to playing Solitaire. What if I cheat while playing? I am not harming anyone else. Why does it matter, then? Simply because that's not Solitaire, that's all.

Voice D

You want me to delete reference to a divine person in an analysis of moral obligation. I am told of the dangers of anthropomorphism. But I am prepared to admit that Divine Command Theory does entail anthropomorphism in a traditional sense. Hume saw this clearly. But this is not the whole story. God is unlike us in all sorts of ways; ways which express truths.

Voice E

But didn't Tillich say that even if we believed in the God you seem to be alluding to, we would have an obligation to ignore him, since we have independent access to moral laws?

Voice C

I repeat that I cannot see how an appeal to God *must* be introduced to account for the varied contexts in which we say 'You ought to help', 'You must do that' and so on. These remarks may refer to the rules of a game whether other people are involved or not. Or it may refer to something like a Hippocratic oath.

Voice D

I do hold a view which, I admit, is not obvious. Mill suggests that moral obligation goes hand in hand with guilt and social punishment. If we feel guilty we feel that it is all right for others to blame and punish. This will apply to the medical case you mentioned. Similarly, if other players in a game do not care, it is hard for us to care.

But if we feel shame, this may show that something is bad, but not necessarily wrong. This is an important distinction which Rawls attempts to obliterate. He does not want the moral appeal to be dependent on either God or society.

Voice E

If we do not have a fundamental duty to ourselves, we can't have it for others. But the duties are to ourselves. They are not duties to obey a command.

Voice D

It does not follow from Divine Command Theory that there are no reasons why things are wrong. But I want to distinguish between seeing or knowing that something is wrong and seeing how bad it is. When I see something as cruel, that is not captured by Divine Command Theory. I may see something as horrible whether it is forbidden or not. I see it, not as wrong, but as horrible.

Voice F

We have to confront what is horrible, horrendous evils in human life. Let me say immediately that I share the misgivings that have been expressed about theodicy. Much of what I had to say was directed against those attempts to justify the ways of God which are responses to demands in analytical philosophy to furnish morally sufficient reasons as to why God does not prevent or eliminate evils. This search for sufficient reasons easily tempts us, like Job's friends, to underestimate the depths of evils, to turn a deaf ear to the sufferers' complaints, insisting that God is morally right no matter how much this seems to be costing them. I want to insist that we shift focus from vague and genuine talk of 'turps' of evils on to the worst cases of suffering, from morally sufficient reasons-why, to soteriological explanations – how God can furnish each created person a life that is a great good by overcoming the corrosive effects of even the worst evils on the individual's attempt to find positive meaning in his or her life. My perhaps crude size-metaphors – that no package of merely created goods can overcome horrors, that only God is a good 'big' enough for that – are attempts to measure how bad some suffering is for certain people.

Nevertheless, I don't believe that trying to answer theological arguments from evil or explain how divine good will might be comparable with horrendous suffering *ipso facto* abandons the sufferer's point of view. My main reason is that many, though to be sure, not all, participants in what I have called horrors raise this question themselves. Philosophers and theologians are not above the human condition; we, too, suffer terrible things, and ask 'why?' and 'how?' We, too, are friends and pastors, honoured by invitations to share intimately in the agonies of others. Some want us not only to 'sit *shiva*' with them, but turn to us for help in making sense of their experience, sometimes desperately demand hints, beg for coaching as they embrace, struggle to sustain the spiritually difficult assignment of integrating their experiences of the goodness of God and horrendous evil into the whole of a meaningful life. I agree, the task of attempting such help is delicate and perilous. We must neither lose our bearings in the sufferer's point of view, nor claim to know more than we can (which, in my judgement, includes morally sufficient reasons-why). For those who ask, it is usually spiritually fruitful to imitate Job, and press the why-questions with God. But soteriology exists in no small part because such pastoral care has traditionally been thought to have an intellectual dimension. 'Who was it for?' It was for me, and my parish.

Two claims, central to my position, may have reinforced the impression that I was reasoning from the observers' viewpoint. First, my definition makes classification as 'horrendous' *objective, yet person-relative*, while denying incorrigibility to the sufferer's judgement about it. My intention, however, was to rule out the superficial pessimisms of curmudgeons and habitual complainers, who in fact find much positive meaning in their self-assigned roles, and to emphasise how others may reasonably agree that participation in evils constitutes the *prima facie* ruin of a person's life. I did not take myself to be thereby *abandoning* the sufferer's point of view, because what is at stake is the positive meaning of life for him or her, an issue about which the individual is in a highly privileged position. And I have repeatedly insisted against 'global' approaches that defeat must come, not merely within the cosmic 'big picture', but within the context of the individual's own life.

My appeals to aesthetics were found to be offensive where the overcoming of evil is concerned. This disagreement may be partially verbal, because I construe 'aesthetic value' broadly to cover *the meanings* of lives. Implicitly, and for the sake of argument, I have borrowed from developmental psychology the neo-Kantian model which pictures subjects of experience as scientists who, consciously and/or unconsciously, seek and impose organising theories on the data of their experience, indeed who – as cognitive, emotional, and spiritual capacities enlarge – impose a succession of ever more subtle theories to integrate larger and more complex data-sets with greater simplicity. Alternatively, we may think of the subject as an artist trying to arrange experiences of his or her life into a stained-glass window – always acquiring new pieces, inventing new designs. Either way, I have taken for granted what common parlance would also concede – namely, that what is in some sense, though even from my standpoint not in every sense, the same experience, may be understood by the subject to have different meanings. Accordingly, I have assumed that talk of value parts and wholes here would serve well enough to convey certain contrasts, most particularly the Chisholmian distinction between 'balancing-off', where opposed values of mutually exclusive parts are 'added' in Benthamite fashion, from 'defeat' which overcomes negative value in a value-part via organic integration into a larger whole. If difficult to make precise, this distinction is crucial for the problem of evil, precisely because roughly speaking 'otherwise unconnected' horrors now and heavenly bliss later, like the painful hour in the dentist's chair and the sublime concert afterwards, offer different possibilities for the subject's meaning-making efforts than do horrors that are susceptible of organic integration into the dominant meaning-making structures of the participant's life.

Second, the charge that I have abandoned the sufferer's point of view may seem vindicated by my suggestion that God and creatures literally share the same experience, as if the same piece of glass could be a constituent in two windows simultaneously, and that suffering may be a vision into the inner life of God, *whether or not the creature recognises this.* Here, my twin concerns were to acknowledge the empirical fact that many do not so regard their participation in horrors before they die, and to ensure that enough of the right sort of materials are available in the ante-mortem life for the subject to find and eventually integrate into the perhaps new-found meaning-making structure of his or her relationship with God. A piece of glass may be just the right shape to fit with others to form a glorious window, and this even if the artist has not yet acquired other important pieces and/or noticed their connection. But the as yet unrecognised and unexploited feature depends on the objective fact of its shape in the first place. In this case, the *de facto* presence of God in our experience of horrors furnishes what is needed.

My concession that symbolic defeat of evil might be possible apart from the sufferer's recognition may have led my critics into a further error about my position. For I am charged with viewing *symbolic* defeat as something observers look to, while positing *concrete* post-mortem defeat to satisfy the sufferer's point of view.

Like other Stoics, Simone Weil herself looks to symbolic defeat to make her own affliction meaningful. Following another strand of Christian tradition, I suggest that the symbolic values she appreciates will be transformed by an at least post-mortem context of concrete compensations.

My critics and I agree on the incommensurability of divine and created agency. Yet, some scorn the notion Wiles and I share – that it is metaphysically possible for God to act contrary to natural laws to do something in particular – as 'anthropomorphic' and 'mythological', contrary to the 'classical' and 'orthodox' view so admirably formulated by Burrell's *Aquinas: God and action* (pp. 18–21). So far from theologically normative, I find Burrell's an at best dubious interpretation of Aquinas, one that conflates many logically independent issues. Consider the following theses:

(T1) God wills whatever God wills by a single act that is identical with the divine essence as such eternal, immutable, and impassable.

(T2) So far as creation is concerned, the intensional content of the divine act of will could have been (can be) otherwise than it is.

(T3) Some of the contents of the divine will exhibit a means–end structure, so that some constitute God's reasons for willing others.

(T4) Among the contents eternally and immutably willed by God are some created events that are contrary to or above nature.

(T5) That some created state of affairs is an intensional object of the divine will is always prior in the order of explanation to its occurrence.

More than once, G insinuates that to affirm (T4) miracles would be to compromise (T1) the eternity, immutability, and impassability of the divine act of willing. But Aquinas himself recognised no problem in God's ordaining some supranatural events (for example, the three men in the fiery furnace) into the eternally cosmic order. Nor would Aquinas, Bonaventure, or Scotus befriend G's equation of (T3) means–end structuring of intensional contents with treating divine agency as unacceptably 'reactive' or contextualised. Aquinas and Bonaventure both declare how God made the rest of nature for the sake of human beings, predestined Christ in part for the purpose of making satisfaction for human sin, while Scotus advertised God as the most well-organised of lovers. Yet, none would concede that anything other than God makes God act, in the sense (contra-(T1)) of *efficiently causing* the divine act of will, or even *efficiently causing* certain created events or states of affairs to be among the intensional objects of the divine will. Ockham saw no difficulty in denying (T5) for created acts of free choice, while all along insisting on (T1). Thus, I would not be alone in assuming that my hypothesis that 'God does something in particular to solve the problem of evil' – that is, that God wills some *supranatural* events *in order* to remedy faulty human choices and their consequences – does not entail any denial of (T1). Consequently, the metaphysical entrenchment of (T1) in medieval theological models by itself creates no presumption against either (T3) or (T4).

What commits me to a rejection of (T1) is neither my endorsement of (T2)–(T4) nor my denial of (T5), but my claim that the passion of Christ in His human nature is a sacramental sign of God's suffering in the divine nature. My own attempted solution to the logical problem of evil does run clean contrary to patristic and medieval tradition in its acceptance of patripassianism. Frankly, I find that having abandoned one dimension of divine impassibility – namely, the one that denies that God experiences any emotions – I feel free to let go of the other – that is, to give up the idea that no creature can be an *efficient cause* of any real state in God. Charged with hopelessly compromising the incommensurability of divine agency, I counter-challenge. Divine impassibility portrays the perfection of divine agency in terms of power exercised to maintain invulnerable defences against alien incursion. It protects by controlling and cutting off interaction. But which is more impressive? The warrior who builds and stays behind the impregnable fort, or the one who engages any and all comers, dares them to do their worst, can take any wound and still rise from the dead? Which government is to be preferred: the police state that micromanages its citizens' lives, or the one that 'rolls with the punches', creative and resourceful enough to resolve any situation for individual and common good? The difference between so-called 'classical' appreciations of divine incommensurability and the more 'interactive' model I have presupposed is not that one is 'anthropomorphic' or 'mythological' while the other is enlightened and philosophical, but rather that they are inspired by fundamentally contrasting political models.

Nor is it fair to accuse me of turning divine government into crisis management. Because I was arguing with Wiles, who admits both the logical and metaphysical possibility of miracles and the depth of current evils, I attempted to turn the latter into a persuasive ground for reconsidering the theoretical desirability of miracles. My appeal to the mother–infant analogy should have dispelled any notion that I was advocating a *deus ex machina* who contravenes natural processes only to clean up messes.

G dismisses my suggestion – that intimate experience of God will defeat horrendous evils within the context of the individual participant's life – as 'pietistic'. I am accused of regarding the world as a barrier to experience of God, and of appealing to divine love as a kind of eschatological solvent threatening to liquidate both problematic evils and the particular subject alike. Although surprised and delighted that my views might be 'fashionable', I am on the whole baffled by these complaints.

On the one hand, Bonaventure and John of the Cross are cited as claiming that in heaven we will see God in ourselves and all things. So far from disagreeing with this, I affirm with the psalmist that both objective and subjective created worlds are 'God-infested', full of God's glory. My hypothesis that present sufferings (as elaborated elsewhere, present joy) are windows into divine life does not strike me as inconsistent with that claim. On the other hand, G claims that Bonaventure and John of the Cross deny that we will see 'naked Divinity' in heaven. Yet, in his *Sentence*-commentary, Bonaventure joins the school theologians' consensus in positing a post-mortem beatific vision of the divine essence for the elect, where the beatific vision is not simply a seeing of God in and through the world. Similarly, in the *Itinerarium*, he suggests that we will first see Divine Being, then Divine Goodness. My own claim of face-to-face divine intimacy in heaven was not so much pietistic as scholastic!

In the *Itinerarium*, Bonaventure hints that the soul's journey culminates in intellectual repose. Certainly, I was not endorsing the view that experience of God would so monopolise our consciousness that our efforts of subjective world-construction would cease right away. On the contrary, my thought was that unmediated vision of God would force a dramatic developmental crisis or series thereof, which would revolutionise the sense we make of our lives.

My notion – that identifying suffering with witting or unrecognised intimacy with God would help – rests on an unabashedly 'anthropomorphic' analogy. The closest of human relationships include a wide variety of experiences: the hug, the wink, the kiss; the spoken words ('sweet nothings', grocery lists, theological and political exchange); the fun, the drudgery and risks, the sheer hard work of collaborative activities; the wordless contact, soul meeting soul. The tactile sensation of being squeezed, the sounds and sights, are indeterminate and determinable with respect to their meanings, but take on special negative and positive significance as they are woven into the relationship. Similarly, to appeal to one of G's favourites, Simone Weil compares affliction to the crushing hug of the lover who presses the beloved tightly to himself. In the same vein, beatific vision would represent another moment in the same love affair, one like those silent, awe-struck occasions of unmediated contact when time stops and love absorbs.

Voice G

We are agreed that the presence of God in suffering is said to make sense of things. Where we differ is in what this comes to. I have a genuine puzzlement about what you want to say. You speak of an experience of God in the afterlife and an experience of God through the world. If people cannot make sense of the way you speak of the afterlife, that will reflect on what they understand by an experience of God through the world. It still seems to me as though you talk of God coming in at the point when other resources run out. I do not see how you can generalise about this in the way you do.

For example, when people have talked of divine action as a miracle, they have thought it to be present at a particular time, not as something postponed to a distant eventuality. Even if we think of the world as a single act of divine grace, this need not lead to a totalitarian conception of the governance of the universe, unless you think of divine action as an enlarged version of human action.

I have serious areas of concern. Some have to do with soteriology. I too am not looking for sufficient reasons to explain suffering, but one is looking for soteriological reasons for how suffering is overcome. One may begin with Christology, but I am suspicious of any generalised 'how' in this matter of 'overcoming'. There is a tendency to link the divine response too closely to specific cases as 'exceptional' instead of concentrating on how ills as ills are overcome.

The reference to aesthetics in this context is relevant. It is not that I object to talk of making a whole out of our experiences, but I do have difficulty about the way you put the matter. You speak of incorporating experiences as though they are discrete elements, but experiences are not like that. They are not discrete elements waiting to be woven into a greater whole. We have to pay attention to the sheer variety of ways in which suffering is lived in and made sense of. How can there be a general reaction to the unevenness of that?

Voice F
You must realise that much of what I said was directed against what is said in contemporary, analytic philosophy of religion. Attempts at explaining and justifying evils are made in terms of appeals to possible worlds and the free will defence. None of this seems relevant to the experience of horrendous evils. As Ivan Karamazov showed, such theories simply do not work. Things are just too bad to simply say in face of them 'you're free'. These appeals do not work as sufficient reasons. In fact of certain evils people say, 'That is morally outrageous'. It's a way of saying 'Nuts to God'.

I don't go along with that, but do we simply say that the problem of evil is insoluble? Stoicism is deep, but doesn't Christianity promise more? 'God will be with you, even though you went through that!' You have stared into the pit and nothing earthly can compensate for that. That is why I emphasise seeking naked beatific union. That is more personal than any other theological model.

Voice H
I agree that talk of 'turps' of evil is limited, but those Christian analytic philosophers did us a great service. They showed that there is no reason to say that evil is logically incompatible with the existence of God. Given what had gone on previously in analytic philosophy that was a big advance.

With respect to theodicy, do we not have to bring in the notion of covenantal religion? That does seem to involve God saying, 'If you do *a*, I'll do *b*.'

Voice F
I agree with what you say about the analytical philosophers. But talk of a covenant is a political analogy. It makes us feel secure.

How do we know God will follow through? It seems to be a concern connected with human fear.

Voice B
You have spoken a lot about the victims of evil. What about its perpetrators?

Voice F
I was asked earlier about soteriology. Do I begin with Christology or suffering. I reply: both. Christ identifies himself with suffering – that is the easy part. Yet, according to liturgical law, anyone who dies as Christ did is cursed and cut off from God. So God has identified himself with a situation in which someone is cursed. But that situation includes the perpetrators. Even what is done here cannot cut us or them off from God. This is because God has identified himself even with horrendous horrors. In that way, even such horrors, ultimately, are turned into a greater good.

Voice B
And is this really supposed to happen in the case of Hitler? Are we to say that no matter what he has done everything is to end in a happy result?

Voice F
Part of my view about what is possible depends on what will happen in post-mortem experiences. What God teaches us then will defeat the contrary perspectives we may hold now. Of course, in Hitler's case this will be a long haul.

Voice I
We can contrast talk of the best of all possible worlds with intense interest in the individual. In the latter context we see an enormous variety: we see incredible strength in concentration camps and at the same time people broken by trivial incidents.

Voice G
I think people are still talking of experiences as though they are atomic events, the problem being how to fit them into some kind of calculus.

Voice F

I don't want to say that experiences are atomic. On the contrary, I am concerned to show how these experiences are woven into the rest of our lives. I am concerned with people who say, 'I can't go on'. They may say that to God.

Voice J

But how seriously are you prepared to take the inability to go on? Socrates dies an informed death: 'You will see me facing my death with equanimity.' But I am told that Jesus' last words from the Cross may well have been, 'My God, my God, why hast thou forsaken me?' And what of the children executed in concentration camps? Do they die informed deaths? Not if Socrates is your model. Little wonder that Camus in *The Plague* makes a child's suffering the hardest case for the priest trying to preach about it. Faced with the suffering of an innocent child, the priest says he will answer with his back to the wall. That's the only way we should answer, I think. You can think of cases where degradation is willingly embraced. A prostitute may decide to stay with her friend because she is the only friend she has, although she realises they will go down together. We may say that the remarkable decision envelops the degradation – though not everyone would say that. But with the children it is different. There is no decision which makes sense of their fate. A retarded girl may inspire a poet to write a poem about her – but.song is denied her. What is one to say about this?

I can only say this. When such evils are perpetrated an absolute good is violated. One cannot appreciate the sufferings of the innocent without a sense of this violation. What cannot be denied is their story. But it is not a story that compensates, explains or justifies the suffering. Sometimes what is good, what is divine, simply suffers – it goes dumb like a lamb to the slaughter. It is the apologists who think they have to speak when the divine is dumb. I do not regard the Resurrection as a postscript to the Crucifixion – no, it is the crucified one who is raised up, exalted, raised on high. Theologically, I might say that the sorrow is part of eternity, not something to be explained away. But I suspect this is too bleak for you.

Voice F

It is certainly too bleak for me. I do not accept your view of the Resurrection. Thomas doubted, but when Jesus showed up, displaying his wounds, it was to answer those doubts and to go beyond them.

Voice C

I find your offered explanations puzzling. Would they include reasons why my intense pain, say my migraine, couldn't be two minutes less?

Voice F

I don't know. You'll have to ask God, but I am not arguing in terms of pain now, bliss later. I am saying that in our post-mortem experiences with God our sufferings will be integrated into a new meaning.

Voice J

Jesus' wounds weren't bandaged, were they?

Voice F

No, but their meaning changed.

Voice G

But in what sense? Is it as though the sufferings had never been? You say the meaning is changed, but I am uneasy about this talk of *the* meaning. There are different perspectives which set sufferings in different contexts.

Voice K

I want to ask whether there cannot be something so evil that it cannot be defeated.

Voice F

As you know, I'm a universalist.

Voice K

What about a Hitler who, after death, simply gets worse and worse?

Voice F

The experience of God after death will make it impossible not to embrace the new perspective he gives. I see no reason why the good it involves would not justify bringing its acceptance about by coercion. We often say that coercion is justified when something morally important is involved. Here we would be dealing with the source of highest value.

Voice L

Suppose I accept that I come to this new understanding after death. Does this mean that the horrendous evils people suffered were only apparent evils? What of other people? If I care about them, I shall not be satisfied only with my own transformation. If the same does not happen in their case I shall be morally dissatisfied. Yet, these outcomes involve treating the evils as real evils, in which case it seems that I end up having to forgive God.

Voice F

No, the horrendous evils are not apparent. They remain horrendous. But as love of God grows after death, so love of one's neighbour grows at the same time. As for the belief in hell, I think it is too bad for the guilt. If you don't think you have to be guilty in order to be forgiven, then you would forgive God, for the experiences of suffering have certainly been alienating.

Voice M

Why not admit that God is limited? He does what he can. The irreducible datum of evil gives us good reason to believe that the Devil is at work.

Voice F

We do have experiences of evil which seem to suggest something greater than the human agents involved. The trouble with the Devil hypothesis is that it suggests a one-dimensional person, whereas it seems unlikely that God would create a creature which was beyond his own powers of redemption.

Voice K

If we gave an example of an evil which most of us would agree about, surely torture would be an obvious candidate. I think it is important to concentrate on a particular example to bring out how the issue regarding the relation of religion to morality has practical import.

Can you justify torture? To whom and for what reason? Is it true that torture is wrong anywhere and everywhere? If it is, can it be justified to everyone? By what means; by moral or religious arguments? Torture is often a horrendous evil. But even if such evils are horrendous and wrong, this does not yield the conclusion that torture is always wrong. We can say that most of the time it is wrong.

If we hold certain religious beliefs we can give arguments for saying that torture is wrong. Torture is wrong because it degrades human beings who are made in the likeness of God and that is wrong. Human beings are sacred, a fact that is derived from their being created by God. The sacredness, it seems to me, is a metaphysical sacredness, albeit derived from religion. It grounds the perceived sacredness. I agree with the suggestion that sometimes this sacredness may stand alone, or that it may be grounded in something other than its metaphysical grounding. According to Divine Command Theory, the sacredness of human beings would make torture bad, and the command would make it wrong.

But even if this religious argument is sound, it is not persuasive with everyone. I am not suggesting that such a justification could not work. My conclusion is based on an inductive pessimism from past failures. I think we have seen the demise of the post-liberal self. We now have to recognise diverse selves capable of plotting the narratives of their own lives. In the light of this situation, what is to be done?

I have two suggestions. First, the exceptionless rule against torture might be achieved through reforming the teaching of children. It could be taught as a commonly held basic belief. Such teaching would not be driven by reason, but it would be pragmatically rational. We have the kind of practical rationality found in Alston's notion of doxastic practices. Second, we might look for a Rawlsian overlapping consensus. Some of these overlaps would be religious, while others would not.

But some in this conference have a far more ambitious aim. This is because they claim that there is such a thing as *the* moral point of view. It is supposed to have four characteristics: taking others into account in one's actions because one respects them as persons; willingness to take into account how one's actions affect others by taking into account the good of everyone equally; abiding by the principles of universalisability; and willingness to be committed to some set of normative moral principles. I want to challenge the claim that there is the moral point of view which has these characteristics; that it is taken as obligatory; that this point of view is violated by torture; and that that is why torture is always wrong.

Will the four characteristics of the moral point of view do the trick? What of the first two? Well, notice that they represent the uneasy alliance of deontology and consequentialism we find in most of the current ethics textbooks. The game is given away when the first characteristic is spelled out in terms of the second formulation of Kant's categorical imperative. What is being touted as the moral point of view is actually something more local, one moral point of view among others. It is a moral point of view typical of Western Enlightenment Liberalism. Mind you, it is a moral point of view of which I personally am very fond. I do my best to defend it against the attacks of assorted natural lawyers, communitarians and virtue theorists who hang out in my neck of the woods. But I am not under the illusion that we liberals alone occupy the moral point of view while our opponents reside in outer darkness.

Moreover, commitment to the first two items on the so-called moral point of view does not add enough to the formal features to generate the conclusion that torture is always wrong. Imagine two moral theorists arguing about whether torturing terrorists is always wrong. One claims it is because torture always shows a lack of respect for the victim as a person. The other responds that, though there is a *prima facie* duty not to torture, it is overridden in the terrorist's case by the duty to take account of the good of everyone, including the victims of the terrorist, equally. The first theorist thinks the deontology always trumps the consequentialism; the second holds that the consequentialism sometimes trumps the deontology. This is, of course, a familiar dispute within the moral tradition of Enlightenment Liberalism. What are we to do in order to resolve it?

Someone might try building the preference for deontology into the moral point of view itself. He might insist that the moral point of view dictates that it is always *ultima facie* wrong to treat a human person as a mere means or simply as a means. But if this were the case, then only deontologists or, more narrowly, Kantians, would be able to occupy the moral point of view as construed. All others would remain outside it; hence, they would be in violation of the obligation to take the moral point of view. But this is absurd. There is no moral obligation to be a deontologist or Kantian in moral theory.

Besides, it is not clear that even the Kantians can justify an absolute prohibition of torture. To be sure, the terrorist who is tortured to save the lives of potential victims is being treated as a mere means to benefits for them. But what of the inquisitor who tortures a heretic, not to benefit someone else, but for the sake of the heretic's own immoral soul and its eternal salvation? Does the inquisitor treat the heretic simply as a means? I doubt it. But if the inquisitor does, so too do parents who spank their young children for the children's own good. But it seems to me silly to think that parents who spank their children, provided they are not abusive, flout a duty of respect for persons.

It has become a cliché of our era that Enlightenment modernity hoped that Reason Itself or The Moral Point of View Itself would underwrite a substantive moral code down to the level of fine detail. The postmoderns have abandoned this hope. Judged in these terms, my opponent remains a modern, but I have entered into postmodernity. Considerable moral pluralism is here to stay – but I say it with some regret.

Voice I

We agree that the prohibition of torture is a universal rule. So the question is how it can be supported. Utilitarianism doesn't work. Religious and secular overreaching arguments do not work. They do not appeal to a wide enough audience. Moral religion may be correct, but how does it show that torture is wrong? There are three reasons why an appeal to religion does not work. First, one could not know with any more certainty that one's religious position was warranted. Morality and religion are on the same epistemological footing, so we cannot appeal to religion. Second, there are cases where moral considerations would override the religious. The Inquisition is an example. Third, justice is contextual, so Divine Command Theory, or any other, will always work for those who accept that argument or point of view.

So suppose conceptual or moral relativism were true, what would you do? First, there is a radical relativism in which no judgement within one scheme is applicable to other schemes. That won't work. If relativity is to work and truth is relative to schemes, there must be overlap if there is to be disagreement or attempts to argue with others. Otherwise, we can't have a public dispute. They overlap in the demarcation of subject-matter. The differences come in how each scheme plays out in particular cases.

I support the characteristics of the moral point of view. I want to emphasise the willingness to so act that you take others into account because you respect them as persons. The failure to prohibit torture then becomes the expression of lack of respect for the victim. It will override the consequentialist argument that it would do good if you tortured a person. You can make a further move and say that taking the moral point of view is a reflection of seeing others in the image of God. This won't work, however, because people simply won't make that further move.

I agree that universal assent cannot be achieved. I also agree with the previous remark about deontology and consequentialism. But I want to say that the first is primary and that the second is derivative. I also want to say that people are deontologists whether they recognise it or not.

Voice N
Anonymous deontologists.

Voice I
Quite so. I am not impressed with the example of the lack of respect not applying to spanking the young child. The whole point is that we are talking of a child, someone who has not yet attained autonomy. But if it was done to an older child, then it would constitute a violation of the respect due to a person.

Voice J
I find that extraordinary. It would involve you in arguing as follows: we can only abuse human beings when they have autonomy; a child does not have autonomy yet, therefore, there is no such thing as child abuse!

Voice E
I do not see how we can say that torture is never justified. Suppose you discover a plot to blow up sectors of New York and you have one of the terrorists in captivity who knows where the bomb has been planted. Wouldn't we be justified in torturing him if that was the only way of finding out the location of the bomb? Not only would it be a way of stopping the terrorist carrying out his plans, it would also be treating other people as ends, including

himself. If we do not do this we are aiding and abetting the terrorist. So this situation is not one which casts doubt on the ultimate Kantian principle of respect for others. We have to distinguish between that principle and what its application may come to in the particular case. In the context I have envisaged its application justifies the use of torture.

Voice K

Someone might say, however, that these considerations do not override the rule. He may say that evil should not be done that good may come. He may look on situations such as the one you have described as a test of faith. He may say that you can never rule out that some other alternative will emerge such that the bombing will be avoided without recourse to torture. To try to intervene by using torture, it may be said, is to try to do God's business for him. It is something we should not meddle in.

Voice I

I am worried about arguments which justify the selective use of torture. Persuading others or ourselves to torture is the beginning of the slippery slope. All sorts of excesses may be justified in this way. That is how the Inquisition got started.

Voice J

I'd like to comment on a number of features of the way this discussion is going. First, there is the issue of the context in which we are discussing whether torture is wrong. In one sense the matter is already settled, since 'torture' is a pejorative word; it is already a word of moral condemnation. So we do not decide, in general, whether torture is wrong. One might say that 'Torture is wrong' gives us one use of the word 'wrong'.

With respect to conceptual relativism, one issue is whether we can call something 'torture' irrespective of the concepts being used in the context in question. For example, it may be a practice among warrior tribes to prod a captured warrior with a hot stick. To be captured is a disgrace among these tribes. The disgrace is removed by a ritual in which the captured warrior is given an opportunity to bear pain without flinching. 'Torture' is not a concept which operates, in this context, with either the inflicter or bearer of the pain. Now, I do not want to say that, knowing this, someone cannot call the practice 'torture' and want to stop it. Others may not want to do so, and some may admire the practice. But the person who wants to change it must, at least, recognise the difference between this situation and acts of wilful torture in his own society. That's the first point.

Second, it seems to me that you are assuming that if torture is done, it follows that a rule has been broken such that we cannot treat 'Torture is wrong' as an absolute judgement, and that the situation in question must be called an exception to the rule. Peter Winch has discussed an example from the film *Black Saturday* which shows that these conclusions do not necessarily follow at all. The example concerns a pacifist rural community, one of whose farms is taken over by gangsters. One of them is playing Russian roulette with a young girl and it is certain that sooner or later he will kill her. With a look of doubt and horror on his face the leader of the sect picks up a pitchfork and buries it in the gangster's back. Now what is obvious from the film is that the leader of the sect thinks he has done something wrong. He does not regard the situation as an exception to the pacifist rule. On the contrary, he thinks that he has to do penance for what he has done – killed a human being, something which went against his most cherished beliefs. But, of course, if he had not killed the gangster he would have been guilty of standing idly by while a young girl was murdered. The most natural way of putting the matter is to say that he did what he had to do.

Some of the responses made in the present discussion, it seems to me, cannot capture this situation. It will not do to say that he should not kill the gangster because we cannot rule out *a priori* that a third alternative won't turn up. As Beardsmore showed in a discussion of such a suggestion by Elizabeth Anscombe, the *a priori* works both ways. If we cannot say *a priori* that nothing else will turn up, we cannot say *a priori* that it will. It would also be odd to imagine the leader of the sect saying, 'This is nothing to do with me. This is God's business so I'll not meddle with it.' That would be moral and religious evasion. He does what he has to do, and later throws himself on God's mercy. It would also be odd to generalise and apply, in this case, fears about the beginnings of a slippery slope. It would simply be silly to say, given the example, that this would encourage the sect-leader to hurl pitchforks into people's backs in all sorts of unjustified situations!

Voice K
I readily accept that before we condemn something as torture we have to be sure that we have got an accurate account of the situation in which we make this judgement. I also agree that we have to recognise that there are tragic moral dilemmas where, whatever one does, one is going to do something wrong.

Voice C
The use of 'first principles' in this discussion seems to promise us more than it actually delivers. 'Torture is wrong', as has been said, gives us one use for the word 'wrong', but if you try to cash it out in certain ways, you'll get into trouble. For example, if you said that not indulging in torture was of benefit to everyone, this is simply false, because it is not of benefit to the torturer. So you have not provided any kind of 'plus' that goes beyond the principle.

This applies to other ways of going 'beyond' the principle 'Torture is wrong'. Some of you have argued in terms of 'respect'. We ought to respect persons. Torturing is a failure to respect them, therefore torture is wrong. It looks as if we have been told why torture is wrong. But this is an illusion. This is because you can only cash out 'respect' in moral terms. The same is true of 'treating others as ends'. If we ask what this comes to, we'll talk of using others for our own selfish purposes, in extreme cases torturing them, and so on. So our moral relations are not underwritten or cashed out by reference to the general principles. On the contrary, it is the moral relations which give the general observations such purchase as they have. So if you ask what counts as 'respect', you can only give a list of examples and say, 'And so on'.

Voice I
I don't agree with that. As circumstances change, what we mean by 'respect' changes. Women may note what counts now as respect in relation to themselves and want it changed. 'You are not treating me with respect' does not mean 'Add me to your list', but, rather, 'Change your attitude'.

Voice C
No, the new case extends the concept of 'respect'.

Voice K
'Respect' seems to be a highly theoretical concept of a Kantian or Hegelian kind. The list referred to does not capture 'agency'. Apart from that aspect, I'd simply be referring to the list and that does not give us what we're looking for.

Voice G
If I may return to the example of torture, it is important not to equate it simply with force. If we punish, we are doing something within specified limits. With torture, those limits are absent. People are trained to torture, trained to ignore certain moral reactions. The damage we are talking about, therefore, is not only damage to the victim, but to the torturer as well.

Voice K
The question of when force becomes torture is a deep one. It is very hard to give a philosophical analysis. Legal analyses tend to be far too narrow.

You are quite right in what you say about damage to the torturer. When people are trained to torture their blindness becomes worse. And when they torture not once, but over and over again, the torturing becomes a horrendous evil in their lives.

Voice I
I would say that if a society sanctioned torture it has lost sight of the moral point of view.

Voice D
I think there are some difficulties with some of the rationales we have been offered. I am doubtful whether there is any penal system which has not damaged the wrong-doer in some way, and yet we wouldn't be prepared to live without a penal system. Sometimes, through a convention, such as the Geneva Convention, we try to mark off something as specially wrong.

Perhaps there is a way forward by making us of Rawls's 'original position' and indirect utilitarianism. We try to see what rules are acceptable as we endeavour to create the conditions we want to live under. So moral dilemmas do not lead me to condone torture or the activities of a police force which wonders, when it has someone in custody, whether this is one of those exceptions to the principle. It is better to say 'It is always wrong' while knowing that if it would stop someone blowing up New York someone will do a third degree on him.

Voice K

I am inclined to think that way when I reflect on the penal system. I also like the appeal to Rawls's 'original position'. My criticism of him is that he smuggles a liberal, democratic society into it. You won't get the same results if you're addressing the Israeli security forces.

Voice H

If you look for some kind of contractual relation about which everyone agrees, you are going to leave out a lot of people from the moral conversation. You are going to leave out those who don't care along with those who find themselves in a moral dilemma. Do you rule Bentham out simply because he does not agree? I do not think that you can simply read people out of the conversation by means of your definitions.

Voice I

I have no problem with saying that a small number are actually read out. We will not convince everyone. We do not ask Hitler whether he thinks torture is wrong. We don't ask alchemists what science is. The latter lacks the scientific point of view and the former lacks the moral point of view.

Voice B

I do not believe that either 'respect' or 'disrespect' are philosophical concepts.

There are also plenty of forms of torture which exert pressure for a limited time, but have no long-term effects. If you had me in captivity and played a certain Rosemary Clooney record over and over I'd tell all! You would make it intolerable for me, but there would be no permanent scars.

So are you speaking of torture as though it is anything that brings pressure on people to make them do what you want them to?

Voice K

I do not deny that there is a common conception of respect which goes along with the possibility of producing lists of examples of what constitutes respect and disrespect. But I wanted to get at those philosophers who go in for grand philosophical principles such as treating people as ends in themselves. So perhaps the two concepts of respect are related, though they are not identical.

I agree that we do not possess a good philosophical analysis of torture, and that there are ways of coercing people which do not constitute torture. So 'torture' is obviously a special kind of coercion, one which need not be restricted to physical torture.

Voice O
My discussion may seem to have little to do with the concerns with the self and others you have been engaged in. I don't have any grand thesis about the self and Zen to put before you. I'm reminded of Frank Ramsey's remark, 'If you can't say it you can't say it, and you can't whistle it either.' I've come to appreciate Wittgenstein's philosophical methods when we think of Zen. All I'll be offering you is some primitive examples and not general or absolute principles. Certain changes have happened in my relation to Zen, and that is why I speak of post-Zen.

I am going to engage in a form of philosophical anthropology in an effort to answer the questions, 'What is it like to be a Buddhist?' 'What is it like to be post-Zen?' What philosophical anthropology says is that if you want to understand what a tribe is doing, go and live with them.

Well, I've been practising Zen and I've noted five points held in common by all the major Buddhist schools: universal causation; the doctrine of karma; rebirth (as opposed to reincarnation); no-self; the possibility of enlightenment. It has been said that this is a form of essentialism. It takes no account of complexities which have occurred in the historical development of Buddhism. But this objection is based on a logical fallacy. All I said was that all schools have these five features. I did not say that they did not have other doctrines as well.

What bothers my critic? He thinks I do not tell you what you need to know in these five doctrines. He will give you lots of details about textual scholarship, definitions, dates, and so on. If you go his way, you go the way of the scholar. That is not my way. I want to reflect on Buddhist practice and ask what it means. It's a view from the pew. I haven't the slightest interest in scholarship – I suppose that's too strong. I've come to the conclusion that the first three features of Buddhism I mentioned are dogmas, whereas the other two features may be viewed in a different light.

What do I mean by 'dogma'? Consider the many people who have a belief in creation or an afterlife. They are taught these things as they grow up. You are told they are true. Perhaps the elders decide it and it is taken as 'given'. 'It is true – it is a say-so truth.' For example, 'Circumcision is not necessary for salvation.'

Zen believes in the doctrines I have outlined, but the last two features of Zen are different – the no-self, and the possibility of enlightenment. Much of this can be understood as part of a mystical quest with the 'void' at its end-point. Why does one have a practice? One wants to become enlightened. That is why people are doing it. 'No-self' is realised through one's practice. One can actually come to this. I compare it with Wittgenstein's notion of a shift of aspect – 'The world of the unhappy man is a different world from the world of the happy man.'

The notion of enlightenment is linked to rebirth. Distinctions are made between enlightenment in this life and final enlightenment. You take a vow that no one is enlightened until everyone is, but we want enlightenment now irrespective of the metaphysical superstructure. I have come to find these tensions problematic.

We are accustomed in philosophy to discussing the self in a theoretical way, and we come across different attempts to deny the self in philosophy. But there is also the 'gut feeling' about no-self, something you struggle to attain. You can write articles or books on 'no-self' and then anxiously peruse the indices of books on the subject to see if you have been named.

Can we make sense of this notion of 'no-self' involved in practice? There was once an athlete whose every movement was imbued with a natural grace. One day, as he bent down to tie his shoes, someone told him that he reminded him of a Greek statue of a god bending down to remove a thorn out of his foot. He never moved with unselfconscious grace after that. You see this grace in the behaviour of young children. We could all be like that.

The self-consciousness you have to get rid of is not the philosophical concept of self-consciousness. It is not awareness of the self as an object, but, for example, going through the world worrying about what others will think of you. 'No-self' is manifested in fine behaviour. We can speak language at a gross level, a medium level or we can attain this fine behaviour. This will show itself, after the loss of self-consciousness, in the way you move in the world. The discovery of 'no-self' will show in people's behaviour. You see it in the way people walk in a Buddhist temple. 'Nonsense', you say. Well, take a look.

'No-self' is contrasted with 'reverie' – self-centred reverie. When 'no-self' is discovered this self-centredness stops. It sounds trivial, but it is not. The philosophical way is to treat 'no-self' as being, not a description, but as having to do with intention. Those who treat it as a description presuppose a practice wherein it has it sense. There are those who recognise it – like a wink between friends.

I confess that I can't stand ethics as a philosophical discipline. But the connection with what I am saying would be that enlightenment would show in a person's life and compassion would open a person up. The other side of ethics, the dark side, can be answered.

But why do I want to distinguish between Zen and post-Zen? Zen schools accept all of the five features of Buddhism I mentioned at the outset. Post-Zen only accepts the last two, not the others. There are institutions linked to Buddhism. Post-Zen can keep them all. What it gives up are doctrines based on metaphysical beliefs. It also gives up the militaristic aspects of some Zen schools. It gives up rituals, prayers, chanting, ritual cleansing of students' houses and the great respect for images.

It keeps the last two features of Buddhism as goals and sees Zen institutions as useful ways of attaining these goals. Krishnamurti also denies the first three features, but keeps some of the metaphysical beliefs.

You may well think that what I am talking about is an attenuated form of Buddhism, but I have only let go that which I could not swallow. My emphasis has been on practice, which should distinguish what I say from fancy Zen – Californian Zen, where all the features of Buddhism are said, but none of them are done.

Voice P
My presentation on Zen is certainly different. Mine is the way of the scholar and I make no apologies for that. We have to look at the main characteristics of Buddhism but I now accept that I have to modify my accusation of essentialism against O in the light of clarification received.

I am claiming that the developments called post-Zen, cut off as they are from central characteristics of Buddhism, have little in common with Buddhism. Why cut off post-Zen from the main tenets of Buddhism? If it is because those tenets are propositional, we have to remember that many have attempted to give a non-propositional account of Christianity without turning their back on its central tenets. When O appeals to practice, I'm afraid I simply do not follow the alleged transition from compassion to no-self.

My suggestion is that the severing-off of post-Zen is too drastic. How could there be a Zen school which is not Buddhistic? Are there comparisons between what has been advocated and 'Death of God' theology? My main question has to do with the conceivability of what is envisaged. It is said that we can have enlightenment without rebirth, but since these notions are correlative concepts, the suggestion is incoherent. So what are we left with in the end? One could go through a number of Buddhistic concepts asking the same question. For example, 'reverie' need not be a case of self-aggrandisement. If the worry is that immortality involves endless duration, immortality can be viewed ethically in Christianity, so why not in Buddhism?

Voice J

May I say that I wholly welcome the emphasis on practice in the attempt to understand Buddhism. I have a question, however, about the reasons given for turning away from Zen to post-Zen. I want to emphasise, however, that I ask it for information because I am ignorant of too much about Buddhism to assert it positively. The turn to post-Zen is a turning away from the metaphysical beliefs in Zen because they simply cannot be accepted. But may there not be an irony here? Has one been over-hasty in accepting the beliefs as metaphysical? What if the metaphysical gloss has hidden from one the point those Zen beliefs have in practice? In turning from them, one would have unwittingly accepted the very metaphysical beliefs which blind us to the significance of practice. What is needed, as with Christianity, is to give an account, a perspicuous representation of the beliefs, which bring out the religious significance of the beliefs, free from the metaphysics which distorts and misunderstands this significance. In the same way, many reject religion as a result of the criticisms of positivists because they cannot see how religion, Christianity or Zen, could be anything else.

Voice O

All I can say is that when I look at the doctrine of rebirth, I cannot believe it. I don't see the connection with practice, or I see a connection I don't like.

Voice J
I can see connections I don't like in certain Christian practices. I may read alongside an altar that if I put money in the box, light the candle, I will have such-and-such time cut from my penalties for my sins. I do not accept that. But that does not make me turn away from altars or stop me lighting a candle for a dead friend.

Voice H
Isn't there a problem of identity for post-Zen? Christianity is a credal religion, so we have some grounds for deciding whether extensions of Christianity are indeed extensions of it or not. And, of course, in Roman Catholicism, you have a far more explicit notion of authority.

Voice O
You ask me whether post-Zen is or is not Buddhism. I suppose it is a borderline case, so any criteria you specify will allow you to go one way or the other. Quite frankly, I couldn't care less what it's called. There are, on the other hand, important connections, from the point of view of communication, in the retention of the Zen institutions.

Voice Q
It may be said that Christianity is what most people at a certain time and place call Christianity. The same may be said about post-Zen. If your group flourishes and enough people acknowledge it, it will be called a branch of Zen. If, on the other hand, it withers away, it will probably be called an aberration.

Voice I
What does it mean to say that there is no ethical theory in Buddhism while at the same time talking about Buddhist ethics?

Voice P
The answer quite simply is that by Buddhist ethics I did not mean ethical theory. For example, compassion may be said to be part of Buddhist ethics.

Voice Q
I think it is important not to impose Western ethical themes on Buddhism. 'Ethical theory' is a Western notion.

Voice D
I can't help thinking of Christian analogues – an interest in the deep things of religion without metaphysics. It reminded me of Protestant piety emerging from metaphysics. The Buddhist tradition is anti-metaphysical and yet metaphysical in other ways. Many Asians are upset precisely because the Hari Krishna group neglect metaphysics.

Voice P
What would be said about the way you speak of post-Zen if you asked eminent Japanese teachers about these new developments?

Voice O
All I can say is that I was lost in many aspects of Japanese practice, for example, the use of 'the stick of mercy'. I had no choice in the matter. Similarly, the metaphysical theses stand no chance with me.

Voice E
I should like to regard Unitarianism as a form of Christianity, but many would refuse to deem it to be such. Or again, Christianity derives from Judaism, the belief in the God of Abraham, Isaac and Jacob, yet we use a new word – Christianity.

Voice Q
Can you say you have left Buddhism behind but still practise?

Voice O
Once again, you can call my practice what you like, I don't care.

Voice K
I appreciate critics wanting to avoid essentialism, but the claim that post-Zen has little to do with Buddhism, as such, creates unnecessary tensions between the other claims critics have made, namely, that differences need not be so great in certain respects. If the critics specify some criteria, even if they do call them the essence of Buddhism, we can then see, in this specific case, to what extent what we have heard of post-Zen is or is not related to these criteria.

Voice R

Post-Zen has been said to retain certain Zen institutions. I do not see why some people find that problematic. Any religion, in its history, will afford continuity, but not identity in many of its doctrine and practices. So I see no special problem here.

Voice P

I certainly do not want to present a set of essential criteria for Buddhism. My aim has been to try to understand what is going on in post-Zen. One of its leading proponents describes what she is doing as leaving Zen to go on to something else. For example, no use is made of 'the stick of mercy'. All this being the case, I was naturally puzzled about what one ought to say in a context such as this.

Voice C

The discussion about whether post-Zen can or cannot make sense independently of Buddhism reminds me of the issues with which this conference began. In the first discussion in the conference, the question arose of whether a sense of other human beings as sacred could mean anything independently of the religious context in which it originated. A related issue emerges in what I want to say about atheism and morality.

I want to make it clear that not everything found in Christianity can be found in atheism. I don't deny that certain concepts depend on religious traditions. So I reject any kind of reductionism. So there will be parts of religion which will have no place in atheism. On the other hand, I also reject the claim that morality has to be based on religion. But I have no general theory to that effect. Like Joe Louis of old, I simply take on each contender. I am not saying that the notion of life as a gift is the strongest contender.

The comments made on my paper centred on the claim of G. E. M. Anscombe that our confusion in modern moral philosophy comes from not realising that many of our moral concepts depend, for their intelligibility, on the notion of God as a law-giver – a notion most people no longer have. My view is that our moral concepts have their sense in different contexts.

Have I, as has been suggested, missed Anscombe's thesis? What *is* her thesis? According to me, she is conflating the thesis that certain words may survive the demise of a law conception of ethics with the thesis that certain *concepts* can do so. There is no diffi-culty with the thesis about words. For example, the use of 'crim-inal' may survive outside the context of law-courts. Again, the term 'bastard' survives as a term of abuse long after it has lost its implications about one's origins. The question, now, is wheth-er expressions such as I'll *have* to help him' are to be understood as surviving in the same way as 'bastard'.

Anscombe claims that the words of the moral expression en-tailed a certain use. What use? She wants to say that talk of a man as bad qua man has become impossible, but what does her claim amount to? On one reading her claim is a tautology: one cannot have a divine law ethics without a conception of the div-ine law. That is true, but uninteresting. Her other thesis is inter-esting, but false. In fact, the thesis that certain words can't survive the demise of their original context is not only false, but pro-foundly false.

If someone professes that life is a gift, and it stands on its own, the claim must be that this is made possible by its derivation from religion. How is that supposed to be known? The philos-opher is not speaking as a historian in making this claim. How does the philosopher know that the religious conception did not develop out of the moral one? In the same way, it cannot be claimed that religious conceptions must have developed out of moral con-ceptions. In making such claims the philosopher is speaking, not as a historian, but as a metaphysician.

Wittgenstein emphasised certain general facts of nature – laugh-ing, crying, reacting to miraculous escapes with gratitude, and so on. Why not say that it is from the last of these that religious and atheistic conceptions are derived?

Voice S

I agreed with so much of what was said in the previous dis-cussion and the original paper that, looking for something to dis-agree with, I reread Anscombe's paper and found it far more difficult to discern than I had thought originally. So I cast myself as her apologist.

Some have claimed that you can't do justice to morality if you are an atheist. If my only options in ethical theory were utilitarian-ism or Divine Command Theory, I'd be interested in the latter. Also, theories which minimise the status of justice tend to be catas-trophes and no purpose is served in attempting to purify them.

Let me begin by stating that morality is compatible with atheism. But I was interested in contexts in which our words begin to founder. This was an abiding interest in Nietzsche and Kierkegaard. They thought that their contemporaries lived under an illusion about how concepts could mean. I placed Anscombe in this company. She is less careful than either Nietzsche or Kierkegaard when she speaks of the survival of *concepts* outside the framework which once made them possible. If that happens, we do not have the concept. All we have is the appearance of the availability of the concepts when its use has gone. Only the nominal words survive. So to say that what she says is tautological is absolutely right. We can only use a concept if conditions are in place. Within religion, the notion of a divine law-giver becomes intelligible.

So let us look to Anscombe's thesis as applying to the survival of words, rather than concepts. We may employ words in contexts which seem to resemble those which gave them their sense, but we do not know what we are doing. This applies, she thinks, to our moral use of 'must'. Anscombe thinks that Divine Command Theory is dead. It was a deep theory, as a matter of fact, it did not get a deep hold on our culture or on modern moral philosophy. If we realise this, we can be clear that we are not borrowing in our contemporary use of 'must'. Her point is a hermeneutic one. We can be thinking clearly in many ways while others become bracketed.

So one does not get to grips with her thesis by simply saying that we do continue to use the words. This is not what she is worried about. She is worried about whether we know what we are saying. In Divine Command Theory she thinks the nature of obligation is to be found in what God commanded. If we give that up, we don't come to anything similar at that level of generality. She believes this leads to disaster in modern moral philosophy. In fact, she thinks it leads to the corruption of morality. You will start thinking of consequences and be tempted to indulge in all sorts of evils, for example, torture. For her, this is a failure to have any kind of moral position. As we have observed already, she reacts to moral dilemmas simply by saying that we cannot know that a third alternative won't turn up which constitutes a way out of them.

All I am saying is that we have to look at the particularity of her claim. She is saying that pseudo-concepts share some of the features of the genuine ones. There are other cases where there is perfectly coherent talk of moral obligation, but those are uses quite independent of Divine Command Theory. Finally, she is saying that there is no coherent concept of moral obligation in modern moral philosophy. So one must not make a generic point against her.

Vioce B

Imagine a science conference without the theistic notion of laws of nature. We can imagine someone suggesting that we drop the theistic account. Yet, whether these features are well lost or sadly lost, we can certainly get on with science without them. We don't think the dispute even gets started now. I don't see how the problems of adjustment are any more serious in the moral case. We, for our part, should get on with the necessary task of interpreting the human condition we find ourselves in.

Voice C

Anscombe is not interested in which concept came first. Concepts change gradually. Country music is not played, in the main, by farmers, but the change was gradual.

Voice S

I agree with that remark about how concepts develop, but Anscombe took herself to be discussing a particular case, namely, modern moral philosophy. I do not think she has a general thesis.

Voice J

There are a number of different issues involved in this dispute. At one level it is clear that atheism presupposes theism for the simple reason that it is a reaction against it. But I do not think her claim is as restricted as has been suggested. MacIntyre claims to have been influenced by her, and his claims are certainly not restricted in the way suggested. We are supposed to be in a moral mess, reflected in moral philosophies which cannot transcend our times. This makes us wonder from where MacIntyre derived the moral energy to point this out. But there have been moral viewpoints, quite independent of religion, ones which simply hold that we should respect others as human beings. Unlike Bentham, they do not attempt to explicate this in terms of criteria. If we try to do so, we shall always come across human beings who do not qualify. Why one should respect them then becomes an insoluble mystery.

So there are different traditions, different movements and some of these have notions of moral necessity, gratitude for life and so on. I am puzzled by the view that our eventual task is one of interpretation or reinterpretation, since it makes me wonder where we are when we do this and where we get our resources from to do so. The idea of the lonely interpreter who does not belong to any movement, or who is not at home in any practice, as *the* condition of human beings is, I think, a romantic illusion. Interpretations are called for. Sometimes they are needed and sometimes not. So I do not see them as defining our essential task as human beings.

Voice S
I take MacIntyre to be saying that, for many, a religious framework no longer has sense. I distance myself from MacIntyre's other remarks precisely because, unlike Anscombe, he refuses to be specific. He starts propounding theses about *all* our moral concepts. He is right in saying that emotivism is the loss of a conception of morality. As for Anscombe, I do not think she has only academic moral philosophy in mind. She wants to identify a site, via Hume, whereby it is suggested to ordinary people that there is a way of avoiding moral pressures.

Voice A
It has never been clear to me what the concept of the law-giver is supposed to deepen. It does not close the alleged gap between 'is' and 'ought' and it is given a place in modern moral philosophy where it cannot retain its force. It seems to me that Anscombe had a rationalist programme, one which is evident in her instrumentalist conception of virtue, which one can contrast with Wittgenstein's absolute conception. The only adequate reason can be given, she thought, by the law-giver. But Wittgenstein's 'Lecture on Ethics' shows how 'You ought' can have application without a religious conception of ethics. If we told someone he ought to play tennis better, but he said he wasn't interested in doing so, we'd have to accept that fact. But if we told someone he ought to act decently and he said he wasn't interested in doing so, we'd say, 'But you ought to'. That use is perfectly intelligible without reference to religion.

Voice C

Anscombe is looking for a 'stopper'. Nothing else will play the same role as Divine Command Theory. But 'It is God's will' is only one stopper among many.

Voice S

If you can show that those other uses are real concepts you have refuted her.

Voice K

I think it would be very interesting if scientists did discuss the idea that the laws of nature depend on God; the idea that without divine law there is no necessity. Hume held the view that 'necessity' is a superstition. Then you have some who say that there is a free-standing notion of physical modalities. Now there are philosophers of science who say that Humean regularities won't do, but who are also dissatisfied with the notion of laws simply existing *in vacuo*. They look for some context to make sense of this. Similarly, I don't think the idea of a deontic ontology makes sense without a wider context.

Voice D

We must not forget that the notions of moral law and scientific law have an intelligible history. They are more evident in modern thought than in pre-Stoic ancient thought. Their prominence in the seventeenth century had much to do with theological voluntarism. These considerations would seem to strengthen Anscombe's hand. I admit that laws of nature and moral laws alone ontologically are not incoherent, but they do seem incredible.

I have a question about the notion of life as a gift. Does the atheistic conception propounded have anything which the theistic notion does not have, or is it like it, but with a little less?

Voice C

When I give a present to my daughter, the idea of a gift seems pretty straightforward. But if I speak of God's gift of life, the use seems stretched, because some features obviously drop out. On the other hand, when believers speak of life as a gift, no matter what happens, while I may be grateful for a lucky escape, what drops out goes the other way. So features may drop out in either direction.

Voice D
But isn't the believer saying that the gift of life is good rather than going into the details?

Voice C
My point is that that is a different use of 'good'.

Voice J
In any case, saying life is good must be mediated through its details to be worth anything, although it is not gratitude for this or that. I must be able to say that the rain falls on the just and the unjust while getting soaked.

Voice E
We seem to ignore the aspect of divine commands which says, 'Do this or burn'. Use is made of rewards to get people to do what is wanted. They are promised a land of milk and honey. All this seems to be a matter of hypothetical imperatives.

Voice O
When we speak of a deontic ontology needing a wider context, I don't think Anscombe was looking for that. She wasn't looking for an overarching account, but one which refers to past moralities.

Voice T
It has been said that the non-believer may feel grateful for life. Is this unnatural? Even if it is natural, isn't there a difference between the natural and the puzzling? It is puzzling that anyone should want to speak in this way. Is it being suggested that we should give up the possibility of exploring this mystery?

Voice C
I referred to Wittgenstein's notion of the natural history of mankind. The difficulty often is in noticing the obvious. We are people who answer questions if asked. We might have been different sorts of beings. We look at paintings. We ask what it is a picture of. We treat it as a real scene in some respects. What we need is not to explain these general features about ourselves, but to notice them.

One of these is that if I narrowly miss death I feel grateful. You may ask, 'To whom?' I don't know. I don't have an explanation.

Now these facts may be part of a religious or a secular morality. Do you find them puzzling?

Voice T

You said it was a mystery.

Voice C

Only in the sense that they are part of our lives, and might not have been. You ask why it is natural, but asking is just as natural. We might say that the ones who didn't ask died out.

Voice T

That sounds like an explanation.

Voice J

At this point, as our discussion draws to a close, I want to ask people to reflect on the course it has taken and make any observations they want to.

Voice I

It has been said that the conception of moral theory is fatally flawed because it is a Western notion, culturally bound. But aren't we still faced by the question of what makes all the different conceptions a moral point of view? Perhaps the answer to *that* question is what makes them all a moral point of view. I still think that would involve the notion of respect for persons.

Voice E

I think we need to extend the notion of respect to include animals. In some ways, the higher animals have the same characteristics as ourselves. They set themselves purposes, but they can't do so freely. They cannot choose not to follow them. We have duties towards them even if they do not have duties towards us. We must turn away from the emphasis on ourselves, regarding animals as created simply for our use. So in our thinking about ethical theories, we need to give more consideration to animals.

Voice H

I wonder whether we don't do ethics with too blunt an instrument. For example, whatever is said of respect, I have to say that I can imagine situations where I would engage in torture. I pray that I may never find myself in such a situation. It seems that theological ethics is stronger: 'Never do evil that good may come', but in complex situations, this, too, is too blunt an instrument. Even Jesus, at times, caused pain that good might come.

Voice K

When I spoke of the difficulties of defining the moral point of view, I did not want to exclude anyone from the moral conversation. I was not looking for sufficient reasons.

I think it would be an extremely useful project to look at non-theistic religions such as Buddhism and compare the cases we discussed in Christianity with their cultural resources now. Of course, there will be substantive differences between secular and theistic moralities. Secular moralities are likely to give their main attention to cruelty, while religious moralities are likely to give it to pride.

Voice G

I have to confess that in discussions with secular moralities, I sometimes feel like the turkey at Christmas who said, 'I feel you are more interested in my meat than in my company'. As religious people faced by secular challenges, we may feel that the only issue is that concerning how much we can salvage. I think we need to pay more attention to the imitation of Christ. What are the desirable states of life involved in religious ethics? We need to explore moral eros as a form of life. This was particularly strong in the moving account we were given of post-Zen. We need a positive account of religion. How does attraction towards the good work?

Voice D

The aspiration towards a transcendent good is more central than obligation in theistic ethics. Divine Command Theory is far less important than the goodness of God. During the conference an important issue was raised: does theistic morality offer a more disciplined reflection on how to live than traditional moral theories, even when these are extended to include the moral virtues? We have to take account of non-theistic religions such as Buddhism, and the fact that even within Christianity there are many who do not hold traditional theistic beliefs.

Perhaps our first question should be: What does it mean to be a religious person? I hesitate to say it has to do with the sacred, since there is the issue of how this is to be translated between theistic and non-theistic religions. But I can think of a range of subjects for future investigation. We ought to be cautious in learning what the social sciences have to teach us. We ought to distrust any homogenous science which focuses on a limited reference in our pluralistic, technological society. So we need different conceptions.

Voice O

My reaction to our discussions is that we should take seriously what Wittgenstein says in his 'Lecture on Ethics' and explore the importance of the mystical tradition for the way we do ethics. In the Roman Empire, it is said that many religions existed together. The masses accepted them all as true. The philosophers rejected them all as false, while the politicians regarded them all as useful. The philosophers got it wrong.

Voice P

The conference enables me to pay far more attention to the notion of 'the path'. Is the path a method, practice? Can it all be method, or is there a way in which belief in propositions of a credal sort enter this context? If not, does a purely pragmatic emphasis on practice leave us bereft?

Voice B

In some ways our discussion of religious experience has been narrow. We have not explored the ecstatic naturalness to be found in Tillich and in Spinoza. Nietzsche talked of it in a different way. Here we have a Dionysian religion which did not presuppose transcendence, but included an intense celebration of life in this world.

As we sort out our human possibilities, we ought to explore whether a significant religion and morality can be grounded in such a relation. Whether it is possible or becomes possible once again. What mileage is there in such a religion if a religion of transcendence is untenable? That might be a thematic project worth exploring. It may be that Nietzsche's attempt is a failed attempt, but the effort is better tried since without it life is grey and uninteresting.

Voice F

I had a feeling of *déjà vu* during our discussions. When I studied the history of ethics in graduate school, I thought the most important thinker was Aquinas. But I was told that religion and morality were independent of each other, and that I could not appeal to God without first proving his existence.

It seems like a false issue to me now. We have to acknowledge that we have different practices which overlap. If we want to explore wonder, how can religion be ignored?

At the level of theory, the different practices beget theories which are analogous to each other. Kant has a conception of law which is different from the medieval concept of law.

So I think we need to relax a little about our firm distinctions. There is no one answer to the question of the relation of religion to morality. What we have is a whole family of answers.

Voice N

Talk about God is a matter of analogical predication. Negation is meant to preserve the transcendence of God who is so different from us in so many ways. I wondered whether this aspect of God, the God of onto-theology, was emphasised too much in our discussions. We need to keep in touch with what theologians such as Rahner and Tillich have shown us, as well as with concepts of ultimacy in other traditions. If we did, we would go beyond the subject–object dichotomy. The concept of mystery would be explored. Can we do so in a way which avoids us ending up as ethical humanists? Religions such as Zen must be put to the test like any other religion. Does it have the resources to generate an existential praxis? We can talk of respect for persons, but we have to ask what it is in human nature which calls forth the response of seeing human beings as worthy of respect. Although answers may be hard to find in contemporary literature, we have to look for them.

Voice A

My concern has been with how moral philosophy can allow space for moral seriousness. To bring out what such seriousness involves I focused in a certain way on the individual as victim. I made 'wronging another' central. If we look at the matter from the point of view of remorse, the wrong caused cannot be captured by expressions such as 'I have violated principles', 'I have violated

reason', 'I have violated motives'. The seriousness doesn't rest
there. It may be right to say that the horrible is not the bad, but
it is important to use the notion of remorse. Only through it can
the experience of guilt be acquired and passed on. *Mystery is that
remorse.*

Wittgenstein shows that one way to use the word 'mystery' is
to draw attention to the mystery of remorse. He doesn't explain
it, but shows us the mystery. This is connected with what I said
about the preciousness of human beings, although I think 'preciousness' is too precious a word. It is a serious question as to
how this sense of human beings can stand independently of religion. I want to say that it can, but if I rewrote my paper, I
wouldn't use the word 'sacred'. So now I am bereft of a way of
speaking.

Voice S

When I went to graduate school, philosophy of religion was not
regarded as serious. Yet, we want to ask questions such as: What
is it to regard something as sacred? What is it to wonder? What
is it to regard with horror? What is it to understand the sanctity
of language? These questions do not seem to belong to moral
philosophy, and many rule them out.

But, then, in the philosophy of religion it is sometimes said
that you have to be a believer to understand religious concepts.

A colleague of mine was in a serious accident and I found myself
praying, although I am not a believer. Do I give a psychological
explanation of this fact?

When I think of the Nazis, I do not say they were wrong. I
react with horror. What they did challenges humanity. It is not a
degree of wrong. I am squeamish about killing a muskrat. Is that
irrational?

What are we to say about these questions? We either say that
they should belong to moral philosophy, or that there are reactions which belong to a religious sensibility which is distinct from
a particular credal system.

The moralist's definition is too narrow, but we are afraid to
give these issues a place, since we think that means going back
to the darkness of theological superstition. We shouldn't shore
up the options in this way.

Voice C
What does it matter what we call them, once we have given a full description of the phenomena in our lives? Whether we call it morality or religion, we need to ask why we need to fit everything into one category or other, come what may. Are we chasing unimportant questions?

Name Index

Subject Index